haole CTO SATO

queue ppdo

URL couchette

REN AT VAT

RFP tender

THE TRAVEL DICTIONARY

GDS

CVD

chip card

SITI ICAR fuselage

boatel pension NUC

T&E fustanella

www OSI hydrofoil SSR

lanai fuselage DBLB

dolme UPC MAP

EEC hostel ASM

CLAUDINE DERVAES pitch

BBR ASM cay

ISBN 0-933143-58-3
LIBRARY OF CONGRESS CARD CATALOG NUMBER 98-060065

For further information and to receive a catalog of all the publications available, contact: SOLITAIRE PUBLISHING
           POB 14508
           TAMPA, FL 33690-4508
           (800) 226-0286 (U.S.)
           (813) 876-0286 phone and fax
            E-mail: PSolitaire@aol.com

TABLE OF CONTENTS

INTRODUCTION

More like an enyclopedia, The Travel Dictionary is designed to assist travel industry personnel/travelers by providing helpful reference information. The standard **Abbreviations for states/provinces** are first. Then a list of **INDUSTRY ORGANIZATIONS** is followed by travel agency co-ops, consortia, licensee groups, and chains. **CITY/AIRPORT CODES** follow - in a decoding and encoding format. **AIRLINE CODES** are next (decoding, then encoding). The "**A to Z of Codes and Terms**" covers a variety of subject areas, such as geography, politics, language, economics, religion, food and art. **As this book is sold in countries other than the U.S., many terms are included for those not familiar with U.S. terminology.** A brief decoding/definition is provided for most items. Further research may be necessary for thorough understanding of terms.

Travel Industry Reference Books, Travel Video Companies, and **Magazines and Newsletters** are listed with addresses, phone/fax numbers, web sites and E-mail addresses. Next are a couple of pages that feature the **Communication Code, 24-hour Clock**, a **Metric Conversion Chart** and a **Clothing Size Comparison Chart**. **WORLD TIME ZONES** is followed with **COUNTRIES, CURRENCIES, AND CURRENCY CODES.**

A page on **U.S. capitals and Canada's capitals** is followed by **COUNTRIES, CAPITALS, AND POPULATIONS. COMPUTERIZATION CODES** are next, with sections on **CAR** and **HOTEL INFORMATION**. A list of **Fare Indicators/Codes** is also provided.

This new edition features lists of **WEB SITES** - for airlines, cruise lines, tour operators, car rental companies, and a miscellaneous list. The section on **World Facts and Trivia** is supplemented with a list of **U.S. States' Nicknames**. The **MINI-ATLAS** and **International Geographical Terms** end the book.

From its beginning, Solitaire Publishing has strived to promote professionalism by providing training materials and publications. I welcome your comments and questions pertaining to this or any other item we offer.

Claudine Dervaes
Tampa, FL

Abbreviations of States and Provinces

To help you with the various lists provided, this book begins with a couple of pages on the abbreviations for U.S. states, Canadian provinces and territories, Australian territories, and the states of Brazil.

TWO-LETTER CODES FOR U. S. STATES AND CAPITAL, OTHER U.S., AND THE PROVINCES/ TERRITORIES OF CANADA

U.S. STATES & CAPITAL

AK	Alaska
AL	Alabama
AR	Arkansas
AZ	Arizona
CA	California
CO	Colorado
CT	Connecticut
DC	District of Columbia
DE	Delaware
FL	Florida
GA	Georgia
HI	Hawaii
IA	Iowa
ID	Idaho
IL	Illinois
IN	Indiana
KS	Kansas
KY	Kentucky
LA	Louisiana
MA	Massachusetts
MD	Maryland
ME	Maine
MI	Michigan
MN	Minnesota
MO	Missouri
MS	Mississippi
MT	Montana
NC	North Carolina
ND	North Dakota
NE	Nebraska
NH	New Hampshire
NJ	New Jersey
NM	New Mexico
NV	Nevada
NY	New York
OH	Ohio
OK	Oklahoma
OR	Oregon
PA	Pennsylvania
RI	Rhode Island

SC	South Carolina
SD	South Dakota
TN	Tennessee
TX	Texas
UT	Utah
VA	Virginia
VT	Vermont
WA	Washington
WI	Wisconsin
WV	West Virginia
WY	Wyoming

U. S. OTHER

AS	American Samoa
GU	Guam
MP	Marianas
PR	Puerto Rico
VI	Virgin Islands

CANADA

AB	Alberta
BC	British Columbia
MB	Manitoba
NB	New Brunswick
NF	Newfoundland
NS	Nova Scotia
NT	Northwest Territories
ON	Ontario
PE	Prince Edward Island
PQ	Quebec
SK	Saskatchewan
YT -	Yukon Territory
NU –	Nunavut

ABBREVIATIONS FOR TERRITORIES OF AUSTRALIA

ACT   Australian Capital Territory
NSW   New South Wales
NT   Northern Territory
QLD   Queensland
VIC   Victoria
SA   South Australia
TAS   Tasmania
WA   Western Australia

ABBREVIATIONS FOR STATES OF BRAZIL

AC   Acre
AL   Alagoas
AM   Amazonas
AP   Amapa
BA   Bahia
CE   Cleara
DF   Brasilia (Capital)
ES   Espiritu Santu
FN   Fernando De Noronha (belongs to Penrnambuco)
GO   Goias
MA   Maranhao
MG   Minas Gerias
MS   Mato Grosso Do Sul
MT   Mato Grosso
PA   Parai
PB   Paraiba
PE   Pernambuco
PI   Piaui
PR   Parana
RJ   Rio De Janeiro
RO   Rondonia
RN   Rio Grande Do Norte
RR   Roraima
RS   Rio Grande Do Sul
SE   Sergipe
SC   Santa Catarina
SP   Sao Paulo
TO   Tocantins

TRAVEL INDUSTRY ORGANIZATIONS

Note: For international phone/fax numbers (shown without parentheses) prefix with the current country digits. Contact your long distance company for help. This list is not all-inclusive. Check with local libraries and other sources for additional organizations and local chapters.

```
AAA - American Automobile     (407) 444-7000
   Association           FAX (407) 444-7380
1000 AAA Drive
Heathrow, FL 32746-5063


AAR - Association of American (202) 639-2100
   Railroads             FAX (202) 639-2156
American Railroads Bldg.
50 F St. NW
Washington, DC 20001


ABA - American Bus Assoc.     (202) 842-1645
1100 New York Ave. NW     FAX (202) 842-0850
Ste. 1050
Washington, DC 20005-3934
                    http://www.buses.org
                 E-mail:abainfo@buses.org


ABTA - Association of British   171-637-2444
   Travel Agents         FAX 171-637-0713
55-57 Newman Street
London, England W1P 4AH


ACI - Assist Card Inter-      (800) 874-2223
   national                  (305) 381-9969
1001 Brickell Bay Dr.     FAX (305) 375-8135
Ste.2302
Miami, FL 33131


ACRA - American Car Rental    (202) 682-4778
   Association           FAX (202) 789-4512
1225 I St. NW, Ste. 500
Washington, DC 20005
```

```
ACTA - Assoc. of Canadian      (613) 521-0474
   Travel Agents          FAX (613) 521-0805
1729 Bank St., Ste. 201
Ottawa, Ont., Canada K1V 7Z5
              E-mail:acta.ntl@sympatico.ca


ACTE - Assoc. of Corporate     (800) 228-3669
   Travel Executives           (202) 546-5746
608 Massachusetts Ave. NW
Washington, DC 20002


Adventure Travel Society       (303) 649-9016
6551 S. Revere Pkwy.,      FAX (303) 649-9017
Ste. 160
Englewood, CO 80111-6410
           http://www.adventuretravel.com
           E-mail: ats@adventuretravel.com


AFA - Association of Flight    (202) 712-9799
   Attendants              FAX (202) 712-9798
1275 K St. NW
Washington, DC 20005
   http://www.flightattendant-afa-inter.net


AGTE - Association of Group     (212) 486-4300
   Travel Executives       FAX (212) 755-2135
c/o The Light Group
424 Madison Ave., Ste. 705
New York, NY 10017
              http://www.wbs.com/light
              E-mail: MIncentive@aol.com


AH & MA - American Hotel and   (202) 289-3100
   Motel Association       FAX (202) 289-3199
1201 New York Ave. NW, Ste. 600
Washington, DC 20005-3931
                 http://www.ahma.com
              E-mail: infoctr@AHMA.com


ALPA - Airline Pilots Asso-    (703) 689-2270
   ciation                 FAX (703) 689-4370
535 Herndon Pkwy., P.O. Box 1169
Herndon, VA 22070
```

American Tourism Society   (212) 532-8845
419 Park Ave. S. #505   FAX (212) 545-9641
New York, NY 10016

AMTRAK - See NRPC

ARC - Airlines Reporting   (703) 816-8000
    Corporation   FAX (703) 816-8104
1530 Wilson Blvd. #800
Arlington, VA 22209-2448

ARTA - Association of Retail   (800) 969-6069
    Travel Agents   (606) 263-1194
501 Darby Creek Rd. #47   FAX (606) 264-0368
Lexington, KY 40509
                http://www.artaonline.com
                E-mail: ARTAHDQ@aol.com

ASAE - American Society of   (202) 626-2723
    Association Executives FAX (202) 371-8825
1575 I St. NW
Washington, DC 20005-1168
                http://www.asaenet.org
                E-mail: asae@asaenet.org

ASTA - American Society of   (800) 828-2712
    Travel Agents   (703) 739-2782
1101 King St., Ste. 200   FAX (703) 684-8319
Alexandria, VA 22314
                http://www.asta.com

ATA - Air Transport Assoc.   (202) 626-4000
1301 Pennsylvania Ave. NW FAX (202) 626-4181
Ste. 1100
Washington, DC 20004
                http://www.air-transport.org

ATME - Association of Travel   (800) 526-0041
    Marketing Executives   FAX (800) 525-3087
305 Madison Ave. Ste 2025   (212) 973-9085
New York, NY 10065-0006

```
CHA - Caribbean Hotel Assoc.    (787) 725-9139
18 Marseilles St., #2B     FAX (787) 725-9166
San Juan, PR 00907-1672


CHRIE - Council on Hotel,       (202) 331-5990
   Restaurant and         FAX (202) 785-2511
   Institutional Education
1200 17th St. NW, 1st Floor
Washington, DC 20036-3097
                    http://www.chrie.org
           E-mail: alliance@access.digex.net


CIEE - Council on Interna-      (888) 268-6245
   tional Educational           (212) 822-2600
   Exchange             FAX (212) 822-2699
205 E. 42nd St.
New York, NY 10017


CITC - Canadian Institute of    (800) 589-5776
Travel Counsellors              (416) 484-4450
55 Eglington Ave. E. #209 FAX (416) 484-4140
Toronto, ONT. Canada M4P 1G8
              http://www.citcontario.com
           E-mail: info@citcontario.com


Citizens Emergency Center       (202) 647-5225
U.S. State Department      FAX (202) 647-6201
2201 C St. NW
Washington, DC 20520


CLIA - Cruise Lines Inter-      (212) 921-0066
   national Association    FAX (212) 921-0549
500 Fifth Ave., Ste. 1407
New York, NY 10010

                    http://ten.io.com/clia


CTO - Caribbean Tourism         (212) 682-0435
   Organization          FAX (212) 697-4258
20 E. 46th St.
New York, NY 10017
           http://www.travelfile.com/get?cto
```

```
DOT - Department of Trans-      (202) 366-2220
    portation
400 7th St. SW, Room 3248
Washington, DC 20590


Ecotourism Society            (802) 447-2121
P.O. Box 755            FAX  (802) 447-2122
N. Bennington, VT 05257
                E-mail: ecotsocy@igc.com


Elderhostel                   (617) 426-7788
75 Federal St.          FAX  (617) 426-8351
Boston, MA 02110-1941


ETC - European Travel         (212) 307-1200
    Commission          FAX  (212) 301-1205
c/o Donald Martin Company
1 Rockefeller Plaza #214
New York, NY 10020


FAA - Federal Aviation        (800) 322-7873
    Administration         Consumer Hotline
APA 200 - FAA                 (202) 366-4000
800 Independence Ave. SW
Washington, DC 20591


FCCA - Florida-Caribbean      (305) 446-7297
    Cruise Assoc.       FAX  (305) 448-0931
2701 Ponce de Leon Blvd.,
    Ste. 203
Coral Gables, FL 33134


HEDNA - Hotel Electronic      (412) 784-8433
    Distribution Network  FAX (412) 781-2871
    Association
303 Freeport Rd.
Pittsburgh, PA 15215


HSMAI - Hospitality Sales     (202) 789-0089
    and Marketing Assoc.  FAX (202) 789-1725
    International
1300 L St. NW, Ste. 1020
Washington, DC 20005
                http://www.hsmai.org
```

IACC - International Assoc.   (314) 993-8575
    of Conference Centers   FAX (314) 993-8919
243 N. Lindbergh Blvd.
St. Louis, MO 63141
                    http://www.oacconline.com

IACVB - International Asso-   (202) 296-7888
    ciation of Convention   FAX (202) 296-7889
    and Visitors Bureaus
2000 L St. NW, Ste. 702
Washington, DC 20036
                      http://www.iacvb.org/
            E-mail: gbarrett@iacvb.org

IAMAT - International Assoc.   (716) 754-4883
    for Medical Assistance FAX (519) 836-3412
    to Travellers
417 Center St.
Lewiston, NY 14092

IAPA - International Airline   (800) 527-5888
    Passengers Association   (972) 404-9980
4125 Keller Sprgs. Rd.#108FAX (972) 233-5348
Dallas, TX 75244

IATA - International Air   (514) 844-6311
    Transport Association FAX (514) 855-5286
2000 Peel St.
Montreal, Que., Canada H3A 2R4

IATAN - International Air-   (516) 747-4716
    lines Travel Agency   FAX (516) 747-4462
    Network
300 Garden City Plaza, Ste. 342
Garden City, NY 11530

IATM - International Assoc.   071-703-9154
    of Tour Managers   FAX 071-703-0358
397 Walworth Rd.
London, England SE17 2AW

```
ICAO - International Civil      (514) 954-8219
   Aviation Organization  FAX (514) 954-6077
999 University St.
Montreal, Que. Canada H3C 5H7
               E-mail: http://icaohq@icao.org


ICCL - International Council  (800) 595-9338
   of Cruise Lines           (202) 296-8463
1211 Conn. Ave. NW #800  FAX (202) 296-1676
Washington, DC 20036


ICTA - Institute for Cer-    (617) 237-0280
   tified Travel Agents  FAX (617) 237-3860
148 Linden St. POB 812059
Wellesly, MA 02181-0012


IFTTA - International Forum   (415) 673-3333
   of Travel and Tourism FAX (415) 673-3548
   Advocates
693 Sutter St., 6th Floor
San Francisco, CA 94102-1076


IFWTO - International Federa- (602) 596-6640
   tion of Womens'       FAX (602) 596-6638
   Travel Organizations
13901 N. 73rd St., Ste. 210B
Scottsdale, AZ 85260-3125
                  http://iftwo.trav.com
            E-mail:iftwohq@primenet.com


IGTA - International Gay      (800) 448-8550
   Travel Association    FAX (305) 296-6633
P.O. Box 4974
Key West, FL 33041


ISMP - International Society  (602) 483-0000
   of Meeting Planners   FAX (602) 998-8022
8383 East Evans Rd.
Scottsdale, AZ 85260-3614
                  http://iami.org/ismp.html
                  E-mail: ismp@iami.org
```

ISTTE - International Society (313) 526-0710
   of Travel and Tourism FAX (313) 526-0710
   Educators
19364 Woodcrest
Harper Woods, MI 48225

                   E-mail: STTE@aol.com

ITTA - Independent Travel   (412) 781-3255
   Technology Association FAX (412) 781-2871
303 Freeport Rd
Pittsburgh, PA 15215
        E-mail: 71513.2343@compuserve.com

MPI - Meeting Professionals   (972) 702-3000
   International   FAX (972) 702-3070
4455 LBJ Freeway, Ste. 1200
Dallas, TX 75244-5903

          http://www.mpiweb.org

NACA - National Air Carrier   (202) 833-8200
   Association   FAX (202) 659-9479
1730 M St. NW, Ste. 806
Washington, DC 20036

NACOA - National Association (305) 663-5626
   of Cruise Oriented   FAX (305) 663-5625
   Agents
7600 Red Rd., Ste. 128
Miami, FL 33143

NACTA - National Association (760) 751-1197
   of Commissioned Travel FAX (619) 751-1309
   Agents
P.O. Box 2398
Valley Center, CA 92082-2398
        E-mail: NACTA@compuserve.com

NATA - National Air Transpor- (703) 845-9000
   tation Association   FAX (703) 845-8176
4226 King St.
Alexandria, VA 22302

```
NBAA - National Business      (202) 783-9000
   Aircraft Association   FAX (202) 331-8364
1200 18th St. NW, Ste. 400
Washington, DC 20036
                       http://www.nbaa.org/


NBTA - National Business      (703) 684-0836
   Travel Association     FAX (703) 684-0263
1650 King St., Ste. 401
Alexandria, VA 22314
                       http://www.nbta.org/nbta


NPF - National Park Found-    (202) 785-4500
   ation                  FAX (202) 785-3539
1101 17th St. NW #1102
Washington, DC 20036


NRPC - National Railroad      (202) 484-7540
   Passenger Corporation (AMTRAK)
60 Mass. Ave.
Washington, DC 20002


NTA - National Tour Assoc.    (606) 226-4444
546 E. Main St.           FAX (606) 226-4404
Lexington, KY 40508
                       http://www.ntaonline.com


OSSN - Outside Sales Support  (800) 771-7327
   Network Association        (407) 743-1900
1061 East Indian Town Rd. FAX (407) 575-4371
Ste. 410
Jupiter, FL 33477
                       http://www.ossn.com


PATA - Pacific Asia Travel    (415) 986-4646
   Association            FAX (415) 986-3458
1 Montgomery St., Ste. 1000
San Francisco, CA 94104
                       http://www.pata.org
                E-mail: parattq@ix.netcom.com
```

PCMA - Professional Conven-   (205) 823-7262
    tion Management Assoc. FAX (205) 822-3891
100 Vestavia Parkway, Ste. 220
Birmingham, AL 35216
                E-mail: PCMA@internetmci.com

RAA - Regional Airline Assoc. (202) 857-1170
1200 19th St. NW, #300   FAX (202) 429-5113
Washington, DC 20036-2412
                        http://www.raa.org

SATH - Society for the   (212) 447-7284
    Advancement of Travel   FAX (212) 725-8253
    for the Handicapped
347 Fifth Ave., Ste. 610
New York, NY 10016

SATW - Society of American   (919) 787-5181
    Travel Writers   FAX (919) 787-4916
4101 Lake Boone Trail, Ste. 201
Raleigh, NC 27607

SCMP - Society of Corporate   (404) 355-9932
    Meeting Professionals FAX (404) 351-3348
1819 Peachtree St. NE, Ste. 620
Atlanta, GA 30309
                E-mail: ASSNHQ@midspring.com

SITE - Society of Incentive   (212) 575-0910
    Travel Executives   FAX (212) 575-1838
21 W. 38th St., 10th Fl.
New York, NY 10018

STAG - Society of Travel   (301) 654-8595
    Agents in Government   FAX (301) 654-6663
6935 Wisconsin Ave., #200
Bethesda, MD 20815

TIA - Travel Industry   (202) 408-8422
    Association of America FAX (202) 408-1255
1100 New York Ave. NW #450
Washington, DC 20005

```
TIAC - Tourism Industry Asso-    (613) 238-3883
    ciation of Canada        FAX (613) 238-3878
1016-130 Albert St.
Ottawa, Ont. Canada K1P 5G4
                        E-mail: tiac@magi.com


TIS - Travel Information Ser-    (215) 456-9600
    vice (phone inquiries only)


TTRA - Travel and Tourism       (606) 226-4344
    Research Association    FAX (606) 226-4355
546 E. Main St.
Lexington, KY 40508
                        http://www.ttra.com
                    E-mail: ttra@mgtserv.com


UFTAA/FUAAV - Universal Federa-  33-92052829
    tion of Travel Agents'   FAX 33-92052987
    Associations
Ave. du Prince Hereditaire Albert
Stade Louis II-Entree H
98000 Monaco


UMA - United Motorcoach         (703) 838-2929
    Association             FAX (703) 838-2950
113 South West St. 4th Fl.
Alexandria, VA 22314


USTOA - United States Tour      (212) 599-6599
    Operators Association   FAX (212) 599-6744
342 Madison, Ste. 1522
New York, NY 10173
                        http://www.ustoa.com
                    E-mail: ustoa@aol.com


WATA - World Association of      022-731-4760
    Travel Agencies        FAX 022-732-8161
14, rue Ferrier CH-102
Geneva, Switzerland
        http://www.watanetwork.kenpubs.co.uk
                    E-mail:watahq@iprolink.ch
```

WTO - World Tourism Organ-   341-571-0628
    ization   FAX 341-571-3733
Calle Captain Haya 42
Madrid 28020 Spain

WTTC - World Travel and   171-222-1955
    Tourism Council   FAX 171-222-4983
181 Chausee de la Hulpe
Box 10, 1170 Brussels Belgium

TRAVEL AGENCY CONSORTIUMS, LICENSEE GROUPS, JOINT MARKETING ORGANIZATIONS, FRANCHISES, AND INDIVIDUAL/CORPORATE OWNED CHAINS

This list is not all-inclusive. It is not meant to endorse any particular organization. Contact the specific companies for information.

Action 6
237 Church St.
Lowell, MA 01852
(978) 459-2104
FAX: (978) 452-7689
E-mail: Action6@aol.com

American Express Co.
100 Church St. 14th Fl.
New York, NY 10007
(212) 640-2449
FAX: (212) 640-5035

API - Allied Percival International
500 Main St., Ste. 400
Ft. Worth, TX 76102-3941
(817) 870-0300
FAX: (817) 870-1050

AURA, Inc.
5 East County Rd. B, Ste 3-4
St. Paul, MN 55117
(612) 487-3223
FAX: (612) 487-2206

Austin Assoc.
1 Apple Hill, Ste. 316
Natick, MA 01760
(508) 653-7890
FAX (508) 655-4066

Boeing International Travel
325 JS McDonnell Blvd. Bldg 303
East Level 1, Mail code 3069236
Hazelwood, MO 63042
(800) 543-4284
(314) 551-4100
FAX: (314) 551-4059

BTI Americas
400 Skokie Blvd.
Northbrook, IL 60062
(847) 480-8400
FAX: (847) 480-3027
http://www.btiamericas.com

BTS Travel Network
5435 Scotts Valley Dr.
Scotts Valley, CA 95066
(800) 358-BELL
(408) 438-6662
FAX: (408) 438-8711
E-mail: btstvlnet@aol.com

Carlson Wagons-Lits Travel
P.O. Box 59159
Minneapolis, MN 55459
(800) 888-8584
FAX: (612) 449-2790

Coast Travel Group
1556 First St.
Napa, CA 94559
(707) 252-7637
FAX (707) 252-2517

Consolidated Travel Services
9800 Centre Parkway, Ste. 860
Houston, TX 77036
(800) 969-9311
(713) 776-0775
FAX: (713) 776-1984
E-mail: ctsi95@aol.com

```
Corp-Net International                    (614) 488-0600
3040 Riverside Dr., Ste. 208    FAX: (614) 488-0619
Columbus, OH 43221

Crown Travel Group                        (800) 848-8756
2701 East Camelback Rd., Ste. 440         (602) 226-5577
Phoenix, AZ 85016               FAX (602) 266-2502

Cruise Holidays International              (800) 866-7245
9665 Chesapeake Dr., Ste. 401              (619) 279-4780
San Diego, CA 92123             FAX: (619) 279-4788

Cruiselink                                 (800) 253-4242
7 West Main St.                            (516) 665-2222
Bay Shore, NY 11706             FAX: (516) 665-0300
              http://www.cruiselink.trav.org

Cruise Shoppes America Ltd.                (800) 375-0199
701 Metaire Rd., Ste. 1A-208               (504) 833-0340
Metaire, LA 70005               FAX: (504) 831-3165
              E-mail: 76726,3357@compuserve.com
              E-mail: gbrown@communique.net
              http://www.cruiseshoppes.com/

Empress Travel Assoc.                      (800) 432-8258
465 Smith St.                              (516) 420-9200
Farmingdale, NY 11735           FAX: (516) 420-0511

First Discount Travel                      (770) 394-0202
7000 Central Pkwy., Ste. 330    FAX: (770) 394-0501
Atlanta, GA 30328

GalaxSea Cruises and Tours                 (972) 671-7245
13150 Coit Rd., Ste. 125        FAX: (972) 671-1151
Dallas, TX 75240

GEM                                        (800) 843-0733
754 Montauk Hwy.                           (516) 422-7700
West Islip, NY 11758            FAX: (516) 422-7790
              http://www.gem.trave.org
              E-mail: gem@ten-io.com

GIANTS                                     (800) 442-6871
2 Park Ave., Ste. 2205                     (212) 545-7460
New York, NY 10016              FAX: (212) 545-7428

Hickory Travel Systems, Inc.               (201) 843-0820
Park 80, Plaza East             FAX: (201) 843-4764
Saddle Brook, NJ 07663

International Tours                        (972) 671-1100
13150 Coit Rd., Ste. 125        FAX: (972) 671-1101
Dallas, TX 75240

Leisure Travel Group                       (310) 574-0883
4640 Admiralty Way, Ste. 306    FAX: (310) 574-0804
Marina del Rey, CA 90292  E-mail: LeisureTvl@aol.com
```

```
MAST (Midwest Agents Selling            (630) 323-0770
   Travel)                    FAX: (630) 323-2662
15 Spinning Wheel Rd., Ste 336
Hinsdale, IL 60521


Maritz Travel Co.                       (314) 827-2425
1395 N. Highway Dr.        FAX: (314) 827-4443
Fenton, MO 63099

                           http://www.maritz.com


Omega World Travel                      (703) 359-0200
3102 Omega Office Park     FAX: (703) 359-8880
Fairfax, VA 22031


Passport Travel, Inc.                   (800) 678-7766
6340 Glenwood                           (913) 677-7777
Overland Park, KS 66202    FAX: (913) 831-1405


Riverside Travel Group, Inc.            (503) 255-2950
Airport Business Center    FAX: (503) 255-7268
6645 NE 78th Ct., Ste. C1
Portland, OR 97218


Rosenbluth Int'l Travel                 (215) 977-4000
2401 Walnut St.            FAX: (215) 977-4028
Philadelphia, PA 19103   http://www.rosenbluth.com


SPACE                                   (800) 223-4523
15 Front St.               FAX: (516) 764-6991
Rockville Centre, NY 11571
                        http://www.ten-uo.com/space
                          E-mail: space@ten-io.com


The Consortium                          (800) 285-0111
151 North Main St., Ste. 301   FAX (914) 639-9136
New City, NY 10956     E-mail: TheConsortium@msn.com


THOR, Inc.                              (800) 862-2111
382 S. Arthur Ave.                      (303) 661-3090
Louisville, CO 80027       FAX: (303) 661-3001


TIME                                    (800) 321-1060
200 W. Main St.                         (516) 321-1030
Babylon, NY 11702          FAX: (516) 321-1035


Travel & Transport                      (800) 228-2545
2120 S 72nd St. #700                    (402) 399-4500
Omaha, NE 68124-6310       FAX: (402) 398-9290
                           http://www.tandt.com


Travel Authority                        (904) 285-9796
100 Executive Way Ste. 214  FAX: (904) 285-9794
Ponte Vedra, FL 32082


Travel Design Associates                (800) 927-7444
2005 De La Cruz Blvd., Ste. 131         (408) 727-8787
Santa Clara, CA 95050      FAX: (408) 727-7557
                           E-mail: tda@best.com
```

```
Travel Network, Ltd.                              (800) 669-9000
560 Sylvan Avenue                                 (201) 567-8500
Englewood Cliffs, NJ 07632        FAX: (201) 567-4405

Travel Professionals Int'l                        (800) 626-2469
10172 Linn Station Rd., Ste. 360                  (502) 423-9966
Louisville, KY 40223              FAX: (502) 423-9914

Travelsavers Inc.                                 (800) 726-7283
71 Audrey Ave.                                    (516) 624-0500
Oyster Bay, NY 11771              FAX: (516) 624-6024

Uniglobe Travel, Uniglobe Bldg.                   (604) 662-3800
Ste. 900 1199 W. Pender           FAX: (604) 662-3878
Vancouver, BC Canada V6E 2R1

WESTA (Western Assoc. of Travel                   (408) 777-8170
    Agencies)                     FAX: (408) 777-8173
12280 S. Saratoga-Sunnyvale Rd., Ste. 111
Saratoga, CA 95070

Woodside Travel Trust                             (301) 718-9500
4330 East-West Highway #1100      FAX: (301) 718-4290
Bethesda, MD 20814-4290
```

DECODING WORLDWIDE CITY/AIRPORT CODES

The airports of the world have designated three-letter codes.
The codes are in alphabetical order. The city, state/province/
territory, and country are provided. Airport names may
also be included when applicable. **Refer to the pages on
"Abbreviations of States and Provinces" for assistance if
necessary.**

OTHER ABBREVIATIONS USED

Dem. Rep. - Democratic Republic
Hlpt - Heliport
P.R. CHINA - People's Republic of China
Rep. - Republic
RR - Railroad

Soc. Rep. - Socialist Republic
Soc. Is. - Society Islands
SPB - Seaplane Base
U.A. Emirates - United Arab Emirates
UK - United Kingdom

AAA - Anaa, Tumato Islands
AAC - Al Arish, Egypt
AAE - Annaba, Algeria
AAL - Aalborg, Denmark
AAN - Al Ain, United Arab
      Emirates
AAQ - Anapa, Russia
AAR - Aarhus, Denmark
AAT - Altay, P. R. China
AAU - Assau, Western Samoa
AAV - Alah, Philippines
AAY - Al Ghaydah. Yemen
ABE - Allentown, PA, USA
ABI - Abilene, TX, USA
ABJ - Abidjan, Cote D'Ivoire
ABK - Kabri Dar, Ethiopia
ABL - Ambler, AK, USA
ABM - Bamaga, QLD, Australia
ABQ - Albuquerque, NM,USA
ABR - Aberdeen, SD, USA
ABS - Abu Simbel, Egypt
ABT - Al-Baha, Saudi Arabia
ABV - Abuja, Nigeria
ABX - Albury, NSW, Australia
ABY - Albany, GA, USA
ABZ - Aberdeen, Scotland, UK
ACA - Acapulco, Mexico
ACC - Accra, Ghana
ACE - Lanzarote, Canary Islands
ACI - Alderney, Channel Islands,
      UK
ACK - Nantucket, MA, USA
ACT - Waco, TX, USA
ACV - Eureka/Arcata, CA,USA
ACY - Atlantic City, NJ-Pomona,
      USA
ADA - Adana, Turkey
ADB - Izmir-Adnan Mend, Turkey
ADD - Addis Ababa, Ethiopia
ADE - Aden, Yemen
ADH - Aldan, Russia
ADK - Adak Island, AK, USA
ADL - Adelaide, SA, Australia
ADQ - Kodiak, AK, USA
ADU - Ardabil, Iran
ADZ - San Andres Is., Colombia
AEO - Aioun El Atrouss,
      Mauritania
AEP - Buenos Aires-Newbery,
      Argentina
AER - Adler/Sochi, Russia
AES - Aalesund, Norway
AET - Allakaket, AK, USA
AEX - Alexandria, LA
AEY - Akureyri, Iceland

AFA - San Rafael, Argentina
AFL - ALta Floresta, MT, Brazil
AGA - Agadir, Morocco
AGB - Munich-Augsburg, Germany
AGE - Wangerooge, Germany
AGF - Agen, France
AGH - Helsingborg, Sweden
AGJ - Aguni, Japan
AGL - Wanigela, Papua New Guinea
AGN - Angoon, AK, USA
AGP - Malaga, Spain
AGR - Agra, India
AGS - Augusta, GA, USA
AGT - Ciudad Del Esté, Paraguay
AGU - Aguascalientes, Mexico
AGV - Acarigua, Venezuela
AHB - Abha, Saudi Arabia
AHN - Athens, GA, USA
AHO - Alghero, Italy
AHS - Ahuas, Honduras
AHU - Al Hoceima, Morocco
AIA - Alliance, NE, USA
AIC - Airok, Marshall Islands
AIM - Ailuk, Marshall Islands
AIN - Wainwright, AK, USA
AIT - Aitutaki, Cook Is., S.
      Pacific
AIU - Atiu, Cook Is., S. Pacific
AIY - Atlantic City, NJ, USA
AJA - Ajaccio, Corsica, France
AJF - Jouf, Saudi Arabia
AJI - Agri, Turkey
AJR - Arvidsjaur, Sweden
AJU - Aracaju, SE, Brazil
AJY - Agades, Niger
AKA - Ankang, P.R. China
AKB - Atka, AK, USA
AKE - Akieni, Gabon
AKG - Anguganak, Papua New Guinea
AKI - Akiak, AK, USA
AKJ - Asahikawa, Japan
AKK - Akhiok, AK, USA
AKL - Auckland, New Zealand
AKN - King Salmon, AK, USA
AKP - Anaktuvuk Pass, AK, USA
AKS - Auki, Solomon Islands
AKU - Aksu, P.R. China
AKV - Akulivik, Que., Canada
AKX - Aktyubinsk, Kazakstan
AKY - Sittwe, Myanmar
ALA - Almaty, Kazakstan
ALB - Albany, NY, USA
ALC - Alicante, Spain
ALF - Alta, Norway
ALG - Algiers, Algeria

ALH - Albany, WA, Australia	ART - Watertown, NY, USA
ALJ - Alexander Bay, South Africa	ARU - Aracatuba, SP, Brazil
ALM - Alamogordo, NM, USA	ARW - Arad, Romania
ALO - Waterloo, IA, USA	ASA - Assab, Ethiopia
ALP - Aleppo, Syria	ASB - Ashkgabat, Turkmenistan
ALS - Alamosa, CO, USA	ASD - Andros Town, Bahamas
ALW - Walla Walla, WA, USA	ASE - Aspen, CO, USA
ALY - Alexandria, Egypt	ASF - Astrakhan, Russia
ALZ - Alitak, AK, USA	ASJ - Amami O Shima, Japan
AMA - Amarillo, TX, USA	ASM - Asmara, Eritrea
AMB - Ambilobe, Madagascar	ASO - Asosa, Ethiopia
AMD - Ahmedabad, India	ASP - Alice Springs, NT,
AMH - Arba Mintch, Ethiopia	Australia
AMI - Mataram, Indonesia	ASR - Kayseri, Turkey
AMM - Amman, Jordan	AST - Astoria, OR, USA
AMQ - Ambon, Indonesia	ASU - Asuncion, Paraguay
AMS - Amsterdam, Netherlands	ASV - Amboseli, Kenya
AMY - Ambatomainty, Madagascar	ASW - Aswan, Egypt
ANC - Anchorage, AK, USA	ATC - Arthur's Town, Bahamas
ANF - Antofagasta, Chile	ATH - Athens, Greece
ANG - Angouleme, France	ATK - Atqasuk, AK, USA
ANI - Aniak, AK, USA	ATL - Atlanta, GA. USA
ANK - Ankara, Turkey	ATM - Altamira, PA, Brazil
ANM - Antalaha, Madagascar	ATN - Namatanai, Papua New Guinea
ANN - Annette Island, AK, USA	ATP - Aitape, Papua New Guinea
ANR - Antwerp, Belgium	ATQ - Amritsar, India
ANS - Andahuaylas, Peru	ATR - Atar, Mauritania
ANU - Antigua, West Indies	ATT - Atmautluak, AK, USA
ANV - Anvick, AK, USA	ATW - Appleton, WI, USA
ANX - Andenes, Norway	ATY - Watertown, SD, USA
AOE - Eskisehir, Turkey	ATZ - Assiut, Egypt
AOI - Ancona, Italy	AUA - Aruba, Aruba
AOJ - Aomori, Japan	AUC - Arauca, Colombia
AOK - Karpathos, Greece	AUG - Augusta, ME, USA
AOO - Altoona, PA, USA	AUH - Abu Dhabi,U. A. Emirates
AOR - Alor Setar, Malaysia	AUJ - Ambunti, Papua New Guinea
AOS - Amook, AK, USA	AUK - Alakanuk, AK,USA
AOT - Aosta, Italy	AUL - Aur, Marshall Islands
APF - Naples, FL,USA	AUP - Agaun, Papua New Guinea
APL - Nampula, Mozambique	AUQ - Atuona, Marquesas Island
APN - Alpena, MI, USA	AUR - Aurillac, France
APO - Apartado, Colombia	AUS - Austin, TX, USA
APP - Asapa, Papua New Guinea	AUU - Aurukun Mission, QLD,
APW - Apia, Western Samoa	Australia
AQA - Araraquara, SP, Brazil	AUV - Aumo, Papua New Guinea
AQG - Anqing, P.R. China	AUW - Wausau, WI, USA
AQI - Qaisumah, Saudi Arabia	AUX - Araguaina, TO, Brazil
AQJ - Aqaba, Jordan	AUY - Aneityum, Vanuatu
AQP - Arequipa, Peru	AVI - Ciego De Avila,Cuba
ARC - Arctic Village, AK, USA	AVL - Asheville, NC, USA
ARH - Arkhangelsk, Russia	AVN - Avignon, France
ARI - Arica, Chile	AVP - Wilkes-Barre/Scranton, PA,
ARM - Armidale, NSW, Australia	USA
ARN - Stockholm-Arlanda, Sweden	AVU - Avu Avu, Solomon Islands
ARP - Aragip, Papua New Guinea	AWD - Aniwa, Vanuatu

AWZ - Ahwaz, Iran	BDL - Hartford-Bradley, CT, USA
AXA - Anguilla, West Indies	BDO - Bandung, Indonesia
AXD - Alexandroupolis, Greece	BDP - Bhadrapur, Nepal
AXK - Ataq, Yemen	BDQ - Vadodara, India
AXM - Armenia, Colombia	BDR - Bridgeport, CT, USA
AXP - Spring Point, Bahamas	BDS - Brindisi, Italy
AXT - Akita, Japan	BDT - Gbadolite, Dem. Rep. of
AXU - Axum, Ethiopia	the Congo
AYP - Ayacucho, Peru	BDU - Bardufoss, Norway
AYQ - Ayers Rock, NT, Australia	BEB - Benbecula, Hebrides,
AYT - Antalya, Turkey	Scotland, UK
AZB - Amazon Bay, Papua New	BEF - Bluefields, Nicaragua
Guinea	BEG - Belgrade, Yugoslavia
AZD - Yazd, Iran	BEH - Benton Harbor, MI, USA
AZN - Andizhan, Uzbekistan	BEI - Beica, Ethiopia
AZO - Kalamazoo, MI, USA	BEJ - Berau, Indonesia
AZR - Adrar, Algeria	BEL - Belem, PA, Brazil
BAA - Bialla, Papua New Guinea	BEO - Belmont, NSW, Australia
BAG - Baguio, Philippines	BER - Berlin, Germany
BAH - Bahrain, Bahrain	BES - Brest, France
BAK - Baku, Azerbaijan	BET - Bethel, AK, USA
BAL - Batman, Turkey	BEU - Bedourie, Qld., Australia
BAQ - Barranquilla, Colombia	BEW - Beira, Mozambique
BAS - Balalae, Solomon Islands	BEY - Beirut, Lebanon
BAT - Barretos, SP, Brazil	BFD - Bradford, PA, USA
BAU - Bauru, SP, Brazil	BFF - Scottsbluff, NE, USA
BAV - Baotou, P. R. China	BFH - Curitiba Bacacheri, PR,
BAX - Barnaul, Russia	Brazil
BAY - Baia Mare, Romania	BFI - Boeing Field Int'l, WA, USA
BBA - Balmaceda, Chile	BFL - Bakersfield, CA, USA
BBI - Bhubaneswar, India	BFN - Bloemfontein, South Africa
BBK - Kasana, Botswana	BFO - Buffalo Range, Zimbabwe
BBM - Battambang, Cambodia	BFQ - Bahia Pinas, Panama
BBN - Bario, Sarawak, Malaysia	BFS - Belfast,N. Ireland, UK
BBO - Berbera, Somalia - BBO	BFV - Buri Ram, Thailand
BBQ - Barbuda, West Indies	BGA - Bucaramanga, Colombia
BBR - Basse Terre, French	BGC - Braganca, Portugal
Antilles	BGF - Bangui, Cen. African
BBU - Baneasa, Romania	Republic
BCA - Baracoa, Cuba	BGI - Barbados, Barbados
BCD - Bacolod, Philippines	BGK - Big Creek, Belize
BCE - Bryce Canyon, UT, USA	BGM - Binghamton, NY, USA
BCI - Barcaldine, QLD, Australia	BGO - Bergen, Norway
BCL - Barra Colorado, Costa Rica	BGR - Bangor, ME,USA
BCN - Barcelona, Spain	BGX - Bage, RS, Brazil
BCO - Jinka, Ethiopia	BGY - Orio Al Serio, Italy
BCP - Bambu, Papua New Guinea	BHB - Bar Harbor, ME, USA
BCW - Benguera Island, Mozambique	BHD - Belfast-City, N. Ireland,
BCX - Beloreck, Russia	UK
BDA - Bermuda, Atlantic Ocean	BHE - Blenheim, New Zealand
BDB - Bundaberg, Qld., Australia	BHG - Brus Laguna, Honduras
BDD - Badu Island, Qld.,	BHI - Bahia Blanca, Argentina
Australia	BHJ - Bhuj, India
BDH - Bandar Lengeh, Iran	BHK - Bukhara, Uzbekistan
BDJ - Banjarmasin, Indonesia	BHM - Birmingham, AL,USA

BHO - Bhopal, India
BHQ - Broken Hill, NSW, Australia
BHR - Bharatpur, Nepal
BHS - Bathurst, NSW, Australia
BHU - Bhavnagar, India
BHV - Bahawalpur, Pakistan
BHX - Birmingham, England, UK
BHY - Beihai, P.R. China
BHZ - Belo Horizonte, MG, Brazil
BIA - Bastia, Corsica, France
BID - Block Island, RI, USA
BII - Bikini Atoll, Marshall
      Islands
BIK - Biak, Indonesia
BIL - Billings, MT,USA
BIM - Bimini, Bahamas
BIO - Bilbao, Spain
BIQ - Biarritz, France
BIR - Biratnagar, Nepal
BIS - Bismarck, ND, USA
BIW - Billiluna, WA, Australia
BJA - Bejaia, Algeria
BJF - Batsfjord, Norway
BJI - Bemidji, MN, USA
BJL - Banjul, Gambia
BJM - Bujumbura, Burundi
BJR - Bahar Dar, Ethiopia
BJS - Beijing, P.R. China
BJV - Bodrum Milas Aprt, Turkey
BJX - Leon/Guanajuato, Mexico
BKA - Bykovo, Russia
BKC - Buckland, AK, USA
BKI - Kota Kinabalu, Sabah,
      Malaysia
BKK - Bangkok, Thailand
BKM - Bakalalan, Sarawak,
      Malaysia
BKO - Bamako, Mali
BKQ - Blackall, QLD, Australia
BKS - Bengkulu, Indonesia
BKW - Beckley, WV, USA
BKX - Brookings, SD, USA
BKY - Bukavu, Dem. Rep. of the
      Congo
BLA - Barcelona, Venezuela
BLE - Borlange, Sweden
BLF - Bluefield, WV, USA
BLG - Belaga, Sarawak, Malaysia
BLI - Bellingham, WA, USA
BLK - Blackpool, England, UK
BLL - Billund, Denmark
BLP - Bellavista, Peru
BLQ - Bologna, Italy
BLR - Bangalore, India
BLT - Blackwater, QLD, Australia

BLZ - Blantyre, Malawi
BMA - Stockholm-Bromma, Sweden
BMB - Bumba, Dem. Rep. of the
      Congo
BMD - Belo, Madagascar
BME - Broome, WA, Australia
BMI - Bloomington, IL, USA
BMM - Bitam, Gabon
BMO - Bhamo, Myanmar
BMP - Brampton Island, QLD,
      Australia
BMV - Ban Me Thuot, Vietnam
BMW - Bordj Badji Mokhtar,
      Algeria
BMY - Belep, New Caledonia
BNA - Nashville, TN, USA
BNB - Boende, Dem. Rep. of the
      Congo
BND - Bandar Abbas, Iran
BNE - Brisbane, QLD, Australia
BNJ - Bonn, Germany
BNK - Ballina, NSW, Australia
BNN - Bronnoysund, Norway
BNP - Bannu, Pakistan
BNU - Blumenau, SC, Brazil
BNY - Bellona Is., Solomon
      Islands
BOB - Bora Bora, Soc. Is., Fr.
      Polynesia
BOC - Bocas Del Toro, Panama Rep.
BOD - Bordeaux, France
BOG - Bogota, Colombia
BOH - Bournemouth, England, UK
BOI - Boise, ID, USA
BOJ - Bourgas, Bulgaria
BOM - Mumbai, Bombay, India
BON - Bonaire, Neth. Antilles
BOO - Bodo, Norway
BOS - Boston, MA, USA
BOV - Boang, Papua New Guinea
BOX - Borroloola, NT, Australia
BOY - Bobo Dioulasso, Burkina
      Faso
BPG - Barra Do Garcas, MT, Brazil
BPN - Balikpapan, Indonesia
BPS - Porto Seguro, BA, Brazil
BPT - Beaumont/Pt. Arthur, TX,
      USA
BPY - Besalampy, Madagascar
BQB - Busselton, WA, Australia
BQE - Bubaque, Guinea-Bissau
BQH - London-Biggin Hill,
      England, UK
BQK - Glynco Jetport, GA, USA
BQL - Boulia, QLD, Australia

BQN - Aguadilla, Puerto Rico
BQS - Blagoveschensk, Russia
BQU - Port Elizabeth, Windward
    Is.
BRA - Barreiras, BA, Brazil
BRC - San Carlos de Bariloche,
    Argentina
BRD - Brainerd, MN, USA
BRE - Bremen, Germany
BRI - Bari, Italy
BRK - Bourke, NSW, Australia
BRL - Burlington, IA, USA
BRM - Barquisimeto, Venezuela
BRN - Berne, Switzerland
BRO - Brownsville, TX, USA
BRQ - Brno, Czech Republic
BRR - Barra, Hebrides Is.,
    Scotland, UK
BRS - Bristol, England, UK
BRT - Bathurst Island, NT,
    Australia
BRU - Brussels, Belgium
BRW - Barrow, AK, USA
BSB - Brasilia, DF, Brazil
BSC - Bahia Solano, Colombia
BSD - Baoshan, P.R. China
BSG - Bata, Equatorial Guinea
BSK - Biskra, Algeria
BSL - Basel/Mulhouse, Switzerland
BSO - Basco, Philippines
BSU - Basankusu, Dem. Rep. of
    the Congo
BTA - Bertoua, Cameroon
BTH - Batam/Batu Besar, Indonesia
BTI - Barter Island, AK, USA
BTJ - Banda Aceh, Indonesia
BTK - Bratsk, Russia
BTM - Butte, MT, USA
BTR - Baton Rouge, LA, USA
BTS - Bratislava, Slovak Republic
BTT - Bettles, AK, USA
BTU - Bintulu, Sarawak, Malaysia
BTV - Burlington, VT, USA
BUA - Buka Is., Papua New Guinea
BUC - Burketown, QLD, Australia
BUD - Budapest, Hungary
BUE - Buenos Aires, Argentina
BUF - Buffalo, NY, USA
BUG - Benguela, Angola
BUH - Bucharest, Romania
BUK - Albuq, Yemen
BUL - Bulolo, Papua New Guinea
BUO - Burao, Somalia
BUQ - Bulawayo, Zimbabwe
BUR - Burbank, CA, USA

BUX - Bunia, Dem. Rep. of the
    Congo
BUZ - Bushehr, Iran
BVA - Paris-Tille, France
BVB - Boa Vista, RR, Brazil
BVC - Boa Vista, Cape Verde
    Islands
BVE - Brive-La-Gaillarde, France
BVG - Berlevag, Norway
BVH - Vilhena, RO, Brazil
BVI - Birdsville, QLD, Australia
BVR - Brava, Cape Verde
BWA - Bhairawa, Nepal
BWD - Brownwood, TX, USA
BWI - Baltimore, MD, USA
BWN - Bandar Seri Begawan, Brunei
BWQ - Brewarrina, NSW, Australia
BWT - Burnie, TS, Australia
BWU - Bankstown, NSW, Australia
BXN - Bodrum, Turkey
BXU - Butuan, Philippines
BXX - Borama, Somalia
BXZ - Bunsil, Papua New Guinea
BYA - Boundary, AK, USA
BYB - Dibaa, Oman
BYK - Bouake, Cote D'Ivoire
BYM - Bayamo, Cuba
BYU - Bayreuth, Germany
BYW - Blakely Island, WA, USA
BZA - Bonanza, Nicaragua
BZB - Bazaruto Island, Mozambique
BZE - Belize City, Belize
BZK - Briansk, Russia
BZL - Barisal, Bangladesh
BZN - Bozeman, MT, USA
BZR - Beziers, France
BZV - Brazzaville, Peop. Rep. of
    the Congo
BZZ - Brize Norton, England, UK
CAB - Cabinda, Angola
CAC - Cascavel, PR, Brazil
CAE - Columbia, SC, USA
CAG - Cagliari, Italy
CAI - Cairo, Egypt
CAJ - Canaima, Venezuela
CAK - Akron/Canton, OH,USA
CAL - Campbeltown, Scotland, UK
CAN - Guangzhou, P. R. China
CAP - Cap Haitien, Haiti
CAQ - Caucasia, Colombia
CAS - Casablanca, Morocco
CAW - Campos, RJ, Brazil
CAY - Cayenne, Fr. Guiana
CAZ - Cobar, NSW, Australia
CBB - Cochabamba, Bolivia

CBE - Cumberland, MD, USA
CBG - Cambridge, England, UK
CBH - Bechar, Algeria
CBL - Ciudad Bolivar, Venezuela
CBO - Cotabato, Philippines
CBQ - Calabar, Nigeria
CBR - Canberra, ACT, Australia
CBT - Catumbela, Angola
CCC - Cayo Coco, Cuba
CCF - Carcassone, France
CCI - Concordia, SC, Brazil
CCJ - Calicut, India
CCM - Crisciuma, SC, Brazil
CCP - Concepcion, Chile
CCS - Caracas, Venezuela
CCU - Calcutta, India
CCV - Craig Cove, Vanuatu
CCZ - Chub Cay, Bahamas
CDB - Cold Bay, AK, USA
CDC - Cedar City, UT, USA
CDG - Paris-De Gaulle, France
CDJ - Conceicao Do Araguaia, PA, Brazil
CDL - Candle, AK, USA
CDR - Chadron, NE, USA
CDV - Cordova, AK, USA
CEB - Cebu, Philippines
CEC - Crescent City, CA, USA
CED - Ceduna, SA, Australia
CEI - Chiang Rai, Thailand
CEK - Chelyabinsk, Russia
CEM - Central, AK, USA
CEN - Ciudad Obregon, Mexico
CEQ - Cannes, France
CER - Cherbourg, France
CEZ - Cortez, CO, USA
CFE - Clermont-Ferrand, France
CFN - Donegal, Rep. of Ireland
CFR - Caen, France
CFS - Coffs Harbour, NSW, Australia
CFU - Kerkyra, Greece
CGA - Craig, AK, USA
CGB - Cuiaba, MT, Brazil
CGC - Cape Gloucester, Papua New Guinea
CGD - Changde, P.R. China
CGH - Congonhas, SP, Brazil
CGI - Cape Girardeau, MO, USA
CGK - Jakarta-Soekarno, Indonesia
CGN - Cologne/Bonn, Germany
CGO - Zhengzhou, P. R. China
CGP - Chittagong, Bangladesh
CGQ - Changchun, P. R. China
CGR - Campo Grande, MS, Brazil

CGX - Chicago, IL-Meigs, USA
CGY - Cagayan de Oro, Philippines
CHA - Chattanooga, TN, USA
CHC - Christchurch, New Zealand
CHH - Chachapoyas, Peru
CHI - Chicago, IL, USA
CHM - Chimbote, Peru
CHO - Charlottesville, VA, USA
CHP - Circle Hot Springs, AK, USA
CHQ - Chania, Crete, Greece
CHS - Charleston, SC, USA
CHT - Chatham Island, New Zealand
CHU - Chuathbaluk, AK, USA
CHX - Changuinola, Panama Rep.
CHY - Choiseul Bay, Solomon Islands
CIA - Rome-Ciampino, Italy
CIC - Chico, CA, USA
CID - Cedar Rapids/Iowa City, IA, USA
CIF - Chifeng, P. R. China
CIJ - Cobija, Bolivia
CIK - Chalkyitsik, AK, USA
CIT - Chimkent, Kazakstan
CIU - Sault Ste. Marie, MI-Chippewa, USA
CIW - Canouan Island, Windward Islands
CIX - Chiclayo, Peru
CJA - Cajamarca, Peru
CJB - Coimbatore, India
CJC - Calama, Chile
CJJ - Cheong Ju City, Rep. of Korea
CJL - Chitral, Pakistan
CJS - Ciudad Juarez, Mexico
CJU - Cheju, Rep. of Korea
CKB - Clarksburg, WV, USA
CKD - Crooked Creek, AK, USA
CKG - Chongqing, P. R. China
CKS - Carajas, PA, Brazil
CKX - Chicken, AK, USA
CKY - Conakry, Guinea
CLD - Carlsbad, CA, USA
CLE - Cleveland, OH, USA
CLJ - Cluj-Napoca, Romania
CLL - College Station, TX, USA
CLM - Port Angeles, WA, USA
CLO - Cali, Colombia
CLP - Clarks Point, AK, USA
CLQ - Colima, Mexico
CLT - Charlotte, NC, USA
CLY - Calvi, Corsica, France
CMA - Cunnamulla, QLD, Australia
CMB - Colombo, Sri Lanka

CMD - Cootamundra, NSW, Australia	CRU - Carriacou, Windward Islands
CME - Ciudad Del Carmen, Mexico	CRV - Crotone, Italy
CMF - Chambery, France	CRW - Charleston, WV, USA
CMG - Corumba, MS, Brazil	CSG - Columbus, GA, USA
CMH - Columbus, OH, USA	CSI - Casino, NSW, Australia
CMI - Champaign, IL, USA	CSK - Cap Skirring, Senegal
CMK - Club Makokola, Malawi	CSL - San Luis Obispo, CA, USA
CMN - Casablanca-Mohamed V., Morocco	CSX - Changsha, P. R. China
CMU - Kundiawa, Papua New Guinea	CTA - Catania, Italy
CMW - Camaguey, Cuba	CTC - Catamarca, Argentina
CMX - Hancock, MI, USA	CTD - Chitre, Panama
CNB - Coonamble, NSW, Australia	CTG - Cartagena, Colombia
CNC - Coconut Island, QLD, Australia	CTL - Charleville, QLD, Australia
CND - Constanta, Romania	CTM - Chetumal, Mexico
CNF - Tancredo Neves Int'l, MG, Brazil	CTN - Cooktown, QLD, Australia
	CTS - Sapporo-Chitose, Japan
CNJ - Cloncurry, QLD, Australia	CTU - Chengdu, P. R. China
CNL - Sindal, Denmark	CUC - Cucuta, Colombia
CNM - Carlsbad, NM, USA	CUE - Cuenca, Ecuador
CNP - Eastgreenland, Greenland	CUF - Cuneo, Italy
CNQ - Corrientes, Argentina	CUG - Orange, NSW-Cudal, Australia
CNS - Cairns, QLD, Australia	CUJ - Culion, Philippines
CNX - Chiang Mai, Thailand	CUK - Caye Caulker, Belize
CNY - Moab, UT, USA	CUL - Culiacan, Mexico
COD - Cody, WY, USA	CUM - Cumana, Venezuela
COG - Condoto, Colombia	CUN - Cancun, Mexico
COJ - Coonabarabran, NSW, Australia	CUQ - Coen, QLD, Australia
COK - Cochin, India	CUR - Curacao, Neth. Antilles
COO - Cotonou, Benin	CUU - Chihuahua, Mexico
COR - Cordoba, Argentina	CUW - Cube Cove, AK, USA
COS - Colorado Springs, CO, USA	CUZ - Cuzco, Peru
COU - Columbia, MO, USA	CVC - Cleve, SA, Australia
CPB - Capurgana, Colombia	CVG - Cincinnati, OH, USA
CPC - San Martin de Los Andes, Argentina	CVJ - Cuernavaca, Mexico
	CVL - Cape Vogel,Papua New Guinea
CPD - Coober Pedy, SA, Australia	CVM - Cuidad Victoria, Mexico
CPE - Campeche, Mexico	CVN - Clovis, NM, USA
CPH - Copenhagen, Denmark	CVQ - Carnarvon, WA, Australia
CPI - Cape Orford, Papua New Guinea	CVU - Corvo Is., Portugal (Azores)
CPO - Copiapo, Chile	CWA - Wausau, Wisconsin Central WI, USA
CPQ - Campinas, SP, Brazil	
CPR - Casper, WY, USA	CWB - Curitiba, PR, Brazil
CPT - Cape Town, South Africa	CWC - Chernovtsy, Ukraine
CPV - Campina Grande, PB, Brazil	CWL - Cardiff, Wales, UK
CPX - Culebra, Puerto Rico	CWS - Center Is., WA, USA
CQA - Canarana, MT, Brazil	CWT - Cowra, NSW, Australia
CRD - Comodoro Rivadavia, Argentina	CXB - Cox's Bazar, Bangladesh
	CXH - Vancouver, BC Harbour-SP, Canada
CRI - Crooked Island, Bahamas	CXJ - Caxias Do Sul, RS, Brazil
CRL - Brussels-South, Belgium	CYB - Cayman Brac, West Indies
CRP - Corpus Christi, TX, USA	CYF - Chefornak, AK, USA
	CYI - Chiayi, Taiwan

CYO - Cayo Lago Del Sur, Cuba
CYS - Cheyenne, WY, USA
CYU - Cuyo, Philippine
CZA - Chichen Itza, Mexico
CZE - Coro, Venezuela
CZF - Cape Romanzof, AK, USA
CZH - Corozal, Belize
CZL - Constantine, Algeria
CZM - Cozumel, Mexico
CZN - Chisana, AK, USA
CZS - Cruzeiro Do Sul, AC, Brazil
CZX - Changzhou, P. R. China
DAB - Daytona Beach, FL, USA
DAC - Dhaka, Bangladesh
DAD - Da Nang, Soc. Rep. of Viet
      Nam
DAL - Dallas/Ft. Worth, TX-Love,
      USA
DAM - Damascus, Syria
DAR - Dar Es Salaam, Tanzania
DAT - Datong, P.R. China
DAU - Daru, Papua New Guinea
DAV - David, Panama Rep.
DAX - Daxian, P.R. China
DAY - Dayton, OH, USA
DBA - Dalbandin, Pakistan
DBM - Debra Marcos, Ethiopia
DBO - Dubbo, NSW, Australia
DBQ - Dubuque, IA, USA
DBT - Debre Tabor, Ethiopia
DBV - Dubrovnik, Croatia
DCA - Washington D.C.- Ronald
      Reagan, USA
DCF - Dominica-Cane, West Indies
DCM - Castres, France
DDC - Dodge City, KS, USA
DDG - Dandong, P. R. China
DDI - Daydream Island, QLD,
      Australia
DDM - Dodoima, Papua New Guinea
DEA - Dera Ghazi Kahn, Pakistan
DEC - Decatur, IL, USA
DEL - Delhi, India
DEM - Dembidollo, Ethiopia
DEN - Denver, CO, USA
DER - Derim, Papua New Guinea
DET - Detroit, MI-City, USA
DEZ - Deirezzor, Syria
DFW - Dallas/Ft. Worth, TX, USA
DGA - Dangriga, Belize
DGE - Mudgee, NSW, Australia
DGO - Durango, Mexico
DGT - Dumaguete, Philippines
DHA - Dhahran, Saudi Arabia
DHI - Dhangarhi, Nepal

DHN - Dothan, AL, USA
DIB - Dibrugarh, India
DIE - Antsiranana, Madagascar
DIJ - Dijon, France
DIK - Dickinson, ND, USA
DIL - Dili, Indonesia
DIN - Dien Bien Phu, Vietnam
DIR - Dire Dawa, Ethiopia
DIS - Loubomo, Peop. Rep. of the
      Congo
DIU - Diu, India
DIY - Diyarbakir, Turkey
DJB - Jambi, Indonesia
DJE - Djerba, Tunisia
DJG - Djanet, Algeria
DJJ - Jayapura, Indonesia
DJN - Delta Junction, AK, USA
DKI - Dunk Island, QLD, Australia
DKR - Dakar, Senegal
DLA - Douala, Cameroon
DLC - Dalian, P. R. China
DLD - Geilo, Norway
DLG - Dillingham, AK, USA
DLH - Duluth, MN/Superior, WI,
      USA
DLI - Dalat, Vietnam
DLM - Dalaman, Turkey
DLO - Dolomi, AK, USA
DLU - Dali City, P.R. China
DLY - Dillons Bay, Vanuatu
DMD - Doomadgee Mission, QLD,
      Australia
DME - Moscow-Domodedovo, Russia
DMU - Dimapur, India
DNB - Dunbar, QLD, Australia
DND - Dundee, Angus, Scotland, UK
DNH - Dunhuang, P. R. China
DNK - Dnepropetrovsk, Ukraine
DNM - Denham, WA, Australia
DNR - Dinard, France
DNZ - Denizli, Turkey
DOF - Dora Bay, AK, USA
DOG - Dongola, Sudan
DOH - Doha, Qatar
DOK - Donetsk, Ukraine
DOM - Dominica, West Indies
DOP - Dolpa, Nepal
DOU - Dourados, MS, Brazil
DPL - Dipolog, Philippines
DPO - Devonport, Tas., Australia
DPS - Denpasar Bali, Indonesia
DRB - Derby, WA, Australia
DRG - Deering, AK, USA
DRO - Durango, CO, USA
DRS - Dresden, Germany

DRT - Del Rio, TX, USA
DRW - Darwin, NT, Australia
DSD - La Desirade, Guadeloupe
DSE - Dessie, Ethiopia
DSK - Dera Ismail Khan, Pakistan
DSM - Des Moines, IA, USA
DTD - Datadawai, Indonesia
DTM - Dortmund, Germany
DTR - Decatur Is., WA, USA
DTT - Detroit, MI, USA
DTW - Detroit, MI-Wayne Co., USA
DUB - Dublin, Rep. of Ireland
DUD - Dunedin, New Zealand
DUE - Dundo, Angola
DUJ - Dubois, PA, USA
DUR - Durban, South Africa
DUS - Duesseldorf, Germany
DUT - Dutch Harbor, AK, USA
DVL - Devils Lake, ND, USA
DVO - Davao, Philippines
DWB - Soalala, Madagascar
DXB - Dubai, U. A. Emirates
DYG - Dayong, P.R. China
DYR - Anadyr, Russia
DYU - Dushanbe, Tajikistan
DZA - Dzaoudzi, Comoros
EAA - Eagle, AK, USA
EAE - Emae, Vanuatu
EAM - Nejran, Saudi Arabia
EAR - Kearney, NE, USA
EAS - San Sebastian, Spain
EAT - Wenatchee, WA, USA
EAU - Eau Claire, WI, USA
EBB - Entebbe/Kampala, Uganda
EBG - El Bagre, Colombia
EBJ - Esbjerg, Denmark
EBO - Ebon, Marshall Islands
EBU - St. Etienne, France
ECN - Ercan, Cyprus
EDA - Edna Bay, AK, USA
EDI - Edinburgh, Scotland, UK
EDR - Edward River, QLD,
    Australia
EEK - Eek, AK, USA
EEN - Keene, NH, USA
EFD - Houston, TX-Ellington, USA
EFG - Efogi, Papua New Guinea
EFL - Kefallinia, Greece
EGC - Bergerac, France
EGE - Vail/Eagle, CO, USA
EGL - Neghelli, Ethiopia
EGM - Sege, Solomon Islands
EGS - Egilsstadir, Iceland
EGX - Egegik, AK, USA
EHM - Cape Newenham, AK, USA

EIA - Eia, Papua New Guinea
EIN - Eindhoven, Netherlands
EIS - Tortola, BVI
EJA - Barrancabermeja, Colombia
EJH - Wedjh, Saudi Arabia
EKO - Elko, NV, USA
ELC - Elcho Island, NT, Australia
ELD - El Dorado, AR, USA
ELE - El Real, Panama
ELG - El Golea, Algeria
ELH - North Eleuthera, Bahamas
ELI - Elim, AK, USA
ELM - Elmira, NY, USA
ELP - El Paso, TX, USA
ELQ - Gassim, Saudi Arabia
ELS - East London, South Africa
ELU - El Oued, Algeria
ELV - Elfin Cove, AK, USA
ELY - Ely, NV, USA
EMA - East Midlands, England, UK
EMD - Emerald, QLD, Australia
EMI - Emirau, Papua New Guinea
EMK - Emmonak, AK, USA
EMN - Nema, Mauritania
EMO - Emo, Papua New Guinea
EMS - Embessa, Papua New Guinea
ENA - Kenai, AK, USA
ENF - Enontekio, Finland
ENS - Enschede, Netherlands
ENT - Enewetak, Marshall Islands
ENU - Enugu, Nigeria
ENY - Yan'an, P.R. China
EOH - Medellin-Herrera, Colombia
EOI - Eday, UK
EPL - Epinal, France
EPR - Esperance, WA, Australia
EPS - El Portillo/Samana,
    Dominican Rep.
EQS - Esquel, Argentina
ERA - Erigavo, Somalia
ERC - Erzincan, Turkey
ERD - Berdyansk, Ukraine
ERF - Erfurt, Germany
ERH - Errachidia, Morocco
ERI - Erie, PA, USA
ERM - Erechim, RS, Brazil
ERS - Windhoek-Eros, Namibia
ERZ - Erzurum, Turkey
ESA - Esa' Ala, Papua New Guinea
ESB - Ankara-Esenboga, Turkey
ESC - Escanaba, MI, USA
ESD - Eastsound, WA, USA
ESR - El Salvador, Chile
ETH - Elat, Israel
ETZ - Metz/Nancy, France

EUA - Eua, Tonga Island
EUG - Eugene, OR, USA
EUN - Laayoune, Morocco
EUX - St. Eustatius, Neth.
      Antilles
EVE - Evenes, Norway
EVG - Sveg, Sweden
EVN - Yerevan, Armenia
EVV - Evansville, IN, USA
EWB - New Bedford, MA, USA
EWN - New Bern, NC, USA
EWR - Newark, NJ, USA
EXI - Excursion Inlet, AK, USA
EXT - Exeter, England, UK
EYL - Yelimane, Mali
EYP - El Yopal, Colombia
EYW - Key West, FL, USA
EZE - Buenos Aires-Pistarini,
      Argentina
EZS - Elazig, Turkey
FAE - Faroe Islands, Denmark
FAI - Fairbanks, AK, USA
FAJ - Fajardo, Puerto Rico
FAK - False Island, AK, USA
FAN - Farsund, Norway
FAO - Faro, Portugal
FAQ - Freida, Papua New Guinea
FAR - Fargo, ND, USA
FAT - Fresno, CA, USA
FAV - Fakarava, Tuamotu Islands
FAY - Fayetteville, NC, USA
FBE - Francisco Beltrao, PR,
      Brazil
FBM - Lubumbashi, Dem. Rep. of
      the Congo
FBU - Fornebu, Norway
FCA - Kalispell/Glacier Nat'l PK,
      MT, USA
FCO - Rome-Da Vinci, Italy
FDE - Forde, Norway
FDF - Fort De France, Martinique
FDH - Friedrichshafen, Germany
FEG - Fergana, Uzbekistan
FEN - Fernando de Noronha, FN,
      Brazil
FEZ - Fez, Morocco
FGI - Apia-Fagali I., Western
      Samoa
FHU - Ft. Huachuca/Sr. Vista, AZ,
      USA
FID - Fishers Island, NY, USA
FIE - Fair Isle, Scotland, UK
FIH - Kinshasa, Dem. Rep. of the
      Congo

FIN - Finschhafen, Papua New
      Guinea
FIZ - Fitzroy Crossing, WA,
      Australia
FJR - Al-Fujairah, United Arab
      Emirates
FKI - Kisangani, Dem. Rep. of
      the Congo
FKL - Franklin, PA, USA
FKS - Fukushima, Japan
FLA - Florencia, Colombia
FLG - Flagstaff, AZ, USA
FLL - Ft. Lauderdale, FL, USA
FLN - Florianopolis, SC, Brazil
FLO - Florence, SC, USA
FLR - Florence, Italy
FLS - Flinders Is., Tas.,
      Australia
FLW - Santa Cruz, Flores,
      Portugal (Azores)
FMA - Formosa, Argentina
FMI - Kalemie, Dem. Rep. of the
      Congo
FMN - Farmington, NM, USA
FMO - Muenster, Germany
FMY - Fort Myers, FL, USA
FNA - Freetown, Sierra Leone
FNC - Funchal, Portugal (Madeira)
FNE - Fane, Papua New Guinea
FNI - Nimes, France
FNJ - Pyongyang, Dem. Peop. Rep.
      of Korea
FNL - Fort Collins/Loveland, CO,
      USA
FNT - Flint, MI, USA
FOC - Fuzhou, P. R. China
FOD - Fort Dodge, IA, USA
FOE - Topeka, KS-Forbes, USA
FOR - Fortaleza, CE, Brazil
FOU - Fougamou, Gabon
FPO - Freeport, Bahamas
FRA - Frankfurt, Germany
FRB - Forbes, NSW, Australia
FRC - Franca, SP, Brazil
FRD - Friday Harbor, WA, USA
FRE - Fera Island, Solomon
      Islands
FRM - Fairmont, MN, USA
FRO - Floro, Norway
FRS - Flores, Guatemala
FRU - Bishkek, Krgyzstan
FRW - Francistown, Botswana
FSC - Figari, Corsica, France
FSD - Sioux Falls, SD, USA
FSM - Ft. Smith, AR, USA

FSP - St. Pierre, St. Pierre and Miquelon
FTA - Futuna Is., Vanuatu
FTU - Ft. Dauphin, Madagascar
FTV - Masvingo, Zimbabwe
FTW - Meachem Field-Ft. Worth, TX, USA
FTX - Owando, Congo
FUE - Fuerteventura, Canary Islands
FUJ - Fukue, Japan
FUK - Fukuoka, Japan
FUN - Funafuti Atol, Tuvalu
FUT - Futuna, Wallis & Futuna Is.
FVL - Flora Valley, WA, Australia
FWA - Ft. Wayne, IN, USA
FYU - Ft. Yukon, AK, USA
FYV - Fayetteville, AR, USA
GAJ - Yamagata, Honshu, Japan
GAL - Galena, AK, USA
GAM - Gambell, AK, USA
GAN - Gan Island, Maldives
GAO - Guantanamo, Cuba
GAQ - Gao, Mali
GAR - Garaina, Papua New Guinea
GAU - Gauhati, India
GAX - Gamba, Gabon
GBD - Great Bend, KS, USA
GBE - Gaborone, Botswana
GBJ - Marie Galante, Fr. Antilles
GCC - Gillette, WY, USA
GCI - Guernsey, Channel Islands, UK
GCK - Garden City, KS, USA
GCM - Grand Cayman, West Indies
GCN - Grand Canyon, AZ, USA
GDE - Gode, Ethiopia
GDL - Guadalajara, Mexico
GDN - Gdansk, Poland
GDQ - Gondar, Ethiopia
GDT - Grand Turk, Turks & Caicos Is.
GDV - Glendive, MT, USA
GDX - Magadan, Russia
GDZ - Gelendzik, Russia
GEA - Noumea-Magenta, New Caledonia
GEG - Spokane, WA, USA
GEL - Santo Angelo, RS, Brazil
GEO - Georgetown, Guyana
GER - Nueva Gerona, Cuba
GES - General Santos, Philippines
GET - Geraldton, WA, Australia
GEV - Gallivare, Sweden
GEW - Gewoya, Papua New Guinea

GFF - Griffith, NSW, Australia
GFK - Grand Forks, ND, USA
GFN - Grafton, NSW, Australia
GGG - Longview, TX, USA
GGT - George Town, Bahamas
GGW - Glasgow, MT, USA
GHA - Ghardaia, Algeria
GHB - Governors Harbour, Bahamas
GHC - Great Harbour Cay, Bahamas
GHD - Ghimbi, Ethiopia
GHE - Garachine, Panama
GIB - Gibraltar, Gibraltar
GIC - Boigu Island, QLD, Australia
GIG - Rio de Janeiro-Int'l, Brazil
GIL - Gilgit, Pakistan
GIS - Gisborne, New Zealand
GIZ - Gizan, Saudi Arabia
GJA - Guanaja Is., Honduras
GJL - Jijel, Algeria
GJT - Grand Junction, CO, USA
GKA - Goroka, Papua New Guinea
GKL - Great Keppel Island, QLD, Australia
GLA - Glasgow, Scotland, UK
GLD - Goodland, KS, USA
GLF - Golfito, Costa Rica
GLH - Greenville, MS, USA
GLI - Glen Innes, NSW, Australia
GLT - Gladstone, QLD, Australia
GLV - Golovin, AK, USA
GMA - Gemena, Dem. Rep. of the Congo
GMB - Gambela, Ethiopia
GME - Gomel, Belarus
GMI - Gasmata, Papua New Guinea
GMR - Gambier Is., Fr. Polynesia
GNB - Grenoble, France
GND - Grenada, Windward Islands
GNR - General Roca, Argentina
GNU - Goodnews Bay, AK, USA
GNV - Gainesville, FL, USA
GOA - Genoa, Italy
GOB - Goba, Ethiopia
GOC - Gora, Papua New Guinea
GOE - Gonalia, Papua New Guinea
GOH - Nuuk, Greenland
GOI - Goa, India
GOJ - Nizhniy Novgorod, Russia
GOM - Goma, Dem. Rep. of the Congo
GON - New London, CT, USA
GOQ - Golmud, P.R. China
GOR - Gore, Ethiopia

```
GOT - Gothenburg, Sweden            GYA - Guayaramerin, Bolivia
GOU - Garoua, Cameroon              GYE - Guayaquil, Ecuador
GOV - Gove, NT,                     GYM - Guaymas, Mexico
GPB - Guarapuava, PR, Brazil        GYN - Goiania, GO, Brazil
GPI - Guapi, Colombia               GYY - Gary, IN, USA
GPN - Garden Point, NT, Australia   GZM - Gozo, Malta
GPT - Gulfport/Biloxi, MS, USA      GZO - Gizo, Solomon Islands
GPZ - Grand Rapids, MN, USA         GZT - Gaziantep, Turkey
GRB - Green Bay, WI, USA            HAA - Hasvik, Norway
GRI - Grand Island, NE, USA         HAC - Hachijo Jima Is., Japan
GRJ - George, South Africa          HAD - Halmstad, Sweden
GRL - Garasa, Papua New Guinea      HAE - Havasupai, AZ, USA
GRP - Gurupi, GO, Brazil            HAH - Moroni-Hahaya, Comoros
GRQ - Groningen, Netherlands        HAJ - Hanover, Germany
GRR - Grand Rapids, MI, USA         HAK - Haikou, P. R. China
GRU - Guarulhos Int'l, SP, Brazil   HAM - Hamburg, Germany
GRW - Graciosa Island, Portugal     HAN - Hanoi, Soc. Rep. of Viet
      (Azores)                            Nam
GRX - Granada, Spain                HAP - Long Island, QLD, Australia
GRY - Grimsey, Iceland              HAQ - Hanimaadhoo, Maldives
GRZ - Graz, Austria                 HAR - Harrisburg, PA, USA
GSA - Long Pasia, Sabah, Malaysia   HAS - Hail, Saudi Arabia
GSE - Gothenburg-Saeve, Sweden      HAU - Haugesund, Norway
GSO - Greensboro/H.PT/Win-Salem,    HAV - Havana, Cuba
      NC, USA                       HBA - Hobart, Tas., Australia
GSP - Greenville/Spartanburg, SC,   HBH - Hobart Bay, AK, USA
      USA                           HBT - Hafr Albatin, Saudi Arabia
GST - Gustavus, AK, USA             HCQ - Halls Creek, WA, Australia
GTE - Groote Is., NT, Australia     HCR - Holy Cross, AK, USA
GTF - Great Falls, MT, USA          HDB - Heidelberg, Germany
GTO - Gorontalo, Indonesia          HDD - Hyderabad, Pakistan
GTR - Columbus-Golden Triangle      HDN - Steamboat Springs-Hayden,
      Reg., MS, USA                       CO, USA
GUA - Guatemala City, Guatemala     HDS - Hoedspruit, Transvaal,
GUB - Guerrero Negro, Mexico              South Africa
GUC - Gunnison, CO, USA             HDY - Hat Yai, Thailand
GUD - Goundam, Mali                 HEH - Heho, Myanmar
GUH - Gunnedah, NSW, Australia      HEL - Helsinki, Finland
GUM - Guam, Guam                    HER - Heraklion, Greece
GUP - Gallup, NM, USA               HET - Hohhot, P. R. China
GUR - Alotau, Papua New Guinea      HEX - Santo Domingo-Herrera Aprt,
GUW - Atyrau, Kazakstan                   Dominican Rep.
GUX - Guna, India                   HFA - Haifa, Israel
GUZ - Guarapari, ES, Brazil         HFD - Hartford, CT/Springield,
GVA - Geneva, Switzerland                 MA, USA
GVI - Green River, Papua New        HFE - Hefei, P. R. China
      Guinea                        HFN - Hornafjordur, Iceland
GVR - Governador Valadares, MG,     HFS - Hagfors, Sweden
      Brazil                        HFT - Hammerfest, Norway
GVX - Gavle, Sweden                 HGA - Hargeisa, Somalia
GWD - Gwadar, Pakistan              HGD - Hughenden, QLD, Australia
GWL - Gwalior, India                HGH - Hangzhou, P. R. China
GWT - Westerland, Germany           HGL - Helgoland, Germany
GWY - Galway, Rep. of Ireland       HGN - Mae Hong Son, Thailand
GXF - Seiyun, Yemen                 HGO - Korhogo, Cote D'Ivoire
```

HGR - Hagerstown, MD, USA
HGU - Mt. Hagen, Papua New Guinea
HHA - Huanghua, P.R. China
HHH - Hilton Head Island, SC, USA
HHN - Hahn, Germany
HIB - Hibbing, MN, USA
HID - Horn Island, QLD, Australia
HII - Lake Havasu City, AZ, USA
HIJ - Hiroshima, Japan
HIL - Shillavo, Ethiopia
HIN - Chinju, Rep. of Korea
HIR - Honiara, Guadalcanal,
     Solomon Islands
HIS - Hayman Is., QLD, Australia
HIW - Hiroshima-West, Japan
HJR - Khajuraho, India
HKB - Healy Lake, AK, USA
HKD - Hakodate, Japan
HKG - Hong Kong, Hong Kong
HKK - Hokitika, New Zealand
HKN - Hoskins, Papua New Guinea
HKT - Phuket, Thailand
HKY - Hickory, NC, USA
HLF - Hultsfred, Sweden
HLN - Helena, MT, USA
HLP - Jakarta-Halim, Indonesia
HLZ - Hamilton, New Zealand
HMA - Malmo-Harbour, Sweden
HME - Hassi Messaoud, Algeria
HMO - Hermosillo, Mexico
HMV - Hemavan, Sweden
HNA - Morioka, Japan
HND - Tokyo-Haneda, Japan
HNH - Hoonah, AK, USA
HNL - Honolulu, Oahu, HI, USA
HNM - Hana, Maui, HI, USA
HNS - Haines, AK, USA
HOB - Hobbs, NM, USA
HOD - Hodeidah, Yemen
HOE - Houeisay, Laos
HOF - Hofuf, Saudi Arabia
HOG - Holguin, Cuba
HOI - Hao Island, Tuamotu Islands
HOK - Hooker Creek, NT, Australia
HOM - Homer, AK, USA
HON - Huron, SD, USA
HOQ - Hof, Germany
HOR - Horta, Portugal (Azores)
HOS - Chos Malal, Argentina
HOT - Hot Springs, AR, USA
HOU - Houston, TX, USA
HOV - Orsta/Volda, Norway
HPA - Ha'Apai, Tonga Island
HPB - Hooper Bay, AK, USA
HPH - Haiphong, Vietnam

HPN - Westchester County, NY, USA
HRB - Harbin, Manchuria, P. R.
     China
HRE - Harare, Zimbabwe
HRG - Hurghada, Egypt
HRK - Kharkov, Ukraine
HRL - Harlingen, TX, USA
HRO - Harrison, AR, USA
HSH - Las Vegas, NV-Henderson,
     USA
HSL - Huslia, AK, USA
HSN - Zhousan, P.R. China
HSV - Huntsville/Decatur, AL, USA
HTA - Chita, Russia
HTI - Hamilton Island, QLD,
     Australia
HTN - Hotan, P. R. China
HTR - Hateruma, Japan
HTS - Huntington, WV, USA
HUE - Humera, Ethiopia
HUF - Terre Haute, IN, USA
HUH - Huahine, Soc. Is., Fr.
     Polynesia
HUI - Hue, Vietnam
HUN - Hualien, Taiwan
HUS - Hughes, AK, USA
HUU - Huanuco, Peru
HUV - Hudiksvall, Sweden
HUX - Santa Cruz Huatulco, Mexico
HUY - Humberside, England, UK
HVB - Hervey Bay, QLD, Australia
HVG - Honningsvag, Norway
HVN - New Haven, CT, USA
HVR - Havre, MT, USA
HWN - Hwange National Park,
     Zimbabwe
HYA - Hyannis, MA, USA
HYD - Hyderabad, India
HYF - Hayfields, Papua New Guinea
HYG - Hydaburg, AK, USA
HYL - Hollis, AK, USA
HYN - Huangyan, P.R. China
HYS - Hays, KS, USA
HZG - Hanzhong, P. R. China
HZK - Husavik, Iceland
IAD - Washington D.C., Dulles,
     USA
IAH - Houston, TX-Int'l, USA
IAM - In Amenas, Algeria
IAN - Kiana, AK, USA
IAS - Iasi, Romania
IBE - Ibague, Colombia
IBI - Iboki, Papua New Guinea
IBZ - Ibiza, Spain
ICI - Cicia, Fiji

ICT - Wichita, KS, USA
IDA - Idaho Falls, ID, USA
IDN - Indagen, Papua New Guinea
IDR - Indore, India
IEV - Kiev, Ukraine
IFJ - Isafjordur, Iceland
IFN - Isfahan, Iran
IFO - Ivano-Frankovsk, Ukraine
IFP - Bullhead City, AZ, USA
IGA - Inagua, Bahamas
IGG - Igiugig, AK, USA
IGM - Kingman, AZ, USA
IGO - Chigorodo, Colombia
IGR - Iguazu, Argentina
IGU - Iguassu Falls, PR, Brazil
IHU - Ihu, Papua New Guinea
IIS - Nissan Island, Papua New
      Guinea
IKI - Iki, Japan
IKO - Nikolski, AK, USA
IKT - Irkutsk, Russia
ILE - Killeen, TX, USA
ILI - Iliamna, AK, USA
ILM - Wilmington, NC, USA
ILO - Iloilo, Philippines
ILP - Ile Des Pins, New Caledonia
ILQ - Ilo, Peru
ILY - Islay, Scotland, UK
ILZ - Zilina, Slovakia
IMF - Imphal, India
IMI - Ine, Marshall Is.
IMK - Simikot, Nepal
IMP - Imperatriz, MA, Brazil
IMT - Iron Mountain, MI, USA
INC - Yinchuan, P. R. China
IND - Indianapolis, IN, USA
INL - Int'l Falls, MN, USA
INN - Innsbruck, Austria
INU - Nauru, Rep. of Nauru
INV - Inverness, Scotland, UK
INZ - In Salah, Algeria
IOA - Ioannina, Greece
IOK - Iokea, Papua New Guinea
IOM - Isle of Man, UK
ION - Impfondo, Congo
IOP - Ioma, Papua New Guinea
IOS - Ilheus, BA, Brazil
IPA - Ipota, Vanuatu
IPC - Easter Island, Pacific
      Ocean
IPH - Ipoh, Malaysia
IPI - Ipiales, Colombia
IPL - El Centro/Imperial, CA, USA
IPN - Ipatinga, MG, Brazil
IPT - Williamsport, PA, USA

IQM - Qiemo, P.R. China
IQQ - Iquique, Chile
IQT - Iquitos, Peru
IRA - Kirakira, Solomon Islands
IRC - Circle, AK, USA
IRG - Lockhart Rivers, QLD,
      Australia
IRJ - La Rioja, Argentina
IRK - Kirksville, MO, USA
IRP - Isiro, Dem. Rep. of the
      Congo
ISA - Mt. Isa, QLD, Australia
ISB - Islamabad/Rawalpindi,
      Pakistan
ISC - Isles of Scilly, UK
ISE - Isparta, Turkey
ISG - Ishigaki, Japan
ISN - Williston, ND, USA
ISO - Kinston, NC, USA
ISP - Long Island Macarthur, NY,
      USA
IST - Istanbul, Turkey
ITB - Itaituba, PA, Brazil
ITH - Ithaca, NY, USA
ITK - Itokama, Papua New Guinea
ITM - Itami, Japan
ITO - Hilo, Hawaii, HI, USA
IUE - Niue Island, Niue
IVA - Ambanja, Madagascar
IVC - Invercargill, New Zealand
IVL - Ivalo, Finland
IVR - Inverell, NSW, Australia
IVW - Inverway, NT, Australia
IWD - Ironwood, MI, USA
IWJ - Iwami, Japan
IXA - Agartala, India
IXB - Bagdogra, India
IXC - Chandigarh, India
IXE - Mangalore, India
IXJ - Jammu, India
IXK - Keshod, India
IXL - Leh, India
IXM - Madurai, India
IXR - Ranchi, India
IXS - Silchar, India
IXU - Aurangabad, India
IXZ - Port Blair, Andaman Is.,
      India
IYK - Inyokern, CA, USA
IZM - Izmir, Turkey
IZO - Izumo, Japan
JAC - Jackson Hole, WY, USA
JAG - Jacobabad, Pakistan
JAI - Jaipur, India
JAN - Jackson, MS, USA

JAQ - Jacquinot Bay, Papua New Guinea
JAT - Jabat, Marshall Is.
JAV - Ilulissat, Greenland
JAX - Jacksonville, FL, USA
JBR - Jonesboro, AR, USA
JCA - Cannes Croisette H/P, France
JCB - Joacaba, SC, Brazil
JCH - Qasigiannguit, Greenland
JCK - Julia Creek, QLD, Australia
JCU - Cueta Heliport, Spain
JDF - Juiz de Fora, MG, Brazil
JDH - Jodhpur, India
JDO - Juazeiro Do Norte, CE, Brazil
JDZ - Jingdezhen, P.R. China
JED - Jeddah, Saudi Arabia
JEG - Aasiaat, Greenland
JEJ - Jeh, Marshall Is.
JER - Jersey, Channel Islands, UK
JFK - New York, NY-Kennedy, USA
JFR - Frederikshab, Greenland
JGA - Jamnagar, India
JGC - Grand Canyon, AZ-Heliport, USA
JGN - Jiayuguan, P. R. China
JGO - Godhavn, Greenland
JGR - Groennedal, Greenland
JHB - Johor Bahru, Malaysia
JHE - Helsingborg-Hlpt, Sweden
JHG - Jinghong, P.R. China
JHM - Kapalua, Maui, HI, USA
JHQ - Shute Harbour, QLD, Australia
JHS - Sisimiut, Greenland
JHW - Jamestown, NY, USA
JIA - Juina, MT, Brazil
JIB - Djibouti, Djibouti
JIK - Ikaria Island, Greece
JIL - Jilin, P.R. China
JIM - Jimma, Ethiopia
JIU - Jiujiang, P.R. China
JIW - Jiwani, Pakistan
JJI - Juanjui, Peru
JJN - Jinjiang, P.R. China
JJU - Qaqortoq, Greenland
JKG - Jonkoping, Sweden
JKH - Chios, Greece
JKR - Janakpur, Nepal
JKT - Jakarta, Indonesia
JLN - Joplin, MO, USA
JMK - Mikonos, Greece
JMM - Malmo-Harbour, Sweden
JMO - Jomsom, Nepal

JMS - Jamestown, ND, USA
JNB - Johannesburg, South Africa
JNN - Nanortalik, Greenland
JNS - Narsaq, Greenland
JNU - Juneau, AK, USA
JNX - Naxos, Cyclades Is., Greece
JNZ - Jinzhou, P.R. China
JOE - Joensuu, Finland
JOG - Yogyakarta, Indonesia
JOI - Joinville, SC, Brazil
JON - Johnston Island, Pacific Ocean
JOS - Jos, Nigeria
JPA - Joao Pessoa, PB, Brazil
JPR - Ji-Parana, RO, Brazil
JQE - Jaque, Panama
JRH - Jorhat, India
JRO - Kilimanjaro, Tanzania
JRS - Jerusalem, Israel
JSA - Jaisalmer, India
JSH - Sitia, Greece
JSI - Skiathos, Greece
JSR - Jessore, Bangladesh
JST - Johnstown, PA, USA
JSU - Manitsoq, Greenland
JSY - Syros Is., Greece
JTR - Santorini, Thira Is., Greece
JTY - Astypalaia Is., Dodekanese, Greece
JUA - Juara, MT, Brazil
JUJ - Jujuy, Argentina
JUL - Juliaca, Peru
JUM - Jumla, Nepal
JUV - Upernavik, Greenland
JUZ - Juzhou, P.R. China
JVA - Ankavandra, Madagascar
JYV - Jyvaskyla, Finland
KAB - Kariba, Zimbabwe
KAC - Kameshli, Syria
KAD - Kaduna, Nigeria
KAE - Kake, AK, USA
KAG - Kangnung, Rep. of Korea
KAJ - Kajaani, Finland
KAL - Kaltag, AK, USA
KAN - Kano, Nigeria
KAO - Kuusamo, Finland
KAT - Kaitaia, New Zealand
KAX - Kalbarri, WA, Australia
KAW - Kawthaung, Myanmar
KBC - Birch Creek, AK, USA
KBL - Kabul, Afghanistan
KBM - Kabwum, Papua New Guinea
KBP - Kiev-Borispol, Ukraine
KBR - Kota Bharu, Malaysia

KBT - Kaben, Marshall Is.
KCA - Kuqa , P.R. China
KCC - Coffman Cove, AK, USA
KCG - Chignik, AK-Fisheries, USA
KCH - Kuching, Sarawak, Malaysia
KCL - Chignik, AK, USA
KCM - Kahramanmaras, Turkey
KCQ - Chignik, AK-Chignik Lk.,
    USA
KCZ - Kochi, Japan
KDD - Khuzdar, Pakistan
KDI - Kendari, Indonesia
KDM - Kaadedhdhoo, Maldives
KDN - N'Dende, Gabon
KDO - Kadhdhoo, Maldives
KDR - Kandrian, Papua New Guinea
KDU - Skardu, Pakistan
KDV - Kandavu, Fiji
KEF - Reykjavik-Keflavik, Iceland
KEJ - Kemerovo, Russia
KEK - Ekwok, AK, USA
KEL - Kiel, Germany
KEM - Kemi, Finland
KEO - Odienne, Cote D'Ivoire
KEP - Nepalganj, Nepal
KER - Kerman, Iran
KET - Kengtung, Myanmar
KEW - Keewaywin, Ont., Canada
KEX - Kanabea, Papua New Guinea
KFA - Kiffa, Mauritania
KFG - Kalkurung, NT, Australia
KFP - False Pass, AK, USA
KGA - Kananga, Dem. Rep. of the
    Congo
KGB - Konge, Papua New Guinea
KGC - Kingscote, SA, Australia
KGD - Kaliningrad, Russia
KGE - Kagau, Solomon Islands
KGF - Karaganda, Kazakstan
KGI - Kalgoorlie, WA, Australia
KGJ - Karonga, Malawi
KGK - Koliganek, AK, USA
KGL - Kigali, Rwanda
KGO - Kirovograd, Ukraine
KGS - Kos, Greece
KGW - Kagi, Papua New Guinea
KGX - Grayling, AK, USA
KHE - Kherson, Ukraine
KHG - Kashi, P. R. China
KHH - Kaohsiung, Taiwan
KHI - Karachi, Pakistan
KHM - Khamti, Myanmar
KHN - Nanchang, Kiangsi, P. R.
    China
KHS - Khasab, Oman

KHV - Khabarovsk, Russia
KIB - Ivanof Bay, AK, USA
KID - Kristianstad, Sweden
KIF - Kingfisher Lake, Ont.,
    Canada
KIJ - Niigata, Japan
KIM - Kimberley, South Africa
KIN - Kingston, Jamaica
KIO - Kili, Marshall Islands
KIQ - Kira, Papua New Guinea
KIR - Kerry County, Rep. of
    Ireland
KIS - Kisumu, Kenya
KIT - Kithira, Greece
KIV - Kishinev, Moldova
KIX - Kansai Int'l, Japan
KJA - Krasnoyarsk, Russia
KJP - Kerama, Japan
KKA - Koyuk, AK, USA
KKB - Kitoi, AK, USA
KKC - Khon Kaen, Thailand
KKD - Kokoda, Papua New Guinea
KKE - Kerikeri, New Zealand
KKH - Kongiganak, AK, USA
KKI - Akiachak, AK, USA
KKJ - Kita Kyushu, Japan
KKN - Kirkenes, Norway
KKR - Kaukura Atoll, Tuamotu
    Islands
KKU - Ekuk, AK, USA
KKX - Kikaiga Shima, Japan
KKZ - Koh Kong, Cambodia
KLG - Kalskag, AK, USA
KLL - Levelock, AK, USA
KLN - Larsen Bay, AK, USA
KLO - Kalibo, Philippines
KLR - Kalmar, Sweden
KLT - Kaiserslauter, Germany
KLU - Klagenfurt, Austria
KLW - Klawock, AK, USA
KLX - Kalamata, Greece
KLZ - Kleinzee, South Africa
KMA - Kerema, Papua New Guinea
KME - Kamembe, Rwanda
KMF - Kamina, Papua New Guinea
KMG - Kunming, P. R. China
KMI - Miyazaki, Japan
KMJ - Kumamoto, Japan
KMO - Manokotak, AK, USA
KMP - Keetmanshoop, Namibia
KMQ - Komatsu, Japan
KMV - Kalemyo, Myanmar
KMY - Moser Bay, AK, USA
KNA - Vina del Mar, Chile

KND - Kindu, Dem. Rep. of the Congo
KNH - Kinmen, Taiwan
KNK - Kakhonak, AK, USA
KNQ - Kone, New Caledonia
KNS - King Island, TAS, Australia
KNW - New Stuyahok, AK, USA
KNX - Kununurra, WA, Australia
KNZ - Kenieba, Mali
KOA - Kona, Hawaii, HI, USA
KOC - Koumac, New Caledonia
KOE - Kupang, Indonesia
KOI - Kirkwall, Orkney Is., Scotland, UK
KOJ - Kagoshima, Japan
KOK - Kokkola, Finland
KOP - Nakhon Phanom, Thailand
KOT - Kotlik, AK, USA
KOU - Koulamoutou, Gabon
KOW - Ganzhou, P. R. China
KOY - Olga Bay, AK, USA
KOZ - Ouzinkie, AK, USA
KPB - Point Baker, AK, USA
KPC - Port Clarence, AK, USA
KPI - Kapit, Sarawak, Malaysia
KPN - Kipnuk, AK, USA
KPO - Pohang, Rep. of Korea
KPR - Port Williams, AK, USA
KPS - Kempsey, NSW, Australia
KPV - Perryville, AK, USA
KPY - Port Bailey, AK, USA
KQA - Akutan, AK, USA
KRB - Karumba, QLD, Australia
KRF - Kramfors, Sweden
KRI - Kikori, Papua New Guinea
KRJ - Karawari, Papua New Guinea
KRK - Krakow, Poland
KRL - Korla, P.R. China
KRN - Kiruna, Sweden
KRP - Karup, Denmark
KRR - Krasnodar, Russia
KRS - Kristiansand, Norway
KRT - Khartoum, Sudan
KRW - Krasnovodsk, Turkmenistan
KRY - Karamay, P.R. China
KSA - Kosrae, Caroline Islands
KSC - Kosice, Slovak Republic
KSD - Karlstad, Sweden
KSH - Kermanshah, Iran
KSJ - Kasos Island, Greece
KSM - St. Mary's, AK, USA
KSN - Kostanay, Kazakstan
KSO - Kastoria, Greece
KSQ - Karshi, Uzbekistan
KSU - Kristiansund, Norway

KSW - Kiryat Shmona, Israel
KSY - Kars, Turkey
KTA - Karratha, WA, Australia
KTB - Thorne Bay, AK, USA
KTD - Kita-Daito, Japan
KTE - Kerteh, Malaysia
KTG - Ketapang, Indonesia
KTM - Kathmandu, Nepal
KTN - Ketchikan, AK, USA
KTP - Kingston-Tinson, Jamaica
KTR - Katherine, NT, Australia
KTS - Brevig Mission, AK, USA
KTT - Kittila, Finland
KTW - Katowice, Poland
KUA - Kuantan, Malaysia
KUD - Kudat, Sabah, Malaysia
KUF - Samara, Russia
KUG - Kubin Island, QLD, Australia
KUH - Kushiro, Japan
KUK - Kasigluk, AK, USA
KUL - Kuala Lumpur, Malaysia
KUM - Yakushima, Japan
KUN - Kaunas, Lithuania
KUO - Kuopio, Finland
KUQ - Kuri, Papua New Guinea
KUS - Kulusuk, Greenland
KUU - Kulu, India
KUV - Kunsan, Rep. of Korea
KUY - Kamusi, Papua New Guinea
KVA - Kavala, Greece
KVB - Skovde, Sweden
KVC - King Cove, AK, USA
KVD - Gyandzha, Azerbaijan
KVE - Kitava, Papua New Guinea
KVG - Kavieng, Papua New Guinea
KVL - Kivalina, AK, USA
KWA - Kwajalein, Marshall Islands
KWE - Guiyang, P. R. China
KWF - Waterfall, AK, USA
KWG - Krivoy Rog, Ukraine
KWI - Kuwait, Kuwait
KWJ - Kwangju, Rep. of Korea
KWK - Kwigillingok, AK, USA
KWL - Guilin, P. R. China
KWM - Kowanyama, QLD, Australia
KWN - Quinhagak, AK, USA
KWO - Kawito, Papua New Guinea
KWP - West Point, AK, USA
KWT - Kwethluk, AK, USA
KWY - Kiwayu, Kenya
KXA - Kasaan, AK, USA
KXF - Koro, Fiji
KYA - Konya, Turkey
KYK - Karluk, AK, USA

```
KYP - Kyaukpyu, Myanmar          LEI - Almeria, Spain
KYS - Kayes, Mali                LEJ - Leipzig, Germany
KYU - Koyukuk, AK, USA           LEL - Lake Evella, NT, Australia
KYX - Yalumet, Papua New Guinea  LEQ - Lands End, England, UK
KZB - Zachar Bay, AK, USA        LER - Leinster, WA, Australia
KZF - Kaintiba, Papua New Guinea LET - Leticia, Colombia
KZI - Kozani, Greece             LEV - Bureta, Fiji
KZN - Kazan, Russia              LEX - Lexington, KY, USA
KZS - Kastelorizo, Greece        LFT - Lafayette, LA, USA
LAA - Lamar, CO, USA             LFW - Lome, Togo
LAB - Lablab, Papua New Guinea   LGA - New York, NY-La Guardia,
LAD - Luanda, Angola                   USA
LAE - Lae, Papua New Guinea      LGB - Long Beach, CA, USA
LAF - Lafayette, IN, USA         LGE - Lake Gregory, WA, Australia
LAI - Lannion, France            LGH - Leigh Creek, SA, Australia
LAJ - Lages, SC, Brazil          LGI - Deadman's Cay, L.I.,
LAN - Lansing, MI, USA                 Bahamas
LAO - Laoag, Philippines         LGK - Langkawi, Malaysia
LAP - La Paz, Mexico             LGL - Long Lellang, Sarawak,
LAR - Laramie, WY, USA                 Malaysia
LAS - Las Vegas, NV, USA         LGN - Linga Linga, Papua New
LAU - Lamu, Kenya                      Guinea
LAW - Lawton, OK, USA            LGP - Legaspi, Philippines
LAX - Los Angeles, CA-Int'l, USA LGS - Malargue, Argentina
LBA - Leeds/Bradford, England, UK LGW - London-Gatwick, England, UK
LBB - Lubbock, TX, USA           LHE - Lahore, Pakistan
LBE - Latrobe, PA, USA           LHG - Lightning Ridge, NSW,
LBF - North Platte, NE, USA            Australia
LBL - Liberal, KS, USA           LHR - London-Heathrow, England,
LBP - Long Banga, Malaysia             UK
LBQ - Lambarene, Gabon           LHW - Lanzhou, P. R. China
LBS - Labasa, Fiji               LIF - Lifou, Loyalty Is.
LBU - Labuan, Sabah. Malaysia    LIG - Limoges,  France
LBV - Libreville, Gabon          LIH - Lihue, Kauai, HI, USA
LBW - Long Bawan, Indonesia      LIJ - Long Island, AK, USA
LBX - Lubang, Philippines        LIK - Likiep, Marshall Islands
LCA - Larnaca, Cyprus            LIL - Lille, France
LCE - La Ceiba, Honduras         LIM - Lima, Peru
LCG - La Coruna, Spain           LIN - Milan, Italy-Linate
LCH - Lake Charles, LA, USA      LIQ - Lisala, Dem. Rep. of  the
LCP - Loncopue, Argentina              Congo
LCY - London-City, England, UK   LIR - Liberia, Costa Rica
LDB - Londrina, PR, Brazil       LIS - Lisbon, Portugal
LDE - Lourdes/Tarbes, France     LIT - Little Rock, AR, USA
LDH - Lord Howe Is., NSW,        LIW - Loikaw, Myanmar
      Australia                  LJA - Lodja, Dem. Rep. of the
LDI - Lindi, Tanzania                  Congo
LDK - Lidkoping, Sweden          LJG - Lijiang City, P.R. China
LDN - Lamidanda, Nepal           LJU - Ljubljana, Slovenia
LDU - Lahad Datu, Sabah, Malaysia LKB - Lakeba, Fiji
LDY - Londonderry N., Ireland, UK LKE - Seattle, WA-Lake Union, USA
LEA - Learmonth, WA, Australia   LKL - Lakselv, Norway
LEB - Lebanon, NH, USA           LKN - Leknes, Norway
LED - St. Petersburg, Russia     LKO - Lucknow, India
LEH - Le Havre, France           LLA - Lulea, Sweden
```

LLI - Lalibela, Ethiopia
LLW - Lilongwe, Malawi
LMA - Lake Minchumina, AK, USA
LMI - Lumi, Papua New Guinea
LML - Lae, Marshall Islands
LMM - Los Mochis, Mexico
LMN - Limbang, Sarawak, Malaysia
LMP - Lampedusa, Italy
LMT - Klamath Falls, OR, USA
LNB - Lamen Bay, Vanuatu
LNE - Lonorore, Vanuatu
LNG - Lese, Papua New Guinea
LNK - Lincoln, NE, USA
LNO - Leonora, WA, Australia
LNS - Lancaster, PA, USA
LNV - Lihir Island, Papua New
    Guinea
LNY - Lanai City, Lanai, HI, USA
LNZ - Linz, Austria
LOD - Longana, Vanuatu
LOF - Loen, Marshall Is.
LON - London, England, UK
LOS - Lagos, Nigeria
LOV - Monclova, Mexico
LPA - Las Palmas, Canary Islands
LPB - La Paz, Bolivia
LPI - Linkoping, Sweden
LPL - Liverpool, England, UK
LPM - Lamap, Vanuatu
LPP - Lappeenranta, Finland
LPQ - Luang Prabang, Laos
LPS - Lopez Island, WA, USA
LPT - Lampang, Thailand
LPU - Long Apung, Indonesia
LPY - Le Puy, France
LRD - Laredo, TX, USA
LRE - Longreach, QLD, Australia
LRH - La Rochelle, France
LRL - Lama-Kara/Niamtougou, Togo
LRM - La Romana, Dominican Rep.
LRS - Leros, Greece
LRT - Lorient, France
LRU - Las Cruces, NM, USA
LSA - Losuia, Papua New Guinea
LSC - La Serena, Chile
LSE - La Crosse WI/Winona, MN,
    USA
LSH - Lashio, Myanmar
LSI - Sumburgh, U.K.
LSM - Long Semado, Sarawak,
    Malaysia
LSP - Las Piedras, Venezuela
LSQ - Los Angeles, Chile
LSS - Terre-De-Haut, Guadeloupe
LST - Launceston, Tas., Australia

LSY - Lismore, NSW, Australia
LTK - Latakia, Syria
LTL - Lastourville, Gabon
LTN - London-Luton Int'l.,
    England, UK
LTO - Loreto, Mexico
LTQ - Le Touquet, France
LUA - Lukla, Nepal
LUC - Laucala Island, Fiji
LUD - Luderitz, Namibia
LUG - Lugano, Switzerland
LUL - Laurel/Hattiesburg, MS, USA
LUM - Luxi, P.R. China
LUN - Lusaka, Zambia
LUP - Kalaupapa, Molokai, HI, USA
LUQ - San Luis, Argentina
LUR - Cape Lisburne, AK, USA
LUX - Luxembourg, Luxembourg
LVB - Livramento, RS, Brazil
LVD - Lime Village, AK, USA
LVI - Livingstone, Zambia
LVO - Laverton, WA, Australia
LWB - Greenbrier, WV, USA
LWK - Lerwick-Tingwall, Scotland,
    UK
LWN - Leninakan, Armenia
LWO - Lvov, Ukraine
LWS - Lewiston, ID, USA
LWT - Lewistown, MT, USA
LWY - Lawas, Sarawak, Malaysia
LXA - Lhasa, P. R. China
LXG - Luang Namtha, Laos
LXR - Luxor, Egypt
LXS - Lemnos, Greece
LYA - Luoyang, P.R. China
LYC - Lycksele, Sweden
LYG - Lianyungang, P. R. China
LYH - Lynchburg, VA, USA
LYP - Faisalabad, Pakistan
LYR - Longyearbyen, Norway
LYS - Lyon, France
LZC - Lazaro Cardenas, Mexico
LZH - Liuzhou, P.R. China
LZO - Luzhou, P.R. China
LZR - Lizard Island, QLD,
    Australia
MAA - Madras, India
MAB - Maraba, PA, Brazil
MAD - Madrid, Spain
MAF - Midland/Odessa, TX, USA
MAG - Madang, Papua New Guinea
MAH - Menorca, Spain
MAJ - Majuro, Marshall Islands
MAM - Matamoros, Mexico
MAN - Manchester, England, UK

MAO - Manaus, AM, Brazil
MAQ - Mae Sot, Thailand
MAR - Maracaibo, Venezuela
MAS - Manus Is., Papua New Guinea
MAT - Matadi, Dem. Rep. of the Congo
MAU - Maupiti, Soc. Is., Fr. Polynesia
MAV - Maloelap, Marshall Islands
MAY - Mangrove Cay, Bahamas
MAZ - Mayaguez, Puerto Rico
MBA - Mombasa, Kenya
MBC - M'Bigou, Gabon
MBD - Mmabatho, South Africa
MBE - Monbetsu, Japan
MBH - Maryborough, QLD, Australia
MBJ - Montego Bay, Jamaica
MBL - Manistee, MI, USA
MBP - Moyobamba, Peru
MBS - Saginaw, MI, USA
MBU - Mbambanakira, Solomon Islands
MBW - Moorabbin, VIC, Australia
MCE - Merced, CA, USA
MCG - Mc Grath, AK, USA
MCI - Kansas City, MO-Int'l, USA
MCK - McCook, NE, USA
MCM - Monte Carlo, Monaco
MCN - Macon, GA, USA
MCO - Orlando, FL-Int'l, USA
MCP - Macapa, AP, Brazil
MCT - Muscat, Oman
MCU - Montlucon, France
MCV - MacArthur River, NT, Australia
MCW - Mason City, IA, USA
MCX - Makhachkala, Russia
MCY - Sunshine Coast, QLD, Australia
MCZ - Maceio, AL, Brazil
MDC - Manado, Indonesia
MDE - Medellin, Colombia
MDG - Mudanjiang, P.R. China
MDI - Makurdi, Nigeria
MDK - Mbandaka, Dem. Rep. of the Congo
MDL - Mandalay, Myanmar
MDQ - Mar Del Plata, Argentina
MDS - Middle Caicos, Turks & Caicos Is.
MDT - Harrisburg, PA, USA
MDU - Mendi, Papua New Guinea
MDW - Chicago, IL-Midway, USA
MDZ - Mendoza, Argentina

MEB - Melbourne, VIC-Essendon, Australia
MED - Madinah, Saudi Arabia
MEE - Mare, Loyalty Is.
MEG - Malange, Angola
MEH - Mehamn, Norway
MEI - Meridian, MS, USA
MEL - Melbourne, VIC, Australia
MEM - Memphis, TN, USA
MES - Medan, Indonesia
MEU - Monte Dourado, PA, Brazil
MEX - Mexico City, Mexico
MEY - Meghauli, Nepal
MFE - Mc Allen, TX, USA
MFF - Moanda, Gabon
MFG - Muzaffarabad, Pakistan
MFJ - Moala, Fiji
MFM - Macau, Macau
MFN - Milford Sound, New Zealand
MFO - Manguna, Papua New Guinea
MFR - Medford, OR, USA
MFT - Machu Picchu, Peru
MFU - Mfuwe, Zambia
MFW - Magaruque, Mozambique
MFZ - Meselia, Papua New Guinea
MGA - Managua, Nicaragua
MGB - Mt. Gambier, SA, Australia
MGD - Magdalena, Bolivia
MGF - Maringa, PR, Brazil
MGH - Margate, South Africa
MGL - Dusseldorf Moenchengladbach, Germany
MGM - Montgomery, AL, USA
MGQ - Mogadishu, Somalia
MGS - Mangaia, Cook Is.
MGT - Millingimbi, NT, Australia
MGV - Margaret River, WA, Australia
MGW - Morgantown, WV, USA
MGX - Moabi, Gabon
MGZ - Myeik, Myanmar
MHD - Mashad, Iran
MHG - Mannheim, Germany
MHH - Marsh Harbour, Bahamas
MHK - Manhattan, KS, USA
MHP - Minsk Int'l, Belarus
MHQ - Mariehamn, Aland Is., Finland
MHT - Manchester, NH, USA
MHX - Manihiki Is. , Cook Is.
MIA - Miami, FL, USA
MID - Merida, Mexico
MII - Marilia, SP, Brazil
MIJ - Mili, Marshall Islands
MIK - Mikkeli, Finland

MIL - Milan, Italy
MIM - Merimbula, NSW, Australia
MIR - Monastir, Tunisia
MIS - Misima, Papua New Guinea
MIU - Maiduguri, Nigeria
MJA - Manja, Madagascar
MJB - Mejit Is., Marshall Is.
MJC - Man, Cote D'Ivoire
MJD - Mohenjo Daro, Pakistan
MJE - Majkin, Marshall Is.
MJF - Mosjoen, Norway
MJK - Monkey Mia, WA, Australia
MJL - Mouila, Gabon
MJM - Mbuji-Mayi, Dem. Rep. of
      the Congo
MJN - Majunga, Madagascar
MJT - Mytilene, Greece
MJV - Murcia, Spain
MKB - Mekambo, Gabon
MKC - Kansas City, MO, USA
MKE - Milwaukee, WI, USA
MKG - Muskegon, MI, USA
MKK - Molokai/Hoolehua, HI, USA
MKL - Jackson, TN, USA
MKM - Mukah, Sarawak, Malaysia
MKN - Malekolon, Papua New Guinea
MKP - Makemo, Tuamotu Islands
MKQ - Merauke, Indonesia
MKR - Meekatharra, WA, Australia
MKS - Mekane Selam, Ethiopia
MKU - Makokou, Gabon
MKY - Mackay, QLD, Australia
MKZ - Malacca, Malaysia
MLA - Malta, Mediterranean Sea
MLB - Melbourne, FL, USA
MLE - Male, Maldives
MLH - Mulhouse/Basel, France
MLI - Moline, IL, USA
MLL - Marshall, AK, USA
MLM - Morelia, Mexico
MLN - Melilla, Spain
MLO - Milos, Greece
MLQ - Malalaua, Papua New Guinea
MLS - Miles City, MT, USA
MLU - Monroe, LA, USA
MLW - Monrovia, Liberia
MLX - Malatya, Turkey
MLY - Manley Hot Sprgs., AK, USA
MMA - Malmo, Sweden
MMB - Memanbetsu, Japan
MMD - Minami Daito Jima, Okinawa
      Islands
MME - Teesside, England, UK
MMJ - Matsumoto, Japan
MMK - Murmansk, Russia

MMO - Maio, Cape Verde Islands
MMX - Malmo-Sturup, Sweden
MMY - Miyako Jima, Japan
MNB - Moanda, Dem. Rep. of the
      Congo
MNF - Mana, Fiji
MNG - Maningrida, NT, Australia
MNJ - Mananjary, Madagascar
MNL - Manila, Philippines
MNT - Minto, AK, USA
MNU - Maulmyine, Myanmar
MNY - Mono Is., Solomon Islands
MOA - Moa, Cuba
MOB - Mobile AL/Pascagoula, MS,
      USA
MOC - Montes Claros, MG, Brazil
MOD - Modesto, CA, USA
MOF - Maumere, Indonesia
MOG - Monghsat, Myanmar
MOI - Mitiaro, Cook Is.
MOL - Molde, Norway
MON - Mount Cook, New Zealand
MOQ - Morondava, Madagascar
MOT - Minot, ND, USA
MOU - Mountain Village, AK, USA
MOW - Moscow, Russia
MOZ - Moorea Is., Soc. Is., Fr.
      Polynesia
MPA - Mpacha, Namibia
MPB - Miami, FL - Public SPB, USA
MPH - Catician, Philippines
MPK - Mokpu, Rep. of Korea
MPL - Montpellier, France
MPM - Maputo, Mozambique
MPN - Mount Pleasant, Falkland
      Is.
MPU - Mapua, Papua New Guinea
MPW - Mariupol, Ukraine
MQF - Magnitogorsk, Russia
MQH - Minacu, GO, Brazil
MQL - Mildura, VIC, Australia
MQN - Mo I Rana, Norway
MQT - Marquette, MI, USA
MQX - Makale, Ethiopia
MRD - Merida, Venezuela
MRE - Mara Lodges, Kenya
MRM - Manare, Papua New Guinea
MRS - Marseille, France
MRU - Mauritius, Mauritius
MRV - Mineralnye Vody, Russia
MRY - Monterey, CA, USA
MRZ - Moree, NSW, Australia
MSA - Muskrat Dam, Ont., Canada
MSH - Masirah, Oman
MSJ - Misawa, Japan

MSL - Muscle Shoals, AL, USA
MSN - Madison, WI, USA
MSO - Missoula, MT, USA
MSP - Minneapolis/St Paul, MN, USA
MSQ - Minsk, Belarus
MSR - Mus, Turkey
MSS - Massena, NY, USA
MST - Maastricht, Netherlands
MSU - Maseru, Lesotho
MSY - New Orleans, LA, USA
MSZ - Namibe, Angola
MTF - Mizan Teferi, Ethiopia
MTH - Marathon, FL, USA
MTI - Mosteiros, Cape Verde Islands
MTJ - Montrose, CO, USA
MTL - Maitland, NSW, Australia
MTM - Metlakatla, AK, USA
MTO - Mattoon, IL, USA
MTR - Monteria, Colombia
MTS - Manzini, Swaziland
MTT - Minatitlan, Mexico
MTV - Mota Lava, Vanuatu
MTY - Monterrey, Mexico
MUA - Munda, Solomon Islands
MUB - Maun, Botswana
MUC - Munich, Germany
MUE - Kamuela, HI, USA
MUK - Mauke, Cook Is.
MUN - Maturin, Venezuela
MUR - Marudi, Sarawak, Malaysia
MUW - Mascara, Algeria
MUX - Multan, Pakistan
MUZ - Musoma, Tanzania
MVB - Franceville, Gabon
MVD - Montevideo, Uruguay
MVN - Mt. Vernon, IL, USA
MVR - Maroua, Cameroon
MVS - Mucuri, BA, Brazil
MVT - Mataiva, Fr. Polynesia
MVX - Minvoul, Gabon
MVY - Martha's Vineyard, MA, USA
MVZ - Masvingo, Zimbabwe
MWA - Marion, IL, USA
MWD - Mianwali, Pakistan
MWF - Maewo, Vanuatu
MWH - Moses Lake, WA, USA
MWI - Maramuni, Papua New Guinea
MWU - Mussau, Papua New Guinea
MWV - Mundulkiri, Cambodia
MWZ - Mwanza, Tanzania
MXH - Moro, Papua New Guinea
MXL - Mexicali, Mexico
MXM - Morombe, Madagascar

MXP - Milan-Malpensa, Italy
MXS - Maota, Savaii Is., Western Samoa
MXT - Maintirano, Madagascar
MXX - Mora, Sweden
MXZ - Meixian, P.R. China
MYA - Moruya, NSW, Australia
MYB - Mayoumba, Gabon
MYD - Malindi, Kenya
MYE - Miyake Jima, Japan
MYG - Mayaguana, Bahamas
MYI - Murray Island, QLD, Australia
MYJ - Matsuyama, Shikoku, Japan
MYR - Myrtle Beach, SC, USA
MYT - Myitkyina, Myanmar
MYU - Mekoryuk, AK, USA
MYW - Mtwara, Tanzania
MYX - Menyamya, Papua New Guinea
MYY - Miri, Sarawak, Malaysia
MZC - Mitzic, Gabon
MZG - Makung, Taiwan
MZI - Mopti, Mali
MZL - Manizales, Colombia
MZO - Manzanillo, Cuba
MZP - Motueka, New Zealand
MZT - Mazatlan, Mexico
MZV - Mulu, Malaysia
NAA - Narrabri, NSW, Australia
NAG - Nagpur, India
NAJ - Nakhichevan, Azerbaijan
NAK - Nakhon Ratchasima, Thailand
NAN - Nadi, Fiji
NAO - Nanchong, P.R. China
NAP - Naples, Italy
NAR - Nare, Colombia
NAS - Nassau, Bahamas
NAT - Natal, RN, Brazil
NAW - Narathiwat, Thailand
NBC - Naberevnye Chelny, Russia
NBO - Nairobi, Kenya
NCA - North Caicos, Turks & Caicos Is.
NCE - Nice, France
NCI - Necocli, Colombia
NCL - Newcastle, England, UK
NCR - San Carlos, Nicaragua
NCU - Nukus, Uzbekistan
NCY - Annecy, France
NDB - Nouadhibou, Mauritania
NDG - Qiqihar, P.R. China
NDI - Namudi, Papua New Guinea
NDJ - N'djamena, Chad
NDK - Namdrik, Marshall Islands
NDM - Mendi, Ethiopia

NDY - Sanday, UK
NDZ - Nordholz-Spieka, Germany
NEF - Neftekamsk, Russia
NEG - Negril, Jamaica
NEJ - Neijo, Ethiopia
NER - Neryungri, Russia
NEU - Sam Neua, Laos
NEV - Nevis, Leeward Islands
NFG - Nefteyugansk, Russia
NFO - Niuafo'ou, Tonga Is.
NGA - Young, NSW, Australia
NGB - Ningbo, P. R. China
NGD - Anegada, BVI
NGE - N'Gaoundere, Cameroon
NGI - Ngau, Fiji
NGO - Nagoya, Japan
NGS - Nagasaki, Japan
NGX - Manang, Nepal
NHA - Nha-Trang, Vietnam
NHV - Nuku Hiva, Fr. Polynesia
NIB - Nikolai, AK, USA
NIM - Niamey, Niger
NIX - Nioro, Mali
NJC - Nizhnevartovsk, Russia
NKC - Nouakchott, Mauritania
NKG - Nanjing, P. R. China
NKI - Naukiti, AK, USA
NKN - Nanknia, Papua New Guinea
NKY - Nkayi, Peop. Rep. of the
    Congo
NLA - Ndola, Zambia
NLD - Nuevo Laredo, Mexico
NLF - Darnley Island, QLD,
    Australia
NLG - Nelson Lagoon, AK, USA
NLK - Norfolk Is., Pacific Ocean
NLP - Nelspruit, South Africa
NLS - Nicholson, WA, Australia
NMA - Namangan, Uzbekistan
NME - Nightmute, AK, USA
NMG - San Miguel, Panama
NNG - Nanning, P. R. China
NNL - Nondalton, AK, USA
NNM - Naryan-Mar, Russia
NNT - Nan, Thailand
NNX - Nunukan, Indonesia
NNY - Nanyang, P. R. China
NOB - Nosara Beach, Costa Rica
NOC - Connaught, Rep. of Ireland
NOJ - Nojabrxsk, Russia
NOS - Nossi-be, Madagascar
NOU - Noumea, New Caledonia
NOV - Huambo, Angola
NPE - Napier, New Zealand
NPL - New Plymouth, New Zealand

NQL - Niquelandia, GO, Brazil
NQN - Neuquen, Argentina
NQU - Nuqui, Colombia
NQY - Newquay, England, UK
NRA - Narrandera, NSW, Australia
NRK - Norrkoping, Sweden
NRL - North Ronaldsay, Scotland,
    UK
NRT - Tokyo-Narita, Japan
NSB - Bimini-North SPB, Bahamas
NSI - Yaounde-Nsimalen, Cameroon
NSK - Norilsk, Russia
NSN - Nelson, New Zealand
NSO - Scone, NSW, Australia
NST - Nakhon Si Thammarat,
    Thailand
NSX - North Sound, BVI
NTE - Nantes, France
NTG - Nantong, P.R. China
NTL - Newcastle, NSW, Australia
NTN - Normanton, QLD, Australia
NTO - Santo Antao, Cape Verde
    Islands
NTT - Niuatoputapu, Tonga Island
NTY - Sun City, South Africa
NUB - Numbulwar, NT, Australia
NUE - Nuremberg, Germany
NUI - Nuiqsut, AK, USA
NUL - Nulato, AK, USA
NUP - Nunapitchuk, AK, USA
NUS - Norsup, Vanuatu
NUX - Novy Urengoy, Russia
NVA - Neiva, Colombia
NVG - Nueva Guinea, Nicaragua
NVK - Narvik, Norway
NVR - Novgorod, Russia
NVT - Navegantes, SC, Brazil
NWI - Norwich, England, UK
NWT - Nowata, Papua New Guinea
NYC - New York, NY-City, USA
NYK - Nanyuki, Kenya
NYM - Nadym, Russia
NYN - Nyngan, NSW, Australia
NYO - Stockholm-Skavsta Arpt,
    Sweden
NYU - Nyaung-U, Myanmar
OAG - Orange, NSW, Australia
OAJ - Jacksonville, NC, USA
OAK - San Francisco, CA-Oakland,
    USA
OAL - Cacoal, TO, Brazil
OAX - Oaxaca, Mexico
OBO - Obihiro, Japan
OBU - Kobuk, AK, USA
OCV - Ocana, Colombia

```
ODE - Odense, Denmark                    ORB - Orebro, Sweden
ODN - Long Seridan, Sarawak,             ORD - Chicago, IL - O'Hare, USA
      Malaysia                           ORF - Norfolf/Va. Beach/WMBG, VA,
ODS - Odessa, Ukraine                          USA
ODW - Oak Harbor, WA, USA                ORH - Worcester, MA, USA
ODY - Oudomxay, Laos                     ORI - Port Lions, AK, USA
OER - Ornskoldsvik, Sweden               ORK - Cork, Rep. of Ireland
OFK - Norfolk, NE, USA                   ORL - Orlando, FL, USA
OFU - Ofu Island, American Samoa         ORN - Oran, Algeria
OGG - Kahului, Maui, HI, USA             ORV - Noorvick, AK, USA
OGN - Yonaguni-Jima, Japan               ORW - Ormara, Pakistan
OGS - Ogdensburg, NY, USA                ORY - Paris-Orly, France
OGX - Ouargla, Algeria                   OSA - Osaka, Japan
OGZ - Vladikavkaz, Russia                OSD - Ostersund, Sweden
OHD - Ohrid, Macedonia                   OSH - Oshkosh, WI, USA
OIM - Oshima Is., Japan                  OSK - Oskarshamn, Sweden
OIR - Okushiri, Japan                    OSL - Oslo, Norway
OIT - Oita, Japan                        OSR - Ostrava, Czech Republic
OKA - Okinawa, Ryukyu Is., Japan         OSS - Osh, Kyrgyzstan
OKC - Oklahoma City, OK, USA             OSW - Orsk, Russia
OKD - Sapporo-Okadama, Japan             OSY - Namsos, Norway
OKE - Okino Erabu, Japan                 OSZ - Koszalin, Poland
OKI - Oki Island, Japan                  OTD - Contadora, Panama Rep.
OKJ - Okayama, Japan                     OTH - North Bend, OR, USA
OKN - Okondja, Gabon                     OTM - Ottumwa, IA, USA
OKR - Yorke Island, QLd,                 OTP - Bucharest-Otopeni, Romania
      Australia                          OTR - Coto 47, Costa Rica
OKU - Mokuti Lodge, Namibia              OTS - Anacortes, WA, USA
OLB - Olbia, Italy                       OTU - Otu, Colombia
OLF - Wolf Point, MT, USA                OTZ - Kotzebue, AK, USA
OLH - Old Harbour, AK, USA               OUA - Ouagadougou, Burkina Faso
OLJ - Olpoi, Vanuatu                     OUD - Oujda, Morocco
OLM - Olympia, WA, USA                   OUE - Ouesso, Peop. Rep. of the
OLP - Olympic Dam, SA, Australia               Congo
OMA - Omaha, NE, USA                     OUL - Oulu, Finland
OMB - Omboue, Gabon                      OUZ - Zouerate, Mauritania
OMD - Oranjemund, Namibia                OVB - Novosibirsk, Russia
OME - Nome, AK, USA                      OVD - Oviedo, Spain
OMH - Urmieh, Iran                       OVL - Ovalle, Chile
OMR - Oradea, Romania                    OWB - Owensboro, KY, USA
OMS - Omsk, Russia                       OXB - Bissau, Guinea-Bissaue
OND - Ondangwa, Namibia                  OXR - Oxnard, CA, USA
ONG - Mornington Is., QLD,               OYE - Oyem, Gabon
      Australia                          OYS - Yosemite Nat'l Park, CA,
ONT - Ontario, CA, USA                         USA
ONX - Colon, Panama Rep.                 OZH - Zaporozhye, Ukraine
OOK - Toksook, AK, USA                   OZZ - Ouarzazate, Morocco
OOL - Gold Coast, QLD, Australia         PAC - Panama City-Paitilla,
OOM - Cooma, NSW, Australia                    Panama Rep.
OPA - Kopasker, Iceland                  PAD - Paderborn, Germany
OPB - Open Bay, Papua New Guinea         PAE - Everett, WA, USA
OPO - Porto, Portugal                    PAH - Paducah, KY, USA
OPS - Sinop, MT, Brazil                  PAJ - Para Chinar, Pakistan
OPU - Balimo, Papua New Guinea           PAP - Port Au Prince, Haiti
ORA - Oran, Argentina                    PAR - Paris, France
```

```
PAS - Paros, Greece                    PHF - Newport News, VA, USA
PAT - Patna, India                     PHL - Philadelphia, PA, USA
PAZ - Poza Rica, Mexico                PHO - Point Hope, AK, USA
PBC - Puebla, Mexico                   PHR - Pacific Harbor, Fiji
PBD - Porbandar, India                 PHS - Phitsanulok, Thailand
PBE - Puerto Berrio, Colombia          PHW - Phalaborwa, South Africa
PBH - Paro, Bhutan                     PHX - Phoenix, AZ, USA
PBI - West Palm Beach, FL, USA         PIA - Peoria, IL, USA
PBJ - Paama, Vanuatu                   PIB - Laurel/Hattiesburg, MS, USA
PBM - Paramaribo, Rep. of              PID - Nassau-Paradise Is.,
      Suriname                               Bahamas
PBO - Paraburdoo, WA, Australia        PIE - St. Petersburg, FL, USA
PBP - Punta Islita, Costa Rica         PIF - Pingtung, Taiwan
PBU - Putao, Myanmar                   PIH - Pocatello, ID, USA
PBZ - Plettenberg Bay, South           PIK - Glasgow-Prestwick,
      Africa                                 Scotland, UK
PCA - Portage Creek, AK, USA           PIP - Pilot Point, AK, USA
PCL - Pucallpa, Peru                   PIR - Pierre, SD, USA
PCM - Playa Del Carmen, Mexico         PIS - Poitiers, France
PCP - Principe Is., Principe           PIT - Pittsburgh, PA, USA
      Island                           PIU - Piura, Peru
PCR - Puerto Carreno, Colombia         PIX - Pico Island, Portugal
PDA - Puerto Inirida, Colombia               (Azores)
PDB - Pedro Bay, AK, USA               PIZ - Point Lay, AK, USA
PDG - Padang, Indonesia                PJC - Pedro Juan Caballero,
PDL - Ponta Delgada, Portugal                Paraguay
      (Azores)                         PJG - Panjgur, Pakistan
PDP - Punta Del Este, Uruguay          PJM - Puerto Jimenez, Costa Rica
PDS - Piedras Negras, Mexico           PKA - Napaskiak, AK, USA
PDT - Pendleton, OR, USA               PKB - Parkersburg, WV, USA
PDX - Portland, OR, USA                PKC - Petropavlovsk-Kamchatsky,
PEC - Pelican, AK, USA                       Russia
PEE - Perm, Russia                     PKE - Parkes, NSW, Australia
PEG - Perugia, Italy                   PKN - Pangkalanbuun, Indonesia
PEI - Pereira, Colombia                PKR - Pokhara, Nepal
PEK - Beijing, P. R. China             PKU - Pekanbaru, Indonesia
PEM - Puerto Maldonado, Peru           PKY - Palangkaraya, Indonesia
PEN - Penang, Malaysia                 PKZ - Pakse, Laos
PER - Perth, WA, Australia             PLB - Plattsburgh, NY, USA
PES - Petrozavodsk, Russia             PLH - Plymouth, England, UK
PET - Pelotas, RS, Brazil              PLJ - Placencia, Belize
PEU - Puerto Lempira, Honduras         PLM - Palembang, Indonesia
PEW - Peshawar, Pakistan               PLN - Pellston, MI, USA
PFB - Passo Fundo, RS, Brazil          PLO - Port Lincoln, SA, Australia
PFN - Panama City, FL, USA             PLP - La Palma, Panama
PFO - Paphos, Cyprus                   PLQ - Palanga, Lithuania
PGA - Page, AZ, USA                    PLS - Providenciales, Turks &
PGF - Perpignan, France                      Caicos Is.
PGK - Pangkalpinang, Indonesia         PLU - Belo Horizonte, MG, Brazil
PGV - Greenville, NC, USA              PLW - Palu, Indonesia
PGX - Perigueux, France                PLX - Semipalatinsk, Kazakstan
PGZ - Ponta Grossa, PR, Brazil         PLZ - Port Elizabeth, South
PHB - Parnaiba, PI, Brazil                   Africa
PHC - Port Harcourt, Nigeria           PMA - Pemba Is., Tanzania
PHE - Port Hedland, WA, Australia      PMC - Puerto Montt, Chile
```

PMD - Palmdale/Lancaster, CA, USA
PMG - Ponta Pora, MS, Brazil
PMI - Palma, Mallorca Is., Spain
PML - Port Moller, AK, USA
PMN - Pumani, Papua New Guinea
PMO - Palermo, Italy
PMR - Palmerston N., New Zealand
PMV - Porlamar, Venezuela
PMW - Palmas, TO, Brazil
PMY - Puerto Madryn, Argentina
PMZ - Palmar, Costa Rica
PNA - Pamplona, Spain
PNB - Porto Nacional, TO, Brazil
PNC - Ponca City, OK, USA
PND - Punta Gorda, Belize
PNH - Phnom Penh, Cambodia
PNI - Pohnpei, Caroline Is.
PNK - Pontianak, Indonesia
PNL - Pantelleria, Italy
PNP - Popondetta, Papua New
      Guinea
PNQ - Poona, India
PNR - Pointe Noire, Peop. Rep. of
      the Congo
PNS - Pensacola, FL, USA
PNZ - Petrolina, PE, Brazil
POA - Porto Alegre, RS, Brazil
POG - Port Gentil, Gabon
POI - Potosi, Bolivia
POL - Pemba, Mozambique
POM - Port Moresby, Papua New
      Guinea
POP - Puerto Plata, Dominican
      Rep.
POR - Pori, Finland
POS - Port of Spain, Trinidad &
      Tobago
POT - Port Antonio, Jamaica
POU - Poughkeepsie, NY, USA
POZ - Poznan, Poland
PPB - Pres. Prudente, SP, Brazil
PPG - Pago Pago, Samoa
PPK - Petropavlovsk, Kazakstan
PPL - Phaplu, Nepal
PPN - Popayan, Colombia
PPP - Proserpine, QLD, Australia
PPQ - Paraparaumu, New Zealand
PPS - Puerto Princesa,
      Philippines
PPT - Papeete, Soc. Is., Fr.
      Polynesia
PPV - Port Protection, AK, USA
PPW - Papa Westray, UK
PQC - Phuquoc, Vietnam
PQI - Presque Isle, ME, USA

PQM - Palenque, Mexico
PQQ - Port Macquarie, NSW,
      Australia
PQS - Pilot Station, AK, USA
PRC - Prescott, AZ, USA
PRG - Prague, Czech Republic
PRH - Phrae, Thailand
PRI - Praslin Is., Seychelles Is.
PRN - Pristina, Yugoslavia
PRS - Parasi, Solomon Islands
PSA - Pisa, Italy
PSC - Pasco, WA, USA
PSE - Ponce, Puerto Rico
PSG - Petersburg, AK, USA
PSI - Pasni, Pakistan
PSO - Pasto, Colombia
PSP - Palm Springs, CA, USA
PSR - Pescara, Italy
PSS - Posadas, Argentina
PSU - Putussibau, Indonesia
PSZ - Puerto Suarez, Bolivia
PTA - Port Alsworth, AK, USA
PTD - Port Alexander, AK, USA
PTF - Malololailai, Fiji
PTG - Pietersburg, South Africa
PTH - Port Heiden, AK, USA
PTJ - Portland, VIC, Australia
PTO - Pato Branco, PR, Brazil
PTP - Pointe A Pitre, Guadeloupe
PTU - Platinum, AK, USA
PTY - Panama City, Panama Rep.
PUB - Pueblo, CO, USA
PUF - Pau, France
PUG - Port Augusta, SA, Australia
PUJ - Punta Cana, Dominican Rep.
PUQ - Punta Arenas, Chile
PUS - Pusan, Rep. of Korea
PUT - Puttaparthi, India
PUU - Puerto Asis, Colombia
PUV - Poum, New Caledonia
PUW - Pullman, WA, USA
PUY - Pula, Croatia
PUZ - Puerto Cabezos, Nicaragua
PVA - Providencia, Colombia
PVC - Provincetown, MA, USA
PVD - Providence, RI, USA
PVH - Porto Velho, RO, Brazil
PVK - Preveza/Lefkas, Greece
PVR - Puerto Vallarta, Mexico
PWM - Portland, ME, USA
PWQ - Pavlodar, Kazakstan
PXM - Puerto Escondido, Mexico
PXO - Porto Santo, Portugal
      (Madeira)
PXU - Pleiku, Vietnam

PYE - Penrhyn Is., Cook Is.
PYH - Puerto Ayacucho, Venezuela
PZB - Pietermaritzburg, South Africa
PZE - Penzance, England, UK
PZH - Zhob, Pakistan
PZO - Puerto Ordaz, Venezuela
PZU - Port Sudan, Sudan
QBC - Bella Coola, BC, Canada
QDU - Duesseldorf, Main RR, Germany
QFK - Selje Harbour, Norway
QFQ - Maloy Harbour, Norway
QFZ - Saarbruecken Hbf Rail Station, Germany
QJY - Kolobrzeg Bus Station, Poland
QKL - Cologne Bonn, Main RR, Germany
QLE - Leeton, NSW, Australia
QRO - Queretaro, Mexico
RAB - Rabaul, Papua New Guinea
RAE - Arar, Saudi Arabia
RAH - Rafha, Saudi Arabia
RAI - Praia, Cape Verde Islands
RAJ - Rajkot, India
RAK - Marrakech, Morocco
RAM - Ramingining, NT, Australia
RAO - Ribeirao Preto, SP, Brazil
RAP - Rapid City, SD, USA
RAR - Rarotonga, Cook Is.
RAS - Rasht, Iran
RAT - Raduzhnyi, Russia
RAZ - Rawala Kot, Pakistan
RBA - Rabat, Morocco
RBE - Ratanankiri, Cambodia
RBJ - Rebun, Japan
RBP - Rabaraba, Papua New Guinea
PBR - Rio Branco, AC, Brazil
RBV - Ramata, Solomon Islands
RBY - Ruby, AK, USA
RCB - Richards Bay, South Africa
RCE - Roche Harbor, WA, USA
RCH - Riohacha, Colombia
RCL - Redcliffe, Vanuatu
RCM - Richmond, QLD, Australia
RCU - Rio Cuarto, Argentina
RDC - Redencao, PA, Brazil
RDD - Redding, CA, USA
RDG - Reading, PA, USA
RDM - Redmond, OR, USA
RDS - Rincon de Los Sauces, Argentina
RDU - Raleigh/Durham, NC, USA
RDV - Red Devil, AK, USA

RDZ - Rodez, France
REC - Recife, PE, Brazil
REG - Reggio Calabria, Italy
REK - Reykjavik, Iceland
REL - Trelew, Argentina
REN - Orenburg, Russia
REP - Siem Reap, Cambodia
RES - Resistencia, Argentina
RET - Rost, Norway
REU - Reus, Spain
REX - Reynosa, Mexico
RFD - Rockford, IL, USA
RFN - Raufarhofn, Iceland
RFP - Raiatea Island, Society Islands
RFS - Rosita, Nicaragua
RGA - Rio Grande, Argentina
RGE - Porgera, Papua New Guinea
RGI - Rangiroa, Fr. Polynesia
RGL - Rio Gallegos, Argentina
RGN - Yangon, Myanmar
RHD - Rio Hondo, Argentina
RHE - Reims, France
RHI - Rhinelander, WI, USA
RHO - Rhodes Island, Greece
RIA - Santa Maria, RS, Brazil
RIB - Riberalta, Bolivia
RIC - Richmond, VA, USA
RIG - Rio Grande, RS, Brazil
RIJ - Rioja, Peru
RIK - Carrillo, Costa Rica
RIM - Rodriguez de Mendoza, Peru
RIN - Ringi Cove, Solomon Islands
RIO - Rio De Janeiro, RJ, Brazil
RIS - Rishiri, Japan
RIW - Riverton, WY, USA
RIX - Riga, Latvia
RIY - Riyan Mukalla, Yemen
RJH - Rajshahi, Bangladesh
RKD - Rockland, ME, USA
RKS - Rock Springs, WY, USA
RKT - Ras Al Khaimah, U. A. Emirates
RKV - Reykjavik Domestic, Iceland
RLG - Rostock-Laage, Germany
RMA - Roma, QLD, Australia
RMI - Rimini, Italy
RMK - Renmark, SA, Australia
RMP - Rampart, AK, USA
RNB - Ronneby, Sweden
RNE - Roanne, France
RNI - Corn Island, Nicaragua
RNJ - Yoron-Jima, Japan
RNL - Rennell Is., Solomon Islands

RNN - Bornholm, Denmark
RNO - Reno, NV, USA
RNS - Rennes, France
ROA - Roanoke, VA, USA
ROC - Rochester, NY, USA
ROK - Rockhampton, QLD, Australia
ROM - Rome, Italy
ROO - Rondonopolis, MT, Brazil
ROP - Rota, Mariana Islands
ROR - Koror, Palau Is.
ROS - Rosario, Argentina
ROT - Rotorua, New Zealand
ROV - Rostov, Russia
ROW - Roswell, NM, USA
RPM - Ngukurr, NT, Australia
RPN - Rosh-Pina, Galilee, Israel
RPR - Raipur, India
RRG - Rodrigues Is., Mauritius
RRS - Roros, Norway
RSA - Santa Rosa, Argentina
RSD - Rock Sound, Bahamas
RSH - Russian Mission, AK, USA
RSJ - Rosario, WA, USA
RST - Rochester, MN, USA
RSU - Yosu, Rep. of Korea
RSW - Fort Myers, FL-Regional,
    USA
RTA - Rotuma, Fiji
RTB - Roatan, Honduras
RTM - Rotterdam, Netherlands
RTS - Rottnest Is., WA, Australia
RTW - Saratov, Russia
RUH - Riyadh, Saudi Arabia
RUN - Reunion Island, Indian
    Ocean
RUR - Rurutu Is., Fr. Polynesia
RUS - Marau, Solomon Islands
RUT - Rutland, VT, USA
RVA - Farafangana, Madagascar
RVK - Roervik, Norway
RVN - Rovaniemi, Finland
RWI - Rocky Mount/Wilson, NC, USA
RXS - Roxas City, Philippines
RYK - Rahim Yar Khan, Pakistan
SAB - Saba, Neth. Antilles
SAC - Sacramento, CA, USA
SAF - Santa Fe, NM, USA
SAH - Sanaa, Yemen
SAK - Saudarkrokur, Iceland
SAL - San Salvador, El Salvador
SAM - Salamo, Papua New Guinea
SAN - San Diego, CA, USA
SAO - Sao Paulo, SP, Brazil
SAP - San Pedro Sula, Honduras
SAQ - San Andros, Bahamas

SAT - San Antonio, TX, USA
SAV - Savannah, GA, USA
SAX - Sambu, Panama
SBA - Santa Barbara, CA, USA
SBH - St. Barthelemy, Leeward
    Islands
SBK - St. Brieuc, France
SBN - South Bend, IN, USA
SBP - San Luis Obispo, CA, USA
SBR - Saibai Island, QLD,
    Australia
SBS - Steamboat Springs, CO, USA
SBT - San Bernardino, CA, USA
SBU - Springbok, South Africa
SBW - Sibu, Sarawak, Malaysia
SBY - Salisbury, MD, USA
SBZ - Sibiu, Romania
SCC - Prudhoe Bay/Deadhorse, AK,
    USA
SCE - State College, PA, USA
SCJ - Smith Cove, AK, USA
SCL - Santiago, Chile
SCM - Scammon Bay, AK, USA
SCN - Saarbruecken, Germany
SCO - Aktau, Kazakstan
SCQ - Santiago De Compostela,
    Spain
SCT - Socotra, Yemen
SCU - Santiago, Cuba
SCV - Suceava, Romania
SCX - Salina Cruz, Mexico
SCY - San Cristobal, Ecuador
SCZ - Santa Cruz, Solomon Islands
SDD - Lubango, Angola
SDE - Santiago Del Estero,
    Argentina
SDF - Louisville, KY-Standiford,
    USA
SDI - Saidor, Papua New Guinea
SDJ - Sendai, Japan
SDK - Sandakan, Sabah, Malaysia
SDL - Sundsvall, Sweden
SDN - Sandane, Norway
SDP - Sand Point, AK, USA
SDQ - Santo Domingo, Dominican
    Rep.
SDR - Santander, Spain
SDT - Saidu Sharif, Pakistan
SDU - Rio De Janeiro-Dumont, RJ,
    Brazil
SDV - Tel Aviv/Yafo-Sde Dov,
    Israel
SDY - Sidney, MT, USA
SDZ - Shetland Is., Scotland, UK
SEA - Seattle/Tacoma, WA, USA

```
SEL - Seoul, Rep. of Korea          SIX - Singleton, NSW, Australia
SEY - Selibaby, Mauritania          SJB - San Joaquin, Bolivia
SEZ - Mahe Is., Seychelles Is.      SJC - San Jose, CA, USA
SFA - Sfax, Tunisia                 SJD - Los Cabos, Mexico
SFD - San Fernando De Apure,        SJI - San Jose, Philippines
      Venezuela                     SJJ - Sarajevo, Bosnia and
SFG - St. Martin, French Antilles         Herzegovina
SFJ - Kangerlussuaq, Greenland      SJK - Sao Jose Dos Campos, SP,
SFL - Sao Filipe, Cape Verde              Brazil
      Islands                       SJO - San Jose, Costa Rica
SFN - Santa Fe, Argentina           SJP - Sao Jose Do Rio Preto, SP,
SFO - San Francisco/Oakland, CA,          Brazil
      USA                           SJT - San Angelo, TX, USA
SFQ - Sanliurfa, Turkey             SJU - San Juan, Puerto Rico
SFS - Subic Bay, Philippines        SJW - Shijiazhuang, P.R. China
SFT - Skelleftea, Sweden            SJY - Seinajoki, Finland
SFU - Safia, Papua New Guinea       SJZ - San Jorge Island, Portugal
SGC - Surgut, Russia                      (Azores)
SGD - Sonderborg, Denmark           SKB - St. Kitts, Leeward Islands
SGF - Springfield, MO, USA          SKD - Samarkand, Uzbekistan
SGN - Ho Chi Minh, Soc. Rep. of     SKE - Skien, Norway
      Viet Nam                      SKG - Thessaloniki, Greece
SGO - St. George, QLD, Australia    SKH - Surkhet, Nepal
SGU - St. George, UT, USA           SKK - Shaktoolik, AK, USA
SGY - Skagway, AK, USA              SKN - Stokmarknes, Norway
SHA - Shanghai, P. R. China         SKO - Sokoto, Nigeria
SHB - Nakashibetsu, Japan           SKP - Skopje, Macedonia
SHC - Indaselassie, Ethiopia        SKS - Vojens, Denmark
SHD - Shenandoah Valley Arpt.,      SKZ - Sukkur, Pakistan
      VA, USA                       SLA - Salta, Argentina
SHE - Shenyang, P. R. China         SLC - Salt Lake City, UT, USA
SHG - Shungnak, AK, USA             SLH - Sola, Vanuatu
SHH - Shishmaref, AK, USA           SLK - Saranac Lake, NY, USA
SHJ - Sharjah, U. A. Emirates       SLL - Salalah, Oman
SHM - Nanki Shirahama, Japan        SLM - Salamanca, Spain
SHO - Sokcho, Rep. of Korea         SLN - Salina, KS, USA
SHP - Qinhuangdao, P. R. China      SLP - San Luis Potosi, Mexico
SHR - Sheridan, WY, USA             SLQ - Sleetmute, AK, USA
SHS - Shashi, P. R. China           SLU - St Lucia, West Indies
SHT - Shepparton, VIC, Australia    SLV - Simla, India
SHV - Shreveport, LA, USA           SLW - Saltillo, Mexico
SHW - Sharurah, Saudi Arabia        SLX - Salt Cay, Turks & Caicos
SHX - Shageluk, AK, USA                   Is.
SIA - Xi An, P. R. China            SLY - Salehard, Russia
SIC - Sinop, Turkey                 SLZ - Sao Luiz, Maranhao, MA,
SID - Sal, Cape Verde Islands             Brazil
SIF - Simra, Nepal                  SMA - Santa Maria, Portugal
SIG - San Juan-Isla Grand, Puerto         (Azores)
      Rico                          SMF - Sacramento, CA, USA
SIL - Sila, Papua New Guinea        SMI - Samos Island, Greece
SIN - Singapore, Singapore          SMK - St. Michael, AK, USA
SIP - Simferopol, Ukraine           SML - Stella Maris, L.I., Bahamas
SIR - Sion, Switzerland             SMM - Semporna, Sabah, Malaysia
SIT - Sitka, AK, USA                SMQ - Sampit, Indonesia
SIU - Siuna, Nicaragua              SMR - Santa Marta, Colombia
```

SMS - St. Marie, Madagascar
SMX - Santa Maria, CA, USA
SNA - Orange County, CA, USA
SNB - Snake Bay, NT, Australia
SNE - Sao Nicolau, Cape Verde
      Islands
SNN - Shannon, Rep. of Ireland
SNO - Sakon Nakhon, Thailand
SNP - St. Paul Island, AK, USA
SNV - Santa Elena, Venezuela
SNW - Thandwe, Myanmar
SOC - Solo City, Indonesia
SOD - Sorocaba, SP, Brazil
SOF - Sofia, Bulgaria
SOG - Sogndal, Norway
SOI - South Molle Is., QLD,
      Australia
SOJ - Sorkjosen, Norway
SOM - San Tome, Venezuela
SON - Espiritu Santo, Vanuatu
SOO - Soderhamn, Sweden
SOP - Pinehurst, NC, USA
SOQ - Sorong, IndonesiA
SOU - Southampton, England, UK
SOY - Stronsay, UK
SPB - St. Thomas SPB, Virgin
      Islands
SPC - Santa Cruz La Palma, Canary
      Islands
SPD - Saidpur, Bangladesh
SPI - Springfield, IL, USA
SPK - Sapporo, Japan
SPN - Saipan, Mariana Islands
SPP - Menongue, Angola
SPR - San Pedro, Belize
SPS - Wichita Falls, TX, USA
SPU - Split, Croatia
SPW - Spencer, IA, USA
SQC - Southern Cross, WA,
      Australia
SQG - Sintang, Indonesia
SQH - Son-La, Vietnam
SQI - Sterling/Rock Falls, IL,
      USA
SQJ - Shehdi, Ethiopia
SQO - Storuman, Sweden
SRA - Santa Rosa, RS, Brazil
SRE - Sucre, Bolivia
SRG - Semarang, Indonesia
SRI - Samarinda, Indonesia
SRJ - San Borja, Bolivia
SRP - Stord, Norway
SRQ - Sarasota/Bradenton, FL, USA
SRV - Stony River, AK, USA
SRY - Sary, Iran

SRZ - Santa Cruz, Bolivia
SSA - Salvador, BA, Brazil
SSB - Seaplane Base, Virgin
      Islands
SSG - Malabo, Equatorial Guinea
SSH - Sharm El Sheik, Egypt
SSI - Brunswick, GA, USA
SSJ - Sandnessjoen, Norway
SSM - Sault Ste. Marie, MI, USA
SSR - Sara, Vanuatu
SSX - Samsum, Turkey
STC - St. Cloud, MN, USA
STD - Santo Domingo, Venezuela
STG - St. George Island, AK, USA
STI - Santiago, Dominican Rep.
STL - St. Louis, MO, USA
STM - Santarem, PA, Brazil
STN - London-Stansted, England,
      UK
STO - Stockholm, Sweden
STR - Stuttgart, Germany
STS - Santa Rosa, CA, USA
STT - St. Thomas, Virgin Islands
STW - Stavropol, Russia
STX - St. Croix, Virgin Islands
SUB - Surabaya, Indonesia
SUF - Lamezia Terme, Italy
SUH - Sur, Oman
SUJ - Satu Mare, Romania
SUL - Sui, Pakistan
SUN - Sun Valley, ID, USA
SUR - Summer Beaver, ON, Canada
SUV - Suva, Fiji
SUX - Sioux City, IA, USA
SVA - Savoonga, AK, USA
SVB - Sambava, Madagascar
SVC - Silver City, NM, USA
SVD - St. Vincent, Windward
      Islands
SVG - Stavanger, Norway
SVJ - Svolvaer, Norway
SVL - Savonlinna, Finland
SVO - Moscow-Sheremetye, Russia
SVP - Kuito, Angola
SVQ - Sevilla, Spain
SVS - Stevens Village, AK, USA
SVU - Savusavu, Fiji
SVX - Ekaterinburg, Russia
SVZ - San Antonio, Venezuela
SWA - Shantou, P.R. China
SWD - Seward, AK, USA
SWF - Newburgh, NY, USA
SWG - Satwag, Papua New Guinea
SWJ - South West Bay, Vanuatu
SWP - Swakopmund, Namibia

SWR - Silur, Papua New Guinea	TBG - Tabubil, Papua New Guinea
SWT - Strzhewoi, Russia	TBI - The Bight, Bahamas
SXB - Strasbourg, France	TBN - Ft. Leonard Wood, MO, USA
SXE - Sale, VIC, Australia	TBO - Tabora, Tanzania
SXF - Berlin-Schoenefld, Germany	TBP - Tumbes, Peru
SXH - Sehulea, Papua New Guinea	TBS - Tbilisi, Georgia
SXL - Sligo, Rep. of Ireland	TBT - Tabatinga, AM, Brazil
SXM - St. Maarten, Neth. Antilles	TBU - Tongatapu, Tonga Island
SXO - Sao Felix Do Araguaia, MT, Brazil	TBZ - Tabriz, Iran
SXP - Sheldon Point, AK, USA	TCA - Tennant Creek, NT, Australia
SXR - Srinagar, India	TCB - Treasure Cay, Bahamas
SXS - Sahabat 16, Malaysia	TCG - Tacheng, P.R. China
SXW - Sauren, Papua New Guinea	TCH - Tchibanga, Gabon
SXZ - Siirt, Turkey	TCI - Tenerife, Canary Islands
SYB - Seal Bay, AK, USA	TCO - Tumaco, Colombia
SYD - Sydney, NSW, Australia	TCP - Taba, Egypt
SYM - Simao, P. R. China	TCQ - Tacna, Peru
SYO - Shonai, Japan	TCT - Takotna, AK, USA
SYP - Santiago, Panama	TDB - Tetabedi, Papua New Guinea
SYQ - San Jose Tobias Bolanos Aprt, Costa Rica	TDD - Trinidad, Bolivia
SYR - Syracuse, NY, USA	TEC - Telemaco Borba, PR, Brazil
SYU - Warraber Island, QLD, Australia	TED - Thisted, Denmark
	TEE - Tbessa, Algeria
SYW - Sehwen Sharif, Pakistan	TEH - Tetlin, AK, USA
SYX - Sanya, P. R. China	TEO - Terapo, Papua New Guinea
SYY - Stornoway, Scotland, UK	TEP - Teptep, Papua New Guinea
SYZ - Shiraz, Iran	TER - Terceira, Portugal (Azores)
SZA - Soyo, Angola	TET - Tete, Mozambique
SZD - Sheffield, UK	TEU - Te Anau, New Zealand
SZG - Salzburg, Austria	TEX - Telluride, CO, USA
SZK - Skukuza, South Africa	TEZ - Tezpur, India
SZT - San Cristobal de las Casas, Mexico	TFF - Tefe, AM, Brazil
	TFI - Tufi, Papua New Guinea
SZX - Shenzhen, P.R. China	TFM - Telefomin, Papua New Guinea
SZZ - Szczecin, Poland	TFN - Tenerife-N.Losrodeo, Canary Is.
TAB - Tobago, Trinidad & Tobago	
TAC - Tacloban, Philippines	TFS - Tenerife-Reinasofia, Canary Islands
TAE - Taegu, Rep. of Korea	
TAG - Tagbilaran, Philippines	TGD - Podgorica, Yugoslavia
TAH - Tanna Island, Vanuatu	TGG - Kuala Terengganu, Malaysia
TAI - Taiz, Yemen	TGH - Tongoa, Vanuatu
TAJ - Tadji, Papua New Guinea	TGI - Tingo Maria, Peru
TAK - Takamatsu, Japan	TGJ - Tiga, Loyalty Is.
TAL - Tanana, AK, USA	TGM - Tirgu Mures, Romania
TAM - Tampico, Mexico	TGN - Traralgon, VIC, Australia
TAO - Qingdao, P. R. China	TGR - Touggourt, Algeria
TAP - Tapachula, Mexico	TGU - Tegucigalpa, Honduras
TAS - Tashkent, Uzbekistan	TGZ - Tuxtla Gutierrez, Mexico
TAT - Tatry/Poprad, Slovak Republic	THE - Teresina, PI, Brazil
	THF - Berlin-Tempelhof, Germany
TAV - Ta'u Island, American Samoa	THG - Thangool, QLD, Australia
TBB - Tuyhoa, Vietnam	THL - Tachilek, Myanmar
TBE - Timbunke, Papua New Guinea	THN - Trollhattan, Sweden
	THO - Thorshofn, Iceland

THR	Tehran, Iran	TMS	Sao Tome Island, Sao Tome Island
THS	Sukothai, Thailand	TMT	Trombetas, PA, Brazil
THU	Pituffik, Greenland	TMU	Tambor, Costa Rica
TIA	Tirana, Albania	TMW	Tamworth, NSW, Australia
TIC	Tinak, Marshall Is.	TMX	Timimoun, Algeria
TID	Tiaret, Algeria	TNA	Jinan, P.R. China
TIE	Tippi, Ethiopia	TNC	Tin City, AK, USA
TIF	Taif, Saudi Arabia	TNE	Tanegashima, Japan
TIH	Tikehau, Fr. Polynesia	TNG	Tangier, Morocco
TIJ	Tijuana, Mexico	TNK	Tununak, AK, USA
TIM	Tembagapura, Indonesia	TNN	Tainan, Taiwan
TIN	Tindouf, Algeria	TNO	Tamarindo, Costa Rica
TIQ	Tinian, Mariana Islands	TNR	Antananarivo, Madagascar
TIR	Tirupati, India	TNX	Stung Treng, Cambodia
TIS	Thursday Is., QLD, Australia	TOD	Tioman, Malaysia
TIU	Timaru, New Zealand	TOE	Tozeur, Tunisia
TIV	Tivat, Yugoslavia	TOF	Tomsk, Russia
TIY	Tidjikja, Mauritania	TOG	Togiak, AK, USA
TIZ	Tari, Papua New Guinea	TOH	Torres, Vanuatu
TJA	Tarija, Bolivia	TOL	Toledo, OH, USA
TJH	Toyooka, Japan	TOM	Tombouctou, Mali
TJI	Trujillo, Honduras	TOP	Topeka, KS, USA
TJK	Tokat, Turkey	TOS	Tromso, Norway
TJM	Tyumen, Russia	TOU	Touho, New Caledonia
TJQ	Tanjung Pandan, Indonesia	TOW	Toledo, PR, Brazil
TJS	Tanjung Selor, Indonesia	TOY	Toyama, Japan
TKB	Tekadu, Papua New Guinea	TPA	Tampa/St. Petersburg, FL, USA
TKE	Tenakee, AK, USA	TPE	Taipei, Taiwan
TKG	Bandar Lampung, Indonesia	TPI	Tapini, Papua New Guinea
TKJ	Tok, AK, USA	TPJ	Taplejung, Nepal
TKK	Truk, Caroline Is.	TPP	Tarapoto, Peru
TKN	Tokuno Shima, Japan	TPQ	Tepic, Mexico
TKP	Takapoto Is., Fr. Polynesia	TPR	Tom Price, WA, Australia
TKQ	Kigoma, Tanzania	TPS	Trapani, Italy
TKS	Tokushima, Japan	TRA	Taramajima, Japan
TKU	Turku, Finland	TRB	Turbo, Colombia
TKX	Takaroa, Tuamotu Islands	TRC	Torreon, Mexico
TLA	Mexico City-Morelos, Mexico	TRD	Trondheim, Norway
TLE	Tulear, Madagascar	TRE	Tiree Island, Scotland, UK
TLH	Tallahassee, FL, USA	TRF	Sandefjord, Norway
TLJ	Tatalina, AK, USA	TRG	Tauranga, New Zealand
TLL	Tallinn, Estonia	TRI	Tri-City Airport, TN, USA
TLM	Tilimsen, Algeria	TRK	Tarakan, Indonesia
TLN	Toulon, Hyeres, France	TRN	Turin, Italy
TLS	Toulouse, France	TRO	Taree, NSW, Australia
TLT	Tuluksak, AK, USA	TRS	Trieste, Italy
TLV	Tel Aviv-Yafo, Israel	TRU	Trujillo, Peru
TMG	Tomanggong, Malaysia	TRV	Trivandrum, India
TMI	Tumlingtar, Nepal	TRW	Tarawa, Kiribati
TMJ	Termez, Uzbekistan	TRZ	Tiruchirapally, India
TMM	Tamatave, Madagascar	TSA	Taipei-Sung Shan, Taiwan
TMP	Tampere, Finland	TSB	Tsumeb, Namibia
TMR	Tamanrasset, Algeria	TSE	Akmola, Kazakstan

TSF - Venice-Treviso, Italy
TSH - Tshikapa, Dem. Rep. of the Congo
TSJ - Tsushima, Japan
TSN - Tianjin, P. R. China
TSO - Isles of Scilly-Tresco, UK
TSR - Timisoara, Romania
TST - Trang, Thailand
TSV - Townsville, QLD, Australia
TTE - Ternate, Indonesia
TTG - Tauranga, New Zealand
TTJ - Tottori, Japan
TTN - Trenton, NJ, USA
TTQ - Tortuquero, Costa Rica
TTS - Tsaratanana, Madagascar
TTT - Taitung, Taiwan
TTU - Tetuan, Morocco
TUB - Tubuai Is., Austral Is.
TUC - Tucuman, Argentina
TUD - Tambacounda, Senegal
TUF - Tours, France
TUG - Tuguegarao, Philippines
TUI - Turaif, Saudi Arabia
TUJ - Tum, Ethiopia
TUK - Turbat, Pakistan
TUL - Tulsa, OK, USA
TUN - Tunis, Tunisia
TUO - Taupo, New Zealand
TUP - Tupelo, MS, USA
TUR - Tucurui, PA, Brazil
TUS - Tucson, AZ, USA
TUU - Tabuk, Saudi Arabia
TUZ - Tucuma, PA, Brazil
TVA - Morafenobe, Madagascar
TVC - Traverse City, MI, USA
TVF - Thief River Falls, MN, USA
TVU - Taveuni, Fiji
TVY - Dawe, Myanmar
TWA - Twin Hills, AK, USA
TWB - Toowoomba, QLD, Australia
TWF - Twin Falls, ID, USA
TWU - Tawau, Sabah, Malaysia
TXG - Taichung, Taiwan
TXK - Texarkana, AR, USA
TXL - Berlin-Tegel, Germany
TXN - Tunxi, P. R. China
TYF - Torsby, Sweden
TYL - Talara, Peru
TYN - Taiyuan, P. R. China
TYO - Tokyo, Japan
TYR - Tyler, TX, USA
TYS - Knoxville, TN-McGhee-Tyson, USA
TZA - Belize City-Municipal, Belize

TZN - South Andros, Bahamas
TZX - Trabzon, Turkey
UAK - Narssarssuaq, Greenland
UAQ - San Juan, Argentina
UAS - Samburu, Kenya
UBA - Uberaba, MG, Brazil
UBB - Mabuiag Island, QLD, Australia
UBI - Buin, Papua New Guinea
UBJ - Ube, Japan
UBP - Ubon Ratchathani, Thailand
UBS - Columbus/Starkville/W. Pt., MS, USA
UCA - Utica, NY, USA
UDI - Uberlandia, MG, Brazil
UDJ - Uzhgorod, Ukraine
UDR - Udaipur , India
UEL - Quelimane, Mozambique
UEO - Kume Jima, Japan
UET - Quetta, Pakistan
UFA - Ufa, Russia
UGB - Pilot Point, AK-Ugashik,
UGC - Urgench, Uzebekistan
UGI - Uganik, AK, USA
UIB - Quibdo, Colombia
UIH - Quinhon, Vietnam
UII - Utila Island, Honduras
UIK - Ust-Ilimsk, Russia
UIN - Quincy, IL, USA
UIO - Quito, Ecuador
UIP - Quimper, France
UIT - Jaluit, Marshall Islands
UJE - Ujae Island, Marshall Islands
UKA - Ukunda, Kenya
UKK - Ust-Kamenogorsk, Kazakhstan
UKU - Nuku, Papua New Guinea
ULB - Ulei, Vanuatu
ULC - Santiago Los Cerillos Arpt., Chile
ULD - Ulundi, South Africa
ULE - Sule, Papua New Guinea
ULN - Ulaanbaatar, Mongolia
ULP - Quilpie, QLD, Australia
UMD - Uummannaq, Greenland
UME - Umea, Sweden
UMR - Woomera, SA, Australia
UNG - Kiunga, Papua New Guinea
UNI - Union Island, Windward Islands
UNK - Unalakleet, AK, USA
UNN - Ranong, Thailand
UNT - Unst. Shetland Is., Scotland, UK
UPG - Ujung Pandang, Indonesia

UPN - Uruapan, Mexico
URA - Uralsk, Kazakstan
URC - Urumqi, P. R. China
URG - Uruguaiana, RS, Brazil
URJ - Uraj, Russia
URO - Rouen, France
URR - Urrao, Colombia
URT - Surat Thani, Thailand
URY - Gurayat, Saudi Arabia
USH - Ushuaia, Argentina
USL - Useless Loop, WA, Australia
USM - Koh Samui, Thailand
USN - Ulsan, Rep. of Korea
USU - Busuanga, Philippines
UTH - Udon Thani, Thailand
UTK - Utirik, Marshall Islands
UTN - Upington, South Africa
UTO - Utopia Creek, AK, USA
UTP - Utapao, Thailand
UTT - Umtata, South Africa
UUD - Ulan-Ude, Russia
UUS - Yuzhno-Sakhalinsk, Russia
UVE - Ouvea, Loyalty Is.
UVF - St. Lucia-Hewanorra, West
      Indies
UVL - New Valley, Egypt
UVO - Uvol, Papua New Guinea
UYN - Yulin, P.R. China
VAA - Vaasa, Finland
VAG - Varginha, MG, Brazil
VAI - Vanimo, Papua New Guinea
VAK - Chevak, AK, USA
VAN - Van, Turkey
VAO - Suavanao, Solomon Is.
VAR - Varna, Bulgaria
VAS - Sivas, Turkey
VAT - Vatomandry, Madagascar
VAV - Vava'U, Tonga Island
VAW - Vardoe, Norway
VBV - Vanuabalavu, Fiji
VBY - Visby, Sweden
VCD - Victoria River Downs, NT,
      Australia
VCE - Venice, Italy
VCT - Victoria, TX, USA
VDA - Ovda, Israel
VDB - Fagernes, Norway
VDC - Vitoria Da Conquista, BA,
      Brazil
VDE - Valverde, Canary Islands
VDM - Viedma, Argentina
VDS - Vadso, Norway
VDZ - Valdez, AK, USA
VEE - Venetie, AK, USA
VEL - Vernal, UT, USA

VER - Veracruz, Mexico
VEY - Vestmannaeyjar, Iceland
VFA - Victoria Falls, Zimbabwe
VGO - Vigo, Spain
VGT - Las Vegas, NE-N. Terminal,
      USA
VHC - Saurimo, Angola
VHM - Vilhemina, Sweden
VIA - Videira, SC, Brazil
VIE - Vienna, Austria
VII - Vinh City, Vietnam
VIJ - Virgin Gorda, BVI
VIL - Dakhla, Morocco
VIS - Visalia, CA, USA
VIT - Vitoria, Spain
VIV - Vivigani, Papua New Guinea
VIX - Vitoria, ES, Brazil
VKO - Moscow-Vnukovo, Russia
VLC - Valencia, Spain
VLD - Valdosta, GA, USA
VLG - Villa Gesell, Argentina
VLI - Port Vila, Vanuatu
VLL - Valladolid, Spain
VLN - Valencia, Venezuela
VLP - Vila Rica, MT, Brazil
VLR - Vallenar, Chile
VLS - Valesdir, Vanuatu
VME - Villa Mercedes, Argentina
VMU - Baimuru, Papua New Guinea
VNO - Vilnius, Lithuania
VNS - Varanasi, India
VNX - Vilanculos, Mozambique
VOG - Volgograd, Russia
VOH - Vohemar, Madagascar
VOZ - Voronezh, Russia
VPE - Ongiva, Angola
VPN - Vopnafjordur, Iceland
VPS - Ft. Walton Beach, FL, USA
VQS - Vieques, Puerto Rico
VRA - Varadero, Cuba
VRC - Virac, Philippines
VRK - Varkaus, Finland
VRL - Vila Real, Portugal
VRN - Verona, Italy
VRY - Vaeroy, Norway
VSA - Villahermosa, Mexico
VST - Vasteras, Sweden
VTE - Vientiane, Laos
VTU - Las Tunas, Cuba
VTZ - Vishakhapatnam, India
VUP - Valledupar, Colombia
VVB - Mahanoro, Madagascar
VVC - Villavicencio, Colombia
VVI - Santa Cruz, Viru Viru,
      Bolivia

VVO - Vladivostok, Russia
VVZ - Illizi, Algeria
VXC - Lichinga, Mozambique
VXE - Sao Vicente, Cape Verde
  Islands
VXO - Vaxjo, Sweden
WAA - Wales, AK, USA
WAE - Wadi-Ad-Dawasir, Saudi
  Arabia
WAG - Wanganui, New Zealand
WAI - Antsohihy, Madagascar
WAM - Ambatondrazaka, Madagascar
WAQ - Antsalova, Madagascar
WAS - Washington, DC, USA
WAT - Waterford, Rep. of Ireland
WAW - Warsaw, Poland
WBB - Stebbins, AK, USA
WBC - Wapolu, Papua New Guinea
WBM - Wapenamanda, Papua New
  Guinea
WBQ - Beaver, AK, USA
WCH - Chaiten, Chile
WDG - Enid, OK, USA
WDH - Windhoek, Namibia
WED - Wedau, Papua New Guinea
WEH - Weihai, P.R. China
WEI - Weipa, QLD, Australia
WFI - Fianarantsoa, Madagascar
WFK - Frenchville, ME, USA
WGA - Wagga-Wagga, NSW, Australia
WGE - Walgett, NSW, Australia
WGP - Waingapu, Indonesia
WHD - Hyder, AK, USA
WHK - Whakatane, New Zealand
WIC - Wick, Scotland, UK
WIL - Nairobi-Wilson, Kenya
WIN - Winton, QLD, Australia
WIR - Wairoa, New Zealand
WJA - Woja, Marshall Is.
WJU - Won-Ju, Rep. of Korea
WKA - Wanaka, New Zealand
WKJ - Wakkanai, Japan
WKK - Aleknagik, AK, USA
WLG - Wellington, New Zealand
WLH - Walaha, Vanuatu
WLK - Selawik, AK, USA
WLS - Wallis Is., Wallis & Futuna
  Is.
WMA - Mandritsara, Madagascar
WME - Mount Keith, WA, Australia
WMH - Mountain Home, AR, USA
WMK - Meyers Chuck, AK, USA
WMN - Maroantsetra, Madagascar
WMO - White Mountain, AK, USA
WMP - Mampikony, Madagascar

WMR - Mananara, Madagascar
WNA - Napakiak, AK, USA
WNN - Wunnummin Lake, ON, Canada
WNP - Naga, Philippines
WNR - Windorah, QLD, Australia
WNS - Nawab Shah, Pakistan
WNZ - Wenzhou, P.R. China
WPB - Port Berge, Madagascar
WRE - Whangarei, New Zealand
WRG - Wrangell, AK, USA
WRL - Worland, WY, USA
WRO - Wroclaw, Poland
WRY - Westray, UK
WSN - South Naknek, AK, USA
WSP - Waspam, Nicaragua
WST - Westerly, RI, USA
WSU - Wasu, Papua New Guinea
WSX - Westsound, WA, USA
WSZ - Westport, New Zealand
WTA - Tambohorano, Madagascar
WTE - Wotje, Marshall Islands
WTK - Noatak, AK, USA
WTL - Tuntatuliak, AK, USA
WTO - Wotho, Marshall Islands
WTP - Woitape, Papua New Guinea
WTS - Tsiroanomandidy, Madagascar
WUD - Wudinna, SA, Australia
WUG - Wau, Papua New Guinea
WUH - Wuhan, P. R. China
WUM - Wasum, Papua New Guinea
WUN - Wiluna, WA, Australia
WUS - Wuyishan, P.R. China
WVB - Walvis Bay, South Africa
WVK - Manakara, Madagascar
WVN - Wilhelmshaven, Germany
WWK - Wewak, Papua New Guinea
WWP - Whale Pass, AK, USA
WWT - Newtok, AK, USA
WWY - West Wyalong, NSW,
  Australia
WXN - Wanxian, P.R. China
WYA - Whyalla, SA, Australia
WYN - Wyndham, WA, Australia
XAP - Chapeco, SC, Brazil
XBE - Bearskin Lake, ON, Canada
XBN - Biniguni, Papua New Guinea
XCH - Christmas Island, Australia
XDB - Europe Railway Service,
  France
XFN - Xiangfan, P.R. China
XGR - Kangiqsualujjuaq, PQ,
  Canada
XIC - Xichang, P.R. China
XIY - Xianyang, P.R. China
XKH - Xieng Khouang, Laos

```
XKS - Kasabonika, ON, Canada          YCH - Chatham, NB, Canada
XLB - Lac Brochet, MB, Canada         YCK - Colville Lake, NT, Canada
XMG - Mahendranagar, Nepal            YCL - Charlo, NB, Canada
XMH - Manihi, Fr. Polynesia           YCN - Cochrane, ON, Canada
XMN - Xiamen, P. R. China             YCO - Kuglutuk Coppermine, NT,
XMY - Yam Island, QLD, Australia            Canada
XNN - Xining, P. R. China             YCR - Cross Lake, MB, Canada
XPK - Pukatawagan, MB, Canada         YCS - Chesterfield Inlet, NT,
XQP - Quepos, Costa Rica                    Canada
XQU - Qualicum, BC, Canada            YCY - Clyde River, NT, Canada
XRY - Jerez De La Frontera, Spain     YDA - Dawson City, YK, Canada
XSC - South Caicos, Turks &           YDF - Deer Lake, NF, Canada
      Caicos Is.                      YDI - Davis Inlet, NF, Canada
XSI - South Indian Lake, MB,          YDL - Dease Lake, BC, Canada
      Canada                          YDN - Dauphin, MB, Canada
XSP - Singapore-Seletar,              YDP - Nain, NF, Canada
      Singapore                       YDQ - Dawson Creek, BC, Canada
XTG - Thargomindah, QLD,              YEA - Edmonton, AB, Canada
      Australia                       YEC - Yechon, Rep. of Korea
XTL - Tadoule Lake, MB, Canada        YEG - Edmonton, AB, Canada
XUZ - Xuzhou, P.R. China              YEK - Arviat, NT, Canada
XYA - Yandina, Solomon Islands        YEL - Elliot Lake, ON, Canada
XYD - Part Dieu Railway Service,      YER - Fort Severn, ON, Canada
      France                          YEV - Inuvik, NT, Canada
YAA - Anahim Lake, BC, Canada         YFA - Fort Albany, ON, Canada
YAB - Arctic Bay, NT, Canada          YFB - Iqaluit, NT, Canada
YAC - Cat Lake, ON, Canada            YFC - Fredericton, NB, Canada
YAG - Fort Frances, ON, Canada        YFH - Fort Hope, ON, Canada
YAI - Chillan, Chile                  YFJ - Snare Lake, NT, Canada
YAK - Yakutat, AK, USA                YFO - Flin Flon, MB, Canada
YAM - Sault Ste. Marie, ON,           YFR - Fort Resolution, NT, Canada
      Canada                          YFS - Ft. Simpson, NT, Canada
YAO - Yaounde, Cameroon               YFX - Fox Harbour/St. Lewis, NF,
YAP - Yap, Caroline Is.                     Canada
YAT - Attawapiskat, ON, Canada        YGB - Gillies Bay, BC, Canada
YAX - Angling Lake, ON, Canada        YGH - Ft. Good Hope, NT, Canada
YAY - St. Anthony, NF, Canada         YGJ - Yonago, Japan
YAZ - Tofino, BC, Canada              YGK - Kingston, ON, Canada
YBA - Banff, AB, Canada               YGL - La Grande, PQ, Canada
YBB - Pelly Bay, NT-Townsite,         YGO - Gods Narrows, MB, Canada
      Canada                          YGP - Gaspe, PQ, Canada
YBC - Baie Comeau, PQ, Canada         YGQ - Geraldton, ON, Canada
YBE - Uranium City, SK, Canada        YGR - Iles De Madeleine, PQ,
YBG - Saguenay, PQ, Canada                  Canada
YBI - Black Tickle, NF, Canada        YGT - Igloolik, NT, Canada
YBK - Baker Lake, NT, Canada          YGV - Havre St. Pierre, PQ,
YBL - Campbell River, BC, Canada            Canada
YBP - Yibin, P.R. China               YGW - Kuujjuarapik, PQ, Canada
YBR - Brandon, MB, Canada             YGX - Gillam, MB, Canada
YBT - Brochet, MB, Canada             YGZ - Grise Fiord, NT, Canada
YBV - Berens River, MB, Canada        YHA - Port Hope Simpson, NF,
YBX - Blanc Sablon, PQ, Canada              Canada
YCB - Cambridge Bay, NT, Canada       YHD - Dryden, ON, Canada
YCD - Nanaimo, BC, Canada             YHF - Hearst, ON, Canada
YCG - Castlegar, BC, Canada           YHG - Charlottetown, NF, Canada
```

YHI - Holman Island, NT, Canada
YHK - Gjoa Haven, NT, Canada
YHM - Hamilton, ON, Canada
YHN - Hornepayne, ON, Canada
YHO - Hopedale, NF, Canada
YHR - Harrington Harbour, PQ,
   Canada
YHY - Hay River, NT, Canada
YHZ - Halifax, NS, Canada
YIF - Pakuashipi, PQ, Canada
YIH - Yichang, P. R. China
YIK - Ivujivik, PQ, Canada
YIN - Yining, P. R. China
YIO - Pond Inlet, NT, Canada
YIV - Island Lake, MB, Canada
YIW - Yiwu, P.R. China
YJT - Stephenville, NF, Canada
YKA - Kamloops, BC, Canada
YKG - Kangirsuk, PQ, Canada
YKL - Schefferville, PQ, Canada
YKM - Yakima, WA, USA
YKN - Yankton, SD, USA
YKQ - Waskaganish, PQ, Canada
YKS - Yakutsk, Russia
YKU - Chisasibi, PQ, Canada
YKX - Kirkland Lake, ON, Canada
YLC - Lake Harbour, NT, Canada
YLD - Chapleau, ON, Canada
YLE - Wha Ti Lac La Martre, NT,
   Canada
YLH - Lansdowne, ON, Canada
YLL - Lloydminster, SK, Canada
YLR - Leaf Rapids, MB, Canada
YLS - Lebel-Sur-Quevillon, PQ,
   Canada
YLW - Kelowna, BC, Canada
YMH - Mary's Harbour, NF, Canada
YMM - Ft. McMurray, AB, Canada
YMN - Makkovik, NF, Canada
YMO - Moosonee, ON, Canada
YMQ - Montreal, PQ, Canada
YMS - Yurimaguas, Peru
YMT - Chibougamau, PQ, Canada
YMX - Montreal, PQ-Mirabel,
   Canada
YNA - Natashquan, PQ, Canada
YNB - Yanbu, Saudi Arabia
YNC - Wemindji, PQ, Canada
YND - Gatineau/Hull, PQ, Canada
YNE - Norway House, MB, Canada
YNG - Youngstown, OH, USA
YNJ - Yanji, P.R. China
YNL - Points North Landing, SK,
   Canada

YNO - North Spirit Lake, ON,
   Canada
YNS - Nemiscau, PQ, Canada
YNT - Yantai, P.R. China
YOC - Old Crow, YK, Canada
YOD - Cold Lake, AB, Canada
YOH - Oxford House, MB, Canada
YOJ - High Level, AB, Canada
YOL - Yola, Nigeria
YOP - Rainbow Lake, AB, Canada
YOW - Ottawa, ON, Canada
YPA - Prince Albert, SK, Canada
YPB - Port Alberni, BC, Canada
YPC - Paulatuk, NT, Canada
YPE - Peace River, AB, Canada
YPH - Inukjuak, PQ, Canada
YPJ - Aupaluk, PQ, Canada
YPL - Pickle Lake, ON, Canada
YPM - Pikangikum, ON, Canada
YPN - Port Menier, PQ, Canada
YPO - Peawanuck, ON, Canada
YPR - Prince Rupert, BC, Canada
YPW - Powell River, BC, Canada
YPX - Puvirnituq, PQ, Canada
YPY - Ft. Chipewyan, AB, Canada
YQB - Quebec, PQ, Canada
YQC - Quaqtaq, PQ, Canada
YQD - The Pas, MB, Canada
YQG - Windsor, ON, Canada
YQH - Watson Lake, YK, Canada
YQI - Yarmouth, NS, Canada
YQK - Kenora, ON, Canada
YQL - Lethbridge, AB, Canada
YQM - Moncton, NB, Canada
YQQ - Comox, BC, Canada
YQR - Regina, SK, Canada
YQT - Thunder Bay, ON, Canada
YQU - Grande Prairie, AB, Canada
YQX - Gander, NF, Canada
YQY - Sydney, NS, Canada
YQZ - Quesnel, BC, Canada
YRA - Rae Lakes, NT, Canada
YRB - Resolute, NT, Canada
YRD - Dean River, BC, Canada
YRF - Cartwright, NF, Canada
YRG - Rigolet, NF, Canada
YRJ - Roberval, PQ, Canada
YRL - Red Lake, ON, Canada
YRS - Red Sucker Lake, MB, Canada
YRT - Rankin Inlet, NT, Canada
YSB - Sudbury, ON, Canada
YSF - Stony Rapids, SK, Canada
YSG - Lutselke Snowdrift, NT,
   Canada
YSJ - Saint John, NB, Canada

```
YSK - Sanikiluaq, NT, Canada          YXY - Whitehorse, YK, Canada
YSL - St. Leonard, NB, Canada         YXZ - Wawa, ON, Canada
YSM - Ft. Smith, NT, Canada           YYB - North Bay, ON, Canada
YSN - Salmon Arm, BC, Canada          YYC - Calgary, AB, Canada
YSO - Postville, NF, Canada           YYD - Smithers, BC, Canada
YSR - Nanisivik, NT, Canada           YYE - Ft. Nelson, BC, Canada
YST - St. Therese Pt., MB, Canada     YYF - Penticton, BC, Canada
YSY - Sachs Harbour, NT, Canada       YYG - Charlottetown, PEI, Canada
YTA - Pembroke, ON, Canada            YYH - Taloyoak, NT, Canada
YTE - Cape Dorset, NT, Canada         YYJ - Victoria, BC, Canada
YTF - Alma, PQ, Canada                YYL - Lynn Lake, MB, Canada
YTH - Thompson, MB, Canada            YYQ - Churchill, MB, Canada
YTL - Big Trout Lake, ON, Canada      YYR - Goose Bay, NF, Canada
YTO - Toronto, ON, Canada             YYT - St. Johns, NF, Canada
YTQ - Tasiujuaq, PQ, Canada           YYU - Kapuskasing, ON, Canada
YTS - Timmins, ON, Canada             YYY - Mont Joli, PQ, Canada
YTZ - Toronto, ON-Toronto Is.,        YYZ - Toronto, ON-Int'l, Canada
      Canada                          YZE - Gore Bay, ON, Canada
YUB - Tuktoyaktuk, NT, Canada         YZF - Yellowknife, NT, Canada
YUD - Umiujaq, PQ, Canada             YZG - Salluit, PQ, Canada
YUF - Pelly Bay, NT, Canada           YZP - Sandspit, BC, Canada
YUL - Montreal, PQ-Dorval Arpt.,      YZR - Sarnia, ON, Canada
      Canada                          YZS - Coral Harbour, NT, Canada
YUM - Yuma, AZ, USA                   YZT - Port Hardy, BC, Canada
YUT - Repulse Bay, NT, Canada         YZV - Sept-Iles, PQ, Canada
YUX - Hall Beach, NT, Canada          ZAC - York Landing, MB, Canada
YUY - Rouyn-Noranda, PQ, Canada       ZAG - Zagreb, Yugoslavia
YVA - Moroni, Comoros                 ZAH - Zahedan, Iran
YVC - La Ronge, SK, Canada            ZAL - Valdivia, Chile
YVM - Broughton, NT, Canada           ZAM - Zamboanga, Philippines
YVO - Val D'or, PQ, Canada            ZAQ - Nuremberg Main Station,
YVP - Kuujjuaq, PQ, Canada                  Germany
YVQ - Norman Wells, NT, Canada        ZAT - Zhaotong, P.R. China
YVR - Vancouver, BC, Canada           ZAZ - Zaragoza, Spain
YVZ - Deer Lake, ON, Canada           ZBF - Bathurst, NB, Canada
YWB - Kangiqsujuaq, PQ, Canada        ZBR - Chah-Bahar, Iran
YWG - Winnipeg, MB, Canada            ZBY - Sayaboury, Laos
YWH - Victoria, BC-Inner Harb.,       ZCL - Zacatecas, Mexico
      Canada                          ZCO - Temuco, Chile
YWJ - Deline, NT, Canada              ZDJ - Berne-RR Station,
YWK - Wabush, NF, Canada                    Switzerland
YWL - Williams Lake, BC, Canada       ZDN - Brno Bus Station, Czech
YWP - Webequie, ON, Canada                  Republic
YXC - Cranbrook, BC, Canada           ZEL - Bella Bella, BC, Canada
YXE - Saskatoon, SK, Canada           ZEM - East Main, PQ, Canada
YXH - Medicine Hat, AB, Canada        ZFD - Fond du Lac, SK, Canada
YXJ - Ft. St. John, BC, Canada        ZFN - Tulita Fort Norman, NT,
YXL - Sioux Lookout, ON, Canada             Canada
YXN - Whale Cove, NT, Canada          ZGI - Gods River, MB, Canada
YXP - Pangnirtung, NT, Canada         ZGS - Gethsemani, PQ, Canada
YXR - Earlton, ON, Canada             ZGU - Gaua, Vanuatu
YXS - Prince George, BC, Canada       ZHA - Zhanyiang, P.R. China
YXT - Terrace, BC, Canada             ZIG - Ziguinchor, Senegal
YXU - London, ON, Canada              ZIH - Ixtapa/Zihuatanejo, Mexico
YXX - Abbotsford, BC, Canada          ZJN - Swan River, MB, Canada
```

```
ZKE - Kaschechewan, ON, Canada
ZKG - Kegaska, PQ, Canada
ZLO - Manzanillo, Mexico
ZLT - La Tabatiere, PQ, Canada
ZNA - Nanaimo, BC-Harbour, Canada
ZNE - Newman, WA, Australia
ZNZ - Zanzibar, Tanzania
ZOS - Osorno, Chile
ZPB - Sachigo Lake, ON, Canada
ZQN - Queenstown, New Zealand
ZRH - Zurich, Switzerland
ZRJ - Round Lake, ON, Canada
ZSA - San Salvador, Bahamas
ZSJ - Sandy Lake, ON, Canada
ZTB - Tete A La Baleine, PQ,
      Canada
ZTH - Zakinthos, Greece
ZTM - Shamattawa, MB, Canada
ZUH - Zhuhai, P.R. China
ZUM - Churchill Falls, NF, Canada
ZVA - Miandrivazo, Madagascar
ZVK - Savannakhet, Laos
ZWL - Wollaston Lake, SK, Canada
ZYL - Sylhet, Bangladesh
ZZU - Mzuzu, Malawi
```

NOTES

ENCODING WORLDWIDE CITIES/AIRPORTS

The cities are in alphabetical order. The city, state/province/ territory, and country are provided with the three-letter code. Airport names may also be included when applicable. **Refer to the pages on "Abbreviations of States and Provinces" for assistance if necessary.**

OTHER ABBREVIATIONS USED

Dem. Rep. - Democratic Republic
Hlpt - Heliport
P.R. CHINA - People's Republic of China
Rep. - Republic
RR - Railroad

Soc. Rep. - Socialist Republic
Soc. Is. - Society Islands
SPB - Seaplane Base
U.A. Emirates - United Arab Emirates
UK - United Kingdom

Aalborg, Denmark - AAL
Aalesund, Norway - AES
Aarhus, Denmark - AAR
Aasiaat, Greenland - JEG
Abbotsford, BC, Canada - YXX
Aberdeen, Scotland, UK - ABZ
Aberdeen, SD, USA - ABR
Abha, Saudi Arabia - AHB
Abidjan, Cote D'Ivoire - ABJ
Abilene, TX, USA - ABI
Abu Dhabi, U. A. Emirates - AUH
Abu Simbel, Egypt - ABS
Abuja, Nigeria - ABV
Acapulco, Mexico - ACA
Accra, Ghana - ACC
Adak Island, AK, USA - ADK
Adana, Turkey - ADA
Addis Ababa, Ethiopia - ADD
Adelaide, SA, Australia - ADL
Aden, Yemen - ADE
Adler/Sochi, Russia - AER
Adrar, Algeria - AZR
Agades, Niger - AJY
Agadir, Morocco - AGA
Agartala, India - IXA
Agaun, Papua New Guinea - AUP
Agen, France - AGF
Agra, India - AGR
Agri, Turkey - AJI
Aguadilla, Puerto Rico - BQN
Aguascalientes, Mexico - AGU
Aguni, Japan - AGJ
Ahmedabad, India - AMD
Ahuas, Honduras - AHS
Ahwaz, Iran - AWZ
Ailuk, Marshall Islands - AIM
Aioun El Atrouss, Mauritania -
   AEO
Airok, Marshall Islands - AIC
Aitape, Papua New Guinea - ATP
Aitutaki, Cook Is., S. Pacific -
   AIT
Ajaccio, Corsica, France - AJA
Akhiok, AK, USA - AKK
Akiachak, AK, USA - KKI
Akiak, AK, USA - AKI
Akieni, Gabon - AKE
Akita, Japan - AXT
Akmola, Kazakstan - TSE
Akron/Canton, OH, USA - CAK
Aksu, P.R. China - AKU
Aktau, Kazakstan - SCO
Aktyubinsk, Kazakstan - AKX
Akulivik, Que., Canada - AKV
Akureyri, Iceland - AEY

Akutan, AK, USA - KQA
Al Arish, Egypt - AAC
Al Ghaydah, Yemen - AAY
Al Hoceima, Morocco - AHU
Al-Baha, Saudi Arabia - ABT
Al-Fujairah, United Arab Emirates
   - FJR
Alakanuk, AK, USA - AUK
Alamogordo, NM, USA - ALM
Alamosa, CO, USA - ALS
Albany, GA, USA - ABY
Albany, NY, USA - ALB
Albany, WA, Australia - ALH
Albuq, Yemen - BUK
Albuquerque, NM, USA - ABQ
Albury, NSW, Australia - ABX
Aldan, Russia - ADH
Alderney, Channel Islands, UK -
   ACI
Aleknagik, AK, USA - WKK
Aleppo, Syria - ALP
Alexander Bay, South Africa - ALJ
Alexandria, Egypt - ALY
Alexandria, LA, USA - AEX
Alexandroupolis, Greece - AXD
Alghero, Italy - AHO
Algiers, Algeria - ALG
Alicante, Spain - ALC
Alice Springs, NT, Australia -
   ASP
Alitak, AK, USA - ALZ
Allakaket, AK, USA - AET
Allentown, PA, USA - ABE
Alliance, NE, USA - AIA
Alma, PQ, Canada - YTF
Almaty, Kazakstan - ALA
Almeria, Spain - LEI
Alor Setar, Malaysia - AOR
Alotau, Papua New Guinea - GUR
Alpena, MI, USA - APN
Alta, Norway - ALF
Alta Floresta, MT, Brazil - AFL
Altamira, PA, Brazil - ATM
Altay, P.R. China - AAT
Altenrhein, Switzerland - ACH
Altoona, PA, USA - AOO
Amami O Shima, Japan - ASJ
Amarillo, TX, USA - AMA
Amazon Bay, Papua New Guinea -
   AZB
Ambanja, Madagascar - IVA
Ambatomainty, Madagascar - AMY
Ambatondrazaka, Madagascar - WAM
Ambilobe, Madagascar - AMB
Ambler, AK, USA - ABL

Ambon, Indonesia - AMQ
Amboseli, Kenya - ASV
Ambunti, Papua New Guinea - AUJ
Amman, Jordan - AMM
Amook, AK, USA - AOS
Amritsar, India - ATQ
Amsterdam, Netherlands - AMS
Anaa, Tuamotu Islands, AAA
Anacortes, WA, USA - OTS
Anadyr, Russia - DYR
Anahim Lake, BC, Canada - YAA
Anaktuvuk Pass, AK, USA - AKP
Anapa, Russia - AAQ
Anchorage, AK, USA - ANC
Ancona, Italy - AOI
Andahuaylas, Peru - ANS
Andenes, Norway - ANX
Andizhan, Uzbekistan - AZN
Andros Town, Bahamas - ASD
Anegada, BVI - NGD
Aneityum, Vanuatu - AUY
Angling Lake, ON, Canada - YAX
Angoon, AK, USA - AGN
Angouleme, France - ANG
Anguganak, Papua New Guinea - AKG
Anguilla, West Indies - AXA
Aniak, AK, USA - ANI
Aniwa, Vanuatu - AWD
Ankang, P.R. China - AKA
Ankara, Turkey - ANK
Ankara-Esenboga, Turkey - ESB
Ankavandra, Madagascar - JVA
Annaba, Algeria - AAE
Annecy, France - NCY
Annette Island, AK, USA - ANN
Anqing, P.R. China - AQG
Antalaha, Madagascar - ANM
Antalya, Turkey - AYT
Antananarivo, Madagascar - TNR
Antigua, West Indies - ANU
Antofagasta, Chile - ANF
Antsalova, Madagascar - WAQ
Antsiranana, Madagascar - DIE
Antsohihy, Madagascar - WAI
Antwerp, Belgium - ANR
Anvick, AK, USA - ANV
Aomori, Japan - AOJ
Aosta, Italy - AOT
Apartado, Colombia - APO
Apia, Western Samoa - APW
Apia-Fagali I., Western Samoa -
    FGI
Appleton, WI, USA - ATW
Aqaba, Jordan - AQJ
Aracaju, SE, Brazil - AJU

Aracatuba, SP, Brazil - ARU
Arad, Romania - ARW
Aragip, Papua New Guinea - ARP
Araguaina, TO, Brazil - AUX
Arapiraca, SP, Brazil - APQ
Arar, Saudi Arabia - RAE
Araraquara, SP, Brazil - AQA
Arauca, Colombia - AUC
Arba Mintch, Ethiopia - AMH
Arctic Bay, NT, Canada - YAB
Arctic Village, AK, USA - ARC
Ardabil, Iran - ADU
Arequipa, Peru - AQP
Arica, Chile - ARI
Arkhangelsk, Russia - ARH
Armenia, Colombia - AXM
Armidale, NSW, Australia - ARM
Arthur's Town, Bahamas - ATC
Aruba, Aruba - AUA
Arviat, NT, Canada - YEK
Arvidsjaur, Sweden - AJR
Asahikawa, Japan - AKJ
Asapa, Papua New Guinea - APP
Asau, Western Samoa - AAU
Asheville, NC, USA - AVL
Ashkhabad, Turkmenistan - ASB
Asmara, Eritrea - ASM
Asosa, Ethiopia - ASO
Aspen, CO, USA - ASE
Assab, Ethiopia - ASA
Assiut, Egypt - ATZ
Astoria, OR, USA - AST
Astrakhan, Russia - ASF
Asturias, Spain - OVD
Astypalaia Is., Greece - JTY
Asuncion, Paraguay - ASU
Aswan, Egypt - ASW
Ataq, Yemen - AXK
Atar, Mauritania - ATR
Athens, Greece - ATH
Athens, GA, USA - AHN
Atiu, Cook Is., S. Pacific - AIU
Atka, AK, USA - AKB
Atlanta, GA, USA - ATL
Atlantic City, NJ, USA - AIY
Atlantic City, NJ-Pomona, USA -
    ACY
Atmautluak, AK, USA - ATT
Atqasuk, AK, USA - ATK
Attawapiskat, ON, Canada - YAT
Atuona, Marquesas Island - AUQ
Atyrau, Kazakstan - GUW
Auckland, New Zealand - AKL
Augsburg, Fed. Rep. of Germany -
    AGB

Augusta, GA, USA - AGS
Augusta, ME, USA - AUG
Auki, Solomon Islands - AKS
Aumo, Papua New Guinea - AUV
Aupaluk, PQ, Canada - YPJ
Aur, Marshall Islands - AUL
Aurangabad, India - IXU
Aurillac, France - AUR
Aurukun Mission, QLD, Australia -
    AUU
Austin, TX, USA - AUS
Avignon, France - AVN
Avu Avu, Solomon Islands - AVU
Axum, Ethiopia - AXU
Ayacucho, Peru - AYP
Ayers Rock, NT, Australia - AYQ
Bacolod, Philippines - BCD
Badu Island, QLD, Australia - BDD
Bagdogra, India - IXB
Bage, RS, Brazil - BGX
Bagotville, PQ, Canada - YBG
Baguio, Philippines - BAG
Bahar Dar, Ethiopia - BJR
Bahawalpur, Pakistan - BHV
Bahia Blanca, Argentina - BHI
Bahia Pinas, Panama - BFQ
Bahia Solano, Colombia - BSC
Bahrain, Bahrain - BAH
Baia Mare, Romania - BAY
Baie Comeau, PQ, Canada - YBC
Baimuru, Papua New Guinea - VMU
Bakalalan, Sarawak, Malaysia -
    BKM
Baker Lake, NT, Canada - YBK
Bakersfield, CA, USA - BFL
Baku, Azerbaijan - BAK
Balalae, Solomon Islands - BAS
Balgo Hills, WA, Australia - BQW
Balikpapan, Indonesia - BPN
Balimo, Papua New Guinea - OPU
Ballina, NSW, Australia - BNK
Balmaceda, Chile - BBA
Baltimore, MD, USA - BWI
Bamaga, QLD, Australia - ABM
Bamako, Mali - BKO
Bambu, Papua New Guinea - BCP
Ban Me Thuot, Vietnam - BMV
Banda Aceh, Indonesia - BTJ
Bandar Abbas, Iran - BND
Bandar Lampung, Indonesia - TKG
Bandar Lengeh, Iran - BDH
Bandar Seri Begawan, Brunei - BWN
Bandung, Indonesia - BDO
Banff, AB, Canada - YBA
Bangalore, India - BLR

Bangkok, Thailand - BKK
Bangor, ME, USA - BGR
Bangui, Cen. African Republic -
    BGF
Banjarmasin, Indonesia - BDJ
Banjul, Gambia - BJL
Bannu, Pakistan - BNP
Baoshan, P.R. China - BSD
Baotou, P.R. China - BAV
Bar Harbor, ME, USA - BHB
Baracoa, Cuba - BCA
Barbados, Barbados - BGI
Barbuda, West Indies - BBQ
Barcaldine, QLD, Australia - BCI
Barcelona, Venezuela - BLA
Barcelona, Spain - BCN
Bardufoss, Norway - BDU
Bari, Italy - BRI
Bario, Sarawak, Malaysia - BBN
Barisal, Bangladesh - BZL
Barnaul, Russia - BAX
Barquisimeto, Venezuela - BRM
Barra Colorado, Costa Rica - BCL
Barra Do Garcas, MT, Brazil - BPG
Barra, Hebrides Is., Scotland, UK
    - BRR
Barrancabermeja, Colombia - EJA
Barranquilla, Colombia - BAQ
Barreiras, BA, Brazil - BRA
Barretos, SP, Brazil - BAT
Barrow, AK, USA - BRW
Barter Island, AK, USA - BTI
Basankusu, Dem. Rep. of the Congo
    - BSU
Basco, Philippines - BSO
Basel/Mulhouse, Switzerland - BSL
Basse Terre, French Antilles -
    BBR
Bastia, Corsica, France - BIA
Bata, Equatorial Guinea - BSG
Batam/Batu Besar, Indonesia - BTH
Bathurst Island, NT, Australia -
    BRT
Bathurst, NB, Canada - ZBF
Bathurst, NSW, Australia - BHS
Batman, Turkey - BAL
Baton Rouge, LA, USA - BTR
Batsfjord, Norway - BJF
Battambang, Cambodia - BBM
Bauru, SP, Brazil - BAU
Bayamo, Cuba - BYM
Bazaruto Island, Mozambique - BZB
Bayreuth, Germany - BYU
Bearskin Lake, ON, Canada - XBE

Beaumont/Pt. Arthur, TX, USA - BPT
Beaver, AK, USA - WBQ
Bechar, Algeria - CBH
Beckley, WV, USA - BKW
Bedourie, Qld., Australia - BEU
Beica, Ethiopia - BEI
Beihai, P.R. China - BHY
Beijing, P.R. China - PEK
Beijing, P.R. China - BJS
Beira, Mozambique - BEW
Beirut, Lebanon - BEY
Bejaia, Algeria - BJA
Belaga, Sarawak, Malaysia - BLG
Belem, PA, Brazil - BEL
Belep, New Caledonia - BMY
Belfast, N. Ireland, UK - BFS
Belfast-City, N. Ireland, UK - BHD
Belgrade, Yugoslavia - BEG
Belize City, Belize - BZE
Belize City-Municipal, Belize - TZA
Bella Bella, BC, Canada - ZEL
Bella Coola, BC, Canada - QBC
Bellavista, Peru - BLP
Bellingham, WA, USA - BLI
Bellona Is., Solomon Islands - BNY
Belo, Madagascar - BMD
Belo Horizonte, MG, Brazil - BHZ
Belo Horizonte-Confins, MG, Brazil - CNF
Beloreck, Russia - BCX
Bemidji, MN, USA - BJI
Benbecula, Herides, Scotland, UK - BEB
Bengkulu, Indonesia - BKS
Benguela, Angola - BUG
Benguera Island, Mozambique - BCW
Benton Harbor, MI, USA - BEH
Berau, Indonesia - BEJ
Berbera, Somalia - BBO
Berdyansk, Ukraine - ERD
Berens River, MB, Canada - YBV
Bergen, Norway - BGO
Bergerac, France - EGC
Berlevag, Norway - BVG
Berlin, Germany - BER
Berlin-Schoenefld, Germany - SXF
Berlin-Tegel, Germany - TXL
Berlin-Tempelhof, Germany - THF
Bermuda, Atlantic Ocean - BDA
Berne, Switzerland - BRN

Berne-Rr Station, Switzerland - ZDJ
Bertoua, Cameroon - BTA
Besalampy, Madagascar - BPY
Bethel, AK, USA - BET
Bettles, AK, USA - BTT
Beziers, France - BZR
Bhadrapur, Nepal - BDP
Bhairawa, Nepal - BWA
Bhamo, Myanmar - BMO
Bharatpur, Nepal - BHR
Bhavnagar, India - BHU
Bhopal, India - BHO
Bhubaneswar, India - BBI
Bhuj, India - BHJ
Biak, Indonesia - BIK
Bialla, Papua New Guinea - BAA
Biarritz, France - BIQ
Big Creek, Belize - BGK
Big Trout Lake, ON, Canada - YTL
Bikini Atoll, Marshall Islands - BII
Bilbao, Spain - BIO
Billiluna, WA, Australia - BIW
Billings, MT, USA - BIL
Billund, Denmark - BLL
Bimini, Bahamas - BIM
Bimini-North SPB, Bahamas - NSB
Binghamton, NY, USA - BGM
Biniguni, Papua New Guinea - XBN
Bintulu, Sarawak, Malaysia - BTU
Biratnagar, Nepal - BIR
Birch Creek, AK, USA - KBC
Birdsville, QLD, Australia - BVI
Birmingham, England, UK - BHX
Birmingham, AL, USA - BHM
Bishkek, Krgyzstan - FRU
Biskra, Algeria - BSK
Bismarck, ND, USA - BIS
Bissau, Guinea-Bissau - OXB
Bitam, Gabon - BMM
Black Tickle, NF, Canada - YBI
Blackall, QLD, Australia - BKQ
Blackpool, England, UK - BLK
Blackwater, QLD, Australia - BLT
Blagoveschensk, Russia - BQS
Blakely Island, WA, USA - BYW
Blanc Sablon, PQ, Canada - YBX
Blantyre, Malawi - BLZ
Blenheim, New Zealand - BHE
Block Island, RI, USA - BID
Bloemfontein, South Africa - BFN
Bloomington, IL, USA - BMI
Bluefield, WV, USA - BLF
Bluefields, Nicaragua - BEF

Blumenau, SC, Brazil - BNU
Boa Vista, RR, Brazil - BVB
Boa Vista, Cape Verde Islands -
    BVC
Boang, Papua New Guinea - BOV
Bobo Dioulasso, Burkina Faso -
    BOY
Bocas Del Toro, Panama Rep. - BOC
Bodo, Norway - BOO
Bodrum, Turkey - BXN
Boeing Field Int'l, WA, USA - BFI
Boende, Dem. Rep. of the Congo -
    BNB
Bogota, Colombia - BOG
Boigu Island, QLD, Australia -
    GIC
Boise, ID, USA - BOI
Bologna, Italy - BLQ
Bonaire, Neth. Antilles - BON
Bonanza, Nicaragua - BZA
Bonn, Germany - BNJ
Bora Bora, Soc. Is., Fr.
    Polynesia - BOB
Borama, Somalia - BXX
Bordeaux, France - BOD
Bordj Badji Mokhtar, Algeria -
    BMW
Borlange, Sweden - BLE
Bornholm, Denmark - RNN
Borroloola, NT, Australia - BOX
Bossaso, Somalia - BSA
Boston, MA, USA - BOS
Bouake, Cote D'Ivoire - BYK
Boulia, QLD, Australia - BQL
Boundary, AK, USA - BYA
Bourgas, Bulgaria - BOJ
Bourke, NSW, Australia - BRK
Bournemouth, England, UK - BOH
Bozeman, MT, USA - BZN
Bradford, PA, USA - BFD
Braganca, Portugal - BGC
Brainerd, MN, USA - BRD
Brampton Island, QLD, Australia -
    BMP
Brandon, MB, Canada - YBR
Brasilia, DF, Brazil - BSB
Bratislava, Slovak Republic - BTS
Bratsk, Russia - BTK
Brava, Cape Verde - BVR
Brazzaville, Peop. Rep. of the
    Congo - BZV
Bremen, Germany - BRE
Brest, France - BES
Brevig Mission, AK, USA - KTS
Brewarrina, NSW, Australia - BWQ

Briansk, Russia - BZK
Bridgeport, CT, USA - BDR
Brindisi, Italy - BDS
Brisbane, QLD, Australia - BNE
Bristol, England, UK - BRS
Brive-La-Gaillarde, France - BVE
Brize Norton, England, UK - BZZ
Brno, Czech Republic - BRQ
Brno Bus Station, Czech Republic
    - ZDN
Brochet, MB, Canada - YBT
Broken Hill, NSW, Australia - BHQ
Bronnoysund, Norway - BNN
Brookings, SD, USA - BKX
Broome, WA, Australia - BME
Broughton, NT, Canada - YVM
Brownsville, TX, USA - BRO
Brownwood, TX, USA - BWD
Brunswick, GA, USA - SSI
Brus Laguna, Honduras - BHG
Brussels, Belgium - BRU
Brussels-South, Belgium - CRL
Bryce Canyon, UT, USA - BCE
Bubaque, Guinea Bissau - BQE
Bucaramanga, Colombia - BGA
Bucharest, Romania - BUH
Bucharest-Baneasa, Romania - BBU
Bucharest-Otopeni, Romania - OTP
Buckland, AK, USA - BKC
Budapest, Hungary - BUD
Buenos Aires, Argentina - BUE
Buenos Aires-Newbery, Argentina -
    AEP
Buenos Aires-Pistarini, Argentina
    - EZE
Buffalo, NY, USA - BUF
Buffalo Range, Zimbabwe - BFO
Buin, Papua New Guinea - UBI
Bujumbura, Burundi - BJM
Buka Is., Papua New Guinea - BUA
Bukavu, Dem. Rep. of the Congo -
    BKY
Bukhara, Uzbekistan - BHK
Bulawayo, Zimbabwe - BUQ
Bullhead City, AZ, USA - IFP
Bulolo, Papua New Guinea - BUL
Bumba, Dem. Rep. of the Congo -
    BMB
Bundabert, Qld., Australia - BDB
Bunia, Dem. Rep. of the Congo -
    BUX
Bunsil, Papua New Guinea - BXZ
Burao, Somalia - BUO
Burbank, CA, USA - BUR
Bureta, Fiji - LEV

Buri Ram, Thailand - BFV
Burketown, QLD, Australia - BUC
Burlington, IA, USA - BRL
Burlington, VT, USA - BTV
Burnie, TS, Australia - BWT
Bushehr, Iran - BUZ
Bussellton, WA, Australia - BQB
Busuanga, Philippines - USU
Butte, MT, USA - BTM
Butuan, Philippines - BXU
Cabin Creek, AK, USA - CBZ
Cabinda, Angola - CAB
Cacoal, TO, Brazil - OAL
Caen, France - CFR
Cagayan de Oro, Philippines - CGY
Cagliari, Italy - CAG
Cairns, QLD, Australia - CNS
Cairo, Egypt - CAI
Cajamarca, Peru - CJA
Calabar, Nigeria - CBQ
Calama, Chile - CJC
Calcutta, India - CCU
Calgary, AB, Canada - YYC
Cali, Colombia - CLO
Calicut, India - CCJ
Calvi, Corsica, France - CLY
Camaguey, Cuba - CMW
Cambridge, England, UK - CBG
Cambridge Bay, NT, Canada - YCB
Campbell River, BC, Canada - YBL
Campbeltown, Scotland, UK - CAL
Campeche, Mexico - CPE
Campina Grande, PB, Brazil - CPV
Campinas, SP, Brazil - CPQ
Campo Grande, MS, Brazil - CGR
Campos, RJ, Brazil - CAW
Canaima, Venezuela - CAJ
Canarana, MT, Brazil - CQA
Canberra, ACT, Australia - CBR
Cancun, Mexico - CUN
Candle, AK, USA - CDL
Cannes, France - CEQ
Cannes Croisette H/P, France -
   JCA
Canouan Island, Windward Islands
   - CIW
Cap Haitien, Haiti - CAP
Cap Skirring, Senegal - CSK
Cape Dorset, NT, Canada - YTE
Cape Girardeau, MO, USA - CGI
Cape Gloucester, Papua New Guinea
   - CGC
Cape Lisburne, AK, USA - LUR
Cape Newenham, AK, USA - EHM

Cape Orford, Papua New Guinea -
   CPI
Cape Romanzof, AK, USA - CZF
Cape Town, South Africa - CPT
Cape Vogel, Papua New Guinea -
   CVL
Capurgana, Colombia - CPB
Caracas, Venezuela - CCS
Carajas, PA, Brazil - CKS
Carcassone, France - CCF
Cardiff, Wales, UK - CWL
Carlsbad, CA, USA - CLD
Carlsbad, NM, USA - CNM
Carnarvon, WA, Australia - CVQ
Carriacou, Windward Islands - CRU
Carrillo, Costa Rica - RIK
Cartagena, Colombia - CTG
Cartwright, NF, Canada - YRF
Casablanca, Morocco - CAS
Casablanca-Mohamed V., Morocco -
   CMN
Casa de Campo, Dominican Republic
   - LRM
Cascavel, PR, Brazil - CAC
Casino, NSW, Australia - CSI
Casper, WY, USA - CPR
Castlegar, BC, Canada - YCG
Castres, France - DCM
Cat Lake, ON, Canada - YAC
Catamarca, Argentina - CTC
Catania, Italy - CTA
Caticlan, Philippines - MPH
Catumbela, Angola - CBT
Caucasia, Colombia - CAQ
Caxias Do Sul, RS, Brazil - CXJ
Caye Caulker, Belize - CUK
Cayenne, Fr. Guiana - CAY
Cayman Brac, West Indies - CYB
Cayo Coco, Cuba - CCC
Cebu, Philippines - CEB
Cedar City, UT, USA - CDC
Cedar Rapids/Iowa City, IA, USA -
   CID
Ceduna, SA, Australia - CED
Center Is., WA, USA - CWS
Central, AK, USA - CEM
Ceuta Heliport, Spain - JCU
Chachapoyas, Peru - CHH
Chadron, NE, USA - CDR
Chah-Bahar, Iran - ZBR
Chaiten, Chile - WCH
Chalkyitsik, AK, USA - CIK
Chambery, France - CMF
Champaign, IL, USA - CMI
Chandigarh, India - IXC

Changchun, P.R. China - CGQ
Changde, P.R. China - CGD
Changsha, P.R. China - CSX
Changuinola, Panama Rep. - CHX
Changzhou, P.R. China - CZX
Chania, Crete, Greece - CHQ
Chapeco, SC, Brazil - XAP
Chapleau, ON, Canada - YLD
Charleston, SC, USA - CHS
Charleston, WV, USA - CRW
Charleville, QLD, Australia - CTL
Charlo, NB, Canada - YCL
Charlotte, NC, USA - CLT
Charlottesville, VA, USA - CHO
Charlottetown, NF, Canada - YHG
Charlottetown, PEI, Canada - YYG
Chatham Island, New Zealand - CHT
Chatham, NB, Canada - YCH
Chattanooga, TN, USA - CHA
Chefornak, AK, USA - CYF
Cheju, Rep. of Korea - CJU
Chelyabinsk, Russia - CEK
Chengdu, P.R. China - CTU
Chennai, India - MAA
Cheong Ju City, Rep. of Korea -
   CJJ
Cherbourg, France - CER
Chernovtsy, Ukraine - CWC
Chesterfield Inlet, NT, Canada -
   YCS
Chetumal, Mexico - CTM
Chevak, AK, USA - VAK
Chevery, PQ, Canada - YHR
Cheyenne, WY, USA - CYS
Chiang Mai, Thailand - CNX
Chiang Rai, Thailand - CEI
Chiayi, Taiwan - CYI
Chibougamau, PQ, Canada - YMT
Chicago, IL, USA - CHI
Chicago, IL - O'Hare, USA - ORD
Chicago, IL-Meigs, USA - CGX
Chicago, IL-Midway, USA - MDW
Chichen Itza, Mexico - CZA
Chicken, AK, USA - CKX
Chiclayo, Peru - CIX
Chico, CA, USA - CIC
Chifeng, P.R. China - CIF
Chignik, AK, USA - KCL
Chignik, AK-Chignik Lk., USA -
   KCQ
Chignik, AK-Fisheries, USA - KCG
Chignik, AK-Lagoon, USA - KCL
Chigorodo, Colombia - IGO
Chihuahua, Mexico - CUU
Chillan, Chile - YAI

Chimbote, Peru - CHM
Chinju, Rep. of Korea - HIN
Chios, Greece - JKH
Chisana, AK, USA - CZN
Chisasibi, PQ, Canada - YKU
Chita, Russia - HTA
Chitral, Pakistan - CJL
Chitre, Panama - CTD
Chittagong, Bangladesh - CGP
Choiseul Bay, Solomon Islands -
   CHY
Chongqing, P.R. China - CKG
Chos Malal, Argentina - HOS
Christchurch, New Zealand - CHC
Christmas Island, Australia - XCH
Chuathbaluk, AK, USA - CHU
Chub Cay, Bahamas - CCZ
Churchill Falls, NF, Canada - ZUM
Churchill, MB, Canada - YYQ
Cicia, Fiji - ICI
Ciego De Avila, Cuba - AVI
Cincinnati, OH, USA - CVG
Circle Hot Springs, AK, USA - CHP
Circle, AK, USA - IRC
Ciudad Bolivar, Venezuela - CBL
Ciudad Del Carmen, Mexico - CME
Ciudad Del Este, Paraguay - AGT
Ciudad Juarez, Mexico - CJS
Ciudad Obregon, Mexico - CEN
Ciudad Victoria, Mexico - CVM
Clarks Point, AK, USA - CLP
Clarksburg, WV, USA - CKB
Clermont-Ferrand, France - CFE
Cleve, SA, Australia - CVC
Cleveland, OH, USA - CLE
Cloncurry, QLD, Australia - CNJ
Clovis, NM, USA - CVN
Club Makokola, Malawi - CMK
Cluj-Napoca, Romania - CLJ
Clyde River, NT, Canada - YCY
Cobar, NSW, Australia - CAZ
Cobija, Bolivia - CIJ
Cochabamba, Bolivia - CBB
Cochin, India - COK
Cochrane, ON, Canada - YCN
Coconut Island, QLD, Australia -
   CNC
Cody, WY, USA - COD
Coen, QLD, Australia - CUQ
Coffman Cove, AK, USA - KCC
Coffs Harbour, NSW, Australia -
   CFS
Coimbatore, India - CJB
Cold Bay, AK, USA - CDB
Cold Lake, AB, Canada - YOD

Colima, Mexico - CLQ
College Station, TX, USA - CLL
Cologne Bonn, Main RR, Germany - QKL
Cologne/Bonn, Germany - CGN
Colombo, Sri Lanka - CMB
Colon, Panama Rep. - ONX
Colorado Springs, CO, USA - COS
Columbia, MO, USA - COU
Columbia, SC, USA - CAE
Columbus, GA, USA - CSG
Columbus, OH, USA - CMH
Columbus/Starkville/W. Pt., MS, USA - UBS
Columbus-Golden Triangle Reg, MS, USA - GTR
Colville Lake, NT, Canada - YCK
Comodoro Rivadavia, Argentina - CRD
Comox, BC, Canada - YQQ
Conakry, Guinea - CKY
Conceicao Do Araguaia, PA, Brazil - CDJ
Concepcion, Chile - CCP
Concordia, SC, Brazil - CCI
Condoto, Colombia - COG
Connaught, Rep. of Ireland - NOC
Constanta, Romania - CND
Constantine, Algeria - CZL
Contadora, Panama Rep. - OTD
Coober Pedy, SA, Australia - CPD
Cooktown, QLD, Australia - CTN
Cooma, NSW, Australia - OOM
Coonabarabran, NSW, Australia - COJ
Coonamble, NSW, Australia - CNB
Cootamundra, NSW, Australia - CMD
Copenhagen, Denmark - CPH
Copiapo, Chile - CPO
Coral Harbour, NT, Canada - YZS
Cordoba, Argentina - COR
Cordova, AK, USA - CDV
Corfu, Greece - CFU
Cork, Rep. of Ireland - ORK
Corn Island, Nicaragua - RNI
Coro, Venezuela - CZE
Corozal, Belize - CZH
Corpus Christi, TX, USA - CRP
Corrientes, Argentina - CNQ
Cortez, CO, USA - CEZ
Corumba, MG, Brazil - CMG
Corvo Is., Portugal (Azores) - CVU
Cotabato, Philippines - CBO
Coto 47, Costa Rica - OTR

Cotonou, Benin - COO
Cowra, NSW, Australia - CWT
Cox's Bazar, Bangladesh - CXB
Cozumel, Mexico - CZM
Craig, AK, USA - CGA
Craig Cove, Vanuatu - CCV
Cranbrook, BC, Canada - YXC
Crescent City, CA, USA - CEC
Crisciuma, SC, Brazil - CCM
Crooked Creek, AK, USA - CKD
Crooked Island, Bahamas - CRI
Cross Lake, MB, Canada - YCR
Crotone, Italy - CRV
Cruzeiro Do Sul, AC, Brazil - CZS
Cube Cove, AK, USA - CUW
Cucuta, Colombia - CUC
Cudal, NS, Australia - CUG
Cuenca, Ecuador - CUE
Cuernavaca, Mexico - CVJ
Cuiaba, Mato Grosso, Brazil - CGB
Culebra, Puerto Rico - CPX
Culiacan, Mexico - CUL
Culion, Philippines - CUJ
Cumana, Venezuela - CUM
Cumberland, MD, USA - CBE
Cuneo, Italy - CUF
Cunnamulla, QLD, Australia - CMA
Curacao, Neth. Antilles - CUR
Curitiba Bacacherim, PR, Brazil - BFH
Curitiba, PR, Brazil - CWB
Cuyo, Philippines - CYU
Cuzco, Peru - CUZ
Da Nang, Soc. Rep. of Viet Nam - DAD
Dakar, Senegal - DKR
Dakhla, Morocco - VIL
Dalaman, Turkey - DLM
Dalat, Vietnam - DLI
Dalbandin, Pakistan - DBA
Dali City, P.R. China - DLU
Dalian, P.R. China - DLC
Dallas/Ft. Worth, TX, USA - DFW
Dallas/Ft. Worth, TX-Love, USA - DAL
Damascus, Syria - DAM
Dandong, P.R. China - DDG
Dangriga, Belize - DGA
Dar Es Salaam, Tanzania - DAR
Darnley Island, QLD, Australia - NLF
Daru, Papua New Guinea - DAU
Darwin, NT, Australia - DRW
Datadawai, Indonesia - DTD
Datong, P.R. China - DAT

Dauphin, MB, Canada - YDN
Davao, Philippines - DVO
David, Panama Rep. - DAV
Davis Inlet, NF, Canada - YDI
Dawe, Myanmar - TVY
Dawson City, YK, Canada - YDA
Dawson Creek, BC, Canada - YDQ
Daxian, P.R. China - DAX
Daydream Island, QLD, Australia - DDI
Dayong, P.R. China - DYG
Dayton, OH, USA - DAY
Daytona Beach, FL, USA - DAB
Deadman's Cay, L.I., Bahamas - LGI
Dean River, BC, Canada - YRD
Dease Lake, BC, Canada - YDL
Debra Marcos, Ethiopia - DBM
Debre Tabor, Ethiopia - DBT
Decatur Is., WA, USA - DTR
Decatur, IL, USA - DEC
Deer Lake, NF, Canada - YDF
Deer Lake, ON, Canada - YVZ
Deering, AK, USA - DRG
Deirezzor, Syria - DEZ
Del Rio, TX, USA - DRT
Delhi, India - DEL
Deline, NT, Canada - YWJ
Delta Junction, AK, USA - DJN
Dembidollo, Ethiopia - DEM
Denham, WA, Australia - DNM
Denizli, Turkey - DNZ
Denpasar Bali, Indonesia - DPS
Denver, CO, USA - DEN
Dera Ghazi Khan, Pakistan - DEA
Dera Ismail Khan, Pakistan - DSK
Derby, WA, Australia - DRB
Derim, Papua New Guinea - DER
Deroches, Seychelles Is. - DES
Des Moines, IA, USA - DSM
Dessie, Ethiopia - DSE
Detroit, MI, USA - DTT
Detroit, MI-City, USA - DET
Detroit, MI-Wayne Co., USA - DTW
Devils Lake, ND, USA - DVL
Devonport, Tas., Australia - DPO
Dhahran, Saudi Arabia - DHA
Dhaka, Bangladesh - DAC
Dhangarhi, Nepal - DHI
Dibaa, Oman - BYB
Dibrugarh, India - DIB
Dickinson, ND, USA - DIK
Dien Bien Phu, Vietnam - DIN
Dijon, France - DIJ
Dili, Indonesia - DIL

Dillingham, AK, USA - DLG
Dillons Bay, Vanuatu - DLY
Dimapur, India - DMU
Dinard, France - DNR
Dipolog, Philippines - DPL
Dire Dawa, Ethiopia - DIR
Diu, India - DIU
Diyarbakir, Turkey - DIY
Djanet, Algeria - DJG
Djerba, Tunisia - DJE
Djibouti, Djibouti - JIB
Dnepropetrovsk, Ukraine - DNK
Dodge City, KS, USA - DDC
Dodoima, Papua New Guinea - DDM
Doha, Qatar - DOH
Dolomi, AK, USA - DLO
Dolpa, Nepal - DOP
Dominica, West Indies - DOM
Dominica-Cane, West Indies - DCF
Donegal, Rep. of Ireland - CFN
Donetsk, Ukraine - DOK
Dongola, Sudan - DOG
Doomadgee Mission, QLD, Australia - DMD
Dora Bay, AK, USA - DOF
Dortmund, Germany - DTM
Dothan, AL, USA - DHN
Douala, Cameroon - DLA
Dourados, MS, Brazil - DOU
Dresden, Germany - DRS
Dryden, ON, Canada - YHD
Du Bois, PA, USA - DUJ
Dubai, U. A. Emirates - DXB
Dubbo, NSW, Australia - DBO
Dublin, Rep. of Ireland - DUB
Dubois, PA, USA - DUJ
Dubrovnik, Croatia - DBV
Dubuque, IA, USA - DBQ
Duesseldorf, Germany - DUS
Duesseldorf, Main RR, Germany - QDU
Duesseldorf Moenchengladbach, Germany - MGL
Duluth, MN/Superior, WI, USA - DLH
Dumaguete, Philippines - DGT
Dundee, Angus, Scotland, UK - DND
Dundo, Angola - DUE
Dunedin, New Zealand - DUD
Dunhuang, P.R. China - DNH
Dunk Island, QLD, Australia - DKI
Durango, Mexico - DGO
Durango, CO, USA - DRO
Durban, South Africa - DUR
Dushanbe, Tajikistan - DYU

Dutch Harbor, AK, USA - DUT
Dzaoudzi, Comoros - DZA
Eagle, AK, USA - EAA
Earlton, ON, Canada - YXR
East London, South Africa - ELS
East Main, PQ, Canada - ZEM
East Midlands, England, UK - EMA
Easter Island, Pacific Ocean -
    IPC
Eastgreenland, Greenland - CNP
Eastsound, WA, USA - ESD
Eau Claire, WI, USA - EAU
Ebon, Marshall Islands - EBO
Eday, UK - EOI
Edinburgh, Scotland, UK - EDI
Edmonton, AB, Canada - YEA
Edmonton-Intl, AB, Canada - YEG
Edna Bay, AK, USA - EDA
Edward River, QLD, Australia -
    EDR
Eek, AK, USA - EEK
Efogi, Papua New Guinea - EFG
Egegik, AK, USA - EGX
Egilsstadir, Iceland - EGS
Eia, Papua New Guinea - EIA
Eindhoven, Netherlands - EIN
Ekaterinburg, Russia - SVX
Ekuk, AK, USA - KKU
Ekwok, AK, USA - KEK
El Bagre, Colombia - EBG
El Centro/Imperial, CA, USA - IPL
El Dorado, AR, USA - ELD
El Golea, Algeria - ELG
El Oued, Algeria - ELU
El Paso, TX, USA - ELP
El Portillo-Samana, Dominican
    Rep. - EPS
El Real, Panama - ELE
El Salvador, Chile - ESR
El Yopal, Colombia - EYP
Elat, Israel - ETH
Elazig, Turkey - EZS
Elcho Island, NT, Australia - ELC
Elfin Cove, AK, USA - ELV
Elim, AK, USA - ELI
Elko, NV, USA - EKO
Elliot Lake, ON, Canada - YEL
Elmira, NY, USA - ELM
Ely, NV, USA - ELY
Emae, Vanuatu - EAE
Embessa, Papua New Guinea - EMS
Emerald, QLD, Australia - EMD
Emirau, Papua New Guinea - EMI
Emmonak, AK, USA - EMK
Emo, Papua New Guinea - EMO

Enewetak, Marshall Islands - ENT
Enid, OK, USA - WDG
Enontekio, Finland - ENF
Enschede, Netherlands - ENS
Entebbe/Kampala, Uganda - EBB
Enugu, Nigeria - ENU
Epinal, France - EPL
Ercan, Cyprus - ECN
Erechim, RS, Brazil - ERM
Erfurt, Germany - ERF
Erie, PA, USA - ERI
Erigavo, Somalia - ERA
Errachidia, Morocco - ERH
Erzincan, Turkey - ERC
Erzurum, Turkey - ERZ
Esa' Ala, Papua New Guinea - ESA
Esbjerg, Denmark - EBJ
Escanaba, MI, USA - ESC
Eskisehir, Turkey - AOE
Esperance, WA, Australia - EPR
Espiritu Santo, Vanuatu - SON
Esquel, Argentina - EQS
Eua, Tonga Island - EUA
Eugene, OR, USA - EUG
Eureka/Arcata, CA, USA - ACV
Europe Railway Service, France -
    XDB
Evansville, IN, USA - EVV
Evenes, Norway - EVE
Everett, WA, USA - PAE
Excursion Inlet, AK, USA - EXI
Exeter, England, UK - EXT
Fagernes, Norway - VDB
Fair Isle, Scotland, UK - FIE
Fairbanks, AK, USA - FAI
Fairmont, MN, USA - FRM
Faisalabad, Pakistan - LYP
Fajardo, Puerto Rico - FAJ
Fakarava, Tuamuto Islands - FAV
False Island, AK, USA - FAK
False Pass, AK, USA - KFP
Fane, Papua New Guinea - FNE
Farafangana, Madagascar - RVA
Fargo, ND, USA - FAR
Farmington, NM, USA - FMN
Faro, Portugal - FAO
Faroe Islands, Denmark - FAE
Farsund, Norway - FAN
Fayetteville, AR, USA - FYV
Fayetteville, NC, USA - FAY
Fera Island, Solomon Is. -   FRE
Fergana, Uzbekistan - FEG
Fernando de Noronha, FN, Brazil -
    FEN
Fez, Morocco - FEZ

Fianarantsoa, Madagascar - WFI
Figari, Corsica, France - FSC
Finschhafen, Papua New Guinea - FIN
Fishers Island, NY, USA - FID
Fitzroy Crossing, WA, Australia - FIZ
Flagstaff, AZ, USA - FLG
Flin Flon, MB, Canada - YFO
Flinders Is., Tas., Australia - FLS
Flint, MI, USA - FNT
Flora Valley, WA, Australia - FVL
Florence, Italy - FLR
Florence, SC, USA - FLO
Florencia, Colombia - FLA
Flores, Guatemala - FRS
Florianopolis, SC, Brazil - FLN
Floro, Norway - FRO
Fond du Lac, SK, Canada - ZFD
Forbes, NSW, Australia - FRB
Forde, Norway - FDE
Formosa, Argentina - FMA
Fornebu, Norway - FBU
Fort Albany, ON, Canada - YFA
Fort Collins/Loveland, CO, USA - FNL
Fort Dauphin, Madagascar - FTU
Fort De France, Martinique - FDF
Fort Dodge, IA, USA - FOD
Fort Frances, ON, Canada - YAG
Fort Good Hope, NT, Canada - YGH
Fort Hope, ON, Canada - YFH
Fort Norman, NT, Canada - ZFN
Fort Resolution, NT, Canada - YFR
Fort Severn, ON, Canada - YER
Fort Worth-Meacham, TX, USA - FTW
Fortaleza, CE, Brazil - FOR
Fougamou, Gabon - FOU
Fox Harbour/St. Lewis - NF, Canada - YFX
Franca, SP, Brazil - FRC
Franceville, Gabon - MVB
Francisco Beltrao, PR, Brazil - FBE
Francistown, Botswana - FRW
Frankfurt, Germany - FRA
Franklin, PA, USA - FKL
Fredericton, NB, Canada - YFC
Frederikshab, Greenland - JFR
Freeport, Bahamas - FPO
Freetown, Sierra Leone - FNA
Freida River, Papua New Guinea - FAQ
Frenchville, ME, USA - WFK

Fresno, CA, USA - FAT
Friday Harbor, WA, USA - FRD
Friedrichshafen, Germany - FDH
Ft. Chipewyan, AB, Canada - YPY
Ft. Huachuca/Sr. Vista, AZ, USA - FHU
Ft. Lauderdale, FL, USA - FLL
Ft. Leonard Wood, MO, USA - TBN
Ft. McMurray, AB, Canada - YMM
Ft. Myers, FL, USA - FMY
Ft. Myers, FL-Regional, USA - RSW
Ft. Nelson, BC, Canada - YYE
Ft. Simpson, NT, Canada - YFS
Ft. Smith, AR, USA - FSM
Ft. Smith, NT, Canada - YSM
Ft. St. John, BC, Canada - YXJ
Ft. Walton Beach, FL, USA - VPS
Ft. Wayne, IN, USA - FWA
Ft. Yukon, AK, USA - FYU
Fuerteventura, Canary Islands - FUE
Fukue, Japan - FUJ
Fukuoka, Japan - FUK
Fukushima, Japan - FKS
Funafuti Atol, Tuvalu - FUN
Funchal, Portugal (Madeira) - FNC
Futuna, Wallis & Futuna Is. - FUT
Futuna Is., Vanuatu - FTA
Fuzhou, P.R. China - FOC
Gaborone, Botswana - GBE
Gainesville, FL, USA - GNV
Galena, AK, USA - GAL
Gallivare, Sweden - GEV
Gallup, NM, USA - GUP
Galway, Rep. of Ireland - GWY
Gamba, Gabon - GAX
Gambela, Ethiopia - GMB
Gambell, AK, USA - GAM
Gambier Is., Fr. Polynesia - GMR
Gan Island, Maldives - GAN
Gander, NF, Canada - YQX
Ganzhou, P.R. China - KOW
Gao, Mali - GAQ
Garachine, Panama - GHE
Garaina, Papua New Guinea - GAR
Garasa, Papua New Guinea - GRL
Garden City, KS, USA - GCK
Garden Point, NT, Australia - GPN
Garoua, Cameroon - GOU
Gary, IN, USA - GYY
Gasmata, Papua New Guinea - GMI
Gaspe, PQ, Canada - YGP
Gassim, Saudi Arabia - ELQ
Gatineau/Hull, PQ, Canada - YND
Gaua, Vanuatu - ZGU

Gauhati, India - GAU
Gavle, Sweden - GVX
Gaziantep, Turkey - GZT
Gbadolite, Dem. Rep. of the Congo
    - BDT
Gdansk, Poland - GDN
Geilo, Norway - DLD
Gelendzik, Russia - GDZ
Gemena, Dem. Rep. of the Congo -
    GMA
General Roca, Argentina - GNR
General Santos, Philippines - GES
Geneva, Switzerland - GVA
Genoa, Italy - GOA
George, South Africa - GRJ
George Town, Bahamas - GGT
Georgetown, Guyana - GEO
Geraldton, ON, Canada - YGQ
Geraldton, WA, Australia - GET
Gethsemani, PQ, Canada - ZGS
Gewoya, Papua New Guinea - GEW
Ghardaia, Algeria - GHA
Ghimbi, Ethiopia - GHD
Gibraltar, Gibraltar - GIB
Gilgit, Pakistan - GIL
Gillam, MB, Canada - YGX
Gillette, WY, USA - GCC
Gillies Bay, BC, Canada - YGB
Gisborne, New Zealand - GIS
Gizan, Saudi Arabia - GIZ
Gizo, Solomon Islands - GZO
Gjoa Haven, NT, Canada - YHK
Gladstone, QLD, Australia - GLT
Glasgow, MT, USA - GGW
Glasgow, Scotland, UK - GLA
Glasgow-Prestwick, Scotland, UK -
    PIK
Glen Innes, NSW, Australia - GLI
Glendive, MT, USA - GDV
Glynco Jetport, GA, USA - BQK
Goa, India - GOI
Goba, Ethiopia - GOB
Gode, Ethiopia - GDE
Godhavn, Greenland - JGO
Gods Narrows, MB, Canada - YGO
Gods River, MB, Canada - ZGI
Goiania, GO, Brazil - GYN
Gold Coast, QLD, Australia - OOL
Golfito, Costa Rica - GLF
Golmud, P.R. China - GOQ
Golovin, AK, USA - GLV
Goma, Dem. Rep. of the Congo -
    GOM
Gomel, Belarus - GME
Gonalia, Papua New Guinea - GOE

Gondar, Ethiopia - GDQ
Goodland, KS, USA - GLD
Goodnews Bay, AK, USA - GNU
Goose Bay, NF, Canada - YYR
Gora, Papua New Guinea - GOC
Gore, Ethiopia - GOR
Gore Bay, ON, Canada - YZE
Goroka, Papua New Guinea - GKA
Gorontalo, Indonesia - GTO
Gothenburg, Sweden - GOT
Gothenburg-Saeve, Sweden - GSE
Goundam, Mali - GUD
Gove, NT, Australia - GOV
Governador Valadares, MG, Brazil
    - GVR
Governors Harbour, Bahamas - GHB
Gozo, Malta - GZM
Graciosa Island, Portugal
    (Azores) - GRW
Grafton, NSW, Australia - GFN
Granada, Spain - GRX
Grand Canyon, AZ, USA - GCN
Grand Canyon, AZ-Heliport, USA -
    JGC
Grand Cayman, West Indies - GCM
Grand Forks, ND, USA - GFK
Grand Island, NE, USA - GRI
Grand Junction, CO, USA - GJT
Grand Rapids, MI, USA - GRR
Grand Rapids, MN, USA - GPZ
Grand Turk, Turks & Caicos Is. -
    GDT
Grande Prairie, AB, Canada - YQU
Grayling, AK, USA - KGX
Graz, Austria - GRZ
Great Bend, KS, USA - GBD
Great Falls, MT, USA - GTF
Great Harbour Cay, Bahamas - GHC
Great Keppel Island, QLD,
    Australia - GKL
Green Bay, WI, USA - GRB
Green River, Papua New Guinea -
    GVI
Greenbrier, WV, USA - LWB
Greensboro/H.PT/Win-Salem, NC,
    USA - GSO
Greenville, MS, USA - GLH
Greenville, NC, USA - PGV
Greenville/Spartanburg, SC, USA -
    GSP
Grenada, Windward Islands - GND
Grenoble, France - GNB
Griffith, NSW, Australia - GFF
Grimsey, Iceland - GRY
Grise Fiord, NT, Canada - YGZ

Groennedal, Greenland - JGR
Groningen, Netherlands - GRQ
Groote Eylandt, NT, Australia - GTE
Guadalajara, Mexico - GDL
Guam, Guam - GUM
Guanaja Is., Honduras - GJA
Guangzhou, P.R. China - CAN
Guantanamo, Cuba - GAO
Guapi, Colombia - GPI
Guarapari, ES, Brazil - GUZ
Guarapuava, PR, Brazil - GPB
Guatemala City, Guatemala - GUA
Guayaquil, Ecuador - GYE
Guayaramerin, Bolivia - GYA
Guaymas, Mexico - GYM
Guernsey, Channel Islands, UK - GCI
Guerrero Negro, Mexico - GUB
Guilin, P.R. China - KWL
Guiyang, P.R. China - KWE
Gulfport/Biloxi, MS, USA - GPT
Gunnedah, NSW, Australia - GUH
Gunnison, CO, USA - GUC
Gurayat, Saudi Arabia - URY
Gurupi, GO, Brazil - GRP
Gustavus, AK, USA - GST
Gwadar, Pakistan - GWD
Gwalior, India - GWL
Gyandzha, Azerbaijan - KVD
Gyoumri, Armenia - LWN
Ha'Apai, Tonga Island - HPA
Hachijo Jima Is., Japan - HAC
Hafr Albatin, Saudi Arabia - HBT
Hagerstown, MD, USA - HGR
Hagfors, Sweden - HFS
Hahn, Germany - HHN
Haifa, Israel - HFA
Haikou, P.R. China - HAK
Hail, Saudi Arabia - HAS
Hailar, P.R. China - HLD
Haines, AK, USA - HNS
Haiphong, Vietnam - HPH
Hakodate, Japan - HKD
Halifax, NS, Canada - YHZ
Hall Beach, NT, Canada - YUX
Hall's Creek, WA, Australia - HCQ
Halmstad, Sweden - HAD
Hamburg, Germany - HAM
Hamilton, New Zealand - HLZ
Hamilton, ON, Canada - YHM
Hamilton Island, QLD, Australia - HTI
Hammerfest, Norway - HFT
Hana, Maui, HI, USA - HNM

Hancock, MI, USA - CMX
Hangzhou, P.R. China - HGH
Hanimaadhoo, Maldives - HAQ
Hanoi, Soc. Rep. of Viet Nam - HAN
Hanover, Germany - HAJ
Hanzhong, P.R. China - HZG
Hao Island, Tuamotu Islands - HOI
Harare, Zimbabwe - HRE
Harbin, Manchuria, P.R. China - HRB
Hargeisa, Somalia - HGA
Harlingen, TX, USA - HRL
Harrington Harbour, PQ, Canada - YHR
Harrisburg, PA, USA - HAR
Harrisburg-Int'l, PA, USA - MDT
Harrison, AR, USA - HRO
Hartford, CT, USA - BDL
Hartford, CT/Springield, MA, USA - HFD
Hassi Messaoud, Algeria - HME
Hasvik, Norway - HAA
Hat Yai, Thailand - HDY
Hateruma, Japan - HTR
Haugesund, Norway - HAU
Havana, Cuba - HAV
Havasupai, AZ, USA - HAE
Havre St. Pierre, PQ, Canada - YGV
Havre, MT, USA - HVR
Hay River, NT, Canada - YHY
Hayfields, Papua New Guinea - HYF
Hayman Is., QLD, Australia - HIS
Hays, KS, USA - HYS
Healy Lake, AK, USA - HKB
Hearst, ON, Canada - YHF
Hefei, P.R. China - HFE
Heho, Myanmar - HEH
Heidelberg, Germany - HDB
Helena, MT, USA - HLN
Helgoland, Germany - HGL
Helsingborg, Sweden - AGH
Helsingborg-Hlpt, Sweden - JHE
Helsinki, Finland - HEL
Hemavan, Sweden - HMV
Heraklion, Greece - HER
Hermosillo, Mexico - HMO
Hervey Bay, QLD, Australia - HVB
Hibbing, MN, USA - HIB
Hickory, NC, USA - HKY
High Level, AB, Canada - YOJ
Hilo, Hawaii, HI, USA - ITO
Hilton Head Island, SC, USA - HHH
Hiroshima, Japan - HIJ

Hiroshima-West Arpt., Japan - HIW
Ho Chi Minh, Soc. Rep. of Viet
   Nam - SGN
Hobart, Tas., Australia - HBA
Hobart Bay, AK, USA - HBH
Hobbs, NM, USA - HOB
Hodeidah, Yemen - HOD
Hoedspruit, Transvaal, South
   Africa - HDS
Hof, Germany - HOQ
Hofuf, Saudi Arabia - HOF
Hohhot, P.R. China - HET
Hokitika, New Zealand - HKK
Holguin, Cuba - HOG
Hollis, AK, USA - HYL
Holman Island, NT, Canada - YHI
Holy Cross, AK, USA - HCR
Homer, AK, USA - HOM
Hong Kong, Hong Kong - HKG
Honiara, Guadalcanal, Solomon
   Islands - HIR
Honningsvag, Norway - HVG
Honolulu, Oahu, HI, USA - HNL
Hooker Creek, NT, Australia - HOK
Hoonah, AK, USA - HNH
Hooper Bay, AK, USA - HPB
Hopedale, NF, Canada - YHO
Horn Island, QLD, Australia - HID
Hornafjordur, Iceland - HFN
Hornepayne, ON, Canada - YHN
Horta, Portugal (Azores) - HOR
Hoskins, Papua New Guinea - HKN
Hot Springs, AR, USA - HOT
Hotan, P.R. China - HTN
Houeisay, Laos - HOE
Houston, TX, USA - HOU
Houston, TX-Ellington, USA - EFD
Houston, TX-Int'l, USA - IAH
Huahine, Soc. Is., Fr. Polynesia
   - HUH
Hualien, Taiwan - HUN
Huambo, Angola - NOV
Huanghua, P.R. China - HHA
Huangyan, P.R. China - HYN
Huanuco, Peru - HUU
Huatulco, Mexico - HUX
Hudiksvall, Sweden - HUV
Hue, Vietnam - HUI
Hughenden, QLD, Australia - HGD
Hughes, AK, USA - HUS
Hultsfred, Sweden - HLF
Humberside, England, UK - HUY
Humera, Ethiopia - HUE
Huntington, WV, USA - HTS
Huntsville/Decatur, AL, USA - HSV

Hurghada, Egypt - HRG
Huron, SD, USA - HON
Husavik, Iceland - HZK
Huslia, AK, USA - HSL
Hwange National Park, Zimbabwe -
   HWN
Hyannis, MA, USA - HYA
Hydaburg, AK, USA - HYG
Hyder, AK, USA - WHD
Hyderabad, India - HYD
Hyderabad, Pakistan - HDD
Iasi, Romania - IAS
Ibague, Colombia - IBE
Ibiza, Spain - IBZ
Iboki, Papua New Guinea - IBI
Idaho Falls, ID, USA - IDA
Igiugig, AK, USA - IGG
Igloolik, NT, Canada - YGT
Iguassu Falls, PR, Brazil - IGU
Iguazu, Argentina - IGR
Ihu, Papua New Guinea - IHU
Ikaria Island, Greece - JIK
Iki, Japan - IKI
Ile Des Pins, New Caledonia - ILP
Iles De Madeleine, PQ, Canada -
   YGR
Ilheus, BA, Brazil - IOS
Iliamna, AK, USA - ILI
Illizi, Algeria - VVZ
Ilo, Peru - ILQ
Iloilo, Philippines - ILO
Ilulissat, Greenland - JAV
Imperatriz, MA, Brazil - IMP
Impfondo, Congo - ION
Imphal, India - IMF
In Amenas, Algeria - IAM
In Salah, Algeria - INZ
Inagua, Bahamas - IGA
Indagen, Papua New Guinea - IDN
Indaselassie, Ethiopia - SHC
Indianapolis, IN, USA - IND
Indore, India - IDR
Ine, Marshall Is. - IMI
Innsbruck, Austria - INN
Int'l Falls, MN, USA - INL
Inukjuak, PQ, Canada - YPH
Inuvik, NT, Canada - YEV
Invercargill, New Zealand - IVC
Inverell, NSW, Australia - IVR
Inverness, Scotland, UK - INV
Inverway, NT, Australia - IVW
Inyokern, CA, USA - IYK
Ioannina, Greece - IOA
Iokea, Papua New Guinea - IOK
Ioma, Papua New Guinea - IOP

Ipatinga, Brazil - IPN
Ipiales, Colombia - IPI
Ipatinga, MG, Brazil - IPN
Ipoh, Malaysia - IPH
Ipota, Vanuatu - IPA
Iqaluit, NT, Canada - YFB
Iquique, Chile - IQQ
Iquitos, Peru - IQT
Irkutsk, Russia - IKT
Iron Mountain, MI, USA - IMT
Ironwood, MI, USA - IWD
Isafjordur, Iceland - IFJ
Isfahan, Iran - IFN
Ishigaki, Japan - ISG
Isiro, Dem. Rep. of the Congo -
    IRP
Islamabad/Rawalpindi, Pakistan -
    ISB
Island Lake, MB, Canada - YIV
Islay, Scotland, UK - ILY
Isle of Man, UK - IOM
Isles of Scilly, UK - ISC
Isles of Scilly-Tresco, UK - TSO
Isparta, Turkey - ISE
Istanbul, Turkey - IST
Itaituba, PA, Brazil - ITB
Itami, Japan - ITM
Ithaca, NY, USA - ITH
Itokama, Papua New Guinea - ITK
Ivalo, Finland - IVL
Ivano-Frankovsk, Ukraine - IFO
Ivanof Bay, AK, USA - KIB
Ivujivik, PQ, Canada - YIK
Iwami, Japan - IWJ
Ixtapa/Zihuatanejo, Mexico - ZIH
Izmir, Turkey - IZM
Izmir-Adnan Menderes, Turkey -
    ADB
Izumo, Japan - IZO
Jabat, Marshall Is. - JAT
Jackson, MS, USA - JAN
Jackson, TN, USA - MKL
Jackson Hole, WY, USA - JAC
Jacksonville, FL, USA - JAX
Jacksonville, NC, USA - OAJ
Jacobabad, Pakistan - JAG
Jacquinot Bay, Papua New Guinea -
    JAQ
Jaipur, India - JAI
Jaisalmer, India - JSA
Jakarta, Indonesia - JKT
Jakarta-Halim, Indonesia - HLP
Jakarta-Soekarno, Indonesia - CGK
Jaluit, Marshall Islands - UIT
Jambi, Indonesia - DJB

Jamestown, ND, USA - JMS
Jamestown, NY, USA - JHW
Jammu, India - IXJ
Jamnagar, India - JGA
Janakpur, Indonesia - JKR
Jaque, Panama - JQE
Jayapura, Indonesia - DJJ
Jeddah, Saudi Arabia - JED
Jeh, Marshall Is. - JEJ
Jerez De La Frontera, Spain - XRY
Jersey, Channel Islands, UK - JER
Jerusalem, Israel - JRS
Jessore, Bangladesh - JSR
Jiayuguan, P.R. China - JGN
Jijel, Algeria - GJL
Jilin, P.R. China - JIL
Jimma, Ethiopia - JIM
Jinan, P.R. China - TNA
Jingdezhen, P.R. China - JDZ
Jinghong, P.R. China - JHG
Jinjiang, P.R. China - JJN
Jinka, Ethiopia - BCO
Jinzhou, P.R. China - JNZ
Ji-Parana, RO, Brazil - JPR
Jiujiang, P.R. China - JIU
Jiwani, Pakistan - JIW
Joacaba, SC, Brazil - JCB
Joao Pessoa, PB, Brazil - JPA
Jodhpur, India - JDH
Joensuu, Finland - JOE
Johannesburg, South Africa - JNB
Johnston Island, Pacific Ocean -
    JON
Johnstown, PA, USA - JST
Johor Bahru, Malaysia - JHB
Joinville, SC, Brazil - JOI
Jomsom, Nepal - JMO
Jonesboro, AR, USA - JBR
Jonkoping, Sweden - JKG
Joplin, MO, USA - JLN
Jorhat, India - JRH
Jos, Nigeria - JOS
Jouf, Saudi Arabia - AJF
Juanjui, Peru - JJI
Juara, PB, Brazil - JUA
Juazeiro Do Norte, CE, Brazil
    - JDO
Juina, MT, Brazil - JIA
Juiz de Fora, MG, Brazil - JDF
Jujuy, Argentina - JUJ
Julia Creek, QLD, Australia - JCK
Juliaca, Peru - JUL
Jumla, Nepal - JUM
Juneau, AK, USA - JNU
Juzhou, P.R. China - JUZ

Jyvaskyla, Finland - JYV
Kaadedhdhoo, Maldives - KDM
Kaben, Marshall Is. - KBT
Kabri Dar, Ethiopia - ABK
Kabul, Afghanistan - KBL
Kabwum, Papua New Guinea - KBM
Kadhdhoo, Maldives - KDO
Kaduna, Nigeria - KAD
Kagau, Solomon Islands - KGE
Kagi, Papua New Guinea - KGW
Kagoshima, Japan - KOJ
Kahramanmaras, Turkey - KCM
Kahului, Maui, HI, USA - OGG
Kaintiba, Papua New Guinea - KZF
Kaiserslauter, Germany - KLT
Kaitaia, New Zealand - KAT
Kajaani, Finland - KAJ
Kake, AK, USA - KAE
Kakhonak, AK, USA - KNK
Kalamata, Greece - KLX
Kalamazoo, MI, USA - AZO
Kalaupapa, Molokai, HI, USA - LUP
Kalbarri, WA, Australia - KAX
Kalemie, Dem. Rep. of the Congo -
    FMI
Kalemyo, Myanmar - KMV
Kalgoorlie, WA, Australia - KGI
Kalibo, Philippines - KLO
Kaliningrad, Russia - KGD
Kalispell/Glacier Nat'l PK, MT,
    USA - FCA
Kalkurung, NT, Australia - KFG
Kalmar, Sweden - KLR
Kalskag, AK, USA - KLG
Kaltag, AK, USA - KAL
Kamembe, Rwanda - KME
Kameshli, Syria - KAC
Kamina, Papua New Guinea - KMF
Kamloops, BC, Canada - YKA
Kamuela, HI, USA - MUE
Kamusi, Papua New Guinea - KUY
Kanabea, Papua New Guinea - KEX
Kananga, Dem. Rep. of the Congo -
    KGA
Kandavu, Fiji - KDV
Kandrian, Papua New Guinea - KDR
Kangerlussuaq, Greenland - SFJ
Kangiqsualujjuaq, PQ, Canada -
    XGR
Kangiqsujuaq, PQ, Canada - YWB
Kangirsuk, PQ, Canada - YKG
Kangnung, Rep. of Korea - KAG
Kano, Nigeria - KAN
Kansas City, MO, USA - MKC
Kansas City, MO-Int'l, USA - MCI

Kaohsiung, Taiwan - KHH
Kapalua, Maui, HI, USA - JHM
Kapit, Sarawak, Malaysia - KPI
Kapuskasing, ON, Canada - YYU
Karachi, Pakistan - KHI
Karaganda, Kazakstan - KGF
Karamay, P.R. China - KRY
Karawari, Papua New Guinea - KRJ
Kariba, Zimbabwe - KAB
Karlstad, Sweden - KSD
Karluk, AK, USA - KYK
Karonga, Malawi - KGJ
Karpathos, Greece - AOK
Karratha, WA, Australia - KTA
Kars, Turkey - KSY
Karshi, Uzbekistan - KSQ
Karumba, QLD, Australia - KRB
Karup, Denmark - KRP
Kasaan, AK, USA - KXA
Kasabonika, ON, Canada - XKS
Kasana, Botswana - BBK
Kaschechewan, ON, Canada - ZKE
Kashi, P.R. China - KHG
Kasigluk, AK, USA - KUK
Kasos Island, Greece - KSJ
Kassel, Germany - KSF
Kastelorizo, Greece - KZS
Kastoria, Greece - KSO
Katherine, NT, Australia - KTR
Kathmandu, Nepal - KTM
Katowice, Poland - KTW
Kaukura Atoll, Tuamotu Islands -
    KKR
Kaunas, Lithuania - KUN
Kavala, Greece - KVA
Kavieng, Papua New Guinea - KVG
Kawito, Papua New Guinea - KWO
Kawthaung, Myanmar - KAW
Kayes, Mali - KYS
Kayseri, Turkey - ASR
Kazan, Russia - KZN
Kearney, NE, USA - EAR
Keene, NH, USA - EEN
Keetmanshoop, Namibia - KMP
Keewaywin, ON, Canada - KEW
Kefallinia, Greece - EFL
Kegaska, PQ, Canada - ZKG
Kelowna, BC, Canada - YLW
Kemerovo, Russia - KEJ
Kemi, Finland - KEM
Kempsey, NSW, Australia - KPS
Kenai, AK, USA - ENA
Kendari, Indonesia - KDI
Kengtung, Myanmar - KET
Kenieba, Mali - KNZ

Kenora, ON, Canada - YQK
Kepi, Indonesia - KEI
Kerama, Japan - KJP
Kerema, Papua New Guinea - KMA
Kerikeri, New Zealand - KKE
Kerkyra, Greece - CFU
Kerman, Iran - KER
Kermanshah, Iran - KSH
Kerry County, Rep. of Ireland -
    KIR
Kerteh, Malaysia - KTE
Keshod, India - IXK
Ketapang, Indonesia - KTG
Ketchikan, AK, USA - KTN
Key West, FL, USA - EYW
Khabarovsk, Russia - KHV
Khajuraho, India - HJR
Khamti, Myanmar - KHM
Kharkov, Ukraine - HRK
Khartoum, Sudan - KRT
Khasab, Oman - KHS
Khon Kaen, Thailand - KKC
Khuzdar, Pakistan - KDD
Kiana, AK, USA - IAN
Kiel, Germany - KEL
Kiev, Ukraine - IEV
Kiev-Borispol, Ukraine - KBP
Kiffa, Mauritania - KFA
Kigali, Rwanda - KGL
Kigoma, Tanzania - TKQ
Kihila, Finland - KTT
Kikaiga Shima, Japan - KKX
Kikori, Papua New Guinea - KRI
Kili, Marshall Islands - KIO
Kilimanjaro, Tanzania - JRO
Killeen, TX, USA - ILE
Kimberley, South Africa - KIM
Kimmirut/Lake Harbour, NT, Canada
    - YLC
Kindu, Dem. Rep. of the Congo -
    KND
King Cove, AK, USA - KVC
King Island, TAS, Australia - KNS
King Salmon, AK, USA - AKN
Kingfisher Lake, Ont., Canada -
    KIF
Kingman, AZ, USA - IGM
Kingscote, SA, Australia - KGC
Kingston-Norman Manley, Jamaica -
    KIN
Kingston-Tinson, Jamaica - KTP
Kingston, ON, Canada - YGK
Kinmen, Taiwan - KNH
Kinshasa, Dem. Rep. of the Congo
    - FIH

Kinston, NC, USA - ISO
Kipnuk, Ak, USA - KPN
Kira, Papua New Guinea - KIQ
Kirakira, Solomon Islands - IRA
Kirkenes, Norway - KKN
Kirkland Lake, ON, Canada - YKX
Kirksville, MO, USA - IRK
Kirkwall, Orkney Is., Scotland,
    UK - KOI
Kirovograd, Ukraine - KGO
Kiruna, Sweden - KRN
Kiryat Shmona, Israel - KSW
Kisangani, Dem. Rep. of the Congo
    - FKI
Kishinev, Moldova - KIV
Kisumu, Kenya - KIS
Kita Kyushu, Japan - KKJ
Kita-Daito, Japan - KTD
Kitava, Papua New Guinea - KVE
Kithira, Greece - KIT
Kitoi, AK, USA - KKB
Kittila, Finland - KTT
Kiunga, Papua New Guinea - UNG
Kivalina, AK, USA - KVL
Kiwayu, Kenya - KWY
Klagenfurt, Austria - KLU
Klamath Falls, OR, USA - LMT
Klawock, AK, USA - KLW
Kleinzee, South Africa - KLZ
Knock, Rep. of Ireland - NOC
Knoxville, TN-McGhee-Tyson, USA -
    TYS
Kobuk, AK, USA - OBU
Kochi, Japan - KCZ
Kodiak, AK, USA - ADQ
Koh Kong, Cambodia - KKZ
Koh Samui, Thailand - USM
Kokkola, Finland - KOK
Kokoda, Papua New Guinea - KKD
Koliganek, AK, USA - KGK
Kolobrzeg Bus Station, Poland -
    QJY
Komatsu, Japan - KMQ
Kona, Hawaii, HI, USA - KOA
Kone, New Caledonia - KNQ
Konge, Papua New Guinea - KGB
Kongiganak, AK, USA - KKH
Konya, Turkey - KYA
Kopasker, Iceland - OPA
Korhogo, Cote D'Ivoire - HGO
Korla, P.R. China - KRL
Koro, Fiji - KXF
Koror, Palau Is. - ROR
Kos, Greece - KGS
Kosice, Slovak Republic - KSC

Kosrae, Caroline Islands - KSA
Kostanay, Kazakstan - KSN
Koszalin, Poland - OSZ
Kota Bharu, Malaysia - KBR
Kota Kinabalu, Sabah, Malaysia - BKI
Kotlik, AK, USA - KOT
Kotzebue, AK, USA - OTZ
Koulamoutou, Gabon - KOU
Koumac, New Caledonia - KOC
Kowanyama, QLD, Australia - KWM
Koyuk, AK, USA - KKA
Koyukuk, AK, USA - KYU
Kozani, Greece - KZI
Krakow, Poland - KRK
Kramfors, Sweden - KRF
Krasnodar, Russia - KRR
Krasnovodsk, Turkmenistan - KRW
Krasnoyarsk, Russia - KJA
Kristiansand, Norway - KRS
Kristianstad, Sweden - KID
Kristiansund, Norway - KSU
Krivoy Rog, Ukraine - KWG
Kuala Lumpur, Malaysia - KUL
Kuala Terengganu, Malaysia - TGG
Kuantan, Malaysia - KUA
Kubin Island, QLD, Australia - KUG
Kuching, Sarawak, Malaysia - KCH
Kudat, Sabah, Malaysia - KUD
Kuglutuk Coppermine, NWT, Canada - YCO
Kuito, Angola - SVP
Kulu, India - KUU
Kulusuk, Greenland - KUS
Kumamoto, Japan - KMJ
Kume Jima, Japan - UEO
Kundiawa, Papua New Guinea - CMU
Kunming, P.R. China - KMG
Kunsan, Rep. of Korea - KUV
Kununurra, WA, Australia - KNX
Kuopio, Finland - KUO
Kupang, Indonesia - KOE
Kuqa, P.R. China - KCA
Kuri, Papua New Guinea - KUQ
Kushiro, Japan - KUH
Kuujjuaq, PQ, Canada - YVP
Kuujjuarapik, PQ, Canada - YGW
Kuusamo, Finland - KAO
Kuwait, Kuwait - KWI
Kwajalein, Marshall Islands - KWA
Kwangju, Rep. of Korea - KWJ
Kwethluk, AK, USA - KWT
Kwigillingok, AK, USA - KWK
Kyaukpyu, Myanmar - KYP

Laayoune, Morocco - EUN
Labasa, Fiji - LBS
Lablab, Papua New Guinea - LAB
Labuan, Sabah, Malaysia - LBU
La Ceiba, Honduras - LCE
La Coruna, Spain - LCG
La Crosse WI/Winona, MN, USA - LSE
La Desirade, Guadeloupe - DSD
La Grande, PQ, Canada - YGL
La Palma, Panama - PLP
La Paz, Bolivia - LPB
La Paz, Mexico - LAP
La Rioja, Argentina - IRJ
La Rochelle, France - LRH
La Romana, Dominican Rep. - LRM
La Ronge, SK, Canada - YVC
La Serena, Chile - LSC
La Tabatiere, PQ, Canada - ZLT
Lac Brochet, MB, Canada - XLB
Lac La Martre, NT, Canada - YLE
Lae, Papua New Guinea - LAE
Lae, Marshall Islands - LML
Lafayette, IN, USA - LAF
Lafayette, LA, USA - LFT
Lages, SC, Brazil - LAJ
Lagos, Nigeria - LOS
Lahad Datu, Sabah, Malaysia - LDU
Lahore, Pakistan - LHE
Laibela, Ethiopia - LLI
Lake Charles, LA, USA - LCH
Lake Evella, NT, Australia - LEL
Lake Gregory, WA, Australia - LGE
Lake Harbour, NT, Canada - YLC
Lake Havasu City, AZ, USA - HII
Lake Minchumina, AK, USA - LMA
Lakeba, Fiji - LKB
Lakselv, Norway - LKL
Lama-Kara/Niamtougou, Togo - LRL
Lamap, Vanuatu - LPM
Lamar, CO, USA - LAA
Lambarene, Gabon - LBQ
Lamen Bay, Vanuatu - LNB
Lamezia Terme, Italy - SUF
Lamidanda, Nepal - LDN
Lampang, Thailand - LPT
Lampedusa, Italy - LMP
Lamu, Kenya - LAU
Lanai City, Lanai, HI, USA - LNY
Lancaster, PA, USA - LNS
Lands End, England, UK - LEQ
Langkawi, Malaysia - LGK
Lannion, France - LAI
Lansdowne, ON, Canada - YLH
Lansing, MI, USA - LAN

Lanzarote, Canary Islands - ACE
Lanzhou, P.R. China - LHW
Laoag, Philippines - LAO
Lappeenranta, Finland - LPP
Laramie, WY, USA - LAR
Laredo, TX, USA - LRD
Larnaca, Cyprus - LCA
Larsen Bay, AK, USA - KLN
Las Cruces, NM, USA - LRU
Las Palmas, Canary Is. - LPA
Las Piedras, Venezuela - LSP
Las Tunas, Cuba - VTU
Las Vegas, NE-N. Terminal, USA -
    VGT
Las Vegas, NV, USA - LAS
Las Vegas, NV-Henderson, USA -
    HSH
Lashio, Myanmar - LSH
Lastourville, Gabon - LTL
Latakia, Syria - LTK
Latrobe, PA, USA - LBE
Laucala Island, Fiji - LUC
Launceston, Tas., Australia - LST
Laurel/Hattiesburg, MS, USA - LUL
Laurel/Hattiesburg-Regional, MS,
    USA - PIB
Laverton, WA, Australia - LVO
Lawas, Sarawak, Malaysia - LWY
Lawton, OK, USA - LAW
Lazaro Cardenas, Mexico - LZC
Le Havre, France - LEH
Le Puy, France - LPY
Le Touquet, France - LTQ
Leaf Rapids, MB, Canada - YLR
Learmonth, WA, Australia - LEA
Lebanon, NH, USA - LEB
Lebel-Sur-Quevillon, PQ, Canada -
    YLS
Leeds/Bradford, England, UK - LBA
Leeton, NSW, Australia - QLE
Legaspi, Philippines - LGP
Leh, India - IXL
Leigh Creek, SA, Australia - LGH
Leinster, WA, Australia - LER
Leipzig, Germany - LEJ
Leknes, Norway - LKN
Lemnos, Greece - LXS
Leninakan, Armenia - LWN
Leon/Guanajuato, Mexico - BJX
Leonora, WA, Australia - LNO
Leros, Greece - LRS
Lerwick-Tingwall, Scotland, UK -
    LWK
Lese, Papua New Guinea - LNG
Lethbridge, AB, Canada - YQL

Leticia, Colombia - LET
Levelock, AK, USA - KLL
Lewiston, ID, USA - LWS
Lewistown, MT, USA - LWT
Lexington, KY, USA - LEX
Lhasa, P.R. China - LXA
Lianyungang, P.R. China - LYG
Liberal, KS, USA - LBL
Liberia, Costa Rica - LIR
Libreville, Gabon - LBV
Lichinga, Mozambique - VXC
Lidkoping, Sweden - LDK
Lifou, Loyalty Is. - LIF
Lightning Ridge, NSW, Australia -
    LHG
Lihir Island, Papua New Guinea -
    LNV
Lihue, Kauai, HI, USA - LIH
Lijiang City, P.R. China - LJG
Likiep, Marshall Islands - LIK
Lille, France - LIL
Lilongwe, Malawi - LLW
Lima, Peru - LIM
Limbang, Sarawak, Malaysia - LMN
Lime Village, AK, USA - LVD
Limoges, France - LIG
Lincoln, NE, USA - LNK
Lindi, Tanzania - LDI
Linga Linga, Papua New Guinea -
    LGN
Linkoping, Sweden - LPI
Linz, Austria - LNZ
Lisala, Dem. Rep. of the Congo -
    LIQ
Lisbon, Portugal - LIS
Lismore, NSW, Australia - LSY
Little Rock, AR, USA - LIT
Liuzhou, P.R. China - LZH
Liverpool, England, UK - LPL
Livingstone, Zambia - LVI
Livramento, RS, Brazil - LVB
Lizard Island, QLD, Australia -
    LZR
Ljubljana, Slovenia - LJU
Lloydminster, SK, Canada - YLL
Lockhart Rivers, QLD, Australia -
    IRG
Lodja, Dem. Rep. of the Congo -
    LJA
Loen, Marshall Is. - LOF
Loikaw, Myanmar - LIW
Lome, Togo - LFW
Loncopue, Argentina - LCP
London, England, UK - LON
London, ON, Canada - YXU

London-Biggin Hill, England, UK - BQH
London-City, England, UK - LCY
London-Gatwick, England, UK - LGW
London-Heathrow, England, UK - LHR
London-Luton Int'l., England, UK - LTN
London-Stansted, England, UK - STN
Londonderry N., Ireland, UK - LDY
Londrina, PR, Brazil - LDB
Long Apung, Indonesia - LPU
Long Banga, Malaysia - LBP
Long Bawan, Indonesia - LBW
Long Beach, CA, USA - LGB
Long Island Macarthur, NY, USA - ISP
Long Island, QLD, Australia - HAP
Long Island, AK, USA - LIJ
Long Lellang, Sarawak, Malaysia - LGL
Long Pasia, Sabah, Malaysia - GSA
Long Semado, Sarawak, Malaysia - LSM
Long Seridan, Sarawak, Malaysia - ODN
Longana, Vanuatu - LOD
Longreach, QLD, Australia - LRE
Longview, TX, USA - GGG
Longyearbyen, Norway - LYR
Lonorore, Vanuatu - LNE
Lopez Island, WA, USA - LPS
Lord Howe Is., NSW, Australia - LDH
Loreto, Mexico - LTO
Lorient, France - LRT
Los Angeles, CA-Int'l, USA - LAX
Los Angeles, Chile - LSQ
Los Cabos, Mexico - SJD
Los Mochis, Mexico - LMM
Losuia, Papua New Guinea - LSA
Loubomo, Peop. Rep. of the Congo - DIS
Louisville, KY-Standiford, USA - SDF
Lourdes/Tarbes, France - LDE
Luanda, Angola - LAD
Luang Namtha, Laos - LXG
Luang Prabang, Laos - LPQ
Lubang, Philippines - LBX
Lubango, Angola - SDD
Lubbock, TX, USA - LBB
Lubumbashi, Dem. Rep. of the Congo - FBM

Lucknow, India - LKO
Luderitz, Namibia - LUD
Lugano, Switzerland - LUG
Lukla, Nepal - LUA
Lulea, Sweden - LLA
Lumi, Papua New Guinea - LMI
Luoyang, P.R. China - LYA
Lusaka, Zambia - LUN
Lutselke Snowdrift, NT, Canada - YSG
Luxembourg, Luxembourg - LUX
Luxi, P.R. China - LUM
Luxor, Egypt - LXR
Luzhou, P.R. China - LZO
Lvov, Ukraine - LWO
Lycksele, Sweden - LYC
Lynchburg, VA, USA - LYH
Lynn Lake, MB, Canada - YYL
Lyon, France - LYS
M'Bigou, Gabon - MBC
Maastricht, Netherlands - MST
Mabuiag Island, QLD, Australia - UBB
Macapa, AP, Brazil - MCP
MacArthur River, NT, Australia - MCV
Macau, Macau - MFM
Maceio, AL, Brazil - MCZ
Machu Picchu, Peru - MFT
Mackay, QLD, Australia - MKY
Macon, GA, USA - MCN
Madang, Papua New Guinea - MAG
Madinah, Saudi Arabia - MED
Madison, WI, USA - MSN
Madrid, Spain - MAD
Madurai, India - IXM
Mae Hong Son, Thailand - HGN
Mae Sot, Thailand - MAQ
Maewo, Vanuatu - MWF
Magadan, Russia - GDX
Magaruque, Mozambique - MFW
Magdalena, Bolivia - MGD
Magnitogorsk, Russia - MQF
Mahanoro, Madagascar - VVB
Mahe Is., Seychelles Is. - SEZ
Mahendranagar, Nepal - XMG
Maiduguri, Nigeria - MIU
Maintirano, Madagascar - MXT
Maio, Cape Verde Islands - MMO
Maitland, NSW, Australia - MTL
Majkin, Marshall Is. - MJE
Majunga, Madagascar - MJN
Majuro, Marshall Islands - MAJ
Makale, Ethiopia - MQX
Makemo, French Polynesia - MKP

Makhachkala, Russia - MCX
Makkovik, NF, Canada - YMN
Makokou, Gabon - MKU
Makung, Taiwan - MZG
Makurdi, Nigeria - MDI
Malabo, Equatorial Guinea - SSG
Malacca, Malaysia - MKZ
Malaga, Spain - AGP
Malalaua, Papua New Guinea - MLQ
Malange, Angola - MEG
Malargue, Argentina - LGS
Malatya, Turkey - MLX
Male, Maldives - MLE
Malekolon, Papua New Guinea - MKN
Malindi, Kenya - MYD
Malmo, Sweden - MMA
Malmo-Harbour HLPT, Sweden - JMM
Malmo City HVC, Sweden - HMA
Malmo-Sturup, Sweden - MMX
Maloelap, Marshall Islands - MAV
Malololailai, Fiji - PTF
Maloy Harbour, Norway - QFQ
Malta, Mediterranean Sea - MLA
Mampikony, Madagascar - WMP
Man, Cote D'Ivoire - MJC
Manado, Indonesia - MDC
Managua, Nicaragua - MGA
Mana Island, Fiji - MNF
Manakara, Madagascar - WVK
Mananara, Madagascar - WMR
Manang, Nepal - NGX
Mananjary, Madagascar - MNJ
Manare, Papua New Guinea - MRM
Manaus, AM, Brazil - MAO
Manchester, England, UK - MAN
Manchester, NH, USA - MHT
Mandalay, Myanmar - MDL
Mandritsara, Madagascar - WMA
Mangaia, Cook Is. - MGS
Mangalore, India - IXE
Mangrove Cay, Bahamas - MAY
Manguna, Papua New Guinea - MFO
Manhattan, KS, USA - MHK
Manihi, Fr. Polynesia - XMH
Manihiki Is., Cook Is. - MHX
Manitsoq, Greenland - JSU
Manila, Philippines - MNL
Maningrida, NT, Australia - MNG
Manistee, MI, USA - MBL
Manizales, Colombia - MZL
Manja, Madagascar - MJA
Manley Hot Sprgs., AK, USA - MLY
Mannheim, Germany - MHG
Manokotak, AK, USA - KMO
Manus Is., Papua New Guinea - MAS

Manzanillo, Cuba - MZO
Manzanillo, Mexico - ZLO
Manzini, Swaziland - MTS
Maota, Savaii Is., Western Samoa - MXS
Mapua, Papua New Guinea - MPU
Maputo, Mozambique - MPM
Mar Del Plata, Argentina - MDQ
Mara Lodges, Kenya - MRE
Maraba, PA, Brazil - MAB
Maracaibo, Venezuela - MAR
Maramuni, Papua New Guinea - MWI
Marathon, FL, USA - MTH
Marau, Solomon Islands - RUS
Mare, Loyalty Is. - MEE
Margaret River, WA, Australia - MGV
Margate, South Africa - MGH
Marie Galante, Fr. Antilles - GBJ
Mariehamn, Aland Is., Finland - MHQ
Marilia, SP, Brazil - MII
Maringa, PR, Brazil - MGF
Marion, IL, USA - MWA
Mariupol, Ukraine - MPW
Maroantsetra, Madagascar - WMN
Maroua, Cameroon - MVR
Marquette, MI, USA - MQT
Marrakech, Morocco - RAK
Marseille, France - MRS
Marsh Harbour, Bahamas - MHH
Marshall, AK, USA - MLL
Martha's Vineyard, MA, USA - MVY
Marudi, Sarawak, Malaysia - MUR
Mary's Harbour, NF, Canada - YMH
Maryborough, QLD, Australia - MBH
Mascara, Algeria - MUW
Maseru, Lesotho - MSU
Mashad, Iran - MHD
Masirah, Oman - MSH
Mason City, IA, USA - MCW
Massena, NY, USA - MSS
Masvingo, Zimbabwe - MVZ
Matadi, Dem. Rep. of the Congo - MAT
Mataiva, Fr. Polynesia - MVT
Matamoros, Mexico - MAM
Mataram, Indonesia - AMI
Matsumoto, Japan - MMJ
Matsuyama, Japan - MYJ
Mattoon, IL, USA - MTO
Maturin, Venezuela - MUN
Mauke, Cook Is. - MUK
Maulmyine, Myanmar - MNU
Maumere, Indonesia - MOF

Maun, Botswana - MUB
Maupiti, Society Is., Fr.
    Polynesia - MAU
Mauritius, Mauritius - MRU
Mayaguana, Bahamas - MYG
Mayaguez, Puerto Rico - MAZ
Mayoumba, Gabon - MYB
Mazatlan, Mexico - MZT
Mbambanakira, Solomon Islands -
    MBU
Mbandaka, Dem. Rep. of the Congo
    - MDK
Mbuji-Mayi, Dem. Rep. of the
    Congo - MJM
Mc Allen, TX, USA - MFE
Mc Grath, AK, USA - MCG
McCook, NE, USA - MCK
Medan, Indonesia - MES
Medellin, Colombia - MDE
Medellin-Herrera, Colombia - EOH
Medford, OR, USA - MFR
Medicine Hat, AB, Canada - YXH
Meekatharra, WA, Australia - MKR
Meghauli, Nepal - MEY
Mehamn, Norway - MEH
Meixian, P.R. China - MXZ
Mejit Is., Marshall Is. - MJB
Mekambo, Gabon - MKB
Mekane Selam, Ethiopia - MKS
Mekoryuk, AK, USA - MYU
Melbourne, FL, USA - MLB
Melbourne, VIC, Australia - MEL
Melbourne, VIC-Essendon,
    Australia - MEB
Melilla, Spain - MLN
Memanbetsu, Japan - MMB
Memphis, TN, USA - MEM
Mendi, Ethiopia - NDM
Mendi, Papua New Guinea - MDU
Mendoza, Argentina - MDZ
Menongue, Angola - SPP
Menorca, Spain - MAH
Menyamya, Papua New Guinea - MYX
Merauke, Indonesia - MKQ
Merced, CA, USA - MCE
Merida, Venezuela - MRD
Merida, Mexico - MID
Meridian, MS, USA - MEI
Merimbula, NSW, Australia - MIM
Meselia, Papua New Guinea - MFZ
Metlakatla, AK, USA - MTM
Metz/Nancy, France - ETZ
Mexicali, Mexico - MXL
Mexico City, Mexico - MEX
Meyers Chuck, AK, USA - WMK

Mfuwe, Zambia - MFU
Miami, FL, USA - MIA
Miami, FL - Public SPB, USA - MPB
Miandrivazo, Madagascar - ZVA
Mianwali, Pakistan - MWD
Middle Caicos, Turks & Caicos Is.
    - MDS
Midland/Odessa, TX, USA - MAF
Mikkeli, Finland - MIK
Mikonos, Greece - JMK
Milan, Italy - MIL
Milan, Italy-Linate - LIN
Milan-Malpensa, Italy - MXP
Milan-Orio Serio, Italy - BGY
Mildura, VIC, Australia - MQL
Miles City, MT, USA - MLS
Milford Sound, New Zealand - MFN
Mili, Marshall Islands - MIJ
Millingimbi, NT, Australia - MGT
Milos, Greece - MLO
Milwaukee, WI, USA - MKE
Minacu, GO, Brazil - MQH
Minami Daito Jima, Okinawa
    Islands - MMD
Minatitlan, Mexico - MTT
Mineralnye Vody, Russia - MRV
Minneapolis/St Paul, MN, USA -
    MSP
Minot, ND, USA - MOT
Minsk, Belarus - MSQ
Minsk-International 1, Belarus -
    MHP
Minto, AK, USA - MNT
Minvoul, Gabon - MVX
Miri, Sarawak, Malaysia - MYY
Misawa, Japan - MSJ
Misima, Papua New Guinea - MIS
Missoula, MT, USA - MSO
Mitiaro, Cook Is. - MOI
Mitzic, Gabon - MZC
Miyake Jima, Japan - MYE
Miyako Jima, Japan - MMY
Miyazaki, Japan - KMI
Mizan Teferi, Ethiopia - MTF
Mmabatho, South Africa - MBD
Mo I Rana, Norway - MQN
Moa, Cuba - MOA
Moab, UT, USA - CNY
Moabi, Gabon - MGX
Moala, Fiji - MFJ
Moanda, Dem. Rep. of the Congo -
    MNB
Moanda, Gabon - MFF
Mobile AL/Pascagoula, MS, USA -
    MOB

Modesto, CA, USA - MOD
Mogadishu, Somalia - MGQ
Mohenjo Daro, Pakistan - MJD
Mokpu, Rep. of Korea - MPK
Mokuti Lodge, Namibia - OKU
Molde, Norway - MOL
Moline, IL, USA - MLI
Molokai/Hoolehua, HI, USA - MKK
Mombasa, Kenya - MBA
Monastir, Tunisia - MIR
Monbetsu, Japan - MBE
Monclova, Mexico - LOV
Moncton, NB, Canada - YQM
Monghsat, Myanmar - MOG
Monkey Mia, WA, Australia - MJK
Mono Is., Solomon Islands - MNY
Monroe, LA, USA - MLU
Monrovia, Liberia - MLW
Mont Joli, PQ, Canada - YYY
Monte Carlo, Monaco - MCM
Monte Dourado, PA, Brazil - MEU
Montego Bay, Jamaica - MBJ
Monterey, CA, USA - MRY
Monteria, Colombia - MTR
Monterrey, Mexico - MTY
Montes Claros, MG, Brazil - MOC
Montevideo, Uruguay - MVD
Montgomery, AL, USA - MGM
Montlucon, France - MCU
Montpellier, France - MPL
Montreal, PQ, Canada - YMQ
Montreal, PQ-Dorval Arpt., Canada
   - YUL
Montreal, PQ-Mirabel, Canada -
   YMX
Montrose, CO, USA - MTJ
Moorabbin, VIC, Australia - MBW
Moorea Is., Soc. Is., Fr.
   Polynesia - MOZ
Moosonee, ON, Canada - YMO
Mopti, Mali - MZI
Mora, Sweden - MXX
Morafenobe, Madagascar - TVA
Moree, NSW, Australia - MRZ
Morelia, Mexico - MLM
Morgantown, WV, USA - MGW
Morioka, Japan - HNA
Mornington Is., QLD, Australia -
   ONG
Moro, Papua New Guinea - MXH
Morombe, Madagascar - MXM
Morondava, Madagascar - MOQ
Moroni, Comoros - YVA
Moroni-Hahaya, Comoros - HAH
Moruya, NSW, Australia - MYA

Moscow, Russia - MOW
Moscow-Bykovo, Russia - BKA
Moscow-Domodedovo, Russia - DME
Moscow-Sheremetye, Russia - SVO
Moscow-Vnukovo, Russia - VKO
Moser Bay, AK, USA - KMY
Moses Lake, WA, USA - MWH
Mosjoen, Norway - MJF
Mosteiros, Cape Verde Islands -
   MTI
Mota Lava, Vanuatu - MTV
Motueka, New Zealand - MZP
Mouila, Gabon - MJL
Mount Cook, New Zealand - MON
Mount Keith, WA, Australia - WME
Mount Pleasant, Falkland Is. -
   MPN
Mountain Home, AR, USA - WMH
Mountain Village, AK, USA - MOU
Moyobamba, Peru - MBP
Mpacha, Namibia - MPA
Mt. Gambier, SA, Australia - MGB
Mt. Hagen, Papua New Guinea - HGU
Mt. Isa, QLD, Australia - ISA
Mt. Vernon, IL, USA - MVN
Mtwara, Tanzania - MYW
Mucuri, BA, Brazil - MVS
Mudanjiang, P.R. China - MDG
Mudgee, NSW, Australia - DGE
Muenster, Germany - FMO
Mukah, Sarawak, Malaysia - MKM
Mulhouse/Basel, France - MLH
Multan, Pakistan - MUX
Mulu, Malaysia - MZV
Mumbai, Bombay, India - BOM
Munda, Solomon Islands - MUA
Mundulkiri, Cambodia - MWV
Munich, Germany - MUC
Munich-Augsburg, Germany - AGB
Murcia, Spain - MJV
Murmansk, Russia - MMK
Murray Island, QLD, Australia -
   MYI
Mus, Turkey - MSR
Muscat, Oman - MCT
Muscle Shoals, AL, USA - MSL
Muskegon, MI, USA - MKG
Muskrat Dam, ON, Canada - MSA
Musoma, Tanzania - MUZ
Mussau, Papua New Guinea - MWU
Muzaffarabad, Pakistan - MFG
Mwanza, Tanzania - MWZ
Myeik, Myanmar - MGZ
Myitkyina, Myanmar - MYT
Myrtle Beach, SC, USA - MYR

Mytilene, Greece - MJT
Mzuzu, Malawi - ZZU
N'Dende, Gabon - KDN
N'djamena, Chad - NDJ
N'Gaoundere, Cameroon - NGE
Naberevnye Chelny, Russia - NBC
Nadi, Fiji - NAN
Nadym, Russia - NYM
Naga, Philippines - WNP
Nagasaki, Japan - NGS
Nagoya, Japan - NGO
Nagpur, India - NAG
Nain, NF, Canada - YDP
Nairobi, Kenya - NBO
Nairobi-Wilson, Kenya - WIL
Nakashibetsu, Japan - SHB
Nakhichevan, Azerbaijan - NAJ
Nakhon Phanom, Thailand - KOP
Nakhon Ratchasima, Thailand - NAK
Nakhon Si Thammarat, Thailand -
    NST
Namangan, Uzbekistan - NMA
Namatanai, Papua New Guinea - ATN
Namdrik Island, Marshall Islands
    - NDK
Namibe, Angola - MSZ
Nampula, Mozambique - APL
Namsos, Norway - OSY
Namudi, Papua New Guinea - NDI
Nan, Thailand - NNT
Nanaimo, BC, Canada - YCD
Nanaimo, BC-Harbour, Canada - ZNA
Nanchang, P.R. China - KHN
Nanchong, P.R. China - NAO
Nanisivik, NT, Canada - YSR
Nanjing, P.R. China - NKG
Nankina, Papua New Guinea - NKN
Nanki Shirahama, Japan - SHM
Nanning, P.R. China - NNG
Nanortalik, Greenland - JNN
Nantes, France - NTE
Nantong, P.R. China - NTG
Nantucket, MA, USA - ACK
Nanyang, P.R. China - NNY
Nanyuki, Kenya - NYK
Napakiak, AK, USA - WNA
Napaskiak, AK, USA - PKA
Napier, New Zealand - NPE
Naples, Italy - NAP
Naples, FL, USA - APF
Narathiwat, Thailand - NAW
Nare, Colombia - NAR
Narrabri, NSW, Australia - NAA
Narrandera, NSW, Australia - NRA
Narsaq, Greenland - JNS

Narssarssuaq, Greenland - UAK
Narvik, Norway - NVK
Naryan-Mar, Russia - NNM
Nashville, TN, USA - BNA
Nassau, Bahamas - NAS
Nassau-Paradise Is., Bahamas -
    PID
Natal, RN, Brazil - NAT
Natashquan, PQ, Canada - YNA
Naukiti, AK, USA - NKI
Nauru, Rep. of Nauru - INU
Navegantes, SC, Brazil - NVT
Nawab Shah, Pakistan - WNS
Naxos, Cyclades Is., Greece - JNX
Ndola, Zambia - NLA
Necocli, Colombia - NCI
Neerlerit Inaat, Greenland - CNP
Neftekamsk, Russia - NEF
Nefteyugansk, Russia - NFG
Neghelli, Ethiopia - EGL
Negril, Jamaica - NEG
Neiva, Colombia - NVA
Nejjo, Ethiopia - NEJ
Nejran, Saudi Arabia - EAM
Nelson, New Zealand - NSN
Nelson Lagoon, AK, USA - NLG
Nelspruit, South Africa - NLP
Nema, Mauritania - EMN
Nemiscau, PQ, Canada - YNS
Nepalganj, Nepal - KEP
Neryungri, Russia - NER
Neuquen, Argentina - NQN
Nevis, Leeward Islands - NEV
New Bedford, MA, USA - EWB
New Bern, NC, USA - EWN
New Haven, CT, USA - HVN
New London, CT, USA - GON
New Orleans, LA, USA - MSY
New Plymouth, New Zealand - NPL
New Stuyahok, AK, USA - KNW
New Valley, Egypt - UVL
New York, NY-City, USA - NYC
New York, NY-Kennedy, USA - JFK
New York, NY-La Guardia, USA -
    LGA
Newark, NJ, USA - EWR
Newburgh, NY, USA - SWF
Newcastle, England, UK - NCL
Newcastle, NSW, Australia - NTL
Newcastle, NSW-Belmont, Australia
    - BEO
Newman, WA, Australia - ZNE
Newport News, VA, USA - PHF
Newquay, England, UK - NQY
Newtok, AK, USA - WWT

Ngaoundere, Camerron - NGE
Ngau, Fiji - NGI
Ngukurr, NT, Australia - RPM
Nha-Trang, Vietnam - NHA
Niamey, Niger - NIM
Nice, France - NCE
Nicholson, WA, Australia - NLS
Nightmute, AK, USA - NME
Niigata, Japan - KIJ
Nikolai, AK, USA - NIB
Nikolski, AK, USA - IKO
Nimes, France - FNI
Ningbo, P.R. China - NGB
Nioro, Mali - NIX
Niquelandia, GO, Brazil - NQL
Nissan Island, Papua New Guinea -
    IIS
Niuafo'ou, Tonga Is. - NFO
Niuatoputapu, Tonga Is. - NTT
Niue Island, Niue - IUE
Nizhnevartovsk, Russia - NJC
Nizhniy Novgorod, Russia - GOJ
Nkayi, Peop. Rep. of the Congo -
    NKY
Noatak, AK, USA - WTK
Nojabrxsk, Russia - NOJ
Nome, AK, USA - OME
Nondalton, AK, USA - NNL
Noorvick, AK, USA - ORV
Nordholz-Spieka, Germany - NDZ
Norfolk/Va. Beach/WMBG, VA, USA -
    ORF
Norfolk Is., Pacific Ocean - NLK
Norfolk, NE, USA - OFK
Norilsk, Russia - NSK
Norman Wells, NT, Canada - YVQ
Normanton, QLD, Australia - NTN
Norrkoping, Sweden - NRK
Norsup, Vanuatu - NUS
North Bay, ON, Canada - YYB
North Bend, OR, USA - OTH
North Caicos, Turks & Caicos Is.
    - NCA
North Eleuthera, Bahamas - ELH
North Platte, NE , USA - LBF
North Ronaldsay, Scotland, UK -
    NRL
North Sound, BVI - NSX
North Spirit Lake, ON, Canada -
    YNO
Norway House, MB, Canada - YNE
Norwich, England, UK - NWI
Nosara Beach, Costa Rica - NOB
Nossi-be, Madagascar - NOS
Nouadhibou, Mauritania - NDB

Nouakchott, Mauritania - NKC
Noumea, New Caledonia - NOU
Noumea-Magenta, New Caledonia -
    GEA
Novgorod, Russia - NVR
Novosibirsk, Russia - OVB
Novy Urengoy, Russia - NUX
Nowata, Papua New Guinea - NWT
Nueva Gerona, Cuba - GER
Nueva Guinea, Nicaragua - NVG
Nuevo Laredo, Mexico - NLD
Nuiqsut, AK, USA - NUI
Nuku, Papua New Guinea - UKU
Nuku Hiva, Fr. Polynesia - NHV
Nukus, Uzbekistan - NCU
Nulato, AK, USA - NUL
Numbulwar, NT, Australia - NUB
Nunapitchuk, AK, USA - NUP
Nunukan, Indonesia - NNX
Nuqui, Colombia - NQU
Nuremberg, Germany - NUE
Nuremberg Main Station, Germany -
    ZAQ
Nuuk, Greenland - GOH
Nyaung-U, Myanmar - NYU
Nyngan, NSW, Australia - NYN
Oak Harbor, WA, USA - ODW
Oakland, CA, USA - OAK
Oaxaca, Mexico - OAX
Obihiro, Japan - OBO
Ocana, Colombia - OCV
Odense, Denmark - ODE
Odessa, Ukraine - ODS
Odienne, Cote D'Ivoire - KEO
Ofu Island, American Samoa - OFU
Ogdensburg, NY, USA - OGS
Ohrid, Macedonia - OHD
Oita, Japan - OIT
Okayama, Japan - OKJ
Oki Island, Japan - OKI
Okinawa, Ryukyu Is., Japan - OKA
Okino Erabu, Japan - OKE
Oklahoma City, OK, USA - OKC
Okondja, Gabon - OKN
Okushiri, Japan - OIR
Olbia, Italy - OLB
Old Crow, YK, Canada - YOC
Old Harbour, AK, USA - OLH
Olga Bay, AK, USA - KOY
Olpoi, Vanuatu - OLJ
Olympia, WA, USA - OLM
Olympic Dam, SA, Australia - OLP
Omaha, NE, USA - OMA
Omboue, Gabon - OMB
Omsk, Russia - OMS

Ondangwa, Namibia - OND
Ongiva, Angola - VPE
Ontario, CA, USA - ONT
Open Bay, Papua New Guinea - OPB
Oradea, Romania - OMR
Oran, Algeria - ORN
Oran, Argentina - ORA
Orange, NSW, Australia - OAG
Orange, NSW-Cudal, Australia - CUG
Orange County, CA, USA - SNA
Oranjemund, Namibia - OMD
Orebro, Sweden - ORB
Orenburg, Russia - REN
Orlando, FL, USA - ORL
Orlando, FL-Int'l, USA - MCO
Ormara, Pakistan - ORW
Ornskoldsvik, Sweden - OER
Orsk, Russia - OSW
Orsta/Volda, Norway - HOV
Osaka, Japan - OSA
Osh, Kyrgyzstan - OSS
Oshima Is., Japan - OIM
Oshkosh, WI, USA - OSH
Oskarshamn, Sweden - OSK
Oslo, Norway - OSL
Osorno, Chile - ZOS
Ostersund, Sweden - OSD
Ostrava, Czech Republic - OSR
Ottawa, ON, Canada - YOW
Ottumwa, IA, USA - OTM
Otu, Colombia - OTU
Ouagadougou, Burkina Faso - OUA
Ouargla, Algeria - OGX
Ouarzazate, Morocco - OZZ
Oudomxay, Laos - ODY
Ouesso, Peop. Rep. of the Congo - OUE
Oujda, Morocco - OUD
Oulu, Finland - OUL
Ouvea, Loyalty Is. - UVE
Ouzinkie, AK, USA - KOZ
Ovalle, Chile - OVL
Ovda, Israel - VDA
Owando, Congo - FTX
Owensboro, KY, USA - OWB
Oxford House, MB, Canada - YOH
Oxnard, CA, USA - OXR
Oyem, Gabon - OYE
Paama, Vanuatu - PBJ
Paamiut, Greenland - JFR
Pacific Harbour, Fiji - PHR
Padang, Indonesia - PDG
Paderborn, Germany - PAD
Paducah, KY, USA - PAH

Page, AZ, USA - PGA
Pago Pago, Samoa - PPG
Pakse, Laos - PKZ
Pakuashipi, PQ, Canada - YIF
Palanga, Lithuania - PLQ
Palangkaraya, Indonesia - PKY
Palembang, Indonesia - PLM
Palenque, Mexico - PQM
Palermo, Italy - PMO
Palm Springs, CA, USA - PSP
Palma, Mallorca Is., Spain - PMI
Palmar, Costa Rica - PMZ
Palmas, TO, Brazil - PMW
Palmdale/Lancaster, CA, USA - PMD
Palmerston N., New Zealand - PMR
Palu, Indonesia - PLW
Pamphula, MG, Brazil - PLU
Pamplona, Spain - PNA
Panama City, Panama Rep. - PTY
Panama City, FL, USA - PFN
Panama City-Paitilla, Panama Rep. - PAC
Pangkalanbuun, Indonesia - PKN
Pangkalpinang, Indonesia - PGK
Pangnirtung, NT, Canada - YXP
Panjgur, Pakistan - PJG
Pantelleria, Italy - PNL
Papa, Westray, UK - PPW
Papeete, Soc. Is., Fr. Polynesia - PPT
Paphos, Cyprus - PFO
Paraburdoo, WA, Australia - PBO
Para Chinar, Pakistan - PAJ
Paramaribo, Rep. of Suriname - PBM
Paraparaumu, New Zealand - PPQ
Parasi, Solomon Islands - PRS
Paris, France - PAR
Paris-De Gaulle, France - CDG
Paris-Orly, France - ORY
Paris-Tille, France - BVA
Parkersburg, WV, USA - PKB
Parkes, NSW, Australia - PKE
Parnaiba, PI, Brazil - PHB
Paro, Bhutan - PBH
Paros, Greece - PAS
Part Dieu Railway Service, France - XYD
Pasco, WA, USA - PSC
Pasni, Pakistan - PSI
Passo Fundo, RS, Brazil - PFB
Pasto, Colombia - PSO
Patna, India - PAT
Pato Branco, PR, Brazil - PTO
Pau, France - PUF

Paulatuk, NT, Canada - YPC
Pavlodar, Kazakstan - PWQ
Peace River, AB, Canada - YPE
Peawanuck, ON, Canada - YPO
Pedro Bay, AK, USA - PDB
Pedro Juan Caballero, Paraguay -
    PJC
Pekanbaru, Indonesia - PKU
Pelican, AK, USA - PEC
Pellston, MI, USA - PLN
Pelly Bay, NT, Canada - YUF
Pelly Bay, NT-Townsite, Canada -
    YBB
Pelotas, RS, Brazil - PET
Pemba, Mozambique - POL
Pemba Is., Tanzania - PMA
Pembroke, ON, Canada - YTA
Penang, Malaysia - PEN
Pendleton, OR, USA - PDT
Penrhyn Is., Cook Is. - PYE
Pensacola, FL, USA - PNS
Penticton, BC, Canada - YYF
Penzance, England, UK - PZE
Peoria, IL, USA - PIA
Pereira, Colombia - PEI
Perigueux, France - PGX
Perm, Russia - PEE
Perpignan, France - PGF
Perryville, AK, USA - KPV
Perth, WA, Australia - PER
Perugia, Italy - PEG
Pescara, Italy - PSR
Peshawar, Pakistan - PEW
Petersburg, AK, USA - PSG
Petrolina, PE, Brazil - PNZ
Petropavlovsk, Kazakstan - PPK
Petropavlovsk-Kamchatsky, Russia
    - PKC
Petrozavodsk, Russia - PES
Phalaborwa, South Africa - PHW
Phaplu, Nepal - PPL
Philadelphia, PA, USA - PHL
Phitsanulok, Thailand - PHS
Phnom Penh, Cambodia - PNH
Phoenix, AZ, USA - PHX
Phrae, Thailand - PRH
Phuket, Thailand - HKT
Phuquoc, Vietnam - PQC
Pickle Lake, ON, Canada - YPL
Pico Island, Portugal (Azores) -
    PIX
Piedras Negras, Mexico - PDS
Pierre, SD, USA - PIR
Pietermaritzburg, South Africa -
    PZB

Pietersburg, South Africa - PTG
Pikangikum, ON, Canada - YPM
Pilot Point, AK, USA - PIP
Pilot Point, AK-Ugashik, USA -
    UGB
Pilot Station, AK, USA - PQS
Pinehurst, NC, USA - SOP
Pingtung, Taiwan - PIF
Pisa, Italy - PSA
Pittsburgh, PA, USA - PIT
Pituffik, Greenland - THU
Piura, Peru - PIU
Placencia, Belize - PLJ
Platinum, AK, USA - PTU
Plattsburgh, NY, USA - PLB
Playa Del Carmen, Mexico - PCM
Pleiku, Vietnam - PXU
Plettenberg Bay, South Africa -
    PBZ
Plymouth, England, UK - PLH
Pocatello, ID, USA - PIH
Podgorica, Yugoslavia - TGD
Pohang, Rep. of Korea - KPO
Pohnpei, Caroline Is. - PNI
Point Baker, AK, USA - KPB
Point Hope, AK, USA - PHO
Point Lay, AK, USA - PIZ
Pointe A Pitre, Guadeloupe - PTP
Pointe Noire, Peop. Rep. of the
    Congo - PNR
Points North Landing, SK, Canada
    - YNL
Poitiers, France - PIS
Pokhara, Nepal - PKR
Ponca City, OK, USA - PNC
Ponce, Puerto Rico - PSE
Pond Inlet, NT, Canada - YIO
Ponta Delgada, Portugal (Azores)
    - PDL
Ponta Grossa, PR, Brazil - PGZ
Ponta Pora, MS, Brazil - PMG
Pontianak, Indonesia - PNK
Poona, India - PNQ
Popayan, Colombia - PPN
Popondetta, Papua New Guinea -
    PNP
Porbandar, India - PBD
Porgera, Papua New Guinea - RGE
Pori, Finland - POR
Porlamar, Venezuela - PMV
Port Alberni, BC, Canada - YPB
Port Alexander, AK, USA - PTD
Port Alsworth, AK, USA - PTA
Port Angeles, WA, USA - CLM
Port Antonio, Jamaica - POT

Port Au Prince, Haiti - PAP
Port Augusta, SA, Australia - PUG
Port Bailey, AK, USA - KPY
Port Berge, Madagascar - WPB
Port Blair, Andaman Is., India - IXZ
Port Clarence, AK, USA - KPC
Port Elizabeth, South Africa - PLZ
Port Elizabeth, Windward Is. - BQU
Port Gentil, Gabon - POG
Port Harcourt, Nigeria - PHC
Port Hardy, BC, Canada - YZT
Port Hedland, WA, Australia - PHE
Port Heiden, AK, USA - PTH
Port Hope Simpson, NF, Canada - YHA
Port Lincoln, SA, Australia - PLO
Port Lions, AK, USA - ORI
Port Macquarie, NSW, Australia - PQQ
Port Menier, PQ, Canada - YPN
Port Moller, AK, USA - PML
Port Moresby, Papua New Guinea - POM
Port of Spain , Trinidad & Tobago - POS
Port Protection, AK, USA - PPV
Port Sudan, Sudan - PZU
Port Vila, Vanuatu - VLI
Port Williams, AK, USA - KPR
Portage Creek, AK, USA - PCA
Portland, ME, USA - PWM
Portland, OR, USA - PDX
Portland, VIC, Australia - PTJ
Porto, Portugal - OPO
Porto Alegre, RS, Brazil - POA
Porto Nacional, TO, Brazil - PNB
Porto Santo, Portugal (Madeira) - PXO
Porto Seguro, BA, Brazil - BPS
Porto Velho, RO, Brazil - PVH
Posadas, Argentina - PSS
Postville, NF, Canada - YSO
Potosi, Bolivia - POI
Poughkeepsie, NY, USA - POU
Poum, New Caledonia - PUV
Powell River, BC, Canada - YPW
Poza Rica, Mexico - PAZ
Poznan, Poland - POZ
Prague, Czech Republic - PRG
Praia, Cape Verde Islands - RAI
Praslin Is., Seychelles Is. - PRI
Pres. Prudente, SP, Brazil - PPB

Prescott, AZ, USA - PRC
Presque Isle, ME, USA - PQI
Preveza/Lefkas, Greece - PVK
Prince Albert, SK, Canada - YPA
Prince George, BC, Canada - YXS
Prince Rupert, BC, Canada - YPR
Prince Rupert, BC-Cove, Canada - ZSW
Principe Is., Principe Island - PCP
Pristina, Yugoslavia - PRN
Proserpine, QLD, Australia - PPP
Providence, RI, USA - PVD
Providencia, Colombia - PVA
Providenciales, Turks & Caicos Is. - PLS
Provincetown, MA, USA - PVC
Prudhoe Bay/Deadhorse, AK, USA - SCC
Pucallpa, Peru - PCL
Puebla, Mexico - PBC
Pueblo, CO, USA - PUB
Puerto Asis, Colombia - PUU
Puerto Ayacucho, Venezuela - PYH
Puerto Berrio, Colombia - PBE
Puerto Cabezos, Nicaragua - PUZ
Puerto Carreno, Colombia - PCR
Puerto Escondido, Mexico - PXM
Puerto Inirida, Colombia - PDA
Puerto Jimenez, Costa Rica - PJM
Puerto Lempira, Honduras - PEU
Puerto Madryn, Argentina - PMY
Puerto Maldonado, Peru - PEM
Puerto Montt, Chile - PMC
Puerto Ordaz, Venezuela - PZO
Puerto Plata, Dominican Rep. - POP
Puerto Princesa, Philippines - PPS
Puerto Suarez, Bolivia - PSZ
Puerto Vallarta, Mexico - PVR
Pukatawagan, MB, Canada - XPK
Pula, Croatia - PUY
Pullman, WA, USA - PUW
Pumani, Papua New Guinea - PMN
Punta Arenas, Chile - PUQ
Punta Cana, Dominican Rep. - PUJ
Punta Del Este, Uruguay - PDP
Punta Gorda, Belize - PND
Punta Islita, Costa Rica - PBP
Pusan, Rep. of Korea - PUS
Putao, Myanmar - PBU
Puttaparthi, India - PUT
Putussibau, Indonesia - PSU
Puvirnituq, PQ, Canada - YPX

Pyongyang, Dem. Peop. Rep. of
   Korea - FNJ
Qaisumah, Saudi Arabia - AQI
Qaqortoq, Greenland - JJU
Qasigiannguit, Greenland - JCH
Qeqertarsuaq, Greenland - JGO
Qiemo, P.R. China - IQM
Qingdao, P.R. China - TAO
Qinhuangdao, P.R. China - SHP
Qiqihar, P.R. China - NDG
Qualicum, BC, Canada - XQU
Quaqtaq, PQ, Canada - YQC
Quebec, PQ, Canada - YQB
Queenstown, New Zealand - ZQN
Quelimane, Mozambique - UEL
Quepos, Costa Rica - XQP
Queretaro, Mexico - QRO
Quesnel, BC, Canada - YQZ
Quetta, Pakistan - UET
Quibdo, Colombia - UIB
Quilpie, QLD, Australia - ULP
Quimper, France - UIP
Quincy, IL, USA - UIN
Quinhagak, AK, USA - KWN
Quinhon, Vietnam - UIH
Quito, Ecuador - UIO
Rabaraba, Papua New Guinea - RBP
Rabat, Morocco - RBA
Rabaul, Papua New Guinea - RAB
Raduzhnyi, Russia - RAT
Rae Lakes, NT, Canada - YRA
Rafha, Saudi Arabia - RAH
Rahim Yar Khan, Pakistan - RYK
Raiatea Island, French Polynesia
   - RFP
Rainbow Lake, AB, Canada - YOP
Raipur, India - RPR
Rajkot, India - RAJ
Rajshahi, Bangladesh - RJH
Raleigh/Durham, NC, USA - RDU
Ramata, Solomon Is. - RBV
Ramingining, NT, Australia - RAM
Rampart, AK, USA - RMP
Ranchi, India - IXR
Rangiroa, Fr. Polynesia - RGI
Rankin Inlet, NT, Canada - YRT
Ranong, Thailand - UNN
Rapid City, SD, USA - RAP
Rarotonga, Cook Is. - RAR
Ras Al Khaimah, U. A. Emirates -
   RKT
Rasht, Iran - RAS
Ratanankiri, Cambodia - RBE
Raufarhofn, Iceland - RFN
Rawala Kot, Pakistan - RAZ

Reading, PA, USA - RDG
Rebun, Japan - RBJ
Recife, PE, Brazil - REC
Red Devil, AK, USA - RDV
Red Lake, ON, Canada - YRL
Red Sucker Lake, MB, Canada - YRS
Redcliffe, Vanuatu - RCL
Redding, CA, USA - RDD
Redencao, PA, Brazil - RDC
Redmond, OR, USA - RDM
Reggio Calabria, Italy - REG
Regina, SK, Canada - YQR
Reims, France - RHE
Renmark, SA, Australia - RMK
Rennell Is., Solomon Islands -
   RNL
Rennes, France - RNS
Reno, NV, USA - RNO
Repulse Bay, NT, Canada - YUT
Resistencia, Argentina - RES
Resolute, NT, Canada - YRB
Reus, Spain - REU
Reykjavik, Iceland - REK
Reykjavik-Domestic, Iceland - RKV
Reykjavik-Keflavik, Iceland - KEF
Reynosa, Mexico - REX
Rhinelander, WI, USA - RHI
Rhodes Island, Greece - RHO
Ribeirao Preto, SP, Brazil - RAO
Riberalta, Bolivia - RIB
Richards Bay, South Africa - RCB
Richmond, QLD, Australia - RCM
Richmond, VA, USA - RIC
Riga, Latvia - RIX
Rigolet, NF, Canada - YRG
Rimini, Italy - RMI
Rincon de Los Sauces, Argentina -
   RDS
Ringi Cove, Solomon Islands - RIN
Rio Branco, AC, Brazil - RBR
Rio Cuarto, Argentina - RCU
Rio De Janeiro, RJ, Brazil - RIO
Rio De Janeiro-Dumont, RJ, Brazil
   - SDU
Rio de Janeiro-Int'l, RJ, Brazil
   - GIG
Rio Gallegos, Argentina - RGL
Rio Grande, Argentina - RGA
Rio Grande, RS, Brazil - RIG
Rio Hondo, Argentina - RHD
Riohacha, Colombia - RCH
Rioja, Peru - RIJ
Rishiri, Japan - RIS
Riverton, WY, USA - RIW
Riyadh, Saudi Arabia - RUH

Riyan Mukalla, Yemen - RIY
Roanne, France - RNE
Roanoke, VA, USA - ROA
Roatan, Honduras - RTB
Roberval, PQ, Canada - YRJ
Roche Harbor, WA, USA - RCE
Rochester, MN, USA - RST
Rochester, NY, USA - ROC
Rock Sound, Bahamas - RSD
Rock Springs, WY, USA - RKS
Rockford, IL, USA - RFD
Rockhampton, QLD, Australia - ROK
Rockland, ME, USA - RKD
Rocky Mount/Wilson, NC, USA - RWI
Rodez, France - RDZ
Rodrigues Is., Mauritius - RRG
Rodriguez De Mendoza, Peru - RIM
Roervik, Norway - RVK
Roma, QLD, Australia - RMA
Rome, Italy - ROM
Rome-Ciampino, Italy - CIA
Rome-Da Vinci, Italy - FCO
Rondonopolis, MT, Brazil - ROO
Ronneby, Sweden - RNB
Roros, Norway - RRS
Rosario, Argentina - ROS
Rosario, WA, USA - RSJ
Rosh-Pina, Galilee, Israel - RPN
Rosita, Nicaragua - RFS
Rost, Norway - RET
Rostock-Laage, Germany - RLG
Rostov, Russia - ROV
Roswell, NM, USA - ROW
Rota, Mariana Islands - ROP
Rotorua, New Zealand - ROT
Rotterdam, Netherlands - RTM
Rottnest Is., WA, Australia - RTS
Rotuma, Fiji - RTA
Rouen, France - URO
Round Lake, ON, Canada - ZRJ
Rouyn-Noranda, PQ, Canada - YUY
Rovaniemi, Finland - RVN
Roxas City, Philippines - RXS
Ruby, AK, USA - RBY
Rurutu Is., Fr. Polynesia - RUR
Russian Mission, AK, USA - RSH
Rutland, VT, USA - RUT
Saarbruecken, Germany - SCN
Saarbruecken Hbf Rail Station,
    Germany - QFZ
Saba, Neth. Antilles - SAB
Sachigo Lake, ON, Canada - ZPB
Sachs Harbour, NT, Canada - YSY
Sacramento, CA, USA - SAC

Sacramento-International, CA, USA
    - SMF
Safia, Papua New Guinea - SFU
Saginaw, MI, USA - MBS
Saguenay, PQ, Canada - YBG
Sahabat 16, Malaysia - SXS
Saibai Is., QLD, Australia - SBR
Saidor, Papua New Guinea - SDI
Saidpur, Bangladesh - SPD
Saidu Sharif, Pakistan - SDT
Saint John, NB, Canada - YSJ
Saipan, Mariana Islands - SPN
Sakon Nakhon, Thailand - SNO
Sal, Cape Verde Islands - SID
Salalah, Oman - SLL
Salamanca, Spain - SLM
Salamo, Papua New Guinea - SAM
Sale, Vic., Australia - SXE
Salehard, Russia - SLY
Salina Cruz, Mexico - SCX
Salina, KS, USA - SLN
Salisbury, MD, USA - SBY
Salluit, PQ, Canada - YZG
Salmon Arm, BC, Canada - YSN
Salt Cay, Turks & Caicos Is. -
    SLX
Salt Lake City, UT, USA - SLC
Salta, Argentina - SLA
Saltillo, Mexico - SLW
Salvador, BA, Brazil - SSA
Salzburg, Austria - SZG
Sam Neua, Laos - NEU
Samara, Russia - KUF
Samarinda, Indonesia - SRI
Samarkand, Uzbekistan - SKD
Sambava, Madagascar - SVB
Sambu, Panama - SAX
Samburu, Kenya - UAS
Samos Island, Greece - SMI
Sampit, Indonesia - SMQ
Samsum, Turkey - SSX
San Andres Is., Colombia - ADZ
San Andros, Bahamas - SAQ
San Angelo, TX, USA - SJT
San Antonio, Venezuela - SVZ
San Antonio, TX, USA - SAT
San Bernardino, CA, USA - SBT
San Borja, Bolivia - SRJ
San Carlos, Nicaragua - NCR
San Carlos de Bariloche,
    Argentina - BRC
San Christobal, Ecuador - SCY
San Christobal De Las Casas,
    Mexico - SZT
San Diego, CA, USA - SAN

San Fernando De Apure, Venezuela
  - SFD
San Francisco, CA-Oakland, USA -
  OAK
San Francisco/Oakland, CA, USA -
  SFO
San Joaquin, Bolivia - SJB
San Jorge Island, Portugal
  (Azores) - SJZ
San Jose, Costa Rica - SJO
San Jose, Philippines - SJI
San Jose, CA, USA - SJC
San Jose Tobias Bolanos, Costa
  Rica - SYQ
San Juan, Argentina - UAQ
San Juan, Puerto Rico - SJU
San Juan-Isla Grand, Puerto Rico
  - SIG
San Luis, Argentina - LUQ
San Luis Obispo, CA, USA - CSL
San Luis Obispo County, CA, USA -
  SBP
San Luis Potosi, Mexico - SLP
San Martin de Los Andes,
  Argentina - CPC
San Miguel, Panama - NMG
San Pedro, Belize - SPR
San Pedro Sula, Honduras - SAP
San Rafael, Argentina - AFA
San Salvador, Bahamas - ZSA
San Salvador, El Salvador - SAL
San Sebastian, Spain - EAS
San Tome, Venezuela - SOM
Sanaa, Yemen - SAH
Sand Point, AK, USA - SDP
Sandakan, Sabah, Malaysia - SDK
Sandane, Norway - SDN
Sanday, UK - NDY
Sandefjord, Norway - TRF
Sandnessjoen, Norway - SSJ
Sandspit, BC, Canada - YZP
Sandy Lake, ON, Canada - ZSJ
Sanikiluaq, NT, Canada - YSK
Sanliurfa, Turkey - SFQ
Santa Barbara, CA, USA - SBA
Santa Cruz, Bolivia - SRZ
Santa Cruz, Solomon Islands - SCZ
Santa Cruz La Palma, Canary
  Islands - SPC
Santa Cruz, Flores, Portugal
  (Azores) - FLW
Santa Cruz, Viru Viru, Bolivia -
  VVI
Santa Elena, Venezuela - SNV
Santa Fe, Argentina - SFN

Santa Fe, NM, USA - SAF
Santa Maria, Portugal (Azores) -
  SMA
Santa Maria, RS, Brazil - RIA
Santa Maria, CA, USA - SMX
Santa Marta, Colombia - SMR
Santa Rosa, Argentina - RSA
Santa Rosa, RS, Brazil - SRA
Santa Rosa, CA, USA - STS
Santander, Spain - SDR
Santarem, PA, Brazil - STM
Santiago, Chile - SCL
Santiago, Cuba - SCU
Santiago, Dominican Rep. - STI
Santiago, Panama - SYP
Santiago De Compostela, Spain -
  SCQ
Santiago Del Estero, Argentina -
  SDE
Santiago Los Cerrillos, Chile -
  ULC
Santo Angelo, RS, Brazil - GEL
Santo Antao, Cape Verde Islands -
  NTO
Santo Domingo, Dominican Rep. -
  SDQ
Santo Domingo, Venezuela - STD
Santorini, Thira Is., Greece -
  JTR
Sanya, P.R. China - SYX
Sao Felix Do Araguaia, MT, Brazil
  - SXO
Sao Filipe, Cape Verde Is. - SFL
Sao Jorge Is., Portugal - SJZ
Sao Jose Do Rio Preto, SP, Brazil
  - SJP
Sao Jose Dos Campos, SP, Brazil -
  SJK
Sao Luiz, MA, Brazil - SLZ
Sao Nicolau, Cape Verde Is. -
  SNE
Sao Paulo, SP, Brazil - SAO
Sao Paulo-Congonhas, SP, Brazil -
  CGH
Sao Paulo-Grarulhos, SP, Brazil -
  GRU
Sao Tome Island, Sao Tome - TMS
Sao Vicente, Cape Verde Is. -
  VXE
Sapporo, Japan - SPK
Sapporo-Chitose, Japan - CTS
Sapporo-Okadama, Japan - OKD
Sara, Vanuatu - SSR
Sarajevo, Bosnia & Herzegovina -
  SJJ

Saranac Lake, NY, USA - SLK
Sarasota/Bradenton, FL, USA - SRQ
Saratov, Russia - RTW
Sarnia, ON, Canada - YZR
Sary, Iran - SRY
Saskatoon, SK, Canada - YXE
Satu Mare, Romania - SUJ
Satwag, Papua New Guinea - SWG
Saudarkrokur, Iceland - SAK
Sault Ste. Marie, MI, USA - SSM
Sault Ste. Marie, MI-Chippewa,
   USA - CIU
Sault Ste. Marie, ON, Canada -
   YAM
Sauren, Papua New Guinea - SXW
Saurimo, Angola - VHC
Savannah, GA, USA - SAV
Savannakhet, Laos - ZVK
Savonlinna, Finland - SVL
Savoonga, AK, USA - SVA
Savusavu, Fiji - SVU
Sayaboury, Laos - ZBY
Scammon Bay, AK, USA - SCM
Schefferville, PQ, Canada - YKL
Scone, NSW, Australia - NSO
Scottsbluff, NE, USA - BFF
Seal Bay, AK, USA - SYB
Seaplane Base, VI, USA - SSB
Seattle, WA-Lake Union, USA - LKE
Seattle/Tacoma, WA, USA - SEA
Sege, Solomon Islands - EGM
Sehulea, Papua New Guinea - SXH
Sehwen Sharif, Pakistan - SYW
Seinajoki, Finland - SJY
Seiyun, Yemen - GXF
Selawik, AK, USA - WLK
Selibaby, Mauritania - SEY
Selje Harbour, Norway - QFK
Semarang, Indonesia - SRG
Semipalatinsk, Kazakstan - PLX
Semporna, Sabah, Malaysia - SMM
Sendai, Japan - SDJ
Seoul, Rep. of Korea - SEL
Sept-Iles, PQ, Canada - YZV
Sevilla, Spain - SVQ
Seward, AK, USA - SWD
Sfax, Tunisia - SFA
Shageluk, AK, USA - SHX
Shaktoolik, AK, USA - SKK
Shamattawa, MB, Canada - ZTM
Shanghai, P.R. China - SHA
Shannon, Rep. of Ireland - SNN
Shantou, P.R. China - SWA
Sharjah, U. A. Emirates - SHJ
Sharm El Sheik, Egypt - SSH

Sharurah, Saudi Arabia - SHW
Shashi, P.R. China - SHS
Sheffield, UK - SZD
Shehdi, Ethiopia - SQJ
Sheldon Point, AK, USA - SXP
Shenandoah Valley Arpt., VA, USA
   - SHD
Shenyang, P.R. China - SHE
Shenzhen, P.R. China - SZX
Shepparton, VIC, Australia - SHT
Sheridan, WY, USA - SHR
Shetland Is., Scotland, UK - SDZ
Shijiazhuang, P.R. China - SJW
Shillavo, Ethiopia - HIL
Shimkent, Kazakstan - CIT
Shiraz, Iran - SYZ
Shishmaref, AK, USA - SHH
Shonai, Japan - SYO
Shreveport, LA, USA - SHV
Shungnak, AK, USA - SHG
Shute Harbour, QLD, Australia -
   JHQ
Sibiu, Romania - SBZ
Sibu, Sarawak, Malaysia - SBW
Sidney, MT, USA - SDY
Siem Reap, Cambodia - REP
Siirt, Turkey - SXZ
Sila, Papua New Guinea - SIL
Silchar, India - IXS
Silur, Papua New Guinea - SWR
Silver City, NM, USA - SVC
Simao, P.R. China - SYM
Simferopol, Ukraine - SIP
Simikot, Nepal - IMK
Simla, India - SLV
Simra, Nepal - SIF
Sindal, Denmark - CNL
Singapore, Singapore - SIN
Singapore-Seletar, Singapore -
   XSP
Singleton, NSW, Australia - SIX
Sinop, MT, Brazil - OPS
Sinop, Turkey - SIC
Sintang, Indonesia - SQG
Sion, Switzerland - SIR
Sioux City, IA, USA - SUX
Sioux Falls, SD, USA - FSD
Sioux Lookout, ON, Canada - YXL
Sisimuit, Greenland - JHS
Sitia, Greece - JSH
Sitka, AK, USA - SIT
Sittwe, Myanmar - AKY
Siuna, Nicaragua - SIU
Sivas, Turkey - VAS
Skagway, AK, USA - SGY

Skardu, Pakistan - KDU
Skelleftea, Sweden - SFT
Skiathos, Greece - JSI
Skien, Norway - SKE
Skopje, Macedonia - SKP
Skovde, Sweden - KVB
Skukuza, South Africa - SZK
Sleetmute, AK, USA - SLQ
Sligo, Rep. of Ireland - SXL
Smara, Morocco - SMW
Smith Cove, AK, USA - SCJ
Smithers, BC, Canada - YYD
Snake Bay, NT, Australia - SNB
Snare Lake, NT, Canada - YFJ
Soalala, Madagascar - DWB
Socotra, Yemen - SCT
Soderhamn, Sweden - SOO
Sofia, Bulgaria - SOF
Sogndal, Norway - SOG
Sokcho, Rep. of Korea - SHO
Sokoto, Nigeria - SKO
Sola, Vanuatu - SLH
Solo City, Indonesia - SOC
Son-La, Vietnam - SQH
Sonderborg, Denmark - SGD
Sorkjosen, Norway - SOJ
Sorocaba, SP, Brazil - SOD
Sorong, Indonesia - SOQ
South Andros, Bahamas - TZN
South Bend, IN, USA - SBN
South Caicos., Turks & Caicos Is. - XSC
South Indian Lake, MB, Canada - XSI
South Molle Is., QLD, Australia - SOI
South Naknek, AK, USA - WSN
South West Bay, Vanuatu - SWJ
Southampton, England, UK - SOU
Southern Cross, WA, Australia - SQC
Soyo, Angola - SZA
Spencer, IA, USA - SPW
Split, Croatia - SPU
Spokane, WA, USA - GEG
Spring Point, Bahamas - AXP
Springbok, South Africa - SBU
Springfield, IL, USA - SPI
Springfield, MO, USA - SGF
Srinagar, India - SXR
St. Anthony, NF, Canada - YAY
St. Barthelemy, Leeward Islands - SBH
St. Brieuc, France - SBK
St. Cloud, MN, USA - STC

St. Croix, Virgin Islands - STX
St. Etienne, France - EBU
St. Eustatius, Neth. Antilles - EUX
St. George Island, AK, USA - STG
St. George, QLD, Australia - SGO
St. George, UT, USA - SGU
St. Johns, NF, Canada - YYT
St. Kitts, Leeward Islands - SKB
St. Leonard, NB, Canada - YSL
St. Louis, MO, USA - STL
St. Lucia, West Indies - SLU
St. Lucia-Hewanorra, West Indies - UVF
St. Maarten, Neth. Antilles - SXM
St. Marie, Madagascar - SMS
St. Martin, French Antilles - SFG
St. Mary's, AK, USA - KSM
St. Michael, AK, USA - SMK
St. Paul Island, AK, USA - SNP
St. Petersburg, Russia - LED
St. Petersburg, FL, USA - PIE
St. Pierre, St. Pierre and Miquelon - FSP
St. Therese Pt., MB, Canada - YST
St. Thomas, Virgin Islands - STT
St. Thomas SPB, Virgin Islands - SPB
St. Vincent, Windward Islands - SVD
State College, PA, USA - SCE
Stavanger, Norway - SVG
Stavropol, Russia - STW
Steamboat Springs, CO, USA - SBS
Steamboat Springs - Hayden, CO, USA - HDN
Stebbins, AK, USA - WBB
Stella Maris, L.I., Bahamas - SML
Stephenville, NF, Canada - YJT
Sterling/Rock Falls, IL, USA - SQI
Stevens Village, AK, USA - SVS
Stockholm, Sweden - STO
Stockholm-Arlanda, Sweden - ARN
Stockholm-Bromma, Sweden - BMA
Stokmarknes, Norway - SKN
Stony Rapids, SK, Canada - YSF
Stony River, AK, USA - SRV
Stony River, AK, USA - SRV
Stord, Norway - SRP
Stornoway, Scotland, UK - SYY
Storuman, Sweden - SQO
Strasbourg, France - SXB
Stronsay, UK - SOY
Strzhewoi, Russia - SWT

Stung Treng, Cambodia - TNX
Stuttgart, Germany - STR
Suavanao, Solomon Is. - VAO
Subic Bay, Philippines - SFS
Suceava, Romania - SCV
Sucre, Bolivia - SRE
Sudbury, ON, Canada - YSB
Sui, Pakistan - SUL
Sukhothai, Thailand - THS
Sukkur, Pakistan - SKZ
Sule, Papua New Guinea - ULE
Sumburgh, UK - LSI
Summer Beaver, ON, Canada - SUR
Sun City, South Africa - NTY
Sun Valley, ID, USA - SUN
Sundsvall, Sweden - SDL
Sunshine Coast, QLD, Australia -
    MCY
Sur, Oman - SUH
Surabaya, Indonesia - SUB
Surat Thani, Thailand - URT
Surgut, Russia - SGC
Surkhet, Nepal - SKH
Suva, Fiji - SUV
Sveg, Sweden - EVG
Svolvaer, Norway - SVJ
Swakopmund, Namibia - SWP
Swan River, MB, Canada - ZJN
Sydney, NSW, Australia - SYD
Sydney, NS, Canada - YQY
Sydney, NS, Canada - YQV
Sylhet, Bangladesh - ZYL
Syracuse, NY, USA - SYR
Syros Is., Greece - JSY
Szczecin, Poland - SZZ
Ta'u Island, American Samoa - TAV
Taba, Egypt - TCP
Tabatinga, AM, Brazil - TBT
Tabora, Tanzania - TBO
Tabriz, Iran - TBZ
Tabubil, Papua New Guinea - TBG
Tabuk, Saudi Arabia - TUU
Tacheng, P.R. China - TCG
Tachilek, Myanmar - THL
Tacloban, Philippines - TAC
Tacna, Peru - TCQ
Tadji, Papua New Guinea - TAJ
Tadoule Lake, MB, Canada - XTL
Taegu, Rep. of Korea - TAE
Tagbilaran, Philippines - TAG
Taichung, Taiwan - TXG
Taif, Saudi Arabia - TIF
Tainan, Taiwan - TNN
Taipei, Taiwan - TPE
Taipei-Sung Shan, Taiwan - TSA

Taitung, Taiwan - TTT
Taiyuan, P.R. China - TYN
Taiz, Yemen - TAI
Takamatsu, Japan - TAK
Takapoto Is., Fr. Polynesia - TKP
Takaroa, French Polynesia - TKX
Takotna, AK, USA - TCT
Talara, Peru - TYL
Tallahassee, FL, USA - TLH
Tallinn, Estonia - TLL
Taloyak, NT, Canada - YYH
Tamanrasset, Algeria - TMR
Tamarindo, Costa Rica - TNO
Tamatave, Madagascar - TMM
Tambacounda, Senegal - TUD
Tambohorano, Madagascar - WTA
Tambor, Costa Rica - TMU
Tampa/St. Petersburg, FL, USA -
    TPA
Tampere, Finland - TMP
Tampico, Mexico - TAM
Tamworth, NSW, Australia - TMW
Tanana, AK, USA - TAL
Tanegashima, Japan - TNE
Tangier, Morocco - TNG
Tanjung Pandan, Indonesia - TJQ
Tanjung Selor, Indonesia - TJS
Tanna Island, Vanuatu - TAH
Tapachula, Mexico - TAP
Tapini, Papua New Guinea - TPI
Taplejung, Nepal - TPJ
Tarakan, Indonesia - TRK
Taramajima, Japan - TRA
Tarapoto, Peru - TPP
Tarawa, Kiribati - TRW
Taree, NSW, Australia - TRO
Tari, Papua New Guinea - TIZ
Tarija, Bolivia - TJA
Tartagal, Argentina - TTG
Tashkent, Uzbekistan - TAS
Tasiujuaq, PQ, Canada - YTQ
Tatalina, AK, USA - TLJ
Tatry/Poprad, Slovak Republic -
    TAT
Taupo, New Zealand - TUO
Tauranga, New Zealand - TRG
Taveuni, Fiji - TVU
Tawau, Sabah, Malaysia - TWU
Tbessa, Algeria - TEE
Tbilisi, Georgia - TBS
Tchibanga, Gabon - TCH
Te Anau, New Zealand - TEU
Teesside, England, UK - MME
Tefe, AM, Brazil - TFF
Tegucigalpa, Honduras - TGU

Tehran, Iran - THR
Tekadu, Papua New Guinea - TKB
Tel Aviv-Ben Gurion, Israel - TLV
Tel Aviv-Sde Dov, Israel - SDV
Telefomin, Papua New Guinea - TFM
Telemaco Borba, PR, Brazil - TEC
Teller, AK, USA - TLA
Telluride, CO, USA - TEX
Tembagapura, Indonesia - TIM
Temuco, Chile - ZCO
Tenakee, AK, USA - TKE
Tenerife, Canary Islands - TCI
Tenerife-Norte Los Rodeos, Canary
    Is. - TFN
Tenerife-Sur Reina Sofia, Canary
    Islands - TFS
Tennant Creek, NT, Australia -
    TCA
Tepic, Mexico - TPQ
Teptep, Papua New Guinea - TEP
Terapo, Papua New Guinea - TEO
Terceira, Portugal (Azores) - TER
Teresina, PI, Brazil - THE
Termez, Uzbekistan - TMJ
Ternate, Indonesia - TTE
Terrace, BC, Canada - YXT
Terre-De-Haut, Guadeloupe - LSS
Terre Haute, IN, USA - HUF
Tetabedi, Papua New Guinea - TDB
Tete, Mozambique - TET
Tete A La Baleine, PQ, Canada -
    ZTB
Tetlin, AK, USA - TEH
Tetuan, Morocco - TTU
Texarkana, AR, USA - TXK
Tezpur, India - TEZ
Thandwe, Myanmar - SNW
Thangool, QLD, Australia - THG
Thargomindah, QLD, Australia -
    XTG
The Bight, Bahamas - TBI
The Pas, MB, Canada - YQD
Thessaloniki, Greece - SKG
Thief River Falls, MN, USA - TVF
Thisted, Denmark - TED
Thompson, MB, Canada - YTH
Thorne Bay, AK, USA - KTB
Thorshofn, Iceland - THO
Thunder Bay, ON, Canada - YQT
Thursday Is., QLD, Australia -
    TIS
Tianjin, P.R. China - TSN
Tiaret, Algeria - TID
Tidjikja, Mauritania - TIY
Tiga, Loyalty Is. - TGJ

Tijuana, Mexico - TIJ
Tikehau, Fr. Polynesia - TIH
Tilimsen, Algeria - TLM
Timaru, New Zealand - TIU
Timbunke, Papua New Guinea - TBE
Timimoun, Algeria - TMX
Timisoara, Romania - TSR
Timmins, ON, Canada - YTS
Tin City, AK, USA - TNC
Tinak, Marshall Is. - TIC
Tindouf, Algeria - TIN
Tingo Maria, Peru - TGI
Tinian, Mariana Islands - TIQ
Tioman, Malaysia - TOD
Tippi, Ethiopia - TIE
Tirana, Albania - TIA
Tiree Island, Scotland, UK - TRE
Tirgu Mures, Romania - TGM
Tiruchirapally, India - TRZ
Tirupati, India - TIR
Tivat, Yugoslavia - TIV
Tlemcen, Algeria - TLM
Tobago, Trinidad & Tobago - TAB
Tofino, BC, Canada - YAZ
Togiak, AK, USA - TOG
Tok, AK, USA - TKJ
Tokat, Turkey - TJK
Toksook, AK, USA - OOK
Tokuno Shima, Japan - TKN
Tokushima, Japan - TKS
Tokyo, Japan - TYO
Tokyo-Haneda, Japan - HND
Tokyo-Narita, Japan - NRT
Toledo, PR, Brazil - TOW
Toledo, OH, USA - TOL
Tom Price, WA, Australia - TPR
Tomanggong, Malaysia - TMG
Tombouctou, Mali - TOM
Tomsk, Russia - TOF
Tongatapu, Tonga Island - TBU
Tongoa, Vanuatu - TGH
Toowoomba, QLD, Australia - TWB
Topeka, KS, USA - TOP
Topeka, KS-Forbes, USA - FOE
Toronto, ON, Canada - YTO
Toronto, ON-Int'l, Canada - YYZ
Toronto, ON-Toronto Is., Canada -
    YTZ
Torreon, Mexico - TRC
Torres, Vanuatu - TOH
Torsby, Sweden - TYF
Tortola, BVI - EIS
Tortuquero, Costa Rica - TTQ
Tottori, Japan - TTJ
Touggourt, Algeria - TGR

Touho, New Caledonia - TOU
Toulon-Hyeres, France - TLN
Toulouse, France - TLS
Tours, France - TUF
Townsville, QLD, Australia - TSV
Toyama, Japan - TOY
Toyooka, Japan - TJH
Tozeur, Tunisia - TOE
Trabzon, Turkey - TZX
Trang, Thailand - TST
Trapani, Italy - TPS
Traralgon, VIC, Australia - TGN
Traverse City, MI, USA - TVC
Treasure Cay, Bahamas - TCB
Trelew, Argentina - REL
Trenton, NJ, USA - TTN
Tri-City Airport, TN, USA - TRI
Trieste, Italy - TRS
Trinidad, Bolivia - TDD
Trivandrum, India - TRV
Trollhattan, Sweden - THN
Trombetas, PA, Brazil - TMT
Tromso, Norway - TOS
Trondheim, Norway - TRD
Trujillo, Honduras - TJI
Trujillo, Peru - TRU
Truk, Caroline Is. - TKK
Tsaratanana, Madagascar - TTS
Tshikapa, Dem. Rep. of the Congo
  - TSH
Tsiroanomandidy, Madagascar - WTS
Tsumeb, Namibia - TSB
Tsushima, Japan - TSJ
Tubuai Is., Austral Is. - TUB
Tucson, AZ, USA - TUS
Tucuma, PA, Brazil - TUZ
Tucuman, Argentina - TUC
Tucurui, PA, Brazil - TUR
Tufi, Papua New Guinea - TFI
Tuguegarao, Philippines - TUG
Tuktoyaktuk, NT, Canada - YUB
Tulear, Madagascar - TLE
Tulita Fort Norman, NT, Canada -
  ZFN
Tulsa, OK, USA - TUL
Tuluksak, AK, USA - TLT
Tum, Ethiopia - TUJ
Tumaco, Colombia - TCO
Tumbes, Peru - TBP
Tumlingtar, Nepal - TMI
Tunis, Tunisia - TUN
Tuntatuliak, AK, USA - WTL
Tununak, AK, USA - TNK
Tunxi, P.R. China - TXN
Tupelo, MS, USA - TUP

Turaif, Saudi Arabia - TUI
Turbat, Pakistan - TUK
Turbo, Colombia - TRB
Turin, Italy - TRN
Turkmanbashi, Turkmenistan - KRW
Turku, Finland - TKU
Tuxtla Gutierrez, Mexico - TGZ
Tuyhoa, Vietnam - TBB
Twin Falls, ID, USA - TWF
Twin Hills, AK, USA - TWA
Tyler, TX, USA - TYR
Tyumen, Russia - TJM
Ube, Japan - UBJ
Uberaba, MG, Brazil - UBA
Uberlandia, MG, Brazil - UDI
Ubon Ratchathani, Thailand - UBP
Udaipur, India - UDR
Udon Thani, Thailand - UTH
Ufa, Russia - UFA
Uganik, AK, USA - UGI
Ujae Island, Marshall Islands -
  UJE
Ujung Pandang, Indonesia - UPG
Ukunda, Kenya - UKA
Ulaanbaatar, Mongolia - ULN
Ulan-Ude, Russia - UUD
Ulei, Vanuatu - ULB
Ulsan, Rep. of Korea - USN
Ulundi, South Africa - ULD
Umea, Sweden - UME
Umiujaq, PQ, Canada - YUD
Umtata, South Africa - UTT
Unalakleet, AK, USA - UNK
Union Island, Windward Islands -
  UNI
Unst. Shetland Is., Scotland, UK
  - UNT
Upernavik, Greenland - JUV
Upington, South Africa - UTN
Uraj, Russia - URJ
Uralsk, Kazakstan - URA
Urgench, Uzbekistan - UGC
Uranium City, SK, Canada - YBE
Urmieh, Iran - OMH
Urrao, Colombia - URR
Uruapan, Mexico - UPN
Uruguaiana, RS, Brazil - URG
Urumqi, P.R. China - URC
Useless Loop, WA, Australia - USL
Ushuaia, Argentina - USH
Ust-Ilimsk, Russia - UIK
Ust-Kamenogorsk, Kazakstan - UKK
Utapao, Thailand - UTP
Utica, NY, USA - UCA
Utila Island, Honduras - UII

Utirik, Marshall Islands - UTK
Utopia Creek, AK, USA - UTO
Uummannaq, Greenland - UMD
Uvol, Papua New Guinea - UVO
Uzhgorod, Ukraine - UDJ
Vaasa, Finland - VAA
Vadodara, India - BDQ
Vadso, Norway - VDS
Vaeroy, Norway - VRY
Vail/Eagle, CO, USA - EGE
Val D'or, PQ, Canada - YVO
Valdez, AK, USA - VDZ
Valdivia, Chile - ZAL
Valdosta, GA, USA - VLD
Valencia, Venezuela - VLN
Valencia, Spain - VLC
Valencia, Venezuela - VLN
Valesdir, Vanuatu - VLS
Valladolid, Spain - VLL
Valledupar, Colombia - VUP
Vallenar, Chile - VLR
Valverde, Canary Is. - VDE
Van, Turkey - VAN
Vancouver, BC, Canada - YVR
Vancouver, BC Harbour-SP, Canada
    - CXH
Vanimo, Papua New Guinea - VAI
Vanuabalavu, Fiji - VBV
Varadero, Cuba - VRA
Varanasi, India - VNS
Vardoe, Norway - VAW
Varginha, MG, Brazil - VAG
Varkaus, Finland - VRK
Varna, Bulgaria - VAR
Vasteras, Sweden - VST
Vatomandry, Madagascar - VAT
Vava'U, Tonga Island - VAV
Vaxjo, Sweden - VXO
Venetie, AK, USA - VEE
Venice, Italy - VCE
Venice-Treviso, Italy - TSF
Veracruz, Mexico - VER
Vernal, UT, USA - VEL
Verona, Italy - VRN
Vestmannaeyjar, Iceland - VEY
Victoria, BC, Canada - YYJ
Victoria, BC-Inner Harb., Canada
    - YWH
Victoria, TX, USA - VCT
Victoria Falls, Zimbabwe - VFA
Victoria River Downs, NT,
    Australia - VCD
Videira, SC, Brazil - VIA
Viedma, Argentina - VDM
Vienna, Austria - VIE

Vientiane, Laos - VTE
Vieques, Puerto Rico - VQS
Vigo, Spain - VGO
Vila Real, Portugal - VRL
Vila Rica, MT, Brazil - VLP
Vilanculos, Mozambique - VNX
Vilhemina, Sweden - VHM
Vilhena, RO, Brazil - BVH
Villa Gesell, Argentina - VLG
Villa Mercedes, Argentina - VME
Villahermosa, Mexico - VSA
Villavicencio, Colombia - VVC
Vilnius, Lithuania - VNO
Vinh City, Vietnam - VII
Vina Del Mar, Chile - KNA
Virac, Philippines - VRC
Virgin Gorda, BVI - VIJ
Visalia, CA, USA - VIS
Visby, Sweden - VBY
Vishakhapatnam, India - VTZ
Vitoria, ES, Brazil - VIX
Vitoria, Spain - VIT
Vitoria Da Conquista, BA, Brazil
    - VDC
Vivigani, Papua New Guinea - VIV
Vladikavkaz, Russia - OGZ
Vladivostok, Russia - VVO
Vohemar, Madagascar - VOH
Vojens, Denmark - SKS
Volgograd, Russia - VOG
Vopnafjordur, Iceland - VPN
Voronezh, Russia - VOZ
Wabush, NF, Canada - YWK
Waco, TX, USA - ACT
Wadi-Ad-Dawasir, Saudi Arabia -
    WAE
Wagga-Wagga, NSW, Australia - WGA
Waingapu, Indonesia - WGP
Wainwright, AK, USA - AIN
Wairoa, New Zealand - WIR
Wakkanai, Japan - WKJ
Walaha, Vanuatu - WLH
Wales, AK, USA - WAA
Walgett, NSW, Australia - WGE
Walla Walla, WA, USA - ALW
Wallis Is., Wallis & Futuna Is. -
    WLS
Walvis Bay, South Africa - WVB
Wanaka, New Zealand - WKA
Wanganui, New Zealand - WAG
Wangerooge, Fed. Rep. of Germany
    - AGE
Wanigela, Papua New Guinea - AGL
Wanxian, P.R. China - WXN

Wapenamanda, Papua New Guinea - WBM
Wapolu, Papua New Guinea - WBC
Warraber Island, QLD, Australia - SYU
Warsaw, Poland - WAW
Washington, DC, USA - WAS
Washington-Dulles, DC, USA - IAD
Washington-Ronald Reagan, DC, USA - DCA
Waskaganish, PQ, Canada - YKQ
Waspam, Nicaragua - WSP
Wasu, Papua New Guinea - WSU
Wasum, Papua New Guinea - WUM
Waterfall, AK, USA - KWF
Waterford, Rep. of Ireland - WAT
Waterloo, IA, USA - ALO
Watertown, NY, USA - ART
Watertown, SD, USA - ATY
Watson Lake, YK, Canada - YQH
Wau, Papua New Guinea - WUG
Wausau, WI, USA - AUW
Wausau-Central Wisc., WI, USA - CWA
Wawa, ON, Canada - YXZ
Webequie, ON, Canada - YWP
Wedau, Papua New Guinea - WED
Wedjh, Saudi Arabia - EJH
Weipa, QLD, Australia - WEI
Wellington, New Zealand - WLG
Wemindji, PQ, Canada - YNC
Wenatchee, WA, USA - EAT
Wenzhou, P.R. China - WNZ
West Palm Beach, FL, USA - PBI
West Point, AK, USA - KWP
West Wyalong, NSW, Australia - WWY
Westchester County, NY, USA - HPN
Westerland, Germany - GWT
Westerly, RI, USA - WST
Westport, New Zealand - WSZ
Westray, UK - WRY
Westsound, WA, USA - WSX
Wewak, Papua New Guinea - WWK
Whakatane, New Zealand - WHK
Whale Cove, NT, Canada - YXN
Whale Pass, AK, USA - WWP
Whangarei, New Zealand - WRE
Wha Ti Lac Martre, NT, Canada - YLE
White Mountain, AK, USA - WMO
Whitehorse, YK, Canada - YXY
Whyalla, SA, Australia - WYA
Wichita, KS, USA - ICT
Wichita Falls, TX, USA - SPS

Wick, Scotland, UK - WIC
Wilhelmshaven, Germany - WVN
Wilkes-Barre/Scranton, PA, USA - AVP
Williams Lake, BC, Canada - YWL
Williamsport, PA, USA - IPT
Williston, ND, USA - ISN
Wilmington, NC, USA - ILM
Wiluna, WA, Australia - WUN
Windhoek, Namibia - WDH
Windhoek-Eros, Namibia - WDH
Windorah, QLD, Australia - WNR
Windsor, ON, Canada - YQG
Winnipeg, MB, Canada - YWG
Winton, QLD, Australia - WIN
Woitape, Papua New Guinea - WTP
Woja, Marshall Is. - WJA
Wolf Point, MT, USA - OLF
Wollaston Lake, SK, Canada - ZWL
Woomera, SA, Australia - UMR
Won-Ju, Rep. of Korea - WJU
Woomera, SA, Australia - UMR
Worcester, MA, USA - ORH
Worland, WY, USA - WRL
Wotho, Marshall Islands - WTO
Wotje, Marshall Islands - WTE
Wrangell, AK, USA - WRG
Wrigley, NT, Canada - YWY
Wroclaw, Poland - WRO
Wudinna, SA, Australia - WUD
Wuhan, P.R. China - WUH
Wunnummin Lake, ON, Canada - WNN
Wuyishan, P.R. China - WUS
Wyndham, WA, Australia - WYN
Xi An, P.R. China - SIA
Xiamen, P.R. China - XMN
Xiangfan, P.R. China - XFN
Xianyang, P.R. China - XIY
Xichang, P.R. China - XIC
Xieng Khouang, Laos - XKH
Xining, P.R. China - XNN
Xuzhou, P.R. China - XUZ
Yakima, WA, USA - YKM
Yakushima, Japan - KUM
Yakutat, AK, USA - YAK
Yakutsk, Russia - YKS
Yalumet, Papua New Guinea - KYX
Yam Island, QLD, Australia - XMY
Yamagata, Honshu, Japan - GAJ
Yan'an, P.R. China - ENY
Yanbu, Saudi Arabia - YNB
Yandina, Solomon Islands - XYA
Yangon, Myanmar - RGN
Yanji, P.R. China - YNJ
Yankton, SD, USA - YKN

Yantai, P.R. China - YNT
Yaounde, Cameroon - YAO
Yaounde-Nsimalen, Carevoon - NSI
Yap, Caroline Is. - YAP
Yarmouth, NS, Canada - YQI
Yazd, Iran - AZD
Yechon, Rep. of Korea - YEC
Yelimane, Mali - EYL
Yellowknife, NT, Canada - YZF
Yerevan, Armenia - EVN
Yibin, P.R. China - YBP
Yichang, P.R. China - YIH
Yinchuan, P.R. China - INC
Yining, P.R. China - YIN
Yiwu, P.R. China - YIW
Yogyakarta, Indonesia - JOG
Yola, Nigeria - YOL
Yonago, Japan - YGJ
Yonaguni-Jima, Japan - OGN
York Landing, MB, Canada - ZAC
Yorke Island, QLD, Australia -
   OKR
Yosemite Nat'l Park, CA, USA -
   OYS
Yoron-Jima, Japan - RNJ
Yosu, Rep. of Korea - RSU
Young, NSW, Australia - NGA
Youngstown, OH, USA - YNG
Yulin, P.R. China - UYN
Yuma, AZ, USA - YUM
Yurimaguas, Peru - YMS
Yuzhno-Sakhalinsk, Russia - UUS
Zacatecas, Mexico - ZCL
Zachar Bay, AK, USA - KZB
Zagreb, Yugoslavia - ZAG
Zahedan, Iran - ZAH
Zakinthos, Greece - ZTH
Zamboanga, Philippines - ZAM
Zanzibar, Tanzania - ZNZ
Zapala, Argentina - APZ
Zaporozhye, Ukraine - OZH
Zaragoza, Spain - ZAZ
Zhanyiang, P.R. China - ZHA
Zhaotong, P.R. China - ZAT
Zhengzhou, P.R. China - CGO
Zhob, Pakistan - PZH
Zhoushan, P.R. China - HSN
Zhuhai, P.R. China - ZUH
Ziguinchor, Senegal - ZIG
Zilina, Slovakia - ILZ
Zouerate, Mauritania - OUZ
Zurich, Switzerland - ZRH

NOTES

AIRLINE CODES

Airline codes and accounting numbers are essential for the identification of passenger and cargo traffic documents.

Because of the limited number of possibilities with two-letters, three-letter designations will be necessary. The ATA (Air Transport Association) and IATA (International Air Transport Association) will agree on a conversion date for the use of three-letter designations.

The DECODING list is provided first - showing the two-letter code, the three-letter code (when available), the name of the airline, and the three-digit accounting number (in parentheses).

The ENCODING list follows - showing the name of the airline followed by the two-letter code and the three-letter code (when available).

AIRLINE CODES - DECODING

Not all airlines are listed. Three-letter codes (when available) are given. Three-digit accounting numbers are also provided.

```
AA - AAL - American Airlines (001)
AC - ACA - Air Canada (014)
AF - AFR - Air France ((057)
AI - AIC - Air India (098)
AM - AMX - Aeromexico (139)
AN - AAA - Ansett Australia (090)
AQ - AAH - Aloha Airlines (327)
AR - ARG - Aerolineas Argentinas (044)
AS - ASA - Alaska Airlines (027)
AT - RAM - Royal Air Maroc (147)
AV - AVA - Avianca (134)
AY - FIN - Finnair (105)
AZ - AZA - Alitalia (055)
BA - BAW - British Airways (125)
BD - BMA - British Midland (236)
BW - BWA - BWIA - British West Indies Airlines (106)
CA - CCA - Air China ( 999)
CF - CFP - Faucett Airlines (163)
CI - CAL - China Airlines (297)
CM - CMP - COPA (230)
CO - COA - Continental Airlines (005)
CP - UYC - Canadian Airlines Int'l (018)
CU - CUB - Cubana Airlines (136)
CX - CPA - Cathay Pacific Airways Ltd. (160)
CY - CYP - Cyprus Airlines (048)
CZ - CSN - China Southern Airlines (784)
DE - CFG - CONDOR (881)
DL - DAL - Delta Airlines (006)
EH - SET - SAETA (156)
EI - EIN - Aer Lingus (053)
ET - ETH - Ethiopian Airlines (071)
FI - ICE - Icelandair (108)
FL - AirTran (332)
FQ - ARU - Air Aruba (276)
GA - GIA - Garuda Indonesian (126)
GF - GFA - Gulf Air Co. (072)
GH - GHA - Ghana Airways (237)
GU - GUG - Aviateca (240)
GY - GYA - Guyana Airways (206)
HA - HAL - Hawaiian Airlines (172)
HM - SEY - Air Seychelles Ltd. (061)
HP - AWE - America West (401)
IB - IBE - Iberia (075)
IT - ITF - Air Inter (279)
JL - JAL - Japan Airlines (131)
JM - AJM - Air Jamaica (201)
KE - KAL - Korean Air (180)
```

```
KL - KLM - Royal Dutch Airlines (074)
KP - Kiwi International (538)
KQ - KQA - Kenya Airways (706)
KU - KAC - Kuwait Airways (229)
KW - CAA - Carnival Air Lines (521)
KX - CAY - Cayman Airways Ltd. (378)
LA - LAN - Lan Chile (045)
LB - LLB - Lloyd Aereo Boliviano (051)
LG - LGL - Luxair (149)
LH - DLH - Lufthansa (220)
LI - LIA - Liat (140)
LM - ALM - Antillean Airlines
LO - LOT - Polish Airlines
LR - LRC - LACSA (133)
LT - LTU - LTU International Airways (266)
LY - ELY - El Al Israel Airlines Ltd. (114)
MA - MAH - Malev - Hungarian Airlines (182)
MH - MAS - Malaysian Airline System (232)
MK - MAU - Air Mauritius (239)
MP - MPH - Martinair Holland (129)
MS - MSR - Egyptair (077)
MX - MXA - Mexicana (132)
NH - ANA - All Nippon Airways Co., Ltd. (205)
NW - NWA - Northwest Airlines (012)
NZ - ANZ - Air New Zealand (086)
OA - OAL - Olympic Airways (050)
OK - CSA - Czech Airlines (064)
OS - AUA - Austrian Airlines (257)
OU - CTN - Croatia Airlines (831)
OV - ELL - Estonian Airlines (960)
PB - PBU - Air Burundi (919)
PC - FAJ - Air Fiji (677)
PK - PIA - Pakistan International (214)
PL - PLI - Aeroperu (210)
PR - PAL - Philippine Airlines (079)
PS - AUI - Ukraine International Airlines (566)
PY - SLM - Surinam Airways (192)
QF - QFA - Qantas Airways Ltd. (081)
RA - RNA - Royal Nepal Airlines Corp. (285)
RB - SYR - Syrian Arab Airlines (070)
RG - VRG - Varig (042)
RJ - RJA - Royal Jordanian (512)
SA - SAA - South African Airways (083)
SK - SAS - Scandinavian Airlines System (117)
SN - SAB - Sabena World Airlines (082)
SQ - SIA - Singapore Airlines (618)
SR - SWR - Swissair (085)
SU - AFL - Aeroflot-Russian Airlines (555)
SV - SVA - Saudi Arabian Airlines (065)
TA - TAI - Taca International (202)
TE - LIL - Lithuanian Airlines (874)
TG - THA - Thai Airways International Ltd. (217)
```

```
TP - TAP - TAP Air Portugal (047)
TR - TBA - Transbrazil (653)
TW - TWA - Trans World Airlines (015)
UA - UAL - United Airlines (016)
UC - LCO - LADECO (145)
UK - UKA - Air UK (130)
UM - AZW - Air Zimbabwe (168)
UP - BHS - Bahamasair (111)
US - USA - US Airways (037)
VA - VIA - Viasa (164)
VE - AVE - Avensa (128)
VP - VSP - VASP (343)
VS - VIR - Virgin Atlantic (932)
VT - VTA - Air Tahiti (135)
W7 - Western Pacific (318)
WN - SWA - Southwest Airlines (526)
ZB - MON - Monarch Airlines (974)
```

AIRLINE CODES - ENCODING

Not all airlines are listed. Three-letter codes (when available) are given. Accounting numbers are provided in "decoding" list.

```
Aer Lingus - EI - EIN
Aerolineas Argentinas - AR - ARG
Aeromexico - AM - AMX
Aeroperu - PL - PLI
Air Aruba - FQ - ARU
Air Burundi - PB - PBU
Air Canada - AC - ACA
Air China - CA - CCA
Air Fiji - PC - FAJ
Air France - AF - AFR
Air India - AI - AIC
Air Inter - IT - ITF
Air Jamaica - JM - AJM
Air Mauritius - MK - MAU
Air New Zealand - NZ - ANZ
Air Seychelles Ltd. - HM - SEY
Air Tahiti - VT - VTA
Air UK - UK - UKA
Air Zimbabwe - UM - AZW
AirTran - FL
Alaska Airlines - AS - ASA
Alitalia - AZ - AZA
All Nippon Airlines - NH - ANA
ALM - Antillean Airlines - LM - ALM
Aloha Airlines - AQ - AAH
American Airlines - AA - AAL
America West - HP - AWE
Ansett Australia - AN - AAA
Austrian Airlines - OS - AUA
Avensa - VE - AVE
Avianca - AV - AVA
Aviateca - GU - GUG
Bahamasair - UP - BHS
British Airways - BA - BAW
British Midland - BD - BMA
British West Indies Airlines - BW - BWA
Canadian Airlines Int'l - CP - UYC
Carnival Air Lines - KW - CAA
Cathay Pacific Airways Ltd. - CX - CPA
Cayman Airways - KX - CAY
China Airlines - CI - CAL
China Southern Airlines - CZ - CSN
CONDOR - DE - CFG
Continental Airlines - CO - COA
COPA - CM - CMP
Croatia Airlines - OU - CTN
Cubana Airlines - CU - CUB
Cyprus Airlines - CY - CYP
```

Czechoslovak Airlines - OK - CSA
Delta Airlines - DL - DAL
Egyptair - MS - MSR
El Al Israel Airlines Ltd. - LY - ELY
Estonian Airlines - OV - ELL
Ethiopian Airlines - ET - ETH
Faucett Airlines - CF - CFP
Finnair - AY - FIN
Garuda Indonesia - GA - GIA
Ghana Airways - GH - GHA
Gulf Air Co. - GF - GFA
Guyana Airways - GY - GYA
Hawaiian Airlines - HA - HAL
Iberia - IB - IBE
Icelandair - FI - ICE
Japan Airlines - JL - JAL
Kenya Airways - KQ - KQA
Kiwi International - KP
KLM Royal Dutch Airlines - KL - KLM
Korean Air - KE - KAL
Kuwait Airways - KU - KAC
Lacsa - LR - LRC
LADECO - UC - LCO
Lan Chile - LA - LAN
Liat - LI - LIA
Lithuanian Airlines - TE - LIL
Lloyd Aereo Boliviano - LB - LLB
LOT Polish Airlines - LO - LOT
LTU International Airways - LT - LTU
Lufthansa - LH - DLH
Luxair - LG - LGL
Malaysian Airline System - MH - MAS
Malev - Hungarian Airlines - MA - MAH
Martinair Holland - MP - MPH
Mexicana - MX - MXA
Monarch Airlines - ZB - MON
Northwest Airlines - NW - NWA
Olympic Airways - OA - OAL
Pakistan International Airways - PK - PIA
Philippine Airlines - PR - PAL
Qantas Airways Ltd. - QF - QFA
Royal Air Maroc - AT - RAM
Royal Jordanian - RJ - RJA
Royal Nepal Airlines Corp. - RA - RNA
Ukraine International Airlines - PS - AUI
Sabena World Airlines - SN - SAB
SAETA - EH - SET
SAS Scandinavian Airlines System - SK - SAS
Saudi Arabian Airlines - SV - SVA
Singapore Airlines - SQ - SIA
South African Airways - SA - SAA
Southwest Airlines - WN - SWA

```
Surinam Airways - PY - SLM
Swissair - SR - SWR
Syrian Arab Airlines - RB - SYR
Taca International - TA - TAI
TAP Air Portugal - TP - TAP
Thai Airways Int'l Ltd. - TG - THA
TransBrazil - TR - TBA
Trans World Airlines - TW - TWA
United Airlines - UA - UAL
US Airways - US - USA
Varig - RG - VRG
VASP - VP - VSP
Viasa - VA - VIA
Virgin Atlantic - VS - VIR
Western Pacific - W7
```

L-1011

"A TO Z" OF TERMS, CODES, ABBREVIATIONS, AND ACRONYMS

A wide range of subjects is included in the "A to Z," such as politics, geography, economics, religion, food, art, culture, and language. This reflects how travel knowledge can extend into many topics. As this book is sold to individuals in countries other than the U.S., many words are provided for those not familiar with U.S. terminology. A brief decoding or definition is provided for most items. Further research may be necessary for a thorough understanding of terms.

NOTES

A

A

A - Letter used in computerization for availability (display flights with available seats) or for an arunk or surface segment (no flight involved). Also a class of service code.

a la carte - On a menu it means that there is a separate price for each item. In conjunction with tours it means clients get a choice of what they want from the menu.

A.C. - Alternating current.

a.k.a. - Also known as.

a.m. - Between 12:00 midnight and 12:00 noon.

A.W.O.L. - Absent Without Leave.

a/c - Air conditioning. Also additional collection.

AAA - American Automobile Association. A large association of the U.S. (AA overseas) that provides maps, tour books, insurance, road service and other services to its members. Headquarters in Heathrow, Florida.

AAD - Agent Automated Deduction.

AAL - American Airlines.

AAR - Association of American Railroads.

AARP - American Association of Retired Persons.

ABA - American Bus Association.

Abacus - Asian/Pacific computerized reservations system owned by Cathay Pacific, China Airlines, Malaysian Airlines, Royal Brunei Airlines, Singapore Airlines and others.

ABC - Advanced Booking Charters.

ABC islands - The nickname for the islands of Aruba, Bonaire, and Curacao.

abeam - At right angles to the length of a ship.

ABTA - Association of British Travel Agents.

access code - A combination of characters that will enable the user of a computer to gain entry to a field of information.

ACCL - American Canadian Caribbean Line.

accommodation - A seat/service sold to a passenger.

accordion fold - Folded like an accordion, piece on top of piece, etc.

accreditation - Approval by conferences or associations for allowing the sale of tickets and other travel services.

ACI - Assist Card International.

ACK - Acknowledge.

ACON - Air-Conditioned.

ACRA - American Car Rental Association.

acrophobia - A fear of high places.

ACTA - Alliance of Canadian Travel Associations.

ACTE - Association of Corporate Travel Executives.

ACTOA - Air Charter Tour Operators of America.

actual flying time - The total amount of time in the air.

ACV - Air Cushion Vehicle (see hovercraft).

AD - Agent's discount. Also Advantage Rent-a-Car.

ADA room - Hotel room that complies with the Americans with Disabilities Act requirements (also called a special needs accommodation).

ADB - Advise if Duplicate Booking .

add-on fare - An arbitrary amount to be added to a gateway fare to produce a through fare. For example, an airline that has a New York (gateway) to Madrid fare may have an add-on fare to travel from Philadelphia. You may have to use specific airlines and the add-on fare cannot be used alone. It is also called a proportional fare.

add-ons - Optional tour arrangements that the customer may choose to purchase.

add/coll - Additional Collection.

adiabatic rate - The general rule that for every 1,000 feet of altitude the temperature will be 3.5 degrees Fahrenheit cooler.

adjoining rooms - Two or more hotel rooms or cabins located next to one another, sharing a wall but not an inside door.

ADNO - Advise if not okay.

ADOA - Advise on arrival.

ADR - Average Daily Rate. The principal measure of a hotel's or a hotel market's pricing scale, as determined by dividing the daily room revenue by the total number of rooms available each day.

ADS - Agency Data Systems.

ADT - Alaska or Atlantic Daylight Time.

ADTK - Advise if Ticketed.

ADV - Advise.

aduane - Customs (French).

advertised tour - A travel package presented in a brochure or other written format, meeting specific airline requirements to obtain an IT (Inclusive Tour) number.

ADVN - Advise Names.

ADVR - Advise Rate.

AEA - Association of European Airlines.

aerodynamics - The study of the motion of air and the forces exerted on it.

aeronautics - The study, business, or science of designing, manufacturing, and operating aircraft.

aerospace - The atmosphere of the earth and the space immediately beyond it.

AF - Added phone.

AFA - Association of Flight Attendants.

affidavit - A written declaration under oath, usually notarized.

affinity card - A credit card marketed jointly by a card vendor and another business whose main function is not credit.

affinity charter - An aircraft that has been specifically contracted by an affinity group (see affinity group).

affinity group - Members of an organization, club or association that was formed for purposes other than travel.

affinity group airfare - An airfare that can only apply to an affinity group (see affinity group).

affluent - Wealthy.

aficionado - An enthusiastic devotee to some subject.

AFT - See actual flying time.

aft - Towards the rear part of a vessel or ship.

agency list - Agencies approved by the ARC and/or IATAN to sell airline tickets and other ARC documents.

agenda - List or program of things to be done or presented.

agent - A person authorized to sell the products or services of a supplier.

agent eligibility list - A list registered with the ARC and/or IATAN to be eligible for airline pass benefits. The travel agency managers list those employees who meet the standards of eligibility.

agent sign - An agent's personal identification code (usually two letters).

agoraphobia - The fear of open spaces.

AGT - See Agent.

AGTE - Association of Group Travel Executives.

AH - Auto Host (car rental company).

AH&MA - American Hotel and Motel Association.

AI - American International (car rental company).

air mile - A measure of distance equalling about 6,076 feet.

air piracy - Seizing or taking control of an aircraft by threatened force or violence. Also called hijacking/skyjacking.

air taxi - Aircraft carrying up to 19 passengers, operating usually within a limited radius of 250 miles.

Air Travel Card - An airline sponsored credit card used for airline ticket purchases and accepted by many of the airlines. Also called the Universal Air Travel Plan card.

air walls - Movable panels used to subdivide areas of ballrooms/meeting rooms.

air/sea - Travel programs or airfares that are offered in conjunction with sea transportation.

airbus industrie - A widebody jet having two engines, a cruising speed of 576 miles per hour and a passenger capacity of 201-345 people.

aircraft - The name for any kind of equipment used for flight in the air.

airdrome - An airfield, hangar or airport.

airglow - A radiant emission from the upper atmosphere that appears at night over the middle and low latitudes on the globe.

AIRIMP - ARC/IATA(N) Reservations Interline Message Procedures-Passenger.

airline plate - A plate issued by an airline, used to validate tickets.

airport access fee or airport service charge - A fee paid by car rental companies located off the airport premises in order to operate their vans and buses on airport grounds. Also called privilege fees, gross receipts fees, or gross revenue fees.

airport transfer - The transportation from the airport to hotels or other specified points.

airsickness - Sickness caused by the motions of the aircraft or altitude, characterized by nausea and vertigo.

airworthy - Safe for service in the air.

AITO - Association of Incentive Tour Operators.

akvavit - A dry, clear Scandinavian liquor.

AL - Alamo (car rental company).

alcove - A room offset from the main room.

all expense tour - An inclusive tour that offers many included services for the stated price. It probably includes most, if not all, meals, sightseeing, taxes, tips, and extras.

all-in - Term for all-expense or all-inclusive arrangements.

all-inclusive - The price includes the features specified (hotel, meals, entertainment).

alleyway - Passageway, as on a ship.

allocation - Assignment of seats/rooms/cabins/accommodations to a specific company/organization for exclusive sale (may also be called allotment).

allocentric - Preferring to travel to unusual places.

allotment - A certain number of rooms, cabins or other items held by an operator to sell, usually by a certain date.

all-suite hotels - Properties featuring only suites.

almanac - A book generally comprising a calendar of days, weeks, and months having information on the rising of the sun and moon, changes in the environment, etc.

aloha - Hawaiian expression meaning hello or goodbye.

ALPA - Airline Pilots Association.

alpenglow - A reddish glow often seen at mountain tops before sunrise and after sunset.

alphanumeric - Combination of letters and numbers.

alpine skiing - Downhill skiing.

alternate distribution system - A system to use other than travel agency outlets for selling transportation items. It uses home computers or other persons as designated by the suppliers.

altimeter - An instrument that displays an aircraft's altitude above mean sea level.

altitude - The height of the aircraft above sea level.

Amadeus - A computer system that has merged with SystemOne, and the new global reservation system is called Unison.

amenities - Services and facilities.

America Online - An interactive services company offering access to the Internet and other computer services.

American Plan - Meal plan that includes three meals daily with the hotel room price. Also called Full Pension Plan (See also Modified American Plan).

AMEX or AMEXCO - American Express Company.

AMHA - American Motor Hotel Association.

Amharic - The official language of Ethiopia.

amidship - In or toward the middle of the ship.

Amish - Followers of or pertaining to a Swiss Mennonite's religious sect of the 17th century.

amity - Friendship, harmony, good understanding, especially between nations.

amphibious aircraft - See seaplane.

amphitheater - An oval-shaped theater with seats rising from the center.

AMSI - ASTA Marketing Services, Inc. See ASTA.

Amtrak - The name used by the National Railroad Passenger Corporation that manages the United States passenger railroad service.

AN - Added name.

anachronism - An error misplacing an event, person or thing according to the period of time.

animation - The use of sequenced drawings made into film or giving artificial or waxed characters voice and movement to make them appear real.

animism - Belief giving God-like qualities to the aspects of nature. It is widely practiced in Africa.

answering service - A commercial service to answer telephone calls for clients.

antebellum - Before a war; especially before the U. S. Civil War.

anteroom - A room leading into the main apartment; a waiting room.

antipodean day - Day gained by crossing the IDL (International Date Line).

antipodes - Two places on the earth's surface that are diametrically opposed to each other.

anti-trust - The term in the U.S. for the complex federal and state statutes that protect consumers and businesses from price-fixing, boycotting, and other similar anti-competitive behavior by suppliers or customers.

ANTOR - Association of National Tourist Offices.

AOL - America Online. An interactive services company offering access to the Internet and other computer services.

AP - American Plan. Meal plan that includes three meals daily: breakfast, lunch, and dinner.

apartheid - The policy of separating whites from non-whites.

APEX - Advance purchase excursion fare.

APHIS - Animal and Plant Health Inspection Service.

aphelion - The point of a planet, comet or meteor's orbit when it is most distant from the sun.

API - Associated Press International.

apolitical - Not having an interest in politics.

Apollo - The marketing name in the U.S., Mexico, and Japan for the Galileo International computerized reservation .

appointment - Process of approval by conferences and/or associations for allowing the sale of tickets and other travel services (See accreditation).

apres-ski - Activities which take place after skiing at a ski lodge.

APT - Airline Passenger Tariff.

aquavit - See akvavit.

aqueduct - A channel or structure for conveying water from one place to another.

arbitrary - Referring to a fare that can only be used in combination with other air fares, in order to construct a through fare. Also called "add-on" or "proportional" fare.

ARC - Airlines Reporting Corporation. It regulates ticket sales and reports to the airlines for travel agencies and other ticket outlets.

architectural bias - The presumed ability for a reservation system (not necessarily acknowledged by CRS companies) for a reservation system to present its own products in such a way as to influence users to those products.

archipelago - A group of many islands.

archive - A record or document preserved as evidence of something.

Area Settlement Plan or area bank - Entity or bank authorized to handle the processing and payments of airline tickets and documents as reported by travel agencies and other persons.

ARINC - Aeronautical Radio Incorporated. Company owned by the airlines that provides communication services.

ARNK - arunk - A - Arrival unknown, other than air transportation.

ARR - Arrive, arrived, arriving or arrival.

arrival pattern - The expected dates and times when members of a group will arrive at a destination.

ARTA - Association of Retail Travel Agents.

Articles of Incorporation - Written document setting forth the activities of a corporation in order for the state to approve of its existence.

artifact - A simple ornament or tool.

arunk - ARNK - A - Arrival unknown, used for a surface segment of an itinerary.

AS - Added segment.

ASAE - American Society of Association Executives.

ASAP - As soon as possible.

ASC - Advising schedule change.

ASCII - American Standard Code for Information Interchange.

ASI - American Sightseeing International (company).

ASMs - Available Seat Miles. The number of available seats multiplied by the total distance flown.

ASP - See Area Settlement Plan.

AST - Alaska or Atlantic Standard Time.

ASTA - American Society of Travel Agents. Largest U.S. travel trade association that includes representatives of the airlines, tour operators, railroads, travel agencies and travel industry related products and services.

astern - Aft; to the rear.

asylum - A sanctuary or place of refuge. An institution for treating people who are mentally ill.

AT - Via the Atlantic, as a global indicator shown with airfares.

AT & T - American Telephone and Telegraph.

ATA - Air Transport Association. An airline association of the United States that works to set standards and rules.

ATAC - Air Transport Association of Canada.

ATB - Automated ticket and boarding pass. A ticket stock that combines the ticket and boarding pass into a single document.

ATC - Air Traffic Conference of America. Division of the Air Transport Association replaced by the ARC.

ATFDS - Automated Ticket and Fare Determination System.

Atlantic Standard Time - A Canadian time zone based on the standard of the 60th meridian. Also called Provincial Standard Time.

ATM - Automated Ticketing Machine/Automated Teller Machine.

ATMA - American Tour Managers Association.

ATME - Association of Travel Marketing Executives.

ATO - Airline Ticket Office.

atoll - An island made of a ring or strip of coral, common in the Pacific Ocean.

ATP - Airline Tariff Publishing.

atrium - A central open area usually having a glass ceiling to allow entrance of natural light.

ATV - All Terrain Vehicle.

ATW - Around the World.

au jus - Served with the natural juices of the meat.

au naturel - In a natural state; nude.

au pair - A young woman, usually from abroad, that helps with housework and/or childcare in exchange for room and board.

auditorium style - When seats are arranged in rows facing front.

auditor's coupon - The coupon of an ARC document that is submitted with the sales report.

aurora australis -The aurora of the Southern Hemisphere (see also aurora borealis).

aurora borealis -The northern lights or waves of colors seen in the northern skies at night and in greatest magnificence in the arctic regions.

Australasia - The areas including Australia, Fiji, New Zealand, Samoa, Tahiti and other South Pacific Islands.

auto drop pnr - A passenger name record that automatically appears in the queue when it needs some attention.

autobahn - The name for a highway in Germany and in other areas of Europe.

automated accounting - Accounting system that uses computers for the preparation of business reports and other financial data files.

automated reservation system - Computerized system offering direct access to airlines, hotels, and other suppliers for reservations and ticketing .

Avail - Availability.

available seat mile - One seat available for sale transported one mile.

AVIH - Animal in hold - checked as cargo.

AVS - Availability Status Messages.

A.W.O.L. - Absent Without Leave. An unauthorized absence.

AX - American Express.

axis - The line around which a thing rotates (the earth's axis runs through the poles).

azimuth - A great circle direction, or the angle measured clockwise between a meridian and an intersecting great circle.

B   B

B & B - Bed and breakfast. Plan to include full breakfast (unless otherwise specified) with room accommodations. Accommodations can be rooms in guest houses, homes, or hotel rooms.

baccarat - A game of cards played by any number of players betting against a banker. Also called chemin de fer.

back office automation - Usually refers to computerized accounting systems, which may also provide management reports and word processing services.

back to back - Series of programs or departures where one group leaves as another group arrives. Also used for one to another tour arrangements on a client's itinerary.

back-to-back ticketing - A practice that is generally frowned upon by the airlines because travelers buy two round trip tickets to take advantage of round trip fares but use the segments out of sequence.

backup - To create a copy of an original computer disk.

backwash - Water thrown back by a ship's passage.

Bactrian - A two-humped camel found in Asia.

baggage check - Receipt or claim ticket issued by a carrier for the handled luggage.

baggage, checked and unchecked - Personal possessions of a traveler. Checked baggage is handled by the carrier, unchecked is handled by the passenger.

bait and switch - Advertising intended to lure the customer in for a sale item and have them purchase a higher-priced item because the sale items are sold.

baksheesh or bakshish - A present of money or gratuity; used in Arabic countries.

balance sheet - An itemized statement of assets, liabilities, and capital showing the financial condition of a company on a specific date.

balcony - A platform projecting from the side of a building and enclosed by a railing.

ballpark figure - An estimated amount, not to be taken as a final cost.

bamboo curtain - A barrier created by strict censorship, restricted travel and official secrecy in communist-controlled areas of the Orient (see also iron curtain).

bank buying rate - The rate at which a bank will purchase a given amount of foreign currency.

bankruptcy - In a state of not being able to pay one's debts.

Banquet Event Order (BEO) - The detailed instructions for a particular meeting or other group function. Also called a function sheet.

bareboat charter - A yacht, boat, or other vessel rented without supplies or crew.

barometric pressure - A unit of measurement expressing the density of the atmosphere at any given point.

barter - Exchange of goods or services not involving exchange of money.

base fare - The fare without tax.

base lodge - A lodge at the bottom of a mountain slope, usually offering a variety of services, from ticketing to food and beverage.

BASIC - Beginner's All-Purpose Symbolic Instruction Code. Computer language especially designed for problemsolvers working on remote time-sharing terminals.

basilica - A styled ancient Roman building, a structure in this style, or a church.

basin - A portion of land lower than its surrounding area; also an area drained by a river and its tributaries.

bassinet - Baby bed.

bastion - Projecting tower that is a stronghold of a structure.

batch mode - A way of processing information or ticketing in groups or batches.

batik - A process of executing designs on fabric by covering with melted wax.

bay - Part of an ocean or sea that extends inland.

bayou - A marshy creek or sluggish river tributary.

BB - Buffet Breakfast.

BBML - Baby Meal.

BBR - See bank buying rate.

BCHFT - Beachfront.

beam - The width of a ship at its widest point.

bearing - relative position; direction.

Beaufort scale - A scale for indicating wind force, ranging from calm (0) to hurricane (12) and sometimes to force 17.

bed and breakfast - A meal plan which includes breakfast with hotel or guest house accommodations.

bed night - Statistical measurement based on one person spending one night in hotel/motel.

bedienung - The tip has been included on the bill (German).

bedroom - On railroads, a compartment for two persons with enclosed toilet and washing facilities.

beeper - A device to notify a person that a message is waiting on the telephone number that it is programmed for.

bell captain - Hotel employee who is in charge of the bellhops.

bellhop - Hotel employee who handles baggage or luggage from the check-in desk to the assigned room. Bellhops often explain the features of the room.

benchmarking - Measuring or evaluating against other organizations along the same lines, or in relation to generally recognized standards of the industry.

Benelux - The union of Belgium, the Netherlands, and Luxembourg.

bereavement fare - A fare offered to those traveling due to the illness or death of an immediate family member.

Bermuda triangle - A triangular area originating at Bermuda spreading out in a southern direction. This area has been known to have unexplained disappearances of ships and aircraft.

Bernoulli box - Fixed computer disk with removable cartridges.

berth - Bed, usually attached to a wall. They may fold up against the wall when not in use. Also a space where ships dock, as in the berths (or slips) of a port.

BHC - Backhaul Check.

bias - Giving preference, as in listing a certain airline's schedules first.

bidet - A fixture in some bathrooms used for bathing the external genitals and douching (sometimes called a foot bath).

BIKE - Bicycle.

bilateral agreement - Treaty or agreement for reciprocal services in accordance with details of equipment, scheduling, and other factors.

bilge - The nearly horizontal part of a ship's bottom.

bilingual - Capable of speaking two languages.

bill of fare - Menu or list of foods available at a restaurant.

billabong - A branch of a river flowing away from the main stream; a stream that is dry except during the rainy season (Australian).

billboard - Large signs of advertising.

binnacle - Receptacle for a ship's compass.

biodegradable - Capable of being broken down into products that will not harm the environment.

biorhythm - A biological process in regular recurrence or rhythm sometimes said to account for moods and stress.

birthrate - The number of births per thousand of population per year.

bistro - A small nightclub serving light meals.

bit - A binary digit (0 or 1) in computerization. An elementary unit of information stored by a single electronic component.

bkg - See booking.

black market - Business transactions that are against the law. It can deal with goods or sometimes currency exchanges.

blacked out - See blackout dates.

blackout dates - Certain dates or periods when travel on specific fares is not permitted (usually holidays).

BLCY - Balcony.

blimp - A small, nonrigid dirigible used especially for observation.

BLND - Blind passenger.

block space - A reserved number of rooms, seats, or other space, usually reserved in advance for the purpose of selling those seats or spaces in a tour package.

blue peter - The letter P flag of international code.

board - To go on or get on (also called boarding).

boarding pass - Card or form given to passenger that indicates the seat assignment or other travel space. On ships, it can be called an embarkation card.

boatel - Accommodations designed for clients traveling by boat.

bodegas - Wine cellars; wine warehouses; a bar (Spanish).

bon voyage - French for "good trip," a term for farewell.

bonbini - Papiamento word for welcome.

bond - An insurance agreement pledging surety protection in case the company goes bankrupt or defaults on payments.

booking - A reservation.

booking code - A letter used to make a reservation on a specific fare.

booking fee - Charge incurred for processing a reservation.

boomerang - A curved piece of wood that, when thrown properly, will return.

booth - A covered stall or enclosed table area at a trade show.

bordello - See brothel.

bossanova - A Brazilian-type music and dance.

botel - See boatel.

bottom line - The result, the net profit.

bourse - An exchange where merchants transact business; also the stock exchange in Paris.

boutique hotel - Small hotel that tries to project an intimate character.

bow - The front or forward of a ship.

bowl skiing - Skiing in open, above-tree-line areas, down broad expanses without trails. Bowl skiing is often for more advanced skiers.

BP - Breakfast or Bermuda Plan. Meal plan to include full breakfast with room price (unless otherwise specified).

BPI - Bits per inch. Density measurement of a tape or disk.

BPS - Bytes per second. A measurement of the speed in which data is transmitted. See also byte.

BPR - Prereserved seat/boarding pass (bilateral agreement required).

Brahman - Among the Hindus, the highest class in the caste system, with usually priests and religious people as members.

brasserie - A restaurant serving simple fare, also an inn or a beer garden.

breakdown - The dismantling of a room setup from one function to another.

break-even point - The point at which revenues equal costs (both fixed and variable); below the break-even point would be a loss, above would be a profit.

breaker - A wave that spreads into foam. Also a device for opening an electric circuit.

breakout rooms - Small areas or rooms next to larger meeting rooms that are used for smaller meeting sessions or breaks.

bridge - Area from which a ship is steered, the captain's work area.

briefing tour - Promotional tour or advance information on destinations or procedures/ facilities.

brioche - A small breakfast roll made with yeast containing large amounts of eggs and butter.

Britannia - Personification of Britain, usually depicted as a woman with a shield, helmet, and trident.

Briton - Native or inhabitant of Great Britain, or the British Empire.

BritRail pass - A pass allowing comprehensive train travel in Great Britain, for a specified time frame.

brochure - Printed literature on products or services.

brothel - A house of prostitution.

brown bagging - The practice of bringing one's own food or liquor. In some areas where the sale of liquor is prohibited, customers are allowed to bring liquor into a restaurant or bar.

browser - A term used for software that provides an interface to the Internet, making it easier for the user to locate information.

BSCT - Bassinet.

BSI/BSO - Basic Sign In/Basic Sign Out.

BSP - Bank Settlement Plan.

BTA - British Tourist Authority.

BTD - Business Travel Department.

BTH - Bath.

bubble car - See dome car.

buccaneer - A pirate; an unscrupulous adventurer, especially in politics or business.

bucket shops - A term used for businesses that quietly buy up excess seats/tickets from airlines and then sell them at reduced rates to consumers or to travel agents. Also called consolidators.

buckshee - Something extra or free (British).

bucolic - Rustic, pastoral.

Buddhism - The religious system founded by Buddha (a religious teacher of India in about the 6th century). One of the most prominent beliefs is that a release of all suffering and pain comes through Nirvana.

budget - A plan to limit expenditures. Also low-cost items.

buffer - Area within a computer where data is temporarily stored.

buffer zone - Usually refers to the 225 mile zone extending north and south of the border of the U.S.

buffet - Relating to a style of service, a display of foods and refreshments on a table so that guests serve themselves.

bug - A malfunction or error.

built-up - Densely covered with houses and buildings.

bulk fare - A net fare for a certain number of seats. Similar to blocked space.

bulk mail - Third class mail (U.S.), requiring a bulk mail permit, sorting by zip code, and a certain minimum number of pieces.

bulkhead - An interior wall separating various areas.

bulkhead seats - The seats directly behind a partition wall.

bulwark - A ship's side above the upper deck.

bumping - When a passenger is unable to travel because other passengers have been given higher priority to travel (the term is used largely with respect to airline travel and an overbooking situation).

bundling - Pooling resources or volumes of business in order to earn better discounts or prices from particular suppliers or companies.

bungalow - A small house or cottage.

buoy - A warning float or marker indicating a navigable channel.

burg - A fortress or fortified medieval town; a city.

burgomaster - The chief magistrate of a town in various countries in Europe, similar to a mayor in England and the United States.

burgundy - A reddish wine.

burro - A small donkey used as a pack animal.

bus - Large vehicle used for transportation or chartered service, often called a motorcoach when used for tours and sightseeing. Also a term used for the clearing of tables in a restaurant.

busboy/busperson - Person responsible for clearing dirty dishes from the table in a restaurant or dining room.

bushman - A settler in the bush or forest districts such as those in Australia or in southern Africa.

business class - A class of service on airlines that is usually situated between first class and coach and offers such amenities as larger seats, free cocktails, and early check-in.

business mix - Having clientele in different categories, such as a combination of commercial and leisure travel clients.

bustee - A small inhabited area in India with residents who are very poor.

bustout - Term used when a travel agency official illegally flees with blank ticket stock, occurring most often when agencies change ownership.

buttress - A structure built against a wall like an arch to give it stability.

butte - A conspicuous, isolated hill/mountain, usually with steep sides and a flat top.

buyback agreements - The agreements made between auto manufacturers and car rental companies to buy back vehicles after a certain time and with a certain rate of depreciation.

buyer's market - Indicating a greater supply of products that often leads to lower prices.

buyer's remorse - A tendency to have second thoughts about a purchase that may lead to a cancellation/return of merchandise.

BVI - British Virgin Islands.

BWIA - British West Indies Airline.

bypass - A secondary route, or to take a secondary route, usually avoiding a congested area. Also the strategy of a supplier to sell its products directly to the users instead of using distributors.

byte - Six or eight bits.

Byzantine - Pertaining to the style of the Eastern Empire after 476 A.D., characterized by the rounded arch, the cross, the circle, the dome, and rich mosaic decoration.

C   C

C.E.O. - Chief Executive Officer.

C.O.D. - Cash On Delivery / Collection On Delivery.

CAA - Civil Aeronautics Authority.

CAAC - Air China.

cab - An automobile for hire, usually equipped with a driver and meter for registering the fare or charges.

CAB - Civil Aeronautics Board. Governmental agency dissolved and incorporated into the DOT (Department of Transportation) in 1985.

caballero - A Spanish gentleman.

cabana - Hotel room usually set apart from the main building and usually situated on a beach area. Also a structure for changing clothes or shielding the sun on the beach or at an event.

cabaret - A tavern, a restaurant providing entertainment, or a floor show provided by a night club.

cabin - A sleeping room on a ship. Also the interior of an aircraft. Also a small house.

cabin attendant - Flight attendant.

cabin steward - Person responsible for housekeeping the cabins on a ship.

cable car - A car moved along rails by a cable.

cablegram - A message sent overseas using the submerged telegram cable.

cabotage - An international law that forbids a carrier of one country to transport commerce between two ports of another country.

cabriolet - A light, hooded, one-horse carriage with two wheels and a single seat. Also a type of automobile with a folding top, like a convertible.

cache - A hiding place. An off-the-ground storage place for provisions used in Alaska and other cold-climate areas.

caddie or caddy - A person paid to carry clubs and otherwise assist a golfer. Also a small conveyance for wheeling items not easily handled.

caddy - A small container for storing tea.

cafe - A coffeehouse, a restaurant, a tavern. Also coffee.

cafe au lait - Coffee with milk (French).

cafe noir - Black coffee, without milk or cream (French).

caftan - A long, flowing garment with full-length sleeves and a belted waist. Also kaftan.

CAI - Computer Assisted Instruction.

caldera - A huge crater formed when the top of a volcano collapses or explodes.

calendar - The act of posting deadlines and important dates on a calendar so that meetings, events, and tasks don't get overlooked.

call sign - A code identifying a ship's radio.

cambio - Change, term for currency exchange offices.

canal - An artificial watercourse for inland navigation/irrigation.

cape - Point of land projecting out into a body of water.

cancel - To void reservations.

cancellation clause - The stated provisions outlining charges to be paid in the event of cancellation.

canoe - A slender, open boat propelled by paddles. Also to paddle a canoe.

canton - A small district or territory. A term used for areas in Switzerland and France.

canyon - A deep narrow valley with steep sides.

capacity controlled - Seats/space is limited.

capital - The official seat of the government in a country or state.

Capitol - A building housing the country or state government operations.

capstan - Motor-driven spindle for winding in cables.

capsule hotel - Lodging that features small, coffin-like sleeping compartments (often found near Japanese railway stations and usually accepting men only).

car ferry - Ferry boat used to transport vehicles as well as passengers.

car for hire - Rental car.

car hop - An employee who carries food or other goods to customers in their cars.

carafe - A glass bottle for serving wine or water.

caravan - A company of travelers who journey together; a group of vehicles traveling in a line; a large vehicle used as a living quarters while traveling.

carbon dating - A process where the age of archaeological and geological specimens is determined through the content of carbon 14.

card mill - Term for a company that recruits salespeople with the lure of "instant" benefits said to be obtainable with I.D. the company issues.

carfare - Fare charged to passengers on public vehicles such as a bus.

cargo - Freight.

cargo liner - Ship that carries freight or cargo (See also freighter).

Carib - A member of an Indian people of Northeastern South America and dominant throughout the Lesser Antilles islands of the Caribbean.

Caribbean Sea - The sea between the Lesser Antilles and Central and South America.

carioca - A South American dance and type of music; a resident or person born in Rio de Janeiro, Brazil.

carnet - A customs document allowing cars to be driven across international borders at no cost.

carnival - The season immediately preceding Lent observed with merrymaking and parties In general, a large party or traveling show.

carousel - Mechanism that baggage moves around in transportation terminals for passengers to claim.

carrier - An airline, rail, motorcoach, cruise or other company responsible for the transportation of passengers and/or freight.

carry-on baggage - Unchecked baggage that client is responsible for handling.

cartel - An organization, often international, which controls commercial policy for companies involved in the same production area; an agreement between warring states, usually for providing exchange of prisoners; a combination of various political groups united for a common cause.

cartographer - One who makes or prepares maps or charts.

cartography - Map making.

Casbah - The old native quarter in cities; the portion of the city around the fortress.

cash advance - Monies given to an employee for future expenses.

cash bar - Guests pay for their own drinks.

cash flow - Money immediately available to pay expenses.

cash in - To turn in and receive cash for, as in gambling chips.

casino - Gambling establishment.

casita - Literally "small house," a bungalow-type accommodation.

castaway - One who is shipwrecked; thrown away or abandoned.

caste system - The social distinction made by the Hindu religion that ranks and restricts the members of the society. The divisions include Brahmans, Kshatriyas, , Vaisyas, and Sudras.

Castilian - A native of Castile, Spain; pertaining to, or the language of the area; the accepted literary form of the Spanish language.

catacomb - A subterranean burial place.

Catalan - Area of northeastern Spain, also the dialect of Spanish spoken in that area.

category - A group of similar rooms, cabins, hotels or other travel specifics.

CIS - Commonwealth of Independent States (most of the former USSR).

CATO - Canadian Association of Tour Operators.

caucus - A meeting of a group of members of a political party to nominate or elect delegates or to determine actions on affairs of concern.

caveat emptor - A commercial principle indicating that, if there is no warranty, the buyer makes a purchase at his own risk.

cavern - A deep hollow place in the earth; a cave.

cay - A small low island. Sometimes spelled key.

CBBG - Cabin baggage.

CBI - Computer Based Instruction. Also Caribbean Basin Initiative.

CBN - Cabin.

CCAR - Compact Car.

CCS - Change Segment Status.

CCTV - Abbreviation for Closed Circuit Television.

CDC - Centers for Disease Control.

CD-ROM - Compact Disk - Read Only Memory.

CDT - Central Daylight Time.

CDW - Collision Damage Waiver. Insurance offered to cover accident damages to a rental car, including the deductible amount.

cedilla - A mark, like a comma, shown under a 'c' to show that it has the sound of an 's'.

ceiling - The maximum altitude an aircraft can fly under specified conditions. Also the altitude of the cloud base.

Celsius - The centigrade thermometer.

center spread - The exact middle of a magazine or publication, which can be a premium spot for full-page advertising.

centralized billing - A system by which a supplier or agency sends one bill containing all charges incurred, rather than sending separate bills for each purchase.

CEO - Chief Executive Officer.

certification - A legitimizing by having achieved certain standards or testing.

certified mail - First class mail accompanied by a receipt to be signed by the addressee and returned to the sender to prove that the mail was delivered (in the United States of America).

CFCs - Chlorofluorocarbons. A compound widely used in aerosol sprays, refrigerants, styrofoam, and solvents used to clean microchips and circuit boards. It's believed that CFCs are responsible for a reduction in the ozone layer.

cfmd - Confirmed.

CFO - Chief Financial Officer.

CFY - Clarify.

CGOT - Canadian Government Office of Tourism.

CH - Child.

CHA - Caribbean Hotel Association.

chain - One of a group owned or operated by a company.

chair lift - Motorized moving cable with chair for transporting passengers.

chalet - House that is cabin-like.

chamber - A room.

Chamber of Commerce - Membership association of businesses in a local area that seeks to promote business. Acts as a clearing house of information and often promotes tourism.

chambermaid - One who has the general duties of cleaning rooms.

Chamorro - A member of the native race of Guam and the Mariana Islands; also the language of this race.

change of gauge or change of equipment - When an airline changes aircraft on a schedule without changing flight numbers.

channel - That part of a waterway which is navigable; a wide strait, as between a continent and an island; a means of conveying.

charabanc - A motorcoach.

charges d'affaires - A lower-ranking official who directs diplomatic affairs in the absence of an ambassador or minister.

chart - Map, also a table or graph of information.

charter - An aircraft, cruise ship, motorcoach, or other transportation used solely by a group.

chat lines - The computer equivalent of going to a party or club meeting. You communicate with people by typing and receiving messages.

chauffeur - Driver of a vehicle, hired for transportation.

CHD - Child.

check digit - A number that follows a ticket/document number that is used in accounting.

check-in time - Time when an accommodation is ready to be occupied. Also the time by which passengers should register with a carrier to be transported.

check-out time - Time by which guests are expected to leave or be charged additional monies.

checker - A person who handles the storing of hats, coats, or baggage. Also a cashier in a store.

checkpoint - A place where traffic is stopped for inspection and clearance.

cheerio - An expression used to say goodbye, sometimes used as a toast.

chemin de fer - A card game similar to baccarat (see baccarat).

Chevron setup - Arrangement of chairs in a V-shape, facing a head table or speaker. Also called herringbone setup.

child - Variably defined. Airlines normally classify a child as 2 through 11, but other suppliers classify the range to 14, 16, or even 18 years of age.

Chinook - A member of Indian tribes of the Columbia River region of North America; a wind coming down off the slopes.

chintz - Cotton cloth or calico from India, printed in bright colors and generally glazed or shiny.

chip card - A term used for a card similar to a credit card that contains encoded data allowing customers to use it for services.

chit - Voucher for an amount owed for food, drinks, etc.

CHNG - Change.

CHNT - Change name to.

CHRIE - Council on Hotel, Restaurant and Institutional Education.

Christianity - The religions including the Eastern Orthodox, Roman Catholic and Protestant religions; the system of doctrines taught by Christ.

chronological order - To put in order of time, according to their dates or sequence of occurrence.

chronometer - An instrument that measures time.

CHTR - Charter.

Chunnel - Channel tunnel linking England to France by rail.

churning - Term used for booking, cancelling, and rebooking reservations.

ciao - Word for goodbye, good luck (Italian).

CIEE - Council on International Educational Exchange.

CINET - Convention Industry Network.

circadian dyschronism - Commonly known as jet lag.

circadian rhythm - Rhythmic changes that occur in plant/animals during a 24-hour period when it is isolated from any daily environmental changes.

circle trip - A trip involving more than one destination and returning to the origin city. Example: Tampa to Atlanta to Dallas to Las Vegas to Tampa.

circle trip minimum - The lowest allowable fare for a circle trip, which can't be less that any round trip fare between any two cities on the itinerary.

circumnavigate - To sail around or travel around.

citadel - A fortress or castle in or near a city, used for defense of the city.

CITC - Canadian Institute of Travel Counselors.

CITS - China International Travel Service.

city pair - Two cities, an origin and destination on an itinerary.

city ticket office - Sales office of a carrier located other than at the terminal.

city/airport codes - Usually three letter codes used to identify cities/airports.

civil aviation - Aviation of a commercial or private nature, as opposed to military aviation.

civil law - The law of private rights, as distinguished from criminal law.

civilization - The state of human society characterized by a high level of intellectual, cultural, technological, and social development; in general, populated areas as distinguished from wilderness.

claim PNR - When a record is pulled electronically from the CRS where it was created and transferred to the CRS of the agent who wants to ticket.

clearance - Ready for take-off or landing or permission to depart.

cleat - A device used to secure cables/ropes.

CLIA - Cruise Lines International Association.

client - Customer.

climate - The condition of a region relating to temperature, wind, moisture and other weather elements.

closed dates - Time periods when nothing is available because everything is booked.

club car - A lounge car usually on a train.

club floor - Term used for a section of a hotel offering higher security and other amenities.

Club Med - Club Mediterranee, S.A. An organization offering all-inclusive resort vacations.

CMP - Certified Meeting Professional. Also Complete Meeting Package.

CNL - Cancel.

co-op advertising - When a travel agency shares the expense of advertising with a supplier.

coach class - A section of a plane, also called tourist or economy class.

coaming - Raised partitions around hatches or between doorways to prevent water from entering.

COBOL - Common Business Oriented Language. A procedure-oriented language for computer programming developed to facilitate business functions. COBOL programs have four divisions: identification, environment, data, and procedure.

COC - Country of Commencement (country where travel originates).

cockney - A native of the East End of London; a dialect of that district or quality of speech to the region.

cockpit - Area of a plane where the pilot and controls are located.

code - A system of signals for communication; numbers, letters or combinations to represent things or words.

code sharing - When an airline uses the code of another airline in flight schedule displays.

cog railway - Railroad constructed on a steep incline with cogs or teeth on the rail to blend with a cogwheel on the locomotive to provide traction.

cohost carrier - An airline that agrees to pay the host for display of flights and fares in computers.

cold call - Sales representatives visiting outlets without making appointments.

cold war - The intense political, economic, and psychological competition which does not reach an actual military operations level.

cold wave - A fall in temperature which occurs rapidly and affects a large area.

colleague - A partner or associate.

collective farm - A farm jointly operated by a community or a group under state control, such as in a Communist country.

colloquium - A seminar that several lecturers take turns in leading; a discussion meeting; a lecture prepared for such a seminar.

colonialism - A system of settling or inhabiting an area.

COMM - Commission.

commercial /commercialization - An advertisement/denotes an environment where everything is for sale, usually used in a negative context.

commercial agency - A travel agency that specializes in business travel.

commercial airline - An airline that sells its seats publicly.

commercial rate - A discount rate offered to a company or business traveler.

commission - A percentage amount of money paid to agents for selling a supplier's products (airline tickets, hotel accommodations, cruise tickets, etc.).

commission cap - The maximum dollar amount of commission that a supplier will pay to an agency/agent regardless of the amount of the sales or tickets.

commissionable - When commission can be earned.

committee - A person or group of persons appointed to investigate, report or act in special cases or on certain issues.

commode - A toilet, a low cabinet or chest of drawers. Also a chair containing a chamber pot.

commodity exchange - An organized trading center where commodities such as grain, sugar, wheat or coffee are bought and sold.

common law - Unwritten law as opposed to statute law; a law of general application throughout a political entity.

common market - A customs union or a partnership of nations for trade purposes.

Common Market - See European Economic Community.

common rated - Two or more destinations having the same fares because they are not very far away from each other.

commonwealth - A state, island, or political unit associated with a representative form of government; a colony united with a country on a voluntary basis.

communism - A theory or system of social organization based on common property controlled by the state or government.

commuter - One who travels to and from a location regularly, like from the suburbs to the city daily for work.

commuter plane - Commuter planes are generally classified as those that hold fewer than 31 passengers.

comp - Abbreviation for complimentary meaning free of charge.

comp room - Room at no charge.

companionway - Stairway, as in between the decks of a ship.

compartment - Section of a railroad car or other transportation vehicle.

compass - An instrument used for determining directions such as north, south, east or west. Also to surround. Also curved, as in forming an arc.

compensation - The act of making up for losses or suffering.

competent - Suitable, fit, having all the requirements.

competitive benchmarking - A practice of rating a company's products against an industry leader in order to gauge performance.

competitor - A rival for sales of the same or similar merchandise.

complimentary - Free.

CompuServe - A commercial online service offering interactive computer services.

concentrated hub - An airport where a single airline with a hub operation controls most of the flights.

concession - A place of business that is not open to the general business competition. Usually contracts and bids are presented by a business to run a concession (such as shops on cruise ships).

concierge - The individual or desk in a hotel which attends to guests' needs and services.

concorde jet - See supersonic transport.

concourse - Passageway or area; term used for parts of terminals (departures, arrivals, baggage).

concrete jungle - Area not having much greenery or trees, mostly buildings and highways.

concubine - A woman who cohabits with a man without being married to him; a mistress; a secondary wife in some polygamous societies.

COND - Conditional.

conditional fare - Also called a leisure class fare, which entitles the passenger to fly free on the next available flight if the flight is full.

condo/condominium - Housing similar to an apartment that a person owns rather than rents. It can also mean a multi-ownership arrangement (see time-sharing).

conducted tour - See escorted tour.

conductor - A leader, a guide, the official in charge of a vehicle or train. A director of an orchestra.

confederation - A league or alliance.

conference - Group meeting or an association of carriers who meet for the purpose of regulating activities and setting up standards and rules.

conference style setup - Meeting room setup in which tables are rectangular
or oval shaped, with chairs placed on both sides and ends. Also called a board of directors setup.

confidential - Intended to be kept private or secret.

confidential tariff - A list of rates to be marked up for retail sales.

confidentiality clause - Statements that suppliers may ask you to sign that obligate you to not reveal the details and specifics of the contract or situation involved.

configuration - A diagram of the interior of an aircraft or other equipment.

confirmation - Certifying that the passenger is holding a room, seat, or other travel arrangement space.

confiscate - To seize.

Confucianism - The moral doctrines of Confucious, the Chinese philosopher, advocating filial piety, justice and fidelity.

conga - A Cuban dance, characterized by a group who form a winding line and follow a leader. Also the music for this dance.

congress - A formal meeting or assembly.

conjunction tickets - When more than one ticket is used for an itinerary.

connecting flight - The change of planes on a schedule.

connecting rooms - Two or more rooms with a private connecting door, permitting access without going into the hallway.

connection - Two things related. In airline travel, a change of planes (See offline and online connections).

connoisseur - One who is competent to make judgements or criticize in an art such as music, painting, etc.

conquistador - A conqueror.

consanguineous - Related by birth; related as in having the same ancestor.

consignment - Arrangement whereby goods remain the property of the owner until the agent sells it.

consolidator - A person or company who has a certain inventory of a product (airline seats, cabins on cruises, etc.) to sell at special prices.

consortium - Group of persons/companies that pool together their resources to obtain benefits such as higher commissions, advertising, etc.

consulate - The office or position of a consul, or official of the government of a country. They particularly handle visas and immigration problems.

consultant - One who offers business, professional, or expert advice for a fee. See also travel consultant.

contiguous - In contact; neighboring, bordering.

continent - A continuous tract of land. The continents include: North and South America (sometimes called America), Asia, Europe, Africa, Australia and Antarctica.

continental breakfast - Usually rolls and coffee (may include juice/fruit).

continental code - The international Morse code, used in communications.

Continental Divide - The watershed of North America, separating the rivers that flow west to the Pacific from those that flow east and north to the Atlantic and the Arctic. It coincides with the Rocky Mountains, Mexico's central plateau and the Central American cordilleras.

continental drift - The slow movement of the continents to their present positions.

continental shelf - The submerged edge of a continent.

contingency - The state of being dependent on some condition.

contour map - A map showing topographical features by the relative spacing of lines known as contour intervals.

contraband - Goods which are prohibited or illegal for import or export.

control tower - The housing of the radar and radio communications equipment and personnel at an airport.

CONV - Convertible.

convention - Business or professional meetings, usually attended by large numbers of people.

conventioneer - Person attending a convention.

conversion rate - The rate at which one currency is exchanged for another.

converter - A device for changing electric current, as from direct current to alternating current.

convertiplane - An aircraft that combines the landing and take-off characteristics of a rotary-wing helicopter with the high forward speed of a plane.

convoy - Accompany/escort, especially for protection.

COO - Chief Operating Officer.

co-op advertising - When costs of advertisements are split between the suppliers and retailers.

cooperative - An organization of individuals with similar interests and problems who have joined together to perform certain activities.

cordillera - A chain of mountains, particularly one forming the axis of a large land mass.

cork charge or corkage - A charge made by the establishment for opening and serving bottles of wine or other liquor not purchased there.

corporate rate - A special rate offered to business clientele, or a rate negotiated upon by a supplier and a company.

corporate travel manager - An employee who makes and/or negotiates travel arrangements for other employees of the company.

correspondence - Communication by exchange of letters.

cost of living - The relationship of the average cost of consumer goods and services to the national level of individual or family incomes.

cost-reimbursable contractor - A company under contract to perform work for another entity (usually a government agency), which pays certain expenses incurred because of the work (such as travel costs).

cot - A light portable bed; a small dwelling/cottage.

COT - Abbreviation for cottage, as in accommodations like a small house (also abbreviated CTG).

coterminous - Having a common boundary; bordering.

couchette - A sleeping berth on a European train. Normally there are four to six beds in a compartment.

counterclockwise - A direction opposite that of a clock.

counterfeit - A forgery; an imitation designed to pass as an original.

coup d'etat - A sudden change or measure in politics, especially one affecting a change in government illegally or by force.

coupon - The part of an airline ticket that is surrendered by the passenger for service. A document or voucher to exchange for goods or services.

coupon broker - A person or business that purchases and resells frequent flyer awards. Such brokering is considered illegal by most programs.

courier - A person who carries documents or cargo to a destination. Also the term used in Britain for a tour escort.

cove - A small sheltered bay or inlet; also a small valley in a mountain.

cover charge - Fee for entry, usually imposed for exclusive night clubs or luxury establishments.

cover letter - Introductory letter that accompanies other documents.

CP - Continental Plan. Meal plan that includes continental breakfast (roll and coffee) with the price of accommodations.

CPU - Central Processing Unit. The part of a computer where the work actually takes place.

CR - Changes record.

crew - Those employees who work on board an aircraft, ship, or other transportation vehicle.

cross-border ticketing - The system of issuing a ticket that makes it appear the trip starts out of the country where the real itinerary begins in order to take advantage of a lower fare structure or more favorable exchange rate.

cross-country skiing - Skiing on a generally flat surface, usually through wooded areas, on a specialized type of ski.

cross-ticketing - When an agency tries to maximize its commissions by booking all or most of its business with one airline through one of its offices. Publicly, cross-ticketing is denounced by most of the airlines.

croupier - An employee of a gambling establishment who supervises a gaming table.

crown colony - A British colony over which the crown has some control of legislation and administration as opposed to one having a constitution and representative government.

crow's nest - A platform high on the mast of a ship.

CRS - Computerized Reservation System.

CRT - Cathode ray tube, a computer terminal.

cruise - Voyage for pleasure, rather than transportation, usually departing and returning to the same port city.

cruise broker - Person/company who specializes in last-minute availability of cabins on cruise ships.

cruise director - Acts like a master of ceremonies for all activities on board a ship, and is responsible for the passengers enjoying their trip.

crypt - A subterranean chamber or vault; especially one beneath the main floor of a church, used as a burial place.

CSM - Convention Services Manager.

CSML - Child's Meal.

CST - Central Standard Time.

CT - Central time (U.S.). Also circle trip (see circle trip).

CTC - Contact, also Certified Travel Counselor (a designation obtained from ICTA, after completing coursework and experience).

CTCA - Contact Address.

CTCB - Contact Business phone.

CTCH - Contact Home phone.

CTCT - Contact Travel Agent phone.

CTG - Abbreviation for cottage (like a small house). Also abbreviated COT.

CTM - Circle Trip Minimum. The fare for a circle trip cannot be less than any intermediate round trip fare between cities on the itinerary.

CTO - See city ticket office. Also Caribbean Tourism Organization.

cuesta - A hill having a steep incline on one side and a gradual incline on the other.

cuisine - Style of cooking.

culture - A total of human behavioral characteristics, patterns, and technology as exhibited by a group of people.

culture shock - When a person becomes shocked and disoriented at a place because of the harsh contrast to their known lifestyle and customs.

cupola - A vault or dome built on a circular base and constituting a roof or ceiling.

curacao - A liquor flavored with orange peel, cinnamon and mace named for the island of Curacao, where it was first made.

curare - Poison made from plants that paralyses animals.

curator - The director of a museum or art gallery; a guardian.

curfew - A police or military order requiring people be off the streets and businesses closed at certain times.

curio - Any object or article valued as a curiosity.

currency restrictions - Limitations established by a country to control the amount of money taken in, out, or exchanged within a country.

cursor - The visible reference mark on the CRT screen which shows the next area to place data.

customer-activated ticketing - Computerized system for the issuance of tickets when a customer inserts appropriate credit card or payment procedure.

customs - The normal manners or behavioral procedures of a society. Also the government agency responsible to inspect, restrict, and/or impose taxes on goods brought into a country.

customs declaration - Form for specifying the articles that are being brought into a country.

customs duty - Tax on certain goods being imported.

cut-off date - Last date by which to make reservations because the plans or specific arrangements need to be finalized.

CV - Container Vessel.

CVB - Convention and Visitors Bureau.

CVR - Cockpit Voice Recorder. A device that records all audible sounds in the cockpit.

CWGN - Compact Station Wagon.

cyberspace - Term applied for communications via the Internet.

cyclone - A circular storm revolving around a calm center. See also tornado, typhoon, hurricane.

D   D

d.b.a. - Doing business as.

D.C. - Direct current.

D.O.A. - Dead On Arrival.

dagoba - See stupa.

dahabeah - A boat used on the Nile for transporting travelers. It used to have sails, but is now motorized.

dais - A raised platform in a hall or large room.

daisy wheel - A type of printer for use with computers.

DAPO - Do all possible.

daredevil - One who fears nothing.

data base - Integrated files of data used for processing applications throughout an organization in contrast to an individual data file.

DATAS II - The computer system sponsored by Delta Air Lines. Now part of Worldspan.

davenport - A large sofa, often convertible into a bed.

davit - A crane on board a ship used for hoisting the anchor or lifeboat.

day rate - A special rate offered by hotels and motels to occupy a room for the day.

DBA - Doing Business As.

dbl - See double.

DBLB - Double room with bath.

DBLN - Double room without bath/shower.

DBLS - Double room with shower.

DCSN - Decision.

DEA - Drug Enforcement Agency.

dead calm - No wind.

dead reckoning - Calculating your position by the knowledge of the path taken, speed, etc.

deadhead - A vehicle operating without a payload or revenue producing cargo.

DEAF - Deaf passenger.

death rate - The number of deaths per thousand of population per year. Also known as mortality rate.

debark - To disembark (or get off).

debit memo - A note showing an amount due or payment to be made, usually as a result of your error.

debug - To isolate and remove mistakes.

deck plan - The diagram of a ship showing cabins, public areas, pools, etc.

deck steward - Person on hand to move deck chairs, provide towels and other services on a ship.

decode - To put into the original language or form.

dedicated line - An electrical outlet set aside as a specific power source.

deductible amount - With respect to insurance, the amount you would be responsible for paying should a claim be made.

default - Failure to provide services, products, or refunds.

Delphi - A commercial online service offering interactive computer services.

delta - A triangular-shaped land area formed by sediment at the mouth of a river.

deluxe hotel - A hotel located centrally or in a resort area that has many amenities and luxury accommodations (pools, night clubs, restaurants).

deluxe room - A room in a hotel that is located centrally or with a popular view and has fine accommodation details.

demagogue - A person who makes use of popular emotions and prejudices for personal power; a popular leader.

demi-pension - See half-pension.

demitasse - A small cup, such as that used for black coffee.

demo - A demonstration; something used for demonstration.

democracy - A form of government in which the supreme power is vested in the people and their elected agents.

demographics - See demography.

demography - Study of population according to birth and death rates, age, moving patterns, etc.

denied boarding compensation - The compensation (money, free trip, accommodations) paid to a passenger when they have been involuntarily bumped from the transportation.

denizen - An inhabitant or dweller in a particular place.

denomination - One of the grades or designations such as money divisions. Example: 100 cents is equal to one dollar.

dep /DEP - Deposit. Also departs, departed, departure.

departure tax - A tax levied on departing passengers, usually when leaving a country.

deplane - To get off a plane.

depletion - The reduction of natural resources or other goods.

DEPO - Deportee.

deportation - The lawful removal, from a state or country, of an alien whose presence is undesirable.

deportee - One deported.

deposit - Partial payment to hold space, usually refundable if cancellation is made enough in advance.

depot - Terminal or station.

depreciable asset - Property that is subject to depreciation for tax purposes.

deregulation - By the Federal law enacted in 1978, the elimination of the CAB and governmental regulation of the airlines and other suppliers with regard to routes, fares and other specifics.

designated driver program - A program by which the person driving does not consume alcoholic beverages. In some areas, the designated driver's beverages are free.

destination - To where someone is traveling.

Destination Management Company (DMC) - Local company or supplier that arranges transportation, tours, special events, etc.

DET - Domestic Escorted Tour. See escorted tour.

detached interface - The capability of a system to do accounting and other business functions while issuing tickets.

detente - A release in tension as in lessening hostility between countries.

detention - A keeping in custody, confinement.

deva - In Hinduism, a god or divinity.

devaluation - A reduction in the amount.

devotee - One who is absorbed in religious duties or ceremonies; a fervent admirer.

DEW line - Distant Early Warning line. A line of radar stations around the seventieth parallel of the North American continent for detecting foreign aircraft.

dew point - The temperature at which the air becomes saturated with moisture.

dharma - Conformity to the religious laws of Hinduism or Buddhism.

dharna - The practice in India of sitting at a person's door without tasting food until he complies with some demand. Like a "sit-in" practiced by demonstrators in the United States.

dhow - An Arab vessel.

dicker - To bargain; to haggle.

dictatorship - A government characterized by the absolute authority of a ruler.

diem - Daily, as in per diem meaning per day.

differential - A difference made because of a class of service change. For example, an adjustment to the fare when no first class is available on one segment of a flight.

diggings - An area of excavation.

diglot - Using or containing two languages.

dine-around plan - Plan where guests can choose from a number of establishments for their dining.

diner - Small restaurant or the restaurant car on a train. Also a person eating at a restaurant

dinghy - Small boat.

diplomacy - The science or art of conducting negotiations between nations; skill in managing negotiations of any kind.

diplomat - A person representing a government in negotiations; a person who is tactful.

diplomatic immunity - A provision that exempts diplomats from the laws of of the country in which they are assigned.

direct access - The ability to go into a vendor's system to obtain last seat/product availability.

 direct flight - A flight that does not require the passenger to change planes. It may make stops.

direct mail - Advertising method which sends information to listed consumer markets.

direct reference system - Collection of information, also called a fact file.

directional selling - The practice of selling products that belong to a preferred supplier or company.

dis - Discontinued.

disburse - To pay out monies.

disclaimer of liability - Legal concept where responsibility for problems incurred while traveling is not claimed by the agent who sells those travel arrangements.

disclosure - The revealing of financial details.

discotheque - A nightclub where patrons dance to recorded music.

discount fare - Usually a one way fare offered in a limited quantity.

discretionary income - Income left after all bills have been paid.

discretionary time - Leisure time, the time after all necessary tasks have been completed.

disembark - To get off a ship, rail car, or other transportation vehicle.

disk - A magnetic file (also called a diskette).

disproportionate - Not properly or correctly proportionate.

District Sales Manager (DSM) - Person responsible for administering sales functions at the district office of an airline, tour company or other supplier headquarters.

DIT - Domestic Independent Tour/Traveler.

divan - A long cushioned seat.

divestiture - The compulsory transfer of title or disposal of interests upon government order.

DLX - See deluxe room.

DM - District Manager.

DMC - Directional Minimum Check. The check to make certain the fare used is not less than the applicable fare in either direction. Also, Destination Management Company/Consultants.

DMO - District Marketing Office, sometimes called a district sales office. Also Destination Marketing Organizations.

DMV - Department of Motor Vehicles.

DO - Drop-off.

docent - Guide or paid employee of a facility.

dock - Structure to which a ship attaches itself when in port.

docs - Documents.

docs rec'd - Documents received.

DOD - Department of Defense.

dog and pony show - An expression used for a sales presentation.

dog watch - Nautical term for either of two two-hour watches (4-6 or 6-8 pm).

DOJ - Department of Justice.

doldrums - A region of calms, sudden storms, and variable winds near the equator.

dollar diplomacy - A foreign policy having its primary aim in the promotion and protection of private investments abroad.

dolmen - An ancient structure that consists of an erect stone or stones.

dom - Domestic.

dome car - Also called a bubble car, a car designed with a glass roof for sightseeing.

domestic airline - Carrier providing service within its own country.

domestic escorted tour - Packaged and planned itinerary including a guide or escort for traveling within one's own country.

domestic fare - A fare for travel wholly within a country and/or its territories.

domicile - A house, home, or residence.

dominion - The power or right of governing and controlling; a territory under its own form of government.

Doppler effect - The change in wave frequency when the source moves away from or towards the observer, used in navigation and radar. Also called the Doppler shift.

dormette - See sleeperette.

DOS - Department of State. Also Disk operating System.

DOT - Department of Transportation.

dot-matrix - A type of printer for use with a computer that uses a series of dots to make the letters and numbers.

double - A room to be occupied by two people who don't mind sharing a bed.

double booking - The practice of confirming two or more reservations when only one will be used.

double double - A room with two double beds.

double occupancy - Rate when two persons will occupy the space.

dowager - A widow who has property or a title inherited from her deceased husband.

down time - The time when a computer is inoperative.

down under - An expression referring mainly to Australia and New Zealand.

downgrade -To move down to a lower grade of accommodations or services.

downline - All segments, legs or cities listed below the originating or headline city.

download - Obtaining/transferring software and/or programs/files from one computer to another.

downs - Unforested, chalk hills found in Southern England.

downsizing - Corporate reorganization or restructuring in order to survive as companies under their original name.

DPLX - See duplex.

DPP - Default Protection Plan. Insurance plan to protect against the bankruptcy or failure to provide services and refunds.

DPST - Deposit.

dptr - Departure.

draft - The depth of water a ship draws.

drag - The total air resistance to an aircraft's flight.

draw - Amount given with the purpose of commissions from sales totaling more or at least as much.

drayage - The charge or cost of transporting goods; the transportation of goods.

drive-in - A method of receiving services, such as food or viewing a movie, without leaving your car.

driver-guide - A driver who is authorized to act as a guide on tours.

dromedary - One-humped camel found in Northern Africa and the Middle East.

drop-off charges - Fees added when a renter of a vehicle does not return the vehicle to the original rental location.

DRS - Direct Reference System.

dry dock - A structure used during the cleaning, construction and repairs of ships.

dry lease - Rental of a vehicle without supplies and crew.

DSM - See District Sales Manager.

DSO - District sales office, also called a district marketing office.

DSPL - Display.

dual designated carrier - See code sharing.

DUI - Driving Under the Influence of some narcotics or drugs.

dune - A hill or ridge of sand formed by wind.

dungeon - A prison or cell, usually underground.

dupe - Duplicate.

duplex - A two part house that can be occupied by two families; accommodations that are separate, but share walls.

Dutch treat - A meal or entertainment for which each person pays their own expenses.

duty-free - When items are not subject to tax.

duty-tax - See customs duty.

DWB or DBLB - Double with bath (see double).

DWI - Driving While Intoxicated.

DXA - Deferred Cancellation Area.

E   E

E-mail - Electronic mail. Messages and communications transmitted by computer .

E-ticketing - Electronic ticketing. See ticketless travel.

Eastern hemisphere - See Traffic Conference Areas 2 and 3 only.

EB - Eastbound. Also English Breakfast.

ECAR - Economy Car.

eclipse - To cause a shadow upon; to render dim; any obscuration of the light of the sun, moon, or other heavenly body by the intervention of another heavenly body in the path of viewing it.

ecology - A branch of biology dealing with organisms and their environment.

economy class - Tourist or coach class.

ecosystem - The interacting biological and environmental systems of an area.

ecotourism - Travel that focuses on nature, the preservation of the environment, and a controlled management of resources.

ECU - European Currency Unit.

eddy - A current of air or water moving circularly.

EDP - Electronic Data Processing.

EDT - Eastern Daylight Time.

EEC - See European Economic Community.

eff - Effective.

efficiency - Room that has kitchen facilities, similar to a one room apartment, also called a studio.

elapsed flying time - Actual time spent in the air, when stops and time differences have been deducted.

elderhostel - A term for a program whereby men and women over 60 years of age can continue to learn with travel experiences. Courses are offered during school breaks and include college dormitory accommodations.

electronic ticketing - See ticketless travel.

EMA - Extra Mileage Allowance.

EMAN - Economy car, manual transmission.

embargo - A prohibition preventing certain transportation suppliers into an area.

embark - To go or get on board.

EMER - Emergency travel.

emigrant - One who leaves his native country to settle in another.

emigrate - To leave one country to settle in another.

emissary - A person sent out on a mission.

EMS - Excess Mileage Surcharge.

enclave - An outlying part of a country or a small autonomous territory completely or partially surrounded by another country. Also an area populated by a minority group.

encode - To put into code.

encroachment - The gradual advancement on the rights or area of another.

ENDI - End Item.

English breakfast - Hearty breakfast consisting of eggs, cereals, breads, meats and beverages.

enhancement - An additional feature usually meaning more capabilities in computer software operations.

enplane - To go aboard an aircraft.

enroute - While traveling.

ensign - A flag; an emblem, badge or symbol of office.

entree - In the U.S. the main dish of a meal , in other countries it is an appetizer course.

entrepreneur - A person who organizes, manages and assumes the risks of a business.

entry - A reply to the system or request by the user for information on a computer.

entry fee - Charge for entering a country or establishment.

entry requirements - The official documents required to enter a country which may include a passport, visa, or document showing inoculations.

environment - All the physical, social and cultural factors and conditions influencing the development of an organism.

environs - The vicinity; areas surrounding a place.

eon - An age; a division of geologic time.

EP - European Plan. Meal plan that does not include meals with the price of accommodations.

EPA - Environmental Protection Agency.

epoch - A particular period of time as marked by certain events; an interval of geologic time.

equator - The line dividing the earth's globe into the two hemispheres, northern and southern.

equinox - The two times of the year (about Mar. 21 and Sept. 23) when the sun is directly over the equator.

EQUIV - Equivalent amount.

erosion - The wearing away of soil or rock by the forces of nature.

ERQ - Endorsement request.

errors and omissions insurance - Insurance to pay for damages that occur because of mistakes or omissions made by the agent.

escort - Person traveling with a group as a guide, usually available throughout the tour. See also tour conductor, tour manager.

escorted tour - A tour that includes the services of an escort. Also called a conducted tour.

escrow account - Legally required safeguard of funds held by financial institutions until services have been rendered.

EST - Eastern Standard Time.

estuary - The wide mouth of a river where the tide meets the currents.

ET - Eastern time (U.S.). Also end transaction.

ETA - Estimated time of arrival.

ETC - European Travel Commission.

ETD - Estimated time of departure.

ETDN - Electronic Ticket Delivery Network. A network of ticket printers in public locations for customers to obtain travel documents. Also called STPN (Satellite Ticket Printer Network).

ethnic - Relating to race or a large group of people who have common customs or traits.

ethnocentrism - A tendency to judge all others by one's own standards and to concentrate on that local sphere or environment.

etiquette - Appropriate social behavior as generally prescribed by a society.

EU - Global indicator meaning via Europe.

Eurailpass - A pass allowing unlimited train travel in many European countries for specified time frames.

European Economic Community - Official name of the Common Market-an economic association established in 1958 to increase free trade among member nations and to adopt common import duties on goods from other countries.

Eurostar - The high-speed passenger train service that runs between London, Paris, and Brussels.

Eurotunnel - A private Anglo-French corporation which owns and operates the Channel Tunnel and Le Shuttle.

EWGN - Economy Station Wagon.

excavate - To expose by digging.

excess baggage - Baggage that may cost more to be transported since it exceeds the allowed limit.

exchange order - See voucher.

exclusivity - Reserved for specific persons.

excursion fare - Usually a round trip fare with restrictions such as minimum and maximum stay and advance purchase requirements.

excursionist - A temporary visitor staying less than 24-hours in a country.

executive floor - Floor in a hotel usually reserved for business travelers, with higher rate rooms and often with concierge and other amenities.

exhibition - A showing; a public display.

expatriate - Citizen of a country who resides in another country.

expedition - An excursion, a journey, usually for some purpose.

expense - Cost or charge.

expense account - An account of expenses incurred by the employee which are to be refunded by the employer.

exploration - Travel for the purposes of discovery.

export - To send, as goods for sale in foreign countries.

exposition - See exhibition.

expressway - Highway.

EXST - Extra seat.

extended stay - Generally defined by hotels as a hotel stay of seven or more nights.

extension ladder - A form placed on the fare ladder area of a manual airline ticket when there are more than 13 cities on the itinerary.

extension tours - Optional trips that may be taken before, during, or after a basic tour.

extra section - An additional aircraft placed on a flight schedule (usually during holidays and peak travel times).

F & B - Food and Beverage.

F.O.B. - See Free On Board.

F.U.B.A.R. - Fouled Up Beyond All Recognition.

FAA - Federal Aviation Administration (or Authority).

fact file - Collection of information, also called a direct reference system.

fado - A Portuguese entertainment featuring the singing of lamenting ballads.

Fahrenheit - Measure of temperature where freezing is 32 degrees, boiling point is 212 degrees.

fair dinkum - Australian expression meaning genuine, true, or honest.

fair market value - A proper price for a item.

false horizon - A line marking the apparent meeting of ground and sky used in instruments to measure altitude.

fam - See familiarization trip or tour.

familiarization trip or tour - A trip or tour offered to promote a new product or destination and the services of the supplier, usually at a discount price. Also called a fam trip.

family plan - Plan offering family members discounted/free rates.

family style - A style of serving meals in which the food is brought to the table in dishes so the diners can help themselves.

fandango - A lively Spanish dance or the music for such a dance; a ball or party; childish behavior.

fantail - The rear or aft overhang of a ship.

Fantasia - A joint venture between Qantas and American Airlines to market the Sabre CRS system in the South Pacific.

FAP - Full American Plan. See AP.

fare - Price.

fare basis - The letter, letters, or letters and numbers assigned to a specific fare, like an identification number.

fare break point - The place where a fare ends. For example, traveling from Tampa and connecting in Atlanta to go to New York, you would call New York the fare break point.

fare code - The letter/letters and numbers identifying a fare.

fare construction point - See fare break point.

fascism - An autocratic system of government, headed by an absolute dictator, and characterized by strict social and economic rules.

fathom - A measure of length, containing six feet, used chiefly in determining the depth of water.

faux pas - A social blunder; a breach of etiquette.

FCCA - Florida-Caribbean Cruise Association.

FDIC - Federal Deposit Insurance Corporation.

FDOR - Four Door Car.

feasibility study - Research done to determine whether to proceed with a project, after collecting and analyzing marketing and financial data.

fee-based pricing - An approach to travel agency compensation by which clients pay for services according to an agreed upon schedule.

feeder airline - A small, local airline that "feeds" passenger traffic to larger airlines.

felucca - A small boat particularly used on the Nile River.

feral - Wild, or existing in a state of nature; savage; pertaining to the dead.

feretory - A shrine, usually portable, designed to hold the relics of saints.

feria - A holiday.

ferry - Vessel used to carry passengers across water.

fertility rate - See birth rate.

FET - Foreign Escorted Tour. See escorted tour.

fete - A feast; a holiday.

FFP - Frequent Flyer Program. Program whereby bonuses are offered by the airlines to passengers who accumulate travel mileage.

FHTL - See first class hotel.

fictitious point principle - A principle of international fare construction that allows the use of a fare to a city to which the passenger is not actually traveling. It is not allowed by most airlines.

field - An assigned area of record, like the name, phone, ticketing, received from and form of payment fields.

fifth freedom - Allowing passenger traffic between two countries by the airline of a third.

file - Collection of related records.

filigree - Ornamental work of fine intertwined gold or silver in a lacy design.

final payment - The last amount due from the clients. Used when the client has paid a deposit, the final payment is the remaining balance due.

finger bowl - A bowl of water on a dining table to use for rinsing the fingers after eating.

firming up - Confirming/verifying the arrangements discussed.

first class - Generally, the best and most expensive seats and services. For example, first class on airlines usually includes free drinks and movies, spacious seating, and separate check-in.

first class hotel - Hotel in a good location having extensive facilities and providing excellent services.

first sitting - The earlier of two meal times for dining on a ship.

firth - See estuary.

fiscal year - A 12 month period used for accounting/taxation that may or may not coincide with the calendar year.

FIT - Foreign Independent Tour/Traveler.

fixed costs - Costs which remain constant.

FIYTO - Federation of International Youth Travel Organizations.

fjord - Narrow sea inlet, usually (but not always) bordered by steep cliffs.

flag carrier - Term usually referring to the national airline of a country.

flambe - A cooking technique that usually involves liquor since the dish is "lit" just before serving.

flamenco - A Spanish style of dance and music featuring clapping, stamping and other vigorous movements.

flaps - Extendable, hinged surfaces on the wings of an aircraft used to control lift.

flat - An apartment.

flat rate - The rate not discounted, a fixed rate.

FLIFO - Flight Information.

flight attendant - Person responsible for the welfare of aircraft passengers.

flight bag - A bag used for air travel and designed to fit under the seat.

flight crew - All the employees working on the aircraft.

flightseeing - Sightseeing by air.

FLIP - Floating Instrument Platform. An ocean-going research vessel that can be towed into place horizontally and then flipped up into a vertical position.

float - The income a company or organization saves by not prematurely depleting company funds - as travelers use their own money or credit cards for expenses, rather than using cash advances.

float plane - An airplane equipped with buoyant landing gear.

floodplain - Low-lying, flat land on the sides of a river subject to flooding.

floppy disk - Flexible disk.

flotilla - A little fleet; a fleet of small vessels.

flow chart - A detailed representation which illustrates the nature and sequence of an operation, step by step.

FLT /flt - Flight.

flurry - A short-lived snowfall; a sudden gust of wind; a sudden commotion.

fly-by-night - An unreliable person or business; not lasting; transitory.

fly-drive - Package that includes airfare, car rental and usually accommo-dations.

flyer - A printed advertisement.

Flying Dutchman - A legendary phantom ship supposedly seen off the coast of the Cape of Good Hope believed to predict foul weather or danger.

FMC - Federal Maritime Commission.

folio - Electronic or written record of a hotel guest's account.

folk tale - A traditional story or legend among a group of people.

folklore - A group's beliefs, myths, stories and traditions that continue from a long standing past.

FONE - Telephone.

footpath - Walkway for pedestrians only.

FOP - Form of payment.

force majeure - An event that cannot be controlled or anticipated by the tour operator, cruise line, airline, etc.

fore or forward - Towards the front part.

foreign exchange rate - Rate at which one currency can be exchanged for another currency.

forestry - The science of developing and cultivating trees.

format - A specific arrangement of data on a document or in a file.

fortnight - Fourteen days or two weeks.

FORTRAN - Formula Translator. Any of several alphanumeric coding systems for programming specific procedures.

fortress - A fortified place.

forum - The marketplace or public place of ancient Roman city; an assembly for the discussion of questions.

fossil - Any remains, impression or trace of a plant or animal found in the earth's crust.

foyer - The lobby or entrance hall.

FP - Final payment. Also see Full Pension.

FQTV - Frequent Traveler.

FRAG - Fragile baggage.

franchise - Basically a contract to distribute and sell a parent company's goods and/or services, usually in a specific geographic area.

franchisee - The purchaser of a franchise. See franchise.

franchisor - The parent company offering a franchise. See franchise.

FRAV - First available.

FRB - Federal Reserve Board.

free hits - The number of times an agency can access CRS data before incurring per use charges.

Free On Board - F.O.B. - without charge for delivery to a specified point.

free port - Port where goods are not subject to tax or duty.

free sale - Allowing the reservationist freedom to make reservations without checking the availability.

free-standing - Balanced independently and of itself.

free trade - International trade without governmental regulations or customs duties.

freebies - Items that do not cost anything.

freeboard - The space between the deck and waterline on the side of a ship or boat.

freedoms of the air - Air traffic rights as agreed upon between countries or nations for the purpose of carrying passengers and freight between those nations.

freeway - Highway, expressway. See also autobahn.

freighter - Vessel intended for carrying cargo, but may allow a limited number of passengers (12-15). Also called a cargo ship.

French service - Style of service whereby the items are served at the table rather than a prepared plate coming from the kitchen.

frequent flyer or frequent buyer - A customer who earns benefits or prizes by purchasing a certain quantity of the product (based on mileage of flights taken, nights at hotels, etc.).

frontier - A new or untapped area; that part of a country that borders another country.

front office - Office or counter in the lobby of a hotel for registering guests, and providing key, mail, cashier, and other services.

FS - See free sale.

FTC - Federal Trade Commission.

FTP - File Transfer Protocol.

full amount - The total amount due from the clients.

full board - See Full Pension.

full house - Accommodations or seats are all taken.

Full Pension (FP) - Meal plan that includes three meals daily. Also called American Plan.

fully appointed - Description of a travel agency that has been approved and accredited to sell airline, cruise and other products and services of travel suppliers.

function book - A type of diary used to list meeting space assignments and other group functions at a hotel.

funnel - The smokestack or chimney-like structure on a ship.

funnel flight - A flight involving a change of equipment. See change of gauge.

fuselage - The main structure or central section of an airplane.

fustanella - A stiff, white kilt worn by men in Greece and Albania.

FYI - For your information.

G   G

G.M. - Gentil Membre. Congenial member or the term for a guest at a Club Med resort.

G.O. - Gentil Organisateur. Congenial host at a Club Med resort.

gale - A strong wind.

Galileo Canada - Computerized reservation system owned by Air Canada and using the Galileo International system. See below.

Galileo International - Multinational computerized reservation system owned by a variety of European and U.S. airlines.

galley - A ship's kitchen.

gangway - Where you leave and enter a ship.

GAO - General Accounting Office.

garni - Term used to designate hotels that do not have a restaurant.

garret - A loft; a place of refuge or outlook.

garrison - A fort.

gateway city - City from which there are international flights or transportation vehicle departures.

GATT - General Agreement on Tariffs and Trade. An agreement to eliminate trade barriers and reduce tariffs between countries.

gaucho - A South American cowboy.

gazebo - A structure offering a view.

gazette - A newspaper.

gazpacho - A thick Spanish vegetable soup served cold.

GDN or GDNVW - Garden room or gardenview room.

GDS - Global Distribution System.

geisha - A Japanese girl trained to entertain men with dance, song and conversation.

Gemini - A computer system formed by the merger of the Air Canada and Canadian Airlines International reservations systems.

gendarme - A policeman.

genealogy - An account or record which traces the ancestry of an individual or family.

Genesis - A travel industry project in the U.S. that is aiming at building agent-controlled alternatives to the airline-owned computer reservation systems and ARC.

Genie - A commercial online service offering interactive computer services.

genocide - Deliberate mass murder of a race, people or minority group.

gentlemen's agreement - An agreement which relies entirely on the honor of the persons involved; an unwritten understanding.

geodesic dome - A hemispherical structure of icosahedral facets, developed by R. Buckminster Fuller.

geodesy - Study of applied mathematics to determine the area of large tracts of land, the exact position of geographical points and the shape and dimensions of the earth.

geography - Science which deals with the aspects of topography, climate, plant and animal life, the ocean, etc.

geology - The science of the physical history and structure of the earth.

gesundheit - A German expression wishing good health to someone who just sneezed.

get-together - An informal party.

GETS - Gabriel Extended Travel Services. A neutral, worldwide agency system for booking airlines, hotels, car firms and some ferry services.

geyser - Natural fountains of hot water and steam, characterized by periodic bursts or eruptions.

GFAX - General Facts.

gharry - A cart or carriage; a horse-drawn vehicle, especially in India, Pakistan, and Egypt.

ghetto - An area populated mainly by a minority group usually due to the financial or social restrictions imposed by a majority group.

GI - Global Indicator.

GIANTS - Greater Independent Association of National Travel Services (a consortium, see consortium).

GIT - Group Inclusive Tour. Arrangements requiring a number of people and the purchase of tour arrangements.

glaciation - A region subjected to glacial action, as in the scoring or erosion of rocks.

glacier - A field or body of ice formed in a region where snowfall exceeds melting.

glade skiing - Downhill skiing in open areas surrounded by trees.

Gladstone - A four-wheeled pleasure carriage; a light traveling bag, opening flat into compartments.

glasnost - An official policy of openness concerning the problems and shortcomings of society (originated at the time of the Soviet Union's breakup).

glider - An aircraft without an engine that is towed to a certain height and then set free to soar on air currents (used for sport and sightseeing).

global indicator - Codes shown next to fares indicating over what land mass or body of water the routing of travel must take. For example, AT means via the Atlantic Ocean.

globe trotter - One who travels widely all over the world.

GM - General Manager.

GMT - See Greenwich Mean Time.

GNP - Gross National Product. Measure of a nation's total production, based on the market value of goods and services produced (usually measured for a month or a year).

GNR - Guest Name Record.

go - A Japanese game played by two players with black and white stones on a board marked with squares.

GO - Value (car rental company).

Golden Age Passport - Special card available to those 62 years of age and over, permitting unlimited entrance to parks and sites operated by the National Park Service.

gondola - A long, narrow flat-bottomed boat used on canals. Also a vehicle used in ski areas to transport skiers and sightseers.

gorge - A particularly deep and narrow canyon.

GPST - Group seat request.

gradient - Degree of slope or inclination.

Grand Prix - Any of several major automobile road races held in various countries.

grand tour - An extended tour.

grappa - A brandy processed from a wine press's residue.

gratuity - Tip/payment for services above the cost of the product or service. See also service charge.

graveyard shift - Night shift, usually from 11:00 p.m. to 7:00 a.m.

greasy spoon - An expression to describe a restaurant that is small, inexpensive, and has a somewhat unsavory appearance.

Great Britain - The countries of England, Scotland, and Wales.

Great Circle - The line of intersection of the surface of a sphere and any plane which passes through the sphere.

Greater Antilles - The arc-like area of islands in the Caribbean including Cuba, Jamaica, Puerto Rico, and Hispaniola.

green card - Term used for the identification card issued to non-citizen residents of the U.S. who meet certain qualifications.

Greenwich Mean Time - Solar time at Greenwich, England from which all other time zones are calculated.

gringo - A foreigner in Spain or Spanish America, especially an American or Englishman, frequently a derogatory term.

gross amount - Amount before deducting.

gross profit - The profit or income before expenses have been deducted.

gross registered ton - A measure of size, equal to 100 cubic feet of enclosed space.

grotto - A cave, natural recess, or cavity.

ground arrangements - Land services such as transfers, tours, etc.

ground operator - The company providing land services.

GRPS - Groups.

GRT - See gross registered ton.

GSA - General Services Administration. Also General Sales Agent.

GSP - Generalized System of Preferences. Used by developed nations, it helps developing nations improve their economy by allowing goods made in those countries to be duty-free.

GST - Goods and Services Tax.

gtd - Guaranteed.

GTR - Government transportation request.

guar - Guarantee or guaranteed.

guarantee - Agreement to provide expected services or products.

guaranteed reservation - Used with hotel reservations to mean the room will be held all night in the case of late arrival of the passengers.

guaranteed share - A rate confirmed even if the supplier does not obtain a roommate.

guest history - Personal profile of a client's stays at a hotel.

guest house - A home that has rooms available for tourists to stay.

guest night - see bed night.

guide - Someone who takes visitors on tours or sightseeing.

gulf - Part of an ocean or sea that extends inland and generally larger than a bay.

Gulf Stream - A major warm-water ocean current that moves in an arc from the Gulf of Mexico to the North Atlantic Ocean. It then becomes the Atlantic Drift.

gunwale - The upper edge of a ship's side.

H   H

habitat - The natural locality of a plant or animal; a place where something or someone is usually found.

hacienda - An estate; a ranch building.

hadj or hajj - A pilgrimage to Mecca, considered the duty of every Muslim.

haggis - A Scottish dish consisting of the heart, liver, etc. of a sheep or calf, minced with suet and oatmeal, seasoned, and boiled in the stomach of the animal.

hale - Hawaiian word for house; free from disease or injury; to haul, pull, or drag.

half board - See half pension.

half pension - Hotel rate that includes breakfast and one other meal. Also called Modified American Plan.

halidom - A holy place; a sanctuary.

halo effect - A term used for the incremental business a travel agency gives to an airline that owns the reservation system the agency uses (above the usual revenues the airline might expect).

hand luggage - Baggage carried by the passenger. See unchecked baggage.

hansom - A low, covered, horse-drawn vehicle with a driver, usually used for sightseeing.

haole - Among Hawaiians, one who is not a native Polynesian, especially a white person.

harbor - A protected anchorage area for ships; to give shelter.

harbor master - An officer in charge of a harbor or port.

hard copy - Copy printed on paper and usually the top copy of multiple-part forms.

hard dollar savings - Tangible or easily identifiable savings.

hard drive - A computer's internal storage and operating capability.

hardware - The actual equipment of a computerization system.

hatch - The opening on the deck of a ship that leads to where cargo is stored.

Hausa - The common language of Sudan and Nigeria.

haute cuisine - A refined style of cooking involving elaborate preparation and presentation of foods.

haven - A harbor or port; a place of safety.

hawker - A peddler of merchandise.

hawsehole - A hole in the ship's bow for running cables through.

hawser - A cable or strong rope used to tow or secure a ship.

head - Toilet.

head tax - See entry and departure tax.

HEDNA - Hotel Electronic Distribution Network Association.

hedonism - Pleasure-seeking philosophy.

hegemony - Leadership; predominance; superiority of one state among several.

heli-skiing - Skiing in which the participants are taken by helicopter to an area inaccessible by lifts.

heliport - Landing and take-off area for helicopters.

helm - Apparatus by which a ship is steered.

hemisphere - One-half of the Earth's surface. The equator separates the Northern from the Southern Hemisphere. Conventionally, the Western Hemisphere is North and South America and the Eastern Hemisphere is Europe, Africa, Asia and Australia.

herringbone setup - Room setup where rows of chairs are separated by a center aisle and slanted in a V-shape, facing a head table or speaker. Also called Chevron setup or V-shape setup.

hidden city ticketing - A risky and basically illegal practice of ticketing a passenger to a destination that has a lower fare, but the passenger disembarks at a connection/intermediate city on the itinerary. Also called point beyond ticketing.

hierarchy - Ranking of individuals.

hieroglyphic - Pictographic inscriptions in the form of characters used in ancient Egyptian records.

high season - Time when rates and/or passenger traffic is increased.

higher intermediate point - When a city between the origin and fare break point has a higher fare, the higher fare must be charged.

hijacking - The seizing or taking control of an aircraft by threatened force or violence. Also called aircraft piracy.

Hinduism - The religious and social system with beliefs in the transmigration of the soul, Karma, and veneration for the cow.

hinterland - District behind coastal or river areas; the interior or back country.

HIP - Higher Intermediate Point. A point or city between the origin and fare break point that has a higher fare. That higher intermediate point fare must be charged.

hire car - Term for a rental car.

history - Detailed account or record.

hitch hiking - To travel by signaling vehicles and obtaining a free ride. However, it may be illegal in some areas.

hits - A term used for the number of times access is made to "web sites."

HK - Hold confirmed.

HL - Holds list.

HLSDE - Hillside.

HMS - Her Majesty's Ship.

HN - Holds need.

HNML - Hindu meal.

hold - The interior of a ship where cargo is stored.

holiday - A day to celebrate or rest; to take a vacation.

hollow square setup - Tables arranged in a rectangle or square with an open space in the center of the square and chairs around the perimeter.

Hollywood bed - A box spring and mattress on low legs or casters without a footboard and usually without a headboard.

holocaust - Great loss of life by earthquake, fire, flood, war or other tragedy.

hologram - A three-dimensional image created by laser beams.

hombre - A man.

home stretch - Final phase of an activity or journey.

homebody - One who would rather remain at home.

homepage - The initial or first page of a web site that typically contains a table of contents for the site.

homesick - Ill or depressed while away from home because of a longing for home.

honor system - System where persons are responsible for paying for their goods or services without any supervisor or manager there to enforce it.

honorarium - A fee paid to a speaker or lecturer.

hooker - A prostitute.

Hoosier - A person from Indiana, which is nicknamed the Hoosier State.

hors d'oeuvres - Appetizers.

horse latitudes - One of two regions of calms bordering the tradewind regions, located at about 30 degrees north and south of the equator.

horseshoe setup - Tables set up in a U shape with chairs placed on the outside.

hospitality industry - The industry segment pertaining to guests and entertainment, such as hotels, restaurants, attractions, etc.

hospitality suite - Hotel room used for entertainment rather than sleeping, usually at conventions and meetings or for groups.

host - Person responsible for servicing the clients or passengers.

host computer - Airline computer to which the agent's terminal is connected.

hosted tour - Tour that includes the services of a host, who is available at certain times, maybe having a desk in the lobby of the hotel.

hostel - Accommodations where the facilities may be similar to dormitories.

hostelry - See hostel.

hot line - An open telephone line to assure consumer satisfaction and ease of ordering or reservations.

hotel - Place offering accommodations. Also called inn, motor hotel, motor lodge, motel. Hotels are generally large and may not have extensive parking facilities.

hotel chain - Two or more hotel properties that are owned or managed by one company.

hotel garni - A smaller accommodations property usually without a restaurant.

hotel register - Permanent record of guests.

hotel rep - See hotel representative.

hotel representative - A person or company who represents hotels for the purpose of taking reservations. Also called a hotel rep.

hotel voucher - Coupon that shows payment has been made and it is to be exchanged for the accommodations and services as they are specified on the voucher.

hotelier - Hotel manager or owner.

house exchange - A system of trading the use of a person's home for another's home, usually in a different city, state or country.

house flag - The flag which denotes the company to which the ship belongs.

house limit - The total amount of credit or charges a person can expend until payment is due by the institution or company involved.

houseboat - A boat fitted to be a house, usually having a flat bottom.

housekeeping - The maintenance of a house/rooms of a hotel or institution.

hovercraft - A vehicle or craft that travels by being buoyed or supported by air pressure.

howdah - Large, elegant, canopied chair-seat strapped to an elephant's back, mostly used in East India.

HRI - Hilton Reservations International.

HS - Have sold.

HSMAI - Hotel Sales and Marketing Association International.

HTL - Hotel.

html - Hypertext Markup Language. Used in web page documents.

http - Hypertext Transfer Protocol. Used in web site addresses.

hub - An airport used as a major connection point.

hub and spoke concept - A concept involving the establishing of a particular city as a central point to which many flights are scheduled, then easy connections are made to smaller cities.

hull - The outer walls of a ship.

Humboldt Current - Current flowing northward along the coast of Peru and northern Chile.

hurache - A Mexican sandal whose upperpart is made of interlaced leather strips.

hurling - A traditional Irish sport, similar to field hockey.

hurricane - A tropical storm with winds greater than 75 miles per hour, usually accompanied by rain, thunder and lightning, especially prevalent from August to October in the tropical North Atlantic and Western Pacific.

HVAC - Heating, ventilating and air conditioning unit.

HX - Have cancelled.

hydrofoil - Ship or boat that has attached struts for lifting the hull clear of the water as it gains speed.

hydrostatic release units - Life rafts that are automatically deployed.

hypertext - Using the click of a mouse on a graphic device or on a highlighted word or phrase so that the computer user can go "deeper" into a document or subject and obtain additional information.

I

I/S - Inside, as in the inside cabins of ships.

IACC - International Association of Conference Centers.

IACVB - International Association of Convention and Visitors Bureaus.

IAFE - International Association of Fairs and Expositions.

IAMAT - International Association for Medical Assistance to Travelers.

IAPA - International Airline Passengers Association.

IAS - Insert a Segment.

IATA or IATAN - International Air Transport Association or International Airlines Travel Agency Network. IATAN offers an ID card identifying travel industry personnel who meet certain standards.

IATM - International Association of Tour Managers.

IAWT - International Association for World Tourism.

Iberia or Iberian peninsula - The area of Spain and Portugal.

IC - Independent Contractor.

ICAO - International Civil Aviation Organization.

ICAR - Intermediate Car.

ICC - Interstate Commerce Commission.

ICCL - International Council of Cruise Lines.

icon - A religious image or painting, sometimes done on a wooden plaque.

ICTA - Institute of Certified Travel Agents.

ID - Identification.

IDL - See International Date Line.

IFA - International Franchise Association.

IFR - Instrument Flight Rules. Rules governing flight in certain visibility and cloud conditions.

IFTTA - International Forum of Travel and Tourism Advocates.

IFTO - International Federation of Tour Operators.

IFUN - If unable.

IFWTO - International Federation of Women's Travel Organizations.

igloo - An Eskimo hut, dome-shaped, built out of ice and snow.

IGN - Ignore.

IGTA - International Gay Travel Association.

ILS - Instrument Landing System.

image - A representation; the composite public impression of a person, company, or organization due to its known procedures, philosophy, and values.

IMF - International Monetary Fund.

immigration - Going to a country for the purpose of permanent residency.

immunity - Exemption from obligation, service, or duty; the state of being insusceptible to disease.

impact - The effect or influence; to collide with.

impasse - A road having no way out; a deadlock.

import - To bring in, as in a foreign commodity.

IN - Infant or International, also check-in date.

in bond system - Method of holding goods or purchases until the purchaser departs, or sending purchases directly to the departing ship or plane.

in season - Available at certain times of the year.

in transit - While traveling, momentarily stopping only to continue to some destination.

in-flight magazines - Airline sponsored magazines or publications usually provided free to passengers.

in-house sales - See self-sales.

in-plant - A travel agency owned and operated within a company itself. Also called a corporate agency.

in-room messages - Messages received by guests on their room TVs.

in/out dates - The arrival/departure dates.

INAD - Inadmissible passenger.

inaugural - First time use of a new route, aircraft, or other travel vehicle.

inbound - Going back to the origin, return portion.

inbound travel - Travel bookings related to servicing clients from other countries traveling to your own country.

incentive house - A company that plans/provides incentive travel programs.

incentive travel - Travel as a reward for sales or work performed by employees.

incidentals - Minor items that are not particularly specified.

inclusive resort - Property that offers meals, sports, and other amenities in a single package rate (also called all-inclusive).

inclusive tour - An advertised package or tour that includes accommodations and other components such as transfers and sightseeing. It has received an IT (Inclusive Tour) number for having met certain standards.

indemnification clauses - Clauses in contracts that contain obtuse legal jargon which require that the other party accepts responsibility if they are sued based on your act or omission. Most contracts have "reciprocal indemnification clauses," which basically state "the first party agrees to defend and pay damages if the second party agrees to defend and pay damages if any suit is incurred on the basis of the agreement."

independent contractor - Term used for hired persons/outside sales agents who are not company/agency employees.

independent tour - A package or tour that does not include the services of an escort or host.

Indian Subcontinent - The area including Bangladesh, Pakistan, India, Nepal, Bhutan, and Sri Lanka.

indigenous - Native; originating or produced in that country or region; natural.

indirect - Not direct; deviating from a direct line or course.

indirect tax - A tax which is ultimately paid for by another, such as a customs tax which results in higher prices.

INF - Infant.

infant - Usually classified as a child under the age of 2. Infants often travel free of charge.

Infini - Japan-based computerized reservations system owned by All Nippon Airways and Abacus.

inflation - An expansion of the volume of currency and bank credit out of proportion to available goods and services, resulting in higher prices.

inflationary spiral - A continuing trend in the general price level, resulting from rising costs and higher wages.

information superhighway - A conceptual term for a massive electronic network offering an array of entertainment, shopping, information, and communication services to homes and businesses via computer or video display terminals.

infrastructure - The underlying foundation or basic framework.

inhibited - Restrained, hindered.

inhospitable - Unfriendly, barren or uninviting.

inlet - A narrow passage or strip of water between land areas.

inn - A public lodging place; a small hotel or restaurant; a tavern.

inner city - The central, usually older and more populated area of a city.

innkeeper - One who manages or owns an inn.

innkeeper's lien - The legal right of an innkeeper to keep the property of a guest for unpaid charges.

inoculation - See vaccination.

INS - Immigration and Naturalization Services.

insert - Something placed between the pages of a publication, usually of an advertising nature.

inside cabin - A cabin without a porthole or window.

insignia - Badges or marks of office, honor, or membership.

int'l - International.

interactive video - Computer programming that allows the viewer to respond to the display, with the response initiating a following display.

intercontinental - To travel between continents; pertaining to two or more continents.

interface - Linkage between reservations made and various accounting functions such as invoicing, reports, etc.

interline agreements - Agreements between airlines that allow baggage to be transferred and several different airlines to be written on the same ticket.

interline connection - Change of planes and airlines.

intermodal - Using different types of transportation, as in a tour using rail, air, and motorcoach services combined.

International Date Line - The 180 degrees line of longitude that separates one date from the next. Crossing the line eastbound will cause the gain of a day, westbound the loss of a day.

Internet - Also called "The Net." A huge network of computer-based information and communication resources accessible to almost anyone with a computer and a modem or another computer network connection.

interstate - Between states.

INTOURIST - National travel agency of the C.I.S. (Commonwealth of Independent States).

intrastate - Within the state.

invoice - Form outlining charges or payment due.

IRC - International Route Charge.

iron curtain - A barrier to information and communication, existing between countries which differ in military, ideological, and political beliefs. This used to exist between the Soviet bloc and non-communist countries.

iron horse - A locomotive or railroad engine.

IS - If not holding, sell.

ISI - International Sales Indicator. See SITI, SITO, SOTI, SOTO.

Islam - A religious and social system based on the teachings of Mohammed as preserved in the Koran and the Sunna.

isle - An island.

islet - A small island.

ISLVW - Island view.

ISMP - International Society of Meeting Planners.

ISO - International Standards Organization.

ISO 9000 - This refers to basic international standards for corporate quality control. ISO 9000 certification is necessary for U.S. companies to trade overseas.

isobar - A line drawn on a map connecting places where the barometric pressure is the same.

isthmus - A narrow strip of land between two larger land masses.

ISTTE - International Society of Travel and Tourism Educators.

IT number - Inclusive tour number assigned by the airline showing that a package or tour has met certain standards.

itinerant - One who travels from place to place.

itinerary - Day by day plan.

ITTA - Independent Travel Technology Association.

ITX - Inclusive tour excursion fare. See inclusive tour and excursion fare.

ivory tower - Place of seclusion; spiritual sanctuary.

IWGN - Intermediate Station Wagon.

J   J

jai alai - A game similar to handball where players catch and throw a small ball with a curved wicker basket-type racket.

JAL - Japan Airlines.

jambalaya - A Creole dish of rice, vegetables, spices, and any kinds of meat or fish.

jamboree - A noisy gathering or festivity; a boy scout assembly of national or international scope.

Japan Current - A major warm-water ocean current of the Pacific Ocean similar to the Gulf Stream.

jargon - The terminology used by a particular class, trade, or profession.

JATO - Jet Assisted Take-Off. A take-off assisted by rocket engines.

jaunt - A short trip; an excursion.

jaunting car - A light, open, two-wheeled cart, popular in Ireland.

jaywalk - To walk across a street carelessly and not at a regular crossing.

jeepney - A Philippine transportation vehicle converted from a jeep. See also jitney.

jet lag - The physical condition resulting from long distance travel and changes in time zones, the symptoms include insomnia, lack of appetite, and a short temper.

jet loader - The enclosed ramp that extends from the door of the plane for boarding and disembarking passengers.

jet port - Airport.

jet set - A group of wealthy, sophisticated, and socially prominent people who travel by jet from one place to another.

jet ski - A motorized vehicle for the water in which a person can stand up holding a handlebar-like piece (like a snowmobile for the water).

jet stream - A strong, high-speed wind current or a trailing stream of fluid or gas exhaust from a jet or rocket engine.

jetliner - A jet plane used by a commercial airline.

jetty - A pier or wharf; a part of a building that projects out.

jetway - A registered trademark for a certain kind of aircraft loading ramp.

jitney - Car, van, or small bus to carry a small number of passengers.

JNTO - Japanese National Tourist Office.

joint fare - A fare agreed upon by two or more carriers to provide service from origin to destination, or a fare for an offline connection (within a country).

Jones Act - An 1886 Federal law forbidding foreign registry ships from carrying passengers between U.S. ports. The customs service now conditionally allows foreign cruise ships to do this.

journey - To travel; travel from one place to another.

joystick - A lever used with a computer that can pivot in all directions (normally used with games).

JRSTE - See junior suite.

JT - Joint. See joint fare.

JTBI - Japan Travel Bureau International.

jumbo jet - Term used for a large, wide-bodied aircraft.

junior suite - Larger room that has a separate sitting area in addition to the bedroom.

junket - A trip often offered at the expense of the public or a particular sponsor (gambling casino, hotel, entrepreneur).

justice of the peace - A local civil officer who can perform marriages, administer oaths, etc.

K   K

K - See Kilobyte.

kaaba - A small cube-shaped building in Mecca containing a sacred stone said to have been turned black by the tears of repentant pilgrims or by the sins of those who have touched it.

kabob - See kebab.

Kabuki - Japanese drama with highly stylized singing and dancing.

kaffee klatsch - An informal gathering to drink coffee and talk.

kaftan - See caftan.

kai - Hawaiian word for sea.

KAL - Korean Airlines.

kampong - A local village in countries where the people speak Malay.

karaoke - Form of entertainment in which people sing the lyrics to pre-recorded music. Pronounced "carry-okee."

karma - Destiny, fate; in Buddhism the quality of a person's actions in one existence which determines his destiny in the next.

Kasbah - See Casbah.

kayak - A fishing boat or canoe with a circular opening in the middle for the occupant.

kebab - Meat cut into cubes and placed on skewers with vegetables.

keel - A horizontal steel plate that runs along the bottom of a ship from stem to stern. It literally forms the backbone of the ship.

kg - Kilograms.

KG - Kemwel (car rental company).

Kiimmel - A liquor made in Germany (and other countries) that is flavored with caraway seeds and cumin.

kilo - A thousand; used mainly in names for metric units such as kilometer, kilogram, etc.

kilobyte - A measure of how much information can be stored. One K equals about 1,000 characters or letters.

kilometer - Distance of 1000 meters (.62 of a mile).

kimono - A loose, robe-like garment worn by both Japanese men and women.

king room - A room with a king-size bed.

kiosk - A kind of open pavilion or structure.

KIP - Keep alone If Possible.

KK - Confirmed.

KL - Confirmed waitlist.

km - Kilometer.

knap - The top of a hill or summit.

knoll - A small hill or elevation.

knot - A unit of speed equal to one nautical mile per hour, about 1.15 land miles an hour.

KNTC - Korea National Tourist Corporation.

Koran - The sacred book of the Muslim religion.

kosher - Right, lawful or clean according to Jewish dietary laws.

kow tow - To kneel, bend, and touch the ground with the forehead as an act of deep reverence or respect.

KP - Commission percentage.

KPH - Kilometers per hour.

Kremlin - Formerly the Soviet government; the citadel of Moscow.

KSML - Kosher Meal.

kuchen - Sweet coffee-cake, usually made with fruit (German).

L

L

Labrador Current - A major cold-water ocean current of the North Atlantic.

labyrinth - A maze; a bewildering arrangement.

lacrosse - A game, originating from the North American Indians, with the object of throwing a ball into a goal area with a lacrosse stick.

lagniappe or lagnappe - In Louisiana and southern Texas, a small present given by a storekeeper to a customer; an extra.

lagoon - A shallow body of water, usually calm.

LAN - Local Area Network. A continuing connection between two or more computers that provides the sharing of files, software, and other resources.

lanai - Balcony, porch, or patio.

land arrangements - Trip elements such as transfers, hotels, sightseeing tours, etc.

land mass - A continent; a large body of land.

land only - Transportation to or airfare is not included.

landau - A carriage having four wheels and a divided top; an automobile with a convertible top over the rear seat.

landfall - The first sighting of land on a journey by sea or air.

landing strip - A runway or area where planes land or take off.

landlocked - Enclosed or encompassed by land.

landlubber - An inexperienced person aboard a ship.

landmark - A turning point; an object or conspicuous building that identifies a locality.

landscape - The natural scenery or vista of an area.

lapis lazuli - A semiprecious stone of a rich blue color.

Lapland - The area of northern Finland, Norway and Sweden.

larboard - See port.

last-seat availability - The capability of a computer/electronic reservation system to provide users with up-to-date information on the availability of airline seats.

late charges - Charges incurred too late for inclusion on the hotel bill at checkout.

Latin America - Pertaining to western hemisphere countries south of the U.S. in which languages derived from Latin are spoken.

latitude - The lines of measurement shown east and west on the earth's globe, but measured north and south (with respect to the equator).

launch - To propel; to set out.

lava - Magma that reaches the surface.

lava-lava - A printed, loin cloth type garment worn by Pacific islanders.

lavatory - A bathroom or toilet.

layout - The arrangement of various components.

layover - Time and place where a passenger changes planes, trains, or other transportation specifics.

LCAR - Luxury Car.

LDW - Loss Damage Waiver. Insurance offered to cover all damages to a rental car. LDW differs from CDW (see CDW) because if renters do not accept the option, they are responsible for theft or vandalism to the vehicle, regardless of fault.

Le Shuttle - Modern freight train-style service owned and operated by Eurotunnel that offers passage for passengers and their vehicles through the Channel Tunnel.

lead time - The advance time or length of time between an announcement or initiation of an event and the actual event.

league - Measure of distance equal to about three miles.

lectern - A raised desk usually with a sloping top for holding a speaker's materials.

lee or leeward - The direction away from the wind.

Leeward Islands - The islands in the Caribbean which include Anguilla, Montserrat, Nevis and St. Kitts.

leg - Segment, portion, or part.

lei - In Hawaii, a wreath of flowers worn around the neck or head.

leisure time - Time available after work and necessary tasks are completed. Also called discretionary time.

leisure travel - Vacation travel or travel other than for business purposes.

Lesser Antilles - The lower arc-like area of islands in the Caribbean extending from the Virgin Islands to the coast of South America.

letter of credit - Written document issued by a financial institution allowing the person named to withdraw a certain amount of money.

letterhead - Printed heading on stationery identifying the name and address of a person or business.

LHTL - Luxury class hotel.

liability - The condition of being legally responsible.

licensing - Process to obtain permission for certain business functions.

lido deck - Area around the swimming pool, as on a ship, the deck containing the swimming pool.

lift - Force exerted on an aircraft enabling it to remain airborne. Also the term for an elevator.

limey - A British sailor; an Englishman.

limited service agency - A branch of a travel agency that performs reservations but not ticketing services.

limousine - Large vehicle for transporting passengers; an expensively equipped car with a chauffeur.

lineage - Race; family; line of descendants.

liner - Large ocean-going vessel or ship.

lingo - Language; speech.

linguist - A person skilled in languages.

liquidated damages clause - Provisions in automation contracts for suppliers to be reimbursed for lost revenue if the contract is cancelled before its scheduled end.

lithosphere - The outerpart or crust of the solid earth; earth's surface.

llama - Any of several South American mammals, often used as pack animals.

LNI - See lanai.

load factor - Percentage of carrier capacity sold out of the available.

local fare - A fare for a direct flight or the equivalent to an online fare: a fare which applies to transportation on a single carrier.

lodge - A resort inn or hotel; a small shelter; the meeting place of a society.

lodging - Accommodations; a room.

log - Official daily record of a ship or other vehicle's progress.

loggia - An open-air gallery area of a building.

logo - Symbol of a company or product.

longitude - The lines shown north and south on the earth's globe but measured east and west (from the prime meridian).

longshoreman - A dock laborer.

loo - In British terms, a toilet; a game of cards.

Low Countries - Historically the countries of Belgium, Holland and Luxembourg were referred to as the Low Countries.

low fare search - Refers to any of the automated software programs that monitor CRSs for the lowest available current fares and rates - in order to rebook at the new lower fares.

low season - Time periods when fares and passenger traffic are not high.

loyalty marketing - Term applied to programs designed to attract repeat business/customers.

LSF - Local Selling Fare. The fare in the origin country's currency.

luggage - See baggage, checked and unchecked.

LUX - See luxury or luxurious room.

luxury or luxurious room - One of the hotel's best rooms.

M   M

M.C. - Master of Ceremonies.

M/M - Mr. and Mrs.

MAAS - Meet and assist.

mackintosh - A raincoat.

maglev - Magnetic levitated train.

magma - Molten rock deep within the Earth.

mah-jongg - A Chinese game usually played with four people and 144 small tiles.

mahalo - Hawaiian word for thanks.

maiden name - A woman's surname before her marriage.

maitre d' - The head waiter.

makatea - A broad, uplifted coral reef surrounding an island in the South Pacific.

mall - A public area often designed for walking; an enclosed area for many shops.

mambo - A fast dance and music originating in Haiti.

manana - Tomorrow; a future time (Spanish).

manifest - List, as in the passenger list of a transportation vehicle (ship, plane, etc.).

mansion - A large house or estate.

manual - Handbook or reference book.

MAP - Modified American Plan. Meal plan that includes two meals daily (usually breakfast and dinner) with the price of accommodations.

marina - Port to accommodate small boats with chartering and other marine services available.

market - A group of people with similar characteristics.

marketing - Process of selling goods and services to include advertising and product development.

markup - The difference between the net rate and the retail price.

maroon - To strand; to leave abandoned and helpless.

marquee - A signboard or large tent.

MARS plus - Multi-access reservation system.

martial law - A temporary military rule imposed when civil law cannot maintain law and order.

Mason-Dixon line - The boundary between Pennsylvania and Maryland between the years of 1763 and 1767 dividing the free and slave states.

masseur - A man who practices massage.

masseuse - A woman who practices massage.

massif - A compact portion of a mountain range.

MAST - Midwest Agents Selling Travel.

master account - A form used for recording a group's authorized charges.

matador - See toreador.

matelot - A sailor.

maximum authorized amount - The maximum amount a bank can withdraw from a travel agency's account (for payment of the weekly sales report of airline tickets).

MAXR - Maximum Rate.

mayday - An international distress call.

MCO - See Miscellaneous Charges Order.

MCT - See Minimum Connecting Time.

meadow - A grassland area.

meal sitting - The time for meals. See sitting.

media - Communication systems (newspapers, magazines, radio, TV, etc.).

meet and greet - The service of meeting and assisting a client or group upon arrival in a city, usually at the airport, train terminal, etc. Also called meet and assist.

meeting fare - Typically a special fare/negotiated discount on airfare for travelers going to the same event.

meeting planner - Person who plans the details of conventions and business meetings.

mega-agency - Term used to designate the very large travel agencies that have nationwide operations.

megabyte - One million bytes (units of information in a computer).

megalopolis - A very large city.

mercantile - Pertaining to trade or merchants.

Mercator projection - A projection of the globe as a rectangular plane surface, resulting in distortion of the high latitudinal areas.

mercenary - A soldier hired into foreign service.

merchant marine - The commercial ships belonging to a nation; the crew and officers on such ships.

merengue - A popular ballroom dance typified by a limping step.

merger - The legal combination of corporations; a uniting.

meridians - The lines of longitude on the globe.

mesa - A high, steep-sided plateau.

Meso-america - The area extending from north-central North America to Nicaragua.

mestizo - A person of mixed ancestry, such as Spanish and Indian.

metal detector - A hand-held or walk-through device for detecting concealed metal objects or weapons. Used at security checkpoints.

meteorology - The science of the weather.

metro - See subway.

metroliner - A term used for high speed electronic trains that offer both coach and club car accommodations (such as trains operated by Amtrak in the U.S. between New York City and Washington, DC.).

metropolis - A chief city of a country, state, or region.

Micronesia - A cluster of small islands in the South Pacific.

mid-office system - The management information system of an agency's automation system, distinguishing it from front-office automation (used in reservations) and back-office automation (used for the accounting).

midnight sun - Sun or light visible during the summer nights in arctic and antarctic regions.

midship - The middle of the ship.

migration - The movement of animals or people from one place to another.

mike - Abbreviation for microphone.

mileage allowance - The number of miles a rental car can be driven before additional charges are applied.

mileage based pricing - A method of setting the prices of airfares based on the distance flown.

mileage system - A system allowing stopovers based on a maximum permitted mileage (MPM). It can only be used on certain fares.

military fare - A discounted fare offered to full-time active military personnel. It may also be offered to those within 7 to 10 days of discharge.

milk run - Denotes a trip or itinerary that includes many stops.

millibar - A unit of air pressure, equaling one-thousandth of a bar.

MIN - See minimum room.

mini-bar - Small refrigerators in hotel rooms that are stocked with drinks and snacks. Guests are charged for items consumed. Also called a servi-bar.

minimum connecting time - The amount of time required to change planes established by law.

minimum land package - Minimum tour cost and components as required for the use of special air fares.

minimum room - One of the least expensive rooms of a hotel with the possibility of an upgrade if there are better rooms when the client checks in, also called rack rate or run of the house room.

minimum use clause - The terms of a CRS contract that required a specific level of usage by subscribers. It's no longer allowed by the DOT.

MINR - Minimum Rate.

minshuku - Japanese accommodation with less amenities than a ryokan.

mirador - A feature of a building such as a window to provide a view.

mirage - An optical illusion.

MIS - Management Information System.

Miscellaneous Charges Order - A form used for the payments of deposits or other travel arrangements that is processed through the ARC.

mishima - A method of decorating pottery by carving the raw body and filling the cuts with clay of a different fired color.

missionary - A person under church sponsorship sent to an area to perform charitable activities and/or spread religious beliefs.

mock-up - A model for purposes of display.

mocktail - A non-alcoholic mixed drink.

MOD - Moderate room.

modem - A way to connect one computer to another computer or computer networks through telephone lines.

moderator - A presiding officer.

Modified American Plan - Meal plan that includes two meals (usually breakfast and dinner) daily with the accommodations.

MODR - Moderate Rate.

modular - Term for designed homes or furniture that are easily put together or taken apart.

mogul - A bump on a ski slope.

mom and pop operation - Small business owned and operated by a husband and wife or family.

MOML - Moslem meal.

monarchy - A government headed by a king or monarch.

monsoon - A periodic wind in the area of the Indian Ocean and southern Asia. Also the rainy season of that area.

Montezuma's Revenge - A term used for diarrhea or stomach illness, related to drinking the water in some countries.

monument - A memorial; an archaeological historic building or ruin; an area of natural beauty or significance.

moon blindness - Poor vision at night.

moor - To secure a vessel to the land by means of ropes or chains.

Morse code - A system of dots, dashes, and spaces used in telegraphy.

mortality rate - See death rate.

Moslem - Pertaining to the Islam religion.

mosque - Holy place of the Islam religion.

motel - Accommodations building accessible to highways and roadways, usually with parking available next to the rooms.

motivational climate - Factors and influences in a work or other environment that affect achievement levels.

motor court - See motel.

motor home - A self-contained, self-driving mobile unit containing all the general necessities of a home: kitchen, bathroom, electrical generator, water supply, etc.

motor hotel - See motel.

motorbike - A small, lightweight motorcycle.

motorboat - A boat with an engine; a power boat.

motorcade - A public procession of cars and other vehicles.

motorcoach - Bus designed to carry passengers for touring and it is often equipped with toilet facilities.

mountaintop - A mountain peak.

mouse - A device that manipulates and directs the cursor on a computer screen.

moving sidewalk - A sidewalk constructed like an endless belt to carry a person who steps on it to another place.

MPH - Miles per hour.

MPI - Meeting Professionals International.

MPM - Maximum permitted mileage. The maximum amount of miles allowed between two cities.

MS - Motor Ship.

MSCN - Misconnection.

MSN - Microsoft Network. A commercial online service offering interactive computer services.

MT - Mountain time (U.S.).

MTS - Motor Turbine Ship.

muk-luk - A kind of boot made of sealskin or reindeer skin.

mulatto - A child of parents, one of which is Caucasian and the other Negro.

multi-access system - A computerized reservation system which has direct access to the computers of several airlines and/or other travel suppliers.

multi-level marketing - Technique in which individuals are compensated for sales made through the recruitment of other individuals.

multilingual - Capable of speaking many languages.

mummer - A masked celebrant, especially at holiday festivals.

municipality - A town, city or borough.

mural - A painting on a wall or a ceiling.

murphy bed - A bed that may be folded or swung into a closet when not in use.

Muslim - See Islam.

MV - Motor Vessel.

MY - Motor Yacht.

N

N

NA - Not available, or no answer, also need alternative.

NABTA - National Association of Business Travel Agents.

NAC - No Action taken on Communication.

NACA - National Air Carrier Association.

NACOA - National Association of Cruise Oriented Agents.

NACTA - National Association of Commissioned Travel Agents.

NAOAG - North American Official Airline Guide.

NAR - New Arrival information.

narrow-body aircraft - An aircraft with a single center aisle.

NATA - National Air Transportation Association.

national - A person who has the citizenship of a country, either by birth or naturalization.

national park - Area designated by the U.S. government for public education and enjoyment. In some cases access to the areas is limited to preserve their natural state.

nautical mile - Approximately 6,080 feet, used to measure sea and air navigational distances.

navigable - Capable of being navigated or steered.

NAVSTAR - Navigational system using time and ranging; a world-wide system for locating aircraft and ships utilizing navigation satellites.

NB - Northbound.

NBR - Number.

NBTA - National Business Travel Association.

NC - No Charge.

NCL - Norwegian Cruise Line.

NCP - See North Central Pacific.

NET - See the Internet.

net amount - The amount due to the supplier after commission has been deducted.

net fare - See net rate.

net net - The net rate for a group.

net profit - Profit or income after all expenses have been deducted.

net rate - The wholesale rate that is usually marked up for resale to the client.

net remittance - The sum of a travel agency's total cash sales, less commissions, plus or minus net adjustments.

netiquette - A term used for the rules or appropriate courtesy to use when communicating by computer on the Internet or other online service.

networking - Communications, a system of sharing ideas, thoughts, criticisms for the betterment of the people involved.

NIBS - Neutral Industry Booking System.

NN - Need need.

NO - No action taken on specified segment.

no-frills - Basic service with no extras.

no go - Cancelled service.

no man's land - Unclaimed or uninhabited land.

no name - To place a reservation without a name on the premise that a name will be provided soon.

no-show - When a client or guest does not arrive for services and fails to cancel the reservation.

NOCN - No connection.

Noh - A stylized Japanese drama in which the actors often wear masks. Three drums and a flute usually accompany the drama.

nomad - A wandering person.

non-commissionable - Items which do not allow a commission to be deducted.

non-compete agreement/clause - Usually a part of a contract that prevents an employee from establishing/working for a competitor for a period of time after leaving the present company. However, it is difficult to enforce.

non-refundable - Money cannot be refunded.

non-sked or non-scheduled - An airline or carrier that offers service at irregular times, at less frequent intervals, and often at lower fares than certificated carriers.

non-transferable - Item is not to be used by any other person than the one named on the item.

nonstop - Transportation made without stops or interruption.

NOOP - Not operating.

Nordic skiing - See cross-country skiing.

NOREC - No record.

normal fare - Fare that is basically unrestricted.

North Central Pacific - The part of area 3 north of the equator and including all of Indonesia (see also Traffic Conferences 1,2,3).

North Pole - The northern end of the earth's axis or the northernmost point on the earth.

Northern Lights - See aurora borealis.

NOSH - No Show.

notarize - To authenticate by using the services of a notary public.

notary or notary public - A person authorized by law to attest documents and authenticate contracts or statements.

NOTR - No traffic rights.

nouveau riche - One who has become newly rich.

NPS - National Park Service.

NR - No Rate. Person does not have to pay.

NRC - No record.

NRCF - Not reconfirmed.

NRP - Non-Revenue Passenger (a non-paying passenger).

NRPC - National Railroad Passenger Corporation.

NRS - No Rate Specified. At the time of reserving, a rate has not been given.

NSML - No Salt Meal.

NSST - No Smoking Seat.

NTA - National Tour Association.

NTBA - Name to be advised.

NTI - Need ticketing information.

NTO - National Tourist Office.

NTSB - National Transportation Safety Board.

NUC - Neutral Unit of Construction. A unit that acts as a common denominator for adding together fares in different currencies.

NV - Nuclear Vessel.

O

O

O - Stopover.

O & D traffic - Origin and Destination traffic. Term used for passengers that are starting or ending their trip in a particular city, as opposed to those who are passing through a city on a change of planes (connecting traffic).

O/S - Outside, as in an outside cabin on a ship.

OAG - Official Airline Guide.

occupancy rate - The percentage of rooms occupied as compared with the total number of rooms available (measured in a certain time frame).

OCG - Official Cruise Guide.

OCNFT - Ocean front.

OCNVW - Ocean view.

off-peak/off-season - Season when tourism is slow or not that heavily booked.

offline carrier or airline - In computerization, any airline other than the one whose computer an agent is using as a source of information.

offline connection - When a passenger changes planes as well as airlines.

offline point - A city not serviced by a particular carrier.

OHG - Official Hotel Guide.

OJ - See open jaw trip.

OK - Confirmed.

Olympic games - An international competition in numerous sports, held every four years, each time in a different country.

OMFG - Official Meeting Facilities Guide.

omnibus - A vehicle for public transportation, a collection of writings all having the same theme.

one-armed bandit - A slot machine; a gambling machine.

one way trip - A trip from an origin to a destination with no return.

online carrier - Airlines that provide for immediate action by the computer.

online connection - Changing planes on the same airline.

online marketing - Using the Internet to advertise a company's products or services.

OP - Other Person.

open bar - Liquor service not requiring payment for drinks; free drinks.

open jaw trip - A trip that has a surface or arunk segment in it.

open pay or rate - Meaning the freedom of establishing the rate, as by negotiations.

open segment or ticket - A flight is involved but no reservations are confirmed because passenger is unsure of date of travel.

open seating/sitting - Access to any tables that are unoccupied; tables and seats are not assigned.

open skies agreements - Unrestricted air services between countries.

operator - Owner, manager or company responsible.

OPNS - Operations.

OPT - See option or option date.

option - Side trip offered that is not necessary or date by which payment needs to be made, or the time frame given for payment to be made or reservations will usually be cancelled.

option date - The date by which payment has to be made or reservations will usually be cancelled.

optional - Not necessary.

ORG - Official Recreation Guide. Also Official Railway Guide.

orientation - A program designed to introduce someone into a new situation.

ORIG - Origin, originated, originating.

origami - The Japanese art of folding paper into decorative shapes.

origin - From where you begin.

ORML - Oriental (Asian) meal.

OSI - See Other Service Information.

OSSN - Outside Sales Support Network.

OTC - One-stop inclusive tour charter.

OTD - Official Tour Directory.

Other Service Information - Information that is included in the passenger name record but which does not require specific action by an airline. For example: a VIP customer.

OTHS - Other services.

ottoman - A divan or sofa; a low cushioned seat.

oust - To forcibly remove.

OUT - Check-out date.

out-plant - Travel agency operations whereby records are queued to an off-premises location for ticketing.

outbound - The portion of the trip involved when leaving the origin city and going to the destination.

outfitter - A business providing the equipment necessary for some adventure or activity, such as white-water rafting.

outrigger - A framework extending out from a canoe; a frame extending out from a structure to act as a support.

outside cabin - A cabin with a porthole or window.

outside sales - A commissioned salesperson who solicits business for a travel agency or other retailer.

outskirts - The bordering areas or districts.

outsourcing - A method of cutting operating costs by assigning certain services to contractors who can presumably do them for less.

overbooking - Deliberate or mistaken confirmation of more reservations than available seats or rooms.

overcrowding - The condition of having too many people.

overhead - Business expenses.

overlook - A place having a view; to ignore.

override commission - Extra-commission paid by suppliers for quantity or volume sales.

oversale - The sale of more seats or rooms (or other services) than actually available. This is done to compensate for no-shows.

oversell - To promote something excessively, to sell more seats or stock than can be delivered.

oversupply - Too much of a product or service.

OW - See one way trip.

OX - Cancel only if requested segment is available.

ozone layer - A high atmospheric level that shields the sun's ultraviolet rays. It's believed that CFCs are responsible for reduction of the ozone layer.

P   P

P&L - See profit and loss statement.

P.A.W.O.B. - Passenger Arriving Without Bag.

p.m. - Between 12:00 noon and 12:00 midnight.

P.P.D.O. - Per person, double occupancy.

P/U - Pick up.

PA - Global indicator meaning via the Pacific ocean.

PAC - Personal Accident Coverage. See PIP.

pacing - The scheduling of activities within an itinerary to give a balance of time allotted to sightseeing, meals, free time, and rest.

package - Pre-arranged elements of a trip such as hotel accommodations and transfers. A package is less inclusive than a tour.

page - To call for someone, usually by means of a loud speaker.

pageant - A spectacle or entertainment; a show.

PAI - Personal Accident Insurance. See PIP.

palace - A splendid residence.

palaeontology, paleontology - The science of fossils.

Pan-American - Of or pertaining to North, Central and South America.

panhandle - A narrow projecting strip of land that is not a peninsula, especially when part of a state.

Papiamento - A Spanish-based Creole language, commonly spoken in Aruba, Bonaire, and Curacao.

par - A level of equality; a commonly accepted standard; the number of strokes on a golf course to represent skilled playing.

parador - A castle, abbey or other historic building restored to use for accommodation (Spanish).

parallels - The lines of latitude on the globe.

parameters - A characteristic element or factor.

parapet - A wall or rampart to protect soldiers.

parcel - A package.

pariah - An outcast; one of a low caste in India or Burma.

parish - County; division of a diocese of the church.

parka - A hooded fur coat.

parliamentary procedure - Conducted assemblies using the rules and practices of parliament.

parlor - A living room or sitting room. Often called a salon in Europe.

parlor car - Motorcoach or railroad car with individual swivel seats.

PARS - The computer system sponsored by Trans World Airlines (TWA). Now part of Worldspan.

partnership - A business that has two or more co-owners.

passenger mile - One passenger carried one mile; this is calculated by multiplying the number of miles traveled times the number of passengers.

Passenger Name Record - The assigned information to the reservation file, such as name, phone number etc. The PNR or file number is also called a record locator or confirmation number.

Passenger Network Services Corporation (PNSC) - The corporation of the U.S. created to administer IATAN (See IATA) airline agency affairs under deregulation.

Passenger Sales Agent - A travel agent.

Passenger Service Agent (PSA) - Usually an airline employee who assists passengers with check-in and boarding.

Passenger Service Representative (PSR) - Usually an airline employee who assists passengers needing information, wheelchairs, etc.

Passenger Traffic Manager (PTM) - Person responsible for making travel arrangements for other employees of the company. Also an airline manager at an airport.

passive booking - Segment entered on a CRS that doesn't result in ticket issuance, such as a manual duplication of a record that was created in another CRS, or entering an itinerary on a CRS to use it like a wordprocessor.

passport - Official document proclaiming the citizenship of an individual.

password - A word or set of characters that enables the user to gain access to information stored in a computer.

PATA - Pacific Asia Travel Association.

pate de fois gras - A spread made from the livers of fattened geese.

patron - Client or customer.

pavilion - An open building; a section that projects from a main part of a building.

paw paw or papaw - A papaya; a large edible fruit; childishly improper.

pax - Passengers, people.

payload - The portion of the total weight in a transportation service that produces revenue; it can include passengers or cargo or both.

PCL - Princess Cruise Line.

PCMA - Professional Convention Management Association.

PCO - Professional Congress Organizer. Term used widely in Europe for a a company that handles the logistics of meetings and conventions.

PDM - Possible Duplicate Message.

PDQ - Abbreviation for Pretty Damn Quick; immediately or at once.

PDR - People's Democratic Republic.

PDW - Physical Damage Waiver. The same as Collision Damage Waiver (see CDW).

peak fare - Fare at the time when travel traffic is heavy or busy, higher fares than off-peak or low season.

peak season - Season when travel traffic is heavy or busy, also called high season. Rates are normally higher during this time.

PEC - See Personal Effects Coverage.

peddler - One who sells merchandise.

pelota - See jai alai.

peninsula - Portion of land almost entirely surrounded by water.

pension or pensions - A boarding house or small hotel.

penthouse - An apartment on the roof of a building.

people movers - Motorized vehicles or platforms that can move quantities of people in a short time.

per diem - Per day.

perihelion - The point in the orbit of a planet, comet, or meteor when it is nearest the sun.

peripherals - Units or machines used in combination or conjunction with a computer.

perishable - Goods subject to decay.

peristyle - An open space enclosed by a series of columns.

perks - Abbreviation for perquisites, which are benefits other than salary or wages.

permafrost - Subsoil that is permanently frozen, found in extreme northern and extreme southern latitudes.

Personal Effects Coverage - Protection against the loss of property in a rental car.

PETC - Pet in cabin.

petit dejeuner - This means breakfast in French.

petit point - Needlepoint in fine detail.

petroglyph - A picture carved on a rock, usually from prehistoric times.

petrol - The word for gas or gasoline in some countries.

PFCs - Passenger Facility Charges. Fees earmarked for airports.

photodrama - A motion picture; a movie.

piazza - An open public square; a veranda of a house; an arcade or covered walkway.

pick-up - Term used for the number of hotel rooms actually used out of a block space of rooms.

pictogram or pictograph - An ancient or prehistoric drawing on a rock wall. Also a diagram or symbolic picture used for international signs in order to overcome language barriers.

pidgin English - A composite English resulting in a simplification and combination of grammar, pronunciation, and vocabulary.

pilgrimage - A trip taken for religious or spiritual reasons.

pilot - Person who flies an aircraft. Also to guide along or steer. Also a trial unit or first-time study (as in research).

pilot house - An enclosed place housing the steering gear of a vessel.

pilot program - A test or trial of a system or technique to detect flaws.

PIP - Personal Injury Protection. Insurance offered to cover costs due to an injury. Also called PAI (Personal Accident Insurance).

pitch - The distance between seats on an aircraft or other vessel. Also the up and down motion of a ship or aircraft.

plain - A large area of level land that is treeless.

plate-tectonics - A geological theory that the lithosphere of the earth is divided into plates which float on the mantle and that earthquakes occur on the boundary of these plates.

plateau - A broad, flat area of land, somewhat elevated.

plating away - The practice of validating ticket stock on other carriers to avoid a specific airline's financial instability.

Plimsoll line - A mark along the side of a ship showing the maximum permitted load when carrying cargo.

PLVW - Pool view.

PNR - See Passenger Name Record.

PNSC - Passenger Network Services Corporation, the corporation in the U.S. for IATA/IATAN.

podium - A raised platform used for public speaking. Also called a rostrum.

POE - Port of Embarkation.

point beyond ticketing - See hidden city ticketing.

point of origin - Where you begin.

point to point - A term for using individual fares from city to city.

polar front - The zone acting as a boundary between a mass of cold polar air and warmer air from a temperate climate.

polder - Area of land reclaimed from the sea.

police action - A localized military operation directed against groups thought to be a threat to international peace and security.

police state - A country in which the citizens are under control and supervision by an arbitrary use of police power, especially through a secret police force.

political action committee - A committee involved in collecting contributions and donating them to candidates or causes it supports.

political asylum - Protection or sanctuary granted by a country to citizens being sought for trial or punishment in their native country.

polity - The form or manner of government of a nation, state or other institution.

pollen count - The average number of pollen grains of certain plants in a cubic yard of air, measured over a 24-hour period.

polyglot - An individual who can speak many languages; composed in many languages.

poncho - A garment like a blanket with a slit in the middle for the head to fit through.

pond - A very small body of water.

pontoon - A flat-bottomed boat; a float on a seaplane.

pool route - When two carriers share equally their facilities, total revenues, and borrow planes and crews from each other.

port - Left side of a ship or aircraft. Also the docking facility area for vessels.

port charges/taxes - Fees levied on cruise passengers.

port of entry - Designated port where passengers or goods first enter a country.

portal - A door; the entrance to a mine or tunnel.

porter - Employee who carries baggage and is normally tipped for the service, also called a skycap.

porterage - The service of baggage handling.

porthole - A window on a ship.

ports of call - Scheduled places where a ship stops on its itinerary.

POS system - A Point-of-Sale system incorporates technological tools that automate basic processes and speed up the reservation procedure.

posada - A small hotel (Spanish).

posh - High class or exclusive; derived from "port out, starboard home" passage on cruise ships.

positioning - The moving of an aircraft, ship, or other transportation vehicle to where it will again begin service for revenue. Also called repositioning.

positive space - A confirmed reservation.

post-audits - Audits of completed travel transactions, often performed by third-party auditors, designed to ensure that contracted rates and other terms have been applied correctly and to obtain refunds from vendors if necessary.

post bellum - Concerning the period after a war, especially the U. S. Civil War.

postal code - Zip code.

postdate - To date later than the actual date of execution.

poster - A large printed sign or paper.

postern - A back door or gate; a private entrance.

POT - Point Of Turnaround.

potable - Suitable for drinking.

pousada or posada - A small hotel.

pow wow - To confer; to hold a conference or meeting.

pp - Per person.

PPR - Passenger Profile Record.

PPT - Profit Per Transaction.

prairie - Level or rolling grassy land that has few trees.

PRC - People's Republic of China.

pre-con meeting - Pre-convention meeting.

pre-existing condition - A condition existing beforehand; such as an illness that may not be covered by insurance because it existed prior.

pre-registration - Service provided especially for conventions, towns and large meetings where room assignments and registration cards are completed ahead of time.

pre/post convention tour - An offering of extra days or destinations that can be added to the beginning or end of the convention - at an additional cost.

precipice - A steep cliff; a dangerous situation.

preferred suppliers - Companies recommended in exchange for discounts or other perks.

productivity-based pricing - A way of structuring CRS charges that provides price incentives when an agency maximizes use of its equipment.

pre-trip audit - Audit of proposed travel arrangements to prevent unnecessary expenditures and to secure other savings opportunities.

prejudice - Bias.

premier class - First class service usually to include sleeperette seats.

prepaid - Paid in advance.

Prepaid Ticket Advice - A form used when a person in one city wants to buy an airline ticket that will be issued at the airport in another city. It can be issued in the same city if departure is within 24 hours.

preserve - Area designated to remain in its natural condition, may also be called a park.

PRF - Partial Refund message.

prime meridian - The 0` longitudinal line passing through Greenwich, England from which east and west longitude and time zones are reckoned.

primitive - Crude, unrefined.

principal - The primary supplier of a service or product.

principality - The territory of a prince.

PRISM - Productivity Related Interactive Systems. A software program available through Systemone.

private butler - An employee who stocks and inventories servi-bars. See servi-bar.

private car hire - A car hired to clients that will pay for a driver.

privy - An outdoor toilet; participating in the knowledge of something secret.

prix fixe - A fixed price for a complete meal with no substitutions allowed.

PRM - Premium.

Prodigy - A commercial online service offering interactive computer services.

professional liability insurance - See errors and omissions insurance.

profile system or frequent traveler file - A list of frequent travelers and important customers, with information on their travel preferences, typical methods of payment and other information.

profit and loss statement - A listing showing expenditures and incomes generated by a business.

promenade - A leisurely walk; also a place for walking.

promo - Abbreviation for promotional.

promotional fare - Lower cost fares that are used to create more passenger traffic.

prompt - A message or symbol appearing on a computer screen, asking for information from the user.

proof of citizenship - Documents such as a birth certificate, passport, voter's registration that certify citizenship.

prop - Abbreviation for propeller aircraft.

propaganda - Allegations, facts or opinions spread with the intention of helping or harming some group, entity or individual.

proposal - Something put forth for consideration or acceptance; a bid; an offer to perform some task.

proprietor - An owner.

prorate - To assess or distribute proportionally.

prospective clients - Expected or potential clients.

PROT - Protected reservation.

protected commissions - When commissions will be paid regardless of cancellations.

protocol - Proper or customary conduct for ceremonies and business functions.

prototype - Model exhibiting the features of something to be made at a later time.

Provincial Standard Time - See Atlantic Standard Time.

provisioned charter - Rental of a boat or yacht that includes all fuel and provisions, but no crew.

prow - Toward the front part of a vessel.

PSA - See Passenger Service Agent.

pseudo PNR - A phrase used to describe a reservation or other information stored in an airline computer using the same format as a standard PNR. It's called "pseudo" because it does not include an airline reservation.

psgr - Passenger.

PSR - See Passenger Service Representative.

psychocentric - Preferring to stay close to home.

PT - Pacific Time (U.S.). Also port taxes.

PTA - See Prepaid Ticket Advice.

PTHSE - See Penthouse.

PTM - See Passenger Traffic Manager.

public charter (PC) - Charter available to individuals or groups.

published fare - A fare amount specifically published in the carrier's fares tariff.

pullman - Railroad sleeping car.

PUP - Pick up.

purdah - Curtain or screen; figuratively the system in India where women of rank are secluded from public view.

purser - Person on a ship responsible for the service and care of the passengers, such as providing information, change, a mail drop, safety deposit boxes and telephone or telegraph service.

purveyor - One who provides a product or service.

PWCT - Passenger will contact.

QADB - Quad room with bath.

QADN - Quad room without bath/shower.

QADS - Quad room with shower.

qd - See quad.

QINB - Quin room with bath.

QINN - Quin room without bath/shower.

QINS - Quin room with shower.

QTD - Quarter To Date.

quad - Room for four people.

quad lift - A ski lift that carries up to four people per chair. There are two types. Detachable quads allow chairs to be removed or added and are usually high speed lifts. Fixed-grip quads have chairs that cannot be removed.

qualifying - Making capable by asking questions and giving the knowledge necessary.

quality assurance - The process of checking a record/booking details for accuracy and completeness.

quarry - An open pit where stones are dug or blasted.

quarter deck - The stern or rear part of the upper deck, usually reserved for the ship's officers.

quay - A wharf or pier. See dock.

queasy - Affected with nausea.

queen room - A room with a queen-size bed.

quest - An expedition; to search or seek for.

queue - To line up; an area of messages on file.

quid - One pound sterling.

quin - Room for five people.

quipu - A Peruvian device consisting of a cord with knotted, colored strings attached and used for recording events.

quota - A share or proportion assigned to a person to achieve or maintain.

R   R

R&R - Rest and recreation or rest and relaxation.

RAA - Regional Airline Association.

rack rate - The regular published rate which may possibly be upgraded on arrival at no additional charge, also called minimum or run of the house rate.

rain check - A slip or stub given to a customer in compensation for services that were paid for but not received (such as items out of stock or weather delays/cancellation).

RAM - Randomly Accessible Memory. Computer memory that allows the central processing unit to move or change a character without affecting other characters.

ramp - A sloping passageway connecting different levels.

ramp agent - Airline employee who handles baggage, cargo, and food supplies to the aircraft.

rampart - A defense; an elevation for defense.

range - Extent or scope; a rank; an expanse of open country; the act of wandering around; how far a vehicle can travel before its fuel is exhausted.

ranger - A person patrolling forest areas.

rate desk - A special department of the airline that calculates fare constructions for a travel agent or client.

rate hike - A rate increase.

raze - To tear down; demolish; to level to the ground.

RCCL - Royal Caribbean Cruise Line.

RCVD - Received.

RDB - Reply to duplicate booking enquiry.

RE - Regarding.

rebate - To give back a portion of the expense.

recall commission - Commission that is requested back as ticket was refunded.

receivership - The legal status of a business under the jurisdiction of the court for the purpose of reorganization, liquidation, or trust.

receiving agent - Also called a contractor or ground operator that specializes in providing services to incoming passengers.

reception - A formal occasion or ceremony. The front desk of a hotel.

receptionist - A person employed to greet callers, especially at a business office.

receptive operator - See receiving agent.

receptive services - Services which visitors need and want when traveling in a foreign country, such as transportation, currency exchange, guide and interpretation services, etc.

recession - A business slump during a generally rising economy; a withdrawal; a departure.

reclamation - The process of recovering useful substances from waste matter; waste brought into a condition of cultivation.

recluse - Living apart from the world; a religious devotee who lives isolated.

reconciliation - Matching up information, such as sales or expense reports with their corresponding invoices or statements.

reconfirmation - To confirm again. Airline reservations should be reconfirmed at least 24-72 hours prior to departure.

record locator - Also called a PNR number; the identification to a file or record in the computer.

recorded delivery - See certified mail.

recreational vehicle (RV) - A motorized self-contained camping trailer or a truck or van used for traveling. Also an off the road vehicle such as a dirt bike or dune buggy.

red and green system - A system of customs separating those with items to declare (red) and those without (green).

Red Book - Previously a reference book for hotels and motels published by the American Hotel and Motel Association (AH & MA) that has merged with the OAG Travel Planners.

red light district - Area of a city known for having prostitution houses or prostitutes available.

red-eye flight - A flight late at night or during the early morning hours, usually at a less expensive cost.

referral - The act of making a recommendation.

regatta - A sailing or boat race or any water festival.

regional carrier - A carrier servicing a particular area only.

registered mail - Mail recorded at the post office of origin and at each point of the mailing process with special care in delivery guaranteed (in the United States of America).

registration card key - Plastic card that is used instead of a key for hotel room access. It is operated by computer codes that can be changed for each guest.

registry - A ship's certificate of registration (which does not necessarily indicate any quality of service or safety). The country of registry doesn't have to correspond to the crew's nationality.

regular fare - Fares without restrictions such as coach or first class.

reissue - To write a new ticket because there are changes.

REMF - Reference my fax.

remittance - The act of transmitting money, vouchers, and such for goods or services rendered.

REML - Reference my letter.

remote - Distant; another location other than the main.

remote ticketing - Ticketing at another location.

REMT - Reference my telegram/telex.

REN - Refund/Exchange Notice.

rent-a-plate - A full service, on-the-premises travel agency operation that is staffed by corporate personnel.

REP - Representative.

repeat customer - A customer who has used the services of a business again and again; a regular or frequenting consumer.

replacement cost - The cost of buying new goods when old ones are damaged or lost.

repositioning - See positioning.

REQ - Request.

rerouting - Using different cities in order to get to the destination.

RES - Reservation.

res agent - A person who takes reservations and sometimes issues tickets.

resident - A person living in a particular country, whether a national or not.

residential - An area of homes, as opposed to businesses and hotels.

resort - Area offering a variety of facilities and services for tourists.

responsibility clause - The detailed statement of conditions and liability applicable to the sale of a product or service.

rest area - Area usually located off a highway where travelers can stop to use restroom facilities and in some cases get information and road maps.

restaurateur - Owner or manager of a restaurant.

restricted access - Limited access, such as agencies not accessible to the public; data not easily available in the computer; off-limit areas.

retailer - A person or business that sells to the public.

retroactive - Referring to a prior time and effective as of that time.

revalidation sticker - A sticker used to show a change of carrier, flight, class, date, time and status, placed over the coupon of the ticket being affected. In the U.S., ARC has discontinued its use.

revenue - Income earned by selling a product/service.

revenue sharing - An agreement to rebate a part of the commission/monies earned.

revenue passenger mile (RPM) - One paying passenger carried one mile; a unit of measurement in the airline industry.

revenue sharing - To give back a portion of the expense. Also called rebating.

REYF/REYL/REYT - Reference Your Fax/Reference Your Letter/Reference Your telegram/Telex.

RFD - Full refund message.

RFI - Request for Further Information.

RFP - Request for Proposal. A formal solicitation for bids on a business's operational specifics and/or services.

RHYA - Release for handling by your agency.

Richter scale - A logarithmic scale recording severity of earthquakes.

rig - A vehicle; the arrangements of sails on a boat; to put together; to control by fraud.

right of search - The right of a ship's captain to stop another vessel of a different nationality to examine its papers and cargo.

right of way - Path that may be lawfully used.

riptide - Violent agitation in the water due to opposing currents or tides.

risk capital - See venture capital.

risk insurance - The insurance to cover losses incurred by lawsuits and other personal injuries.

riviera - A coastal resort area usually characterized by a temperate climate; originally the area on the Mediterranean near Marseilles.

RLNG - Releasing.

RLOC - Record locator.

RLSE - Release.

RMKS - Remarks.

RMS - Royal Mail Steamship.

RNP - Reduce Number in Party.

road house - An eating place, bar, or night club, usually situated outside the city limits.

Roaring Forties - Either of two ocean areas between 40 and 50 degrees latitude north and south where strong winds prevail.

ROC - Republic of China. Also Record of Charge.

rococo - A flamboyant style of French decoration and architecture; ornamental; gaudy or overdone.

rodeo - A public performance of cowboy skills including bronco riding and steer wrestling.

ROE - Rate Of Exchange.

ROH - See run of the house rate.

roll - The swaying motion on a ship or boat.

roll away - A bed that is portable and can be moved from place to place.

rollover clauses - Provisions in contracts that indicate a new contract begins if specific changes are made in a company's operations or services.

ROM - Read Only Memory. Computer memory that cannot be rewritten.

room block - Rooms reserved for a group.

room night - One room used for one night.

room service - Delivery available of food and beverages to the room.

roomette - On a train, it is a single bedroom with toilet facilities (which are covered when the bed is folded down).

rooming house - A lodging house where rooms are rented.

rooming list - A list of guest names and data on the rooms they will require, provided in advance of their arrival.

rope tow - Motorized rope that is used to help skiers reach the top of the mountain.

roster - A list.

rostrum - See podium.

ROTH - See run of the house rate.

rotunda - A round building, especially one with a dome.

round trip - A trip to a destination and back. In conjunction with airline fares, a round trip usually means a journey that has the same fare applicable in both directions.

roundabout - Traffic circle.

routing - Tells what cities and airlines have to be used for a fare.

royalty - A percentage of the sales figure paid to the owner of a product or service, such as an amount paid by a franchisee to a franchisor.

RPM - See revenue passenger mile.

RPT - Repeat Previous Transaction or Response.

RQ - On request.

RQID - Request is desired.

RQR - Request for Reply.

RQST - Request seat.

RR - Reconfirmed.

RS - Reserved Seat.

RSO - Receptive Service Operator. A company or individual handling receptive services. Also Regional Sales Office.

RSVP - Repondez s'il vous plait (French). Please respond.

RT - Round trip.

rudder - A movable, vertical device used for steering.

run of the house rate - A flat rate for an accommodation which may possibly be upgraded on arrival at no additional charge. Also called minimum or rack rate.

runner - A messenger.

running lights - Any of the colored lights that a ship or aircraft must display at night. Also called navigation lights.

rural - Pertaining to country life.

rustic - Pertaining to living in the country, simple or unsophisticated.

RV - See recreational vehicle.

ryokan - A traditional-style inn in Japan.

S   S

S&T - Shower and toilet.

S.A.E. - Self-addressed Envelope.

S.A.S.E. - Self-addressed Stamped Envelope.

S.O.S. - The international radio code signal used by aircraft or ships when they are in distress; a request for aid. It consists of three dots, three dashes and three dots in Morse Code.

SA - See space available.

Sabbath - The seventh day of the week; Saturday or Sunday as observed by different religious groups; a day of rest. The Jewish Sabbath is from sundown on Friday to sundown on Saturday.

sabbatical - Providing time for rest and regeneration.

sabra - A native of Israel.

Sabre - The computer system sponsored by American Airlines.

sadhu - A monk; a religious ascetic.

safari - An adventurous trip for experiencing nature and wildlife (possibly for study, photography or hunting).

Sahel - The dry region separating the Sahara Desert from tropical West and Central Africa.

SAI - System Assisted Instruction.

sake - Japanese rice wine.

salaam - Expression for peace, good health, happiness.

salon - A drawing room or reception room; a stylish shop or place of business; a living room or sitting room (also called a parlor).

salt lick - A place where animals lick on exposed salt deposits; a salt spring.

salud - In Spanish, to your health as a toast when drinking, also "God bless you" when sneezing.

samba - A popular Brazilian music and dance.

sampan - A small boat used for river traffic in China and Japan.

samshu - A Chinese liquor made from rice or millet.

sari - The chief garment of a Hindu woman, consisting of a long piece of cloth wound around the waist with one edge hanging down in front and the other taken up and thrown over the head and shoulders.

SAS - Scandinavian Airlines.

SATA - South American Tourism Association.

SATH - Society for the Advancement of the Handicapped.

SATO - Scheduled Airline Traffic Offices. Carrier-run offices in government buildings. They operate as a joint venture among the airlines.

SATW - Society of American Travel Writers.

sauna - A Finnish steam bath or the building in which such baths are taken.

savanna - Grassy portion of land with few trees.

SB - Steamboat. Also Southbound.

SC - Schedule Change.

Scandinavia - The area including the countries of Norway, Sweden and Denmark sometimes Finland, Iceland and the Faroe Islands.

SCAR - Standard/Full Size Car.

scenic route - A path or road that offers visual beauty, usually indirect and more time-consuming.

scheduled carrier - Airline or carrier that publishes its transportation services timetable.

schnapps - A liquor, generally having a high alcohol content.

schoolroom setup - Tables lined up in a row, one behind the other, on each side of a center aisle, with all the chairs facing a head table.

SCMP - Society of Corporate Meeting Professionals.

scooter - See motorbike.

screw - A ship's propeller.

scrimshaw - Any of various carved or engraved articles, especially those made of ivory or whalebone.

scrolling - The method of moving up or down pages of information on a computer screen. Some entries for scrolling are MD -- move down, MU -- move up, MT -- move top, MB -- move bottom.

scupper - An opening which enables water accumulated on deck to flow overboard.

SDR - Special Drawing Right. A fictitious unit of currency based on a composite of five major currencies that is used for comparison when establishing local selling fares (used in international airline faring).

sea legs - The ability to walk without difficulty on the decks of a moving ship.

seabed - The ocean floor.

seaboard - The area bordering on the sea.

seafaring - Travel by the sea.

seagate - A channel giving access to the sea.

seagoing - See seafaring.

seaplane - A plane having floats to land on water.

search engine - Program to navigate on the Internet.

seasickness - Nausea caused by the rolling and swaying of a vessel at sea.

seat pitch - The distance between seats.

seat rotation - System used on tours that involves the changing of seats on the vehicles involved in the transportation so that passengers have an equal opportunity for viewing from the best seats.

seatmate - One who sits next to a person, as in automobile or airplane.

seatrain - A ship equipped to transport rail cars.

seaward - Towards the sea.

seaway - An ocean traffic lane; an inland waterway.

seaworn - Exhausted by the sea.

seaworthy - In good condition for a voyage.

SEC - Securities and Exchange Commission.

second sitting - The later of two meal times for dining on a ship.

sector - See segment.

sector bonus - Bonus offered by airlines to travel agencies for limited periods of time on particular routes (usually international routes).

security surcharge - Fee levied on tickets to pay for security measures.

SEDM - Schedule Exchange Data Message.

segment - A part of a trip, also called a leg or portion.

segmental analysis - The process of analyzing segments of a business to determine which areas are most profitable.

segmenting - A marketing strategy whereby a company operates different types of services or products in order to reach different customers or customer bases.

seismograph - An instrument to measure earthquakes.

self-catering apartment - An efficiency apartment. See efficiency.

self-drive - Car without a driver, also called u-drive.

self-sales - Selling to employees of the company itself.

selling up - The practice of selling the more expensive or more inclusive products or services.

senior citizen - An older person, usually at least 60 years or older.

sentry - A guard or watchman.

Serbo-Croation - A Slavic language.

servi-bar - A stocked cabinet of liquors, beverages, and snacks for the guests in a hotel room. There are charges for the items consumed.

service charge - A fee added to the bill to cover the cost of tipping or any fee as stated for providing the applicable service (used when agencies charge clients for the time and sale of non-commissionable items).

service compris - The tip has been included on the bill (French).

service non compris - The tip has not been included on the bill (French).

set-ups - The providing of glasses, ice and non-alcoholic mixers.

SFML - Seafood Meal.

sgl - See single.

SGLB - Single room with bath.

SGLN - Single room without bath/shower.

SGLS - Single room with shower.

SGMT - Segment.

shakedown cruise - A test cruise for detecting flaws/inefficiencies.

shalom - Expression for hello, goodbye, peace.

shaman - A priest; sorcerer; medicine man.

Shangri-la - An earthly paradise.

shantytown - The part of a town where most of the dwellings are shacks.

share fare/rate - Fares or rates extended to single travelers who are willing to share accommodations.

shared code carrier - An airline using the code of another airline.

sheikdom - The territory ruled by a sheik.

shell - A brochure or flyer available from suppliers that has room available for travel agencies to place their own information or stamp.

Sherpa - A Himalayan person most noted as a guide on mountaineering expeditions.

Shintoism or Shinto - A religion characterized by reverence of natural spirits and the spirits of ancestors.

ship to shore - Radio system communications between ships and land.

shogi - Japanese chess played on a board of 81 squares with 40 pieces to the set.

shogun - A military governor of Japan before the mid-19th century revolution.

shoji - A paper screen serving as a wall, partition, or sliding door.

shooting star - A meteor.

shoptalk - The jargon or subject information relating to a particular occupation; talk about one's work.

shore excursion - Tours or sightseeing as available at the ports on cruise itineraries (usually at an additional cost to the price of the cruise).

short haul - Flight segments or aircraft that involve smaller distances.

shoulder season - Between the high and low season of a fare or traffic period.

showboat - A river steamship containing a theater or other entertainment.

SHTL - Second class hotel.

shuttle - A vehicle traveling back and forth frequently (usually for a short distance).

SI - Service Information; Systeme International - International system of units of measurement.

sic - Intentionally so written, such as indicating exactly what was printed in the original document.

sidereal - Relating to the stars or constellations.

sierra - A range of mountains.

siesta - A nap or rest taken in the heat of midday or early afternoon. Some stores will close from 1:00 pm to 4:00 pm for this convenience.

SIGs - Special Interest Groups.

single - Room for one person.

single entity charter - An individual, company, or group that charters the equipment directly and does not sell it to others.

single supplement - The additional payment to be added to the double cost if the client is traveling alone.

SIPP - Standard Interline Passenger Procedures.

SITs - Special Interest Tour/Traveler.

SITA - Societe Internationale de Telecommunications Aeronautiques Societe Cooperative. The equivalent of ARINC for international airlines.

SITE - Society of Incentive Travel Executives.

site inspection - The procedure of looking at hotels and facilities in a city or at a destination.

SITI - Sold Inside, Ticketed Inside. One of the international sales codes indicated on tickets. (Example: Miami to London to Miami, ticket bought in the U.S.)

SITO - Sold Inside, Ticketed Outside. One of the international sales codes indicated on tickets. (Example: A PTA issued in the U.S. for travel from Los Angeles to Rome, the ticket issued in Mexico City.)

sitting - On a ship, there are usually two serving times for breakfast, lunch, and dinner. The early or first sitting may feature breakfast at 7:30 a.m., lunch at 12:00 noon and dinner at 6:30 p.m.; the second sitting may occur 1 to 1-1/2 hours later for each meal.

sixth freedom - Allowing an airline of one country to carry passengers between two other countries as long as it travels via the home country.

SKAL - A social organization of travel industry executives.

SKD - Schedule or schedule change.

SKED - Schedule.

skeetshooting - A sport in which the shooter fires at clay disks hurled at varying speeds and angles to practice hunting skills.

ski lift - A motor-driven device for carrying skiers up a mountain slope.

skid row - An area of town containing cheap bars, hotels, and restaurants frequented by vagrants and alcoholics.

skiff - A small, light boat.

skijoring - A sport in which a skier is drawn by a horse or vehicle over snow or ice.

skipper - The captain of a ship.

skycap - The porter or baggage carrier at an airport.

skyjacking - See aircraft piracy.

skyscraper - A tall building.

slalom - Skiing on a zigzag or wavy course. Also a race against time over such a course.

sleeper berth - See sleeperette.

sleeperette - A transport seating designed to recline almost like a bed, as available on some of the long-distance aircraft schedules.

SLIP/PPP - Seriel Line Internet Protocol/Point-to-Point Protocol. Two methods of hooking up to the Internet via dial-up connection over standard telephone lines.

slip - Dock space at a marina or port.

slippage - The difference between what a company/corporation has promised and what it actually delivers.

sloop - A small boat.

slot - Area at the airport for planes to land or park; a place or position in an organization; nickname for a slot machine (a coin-operated gambling machine).

SLPR - Sleeper berth. See sleeperette.

SM - Sales Manager.

small circle - Any circle on a sphere smaller than a great circle (all parallels except the equator).

smart card - A card similar to a credit card that has encoded data, allowing customers to receive services by using it.

SMERF market - An acronym for the market specialty comprising of social, military, educational, religious, and fraternal business.

smorgasbord - A buffet consisting of a variety of hot and cold dishes; a conglomeration.

SMST - Smoking Seat.

smuggle - To bring in or out of a country illegally.

SNOOPE - System for Nuclear Observation of Possible Explosives.

snowbird - Term for people from northern climates who go to southern climates during the winter.

snowboarding - A sport which combines the elements of skiing, skateboarding and surfing.

snowcat - A vehicle that grooms ski slopes and also carries skiers/passengers.

snuba - A cross between snorkeling and scuba diving.

SODA - System One Direct Access. A computer reservation system now merged with Amadeus. The new global res system is called Unison.

soft adventure - Outdoor travel experience/trip that is not overly demanding in physical activity.

soft departure or soft sailing - A departure date of a tour/cruise that has a low amount of bookings.

soft dollar savings - Savings that are obtained through cost avoidance (such as discounts and free upgrades). In other words, savings because of money not spent.

soft opening - The time before a grand opening of a business or hotel property.

software - The programming of a computer, available in disks or tapes.

soiree - Party.

sojourner - A traveler.

SOLAS - Safety Of Life At Sea. An international standard of procedures for ships for safety and inspection procedures.

soldier of fortune - A military adventurer ready to serve whenever there is a promise of profit, adventure, or some other gain.

sole proprietorship - A business owned by one person.

solstice - Either of the two times of the year when the sun is at its greatest distance from the equator. It reaches the northernmost point on June 21-22 and its southernmost point on December 22.

SOM - Shortest Operated Mileage. When using the mileage system, this allows you to use the mileage from the origin to a gateway city, skipping the connecting city entirely. Also the abbreviation for Start Of Message.

sommelier - A wine steward; a court official charged with the transportation of suppliers.

son et lumiere - Sound and light. Show that includes music and lights, usually presented at historical sights or tourist attractions.

SOTI - Sold Outside, Ticketed Inside. One of the international sales codes indicated on tickets. (Example: A PTA issued in the U.S. for travel from Paris to Athens, the ticket issued in Paris.)

SOTO - Sold Outside, Ticketed Outside. One of the international sales codes indicated on tickets for international travel. (Example: An Athens to Istanbul ticket, issued in the U.S.)

souk - A marketplace.

sound - A body of water separating an island from the mainland or one that connects two oceans or other bodies of water.

South Pole - The southern end of the earth's axis or southernmost point on the earth.

South West Pacific - Points in the Pacific Ocean that are south of the equator and including Papua New Guinea, New Zealand, Australia and Tahiti.

Southern Lights - See aurora australis.

souvenir - A memento; something that serves as a reminder; a token purchase made on a trip to remember the destination.

spa - Originally named for a city in Belgium, now meaning a resort that features mineral springs.

space - Reserved room or table or accommodation.

space available - Often a reduced fare for travel industry people and airline employees allowing them to travel if there are empty seats available.

spam - Unsolicited commercial e-mail.

SPCL - Special Class/Type car (specify).

special fare - Other than normal fares, special fares have restrictions usually such as advance purchase and a limited number of seats.

special interest tour - A tour catering to a unique interest or hobby such as wine-tasting, canoeing, backpacking, birdwatching, archaeology, etc.

special needs accommodations - Hotel rooms that comply with the Americans with Disabilities act requirements. Also called ADA room.

special service requirement - A request for specific action from the airline providing transportation, such as kosher meal requests, wheel chair requests, special seat requests, etc.

specialty vehicles - Particular vehicles rented or available at tourist destinations for enjoyment, such as paddlewheel boats, jet skis, etc.

specification - A written description or statement containing details; a drawing given detailed information.

spectator sport - An athletic event usually observed by an audience.

speed trap - Where police deliberately try to catch motorists exceeding the speed limit by hiding in the area.

sphinx - A figure usually having the head of a woman or man and the body of a lion.

spinner - A passenger who has boarded but finds his seat taken because a duplicate boarding pass was issued.

split payment transaction - When payment is made by two different forms, such as part cash and part credit card or payment on two different credit cards.

split ticketing - The practice of creating two one-way journey tickets instead of a round trip ticket (usually for a lower total airfare). Also refers to a ticketing process in which the agent's and auditor's coupons go to a host agency, while the flight coupons are issued at a separate location.

SPML - Special meal.

spot - In conjunction with tours it is a term used when a person is designated to meet the motorcoach (or other transportation vehicle) and make sure everything is set for the departure.

SQ - Space Requested.

squall - A sudden violent gust of wind; a disturbance; large waves in the water; a downpour of rain; to cry out.

squash - To mash; a game played with rackets and a rubber ball.

squatter - One who settles on new land.

squire - A young man of aristocratic birth; a personal attendant; to accompany or escort.

SRO - Standing Room Only.

SRVS - Servicing.

SS - Steamship. Also Sold Segment.

SSC or SST - See supersonic transport (also called the concorde jet).

SSM - Segment Status Messages, or Schedule Exchange Data Message Identification.

SSR - See special service requirement.

SST - Self-Service Terminal. Also supersonic transport.

stabilizer - Retractable "fins" that extend from the sides of the ship to reduce sway and rolling and provide smoother sailings.

stack - A tall vertical pipe or chimney on a ship.

STAG - Society of Travel Agents in Government.

staging guide - Detailed outlines of all the specifications for a meeting or convention. Also called a "spec book."

stalactite - A deposit of crystalline calcium carbonate resembling an icicle pendant from the roof of a cavern.

stalagmite - A deposit of crystalline calcium carbonate rising from the floor of a cavern, often cone-shaped.

stalls - The orchestra seats in a theater.

standard hotel - Economy or tourist hotel with few, if any, amenities and may be located inconveniently.

standard of living - The amount and quality of material goods and services which a person or group needs and uses to live a certain way; a higher standard of living usually means higher cost of goods and services.

standard room - One of the basic, lower cost rooms at a hotel or motel.

standby - Refers to passengers who are either: (1) holding tickets on reduced standby fares that do not allow them to make reservations, or (2) on a waiting list seeking an available seat.

Stanford-Binet test - An intelligence test developed at Stanford University as an American revision of the French Binet-Simon scale for intelligence.

stanhope - A light two or four-wheeled carriage without a top and having a high seat.

STAR - Standardized Travel Agency Reporting. A project designed by a group of travel agencies to devise a way for travel industry companies to provide public statistics about their companies in a common manner.

STAR Service - A descriptive guide to hotels and cruise ships.

starboard - The right side of a ship or aircraft.

starling - A projecting enclosure of piles, as used for resisting waves.

stateroom - A cabin on a ship.

station house - A police station; a place or building used as a station.

stationary front - A front of weather conditions in which neither of two dissimilar air masses is replacing the other to any degree.

status codes - Codes that indicate whether a reservation is confirmed (OK/HK), on request (RQ), waitlisted (WL), etc.

statute mile - 5,280 feet, a mile.

stay-over - Term used for a hotel guest that stays longer than the reserved date(s).

STCR - Stretcher passenger.

STD - See standard room.

steamer - A steamship.

steeple - A spire; a tall, tapering structure.

steeple chase - A race with obstacles such as ditches, fences, and hedges.

steerage - Area for the cheapest accommodations on a ship.

stem - The bow of the ship.

step-on guide - A local guide who boards a motorcoach for local sight-seeing.

steppe - Land area with little rainfall, extreme temperature variations and drought-resistant vegetation.

stern - The aft or rear of the ship.

steward - An employee on a ship or aircraft; a cabin or room steward is responsible for housekeeping the staterooms or cabins on a ship.

stiffing - Deliberately withholding a tip.

STO - See studio.

STOL - Short Take-Off and Landing.

stopover - A deliberate interruption of an itinerary.

stowaway - An unregistered passenger; a hiding place.

STP - Satellite Ticket Printer.

STPN - Satellite Ticket Printer Network.

strait - Narrow body of water connecting two larger bodies of water.

streetcar - A public passenger vehicle powered by electric cable and running on rails set in the street. Also called a cable car.

streetwalker - A prostitute who solicits on the street.

strip - To remove one's clothing; to deprive; a long narrow area of land or water; a popular area of a city for nightclubs and entertainment.

strip shops or strip center - Businesses in a row usually connected or consisting of one long building divided into shops.

stripped package - The minimum inclusions as necessary to qualify for an IT (inclusive tour) such as hotel and transfers.

student visa - A visa issued requiring the visitor to be enrolled in educational institutions.

studio - A couch that can be converted into a bed, also a term used for a one-room apartment or efficiency.

stuffers - See insert.

stupa - A dome-shaped structure dedicated as a shrine to Buddha or one of his saints.

STVR - Stopover.

subcontractor - A subordinate company, such as a local tour company used by a larger wholesaler.

subsidiary - A company controlled by another company by virtue of ownership of the controlling stock.

subsidy - Direct or indirect governmental support of a private industry.

subsoil - The bed of earthy matter which lies immediately under the surface soil.

substation - A subordinate station.

substratum - A foundation. See also subsoil.

subtemperate - Pertaining to or occurring in the colder parts of the temperate zone. See temperate zone.

subterranean - Underground; hidden or secret.

subtropical - Characteristic of the regions near the tropics. See tropics.

suburb - A district lying immediately outside a town or city.

suburbia - Group of suburbs. See suburb.

subway - The mostly underground railway in a city. Also called the underground, the tube (London), and the metro (Paris).

suite - Accommodations that include an additional sitting room, as well as the bedroom and bath facilities. Sometimes a suite will include kitchen facilities.

sukiyaki - A Japanese dish made of thinly-sliced meat and vegetables with soy sauce, sugar and sake.

sultan - Any absolute ruler.

sultana - The wife, mother, or sister of a sultan; a concubine or mistress.

sultanate - The territory of a sultan.

summit - The highest point; the top; of or pertaining to diplomacy between high ranking government officials.

sumo - A type of Japanese wrestling. The contestant who forces his opponent out of the ring or causes any part of his opponent's body, except his feet, to touch the ground is declared the winner.

sun deck - A platform used for sunbathing.

sunbathe - To lay down exposed to the sun.

sundial - An instrument indicating time by the shadow of a pointer cast by the sun.

sundries - Various small things.

sunny-side up - Denoting an egg fried only on the under side, with the yolk unbroken.

sunshade - An awning or something used as protection from the sun.

sunspot - One of the relatively dark patches which appear periodically on the sun, and which are regarded as affecting terrestrial magnetism.

sunstroke - A type of heatstroke resulting from exposure to the sun.

SUP - See superior room.

superhighway - A high-speed, multilane highway.

superintendent - A manager; a maintenance supervisor.

superior room - One of the nicer rooms at a hotel or motel, maybe with a view and other amenities.

superliner - A type of train, usually bi-level. Also a luxury ship of exceptional size.

supermarket - A large retail store selling food.

supernova - A rarely-observed exploding star which achieves a brightness as much as 100 million times greater than the sun.

superpower - Power on an extraordinary scale; a nation or bloc of nations with great political power.

supersonic transport - An airplane designed and built to travel faster than the speed of sound.

superstructure - Any structure built on something else.

supertax - See surtax.

Supl info - Supplemental information.

supplement - Additional charge for special or noted features, see also single supplement.

supplier - One who offers the products or services as sold through the retailers or in some cases directly with the public.

SUR - Surface.

surcharge - An additional cost for a certain situation or inclusive feature such as a deluxe room, or better hotel category, or traveling on the weekends.

surety bond - A bond guaranteeing the performance of a contract or obligation.

surface - As a segment of an itinerary, it means ground transportation is being used, also called an arunk segment.

surf the net - An expression for accessing the Internet and going through the interactive information services available.

surname - A person's last name; a second name or added name.

surtax - An additional tax.

survey - Research method of obtaining data using questionnaires.

SV - Sailing Vessel.

SVW - Sea view.

swabbie or swabby - A sailor.

swami or swamy - A Hindu religious teacher.

swamp - Wet, waterlogged, or flooded land.

SWAP - Severe Weather Avoidance Procedure.

swaraj - Self-government in India.

SWATH - Small Water-plane Area Twin Hull ship design. A twin hull ship design that minimizes pitching and rolling.

SWB or SGLB - Single with bath (see single).

swing shift - A work shift from 4 p.m. until midnight, between the day and night shifts.

swizzle stick - A plastic or glass stick used to mix or stir drinks.

SWP - See South West Pacific.

syce - A servant or groom in India.

sycee - A fine silver of China which is cast into ingots of various weights and used as a medium of exchange.

symposium - A panel discussion done by experts or professionals before an audience.

sysops - System operators. People who run forums for on-line services.

SystemOne Amadeus - A computer reservation system used by travel agencies, which is being converted to a global system called Unison.

systemwide revenue - Amount of revenue attributed to all of a supplier's locations, regardless of whether they are corporate-owned or franchises.

T   T

T - Toilet.

T & D - Training and Development.

T & E - Travel and Entertainment. Also Training and Education.

T-bar lift - A ski lift in which skiers stand on their skis and lean across a center crossbar as they are pulled up the slope. See also teleskis.

T.S. or T/S - Twin screw ship.

T/S/S - Turbine steam ship.

T/V - Turbine vessel.

TA - Travel agent.

TAAD - Travel Agent Automated Deduction.

TAAWNY - Travel Agent's Alliance of Western New York, consortium (see consortium).

tab - A bill; to label; a small addition. Also to mark on the edge of a page or folder for easy reference.

table d'hote - Literally "table of the host;" as a meal plan on tours it means a limited choice of entrees.

table talk - Talk at meals; pleasant topics of conversation.

table tent - Folded cards placed on tables for advertising certain items or specials.

tableau - A picture.

tableland - A broad stretch of elevated flat land.

tabloid - A newspaper; a condensed version.

taboo or tabu - Forbidden for general use; to prohibit or forbid.

TAC - Travel Agency Commission.

tachometer - An instrument for measuring the speed of rotation.

TAE - Travel Age East (magazine).

TAF - Travel Agency Fee document. An ARC form that allows agencies to process service fees paid by credit card through the Area Settlement Bank.

Tagalog - One of the languages of the Philippines.

TAI - Travel Agents International.

taiga - The coniferous forests of the far north, especially in Siberia.

Talmud - The body of Jewish civil and canon law or the book that contains the laws.

tandem bicycle - A bicycle built for two or more persons.

tango - A South American dance or the music to the dance.

tank town - A small or unimportant town.

tankard - A large drinking vessel with a hinged lid and a handle, usually of silver or pewter.

Taoism - A religion and philosophy of China teaching conformity to the Tao, the unitary first principle from which all existence and change happens; revering the eternal order of the universe.

tapa cloth - A coarse cloth made in the Pacific islands from the pounded bark of trees and plants, usually decorated with geometric patterns.

tapas - Snacks.

tariff - List or book of fares.

tarmac - A paved area such as that of a runway at an airport.

tartan - A woolen cloth, usually plaid, traditionally worn by Scottish Highlanders; a vessel used in the Mediterranean.

TASC - Travel Agents of Suffolk County (NY).

TAT - Transitional Automated Ticket.

taxi - A taxicab. To ride or travel in a taxicab. To move along a surface under a vehicle's own power, such as an aircraft preparing to take off or after landing.

TBA - To be assigned or announced.

TC1, TC2, TC3 - See Traffic Conference Areas 1, 2, 3.

TCASII - Traffic Alert and Collision Avoidance Systems. Computerized devices that warn pilots of their proximity to other aircraft.

TCP - To complete party of.

TCP/IP - Transmission Control Protocol/Internet Protocol. The basic language of the Internet.

TDC - Tourist Development Council.

TDM - Ticket Delivery Machine.

TDOR - Two Door Car.

teatime - Late afternoon or early evening; the time to have tea (and usually snacks); a rest break around 4 p.m.

TEE - Trans-European Express. High-speed luxury trains in Europe. Also called Euro-City trains.

telecast - To broadcast by television.

telecommunications - Any communications by electronic transmission such as radio, telephone, telegraph, or television.

telecommute - To work at home using computer and telephone hookups.

teleconference - Meeting held via telephone.

teleferic - Transportation vehicle attached to motorized cable such as those used at ski resorts.

telemark - A method of turning in which the outside ski is placed far in advance of the other, and then slowly angled into the turn.

telemarketing - The use of television or telephone for advertising.

telephoto - Denoting a lens which enlarges an image far away so that it can be seen clearly.

teleprompter - An electronic device that displays a script to a lecturer.

teleskis - Motorized cable with a bar or T-bar for one or more persons to hold or sit on for transportation.

teleticketing - An airline-generated automated ticketing procedure that is now obsolete.

temblor - An earthquake.

temperate - Moderate as it regards heat or cold; without extremes in temperature.

temperate zone - Either of two latitudinal belts: North Temperate Zone is between the Arctic Circle and the Tropic of Cancer; the South Temperate Zone is between the Antarctic Circle and the Tropic of Capricorn.

tempura - A Japanese dish of seafood or vegetables coated with batter and fried.

tenant - An occupant; to swell.

tender - A small boat used to carry passengers to port when the ship cannot pull up against the dock, also used as a lifeboat.

tenement house - A house or building divided into sets of rooms.

tenet - Any opinion, principle or doctrine believed by an organized group or profession.

tepee - The American Indian cone-shaped tent.

tequila - An alcoholic liquor made from the agave plant.

terai - A felt sun hat with a wide brim, usually worn in subtropical areas.

tercentenary - The 300th anniversary of any event.

terminal - Area for embarking or disembarking at an airport, train station, etc. Also a term for computer equipment usually involving a monitor and keyboard.

terms and conditions - Paragraph detailing the liability and specifics of the product or service being sold.

terra firma - Firm or solid earth, as opposed to air or water.

terra incognita - An unknown or unexplored region or territory.

terrain - The physical features of a tract of land. See also topography.

terrane - See terrain.

terrestrial - Pertaining to or existing on the earth; pertaining to the world; an inhabitant of the earth.

territory - Any tract of land, region or district; a land belonging to or under the jurisdiction of a state or country.

tetrahedron - A triangular pyramid having four plane faces.

TFC - Traffic.

TGC - Travel group charters.

TGV - "Train a la grand vitesse;" the high speed train in France used primarily between Paris and Lyons.

theater style setup - Room is setup like a theater, with a stage or presentation area. Also called auditorium style setup.

theme cruise - A cruise designated to appeal to a certain interest such as jazz music, wine tasting, archaeology, etc.

theme park - Also called amusement park, attraction/tourist attraction that contains a multitude of experiences from rides and shows to gardens and unique exhibits.

thermal neutron analysis - Technique used for screening baggage.

thermal spring - A spring having water of a higher temperature than found in the surrounding area.

third world - The undeveloped or emerging countries of the world, such as parts of Africa or Asia.

THISCo - The Hotel Industry Switching Co. A service which acts as a translator between airline CRSs and hotel reservation systems.

thoroughfare - A passageway; an unobstructed way.

through fare - A fare for travel from point of origin to point of destination.

through passenger - Passenger at a certain point going on to a final destination and thus is not departing at that time.

throwaway - Items not going to be used. Sometimes a package purchase is necessary for an air fare, but parts of the package become a throwaway when not used.

THTL - Tourist hotel.

thunderclap - A burst of thunder.

thunderhead - A cumulonimbus cloud of dark and dense appearance that produces lightning and thunder.

TIA - Travel Industry Association of America.

TIAC - Tourism Industry Association of Canada.

ticket - Written or printed contract for service or product as outlined on the conditions stated.

ticket designator - Code indicated on a ticket reflecting a discount.

ticketed point mileage - The actual mileage between two cities.

ticketless travel - Also known as "electronic ticketing/E-ticketing," it's the process by which passengers arrive at the airport without tickets or other formal documents to board flights. They present identification and a confirmation number.

tickler file - Method of organizing messages or tasks to be done; files for storing information to have data readily available.

tidal wave - A dangerously large ocean wave produced by an earthquake, windstorm, or extremely high tide.

tide - The rise and fall of an ocean's surface.

tie-in - Cross-marketing arrangement that benefits two different companies (such as earning air mileage for staying at hotels).

tie-up - A slowing or stopping of business, traffic, etc.; a place where a boat can be moored.

tier - One of a series of rows or rings, rising like steps.

TIME - Travel Industry Marketing Enterprises. A consortium.

time sharing - Ownership of an individual dwelling unit in addition to a share of the common property for a specific period of time.

time window - Interval before and after a requested date or time that a traveler will accept for the flights or tour/travel arrangements.

tip - To insure promptness; a gratuity or present of money for services performed; a useful hint or idea.

TKNO - Ticket number.

tkt/tktd - Ticket/ticketed.

TKTL - Ticket time limit.

TN - Telephone Number.

TNA - Thermal Neutron Analysis. Device used at some airports for screening luggage.

TO - Tour order.

toddy - A drink made of liquor, hot water and usually spices.

TOE - Ticket Order Exception.

toll call - A call that costs more than local calls; a long-distance call.

toll road - See tollway.

toll-free number - In the U.S. a number that allows a caller to make the long distance call free, or at the expense of the business being called.

tollway - Highway that costs the traveler money when using it.

tong - To seize, gather, or hold with tongs; Chinese society or organization; a secret Chinese society in the U.S.

tonga - A light, two-wheeled, usually horsedrawn vehicle, used in India.

tonnage - The carrying capacity of a ship expressed in tons of 100 cubic feet; the total weight. See gross registered ton.

tope - See stupa.

topography - The physical features such as mountains, lakes, glaciers, etc.

toreador/torero - A bullfighter.

torii - A form of a decorative entrance, consisting of two upright poles connected at the top by two horizontal crosspieces, and commonly found at the entrance to Shinto shrines.

tornado - A violent squall or whirlwind, a funnel cloud, causing severe damage in some cases.

torrent - A stream of rushing water; a violent downpour of rain.

torrid - Subject to parching or burning heat.

torrid zone - The area between the Tropic of Cancer and the Tropic of Capricorn, see also tropics.

torte - Any rich cake.

Total Quality Management - A 14-step program (attributed to W. Edwards Deming) designed to improve quality processes within a company.

TOTL - Total.

touch-tone telephone - A push-button operated telephone that uses tones to send calls.

tour - A lengthy trip; to make a tour.

tour broker - Person or company that organizes and markets tour products.

tour conductor - See tour escort.

tour de force - An achievement which requires great ability, strength or creativity.

tour desk - Desk at a hotel or airline that is used specifically for selling tours and packages.

tour documents - Vouchers, itineraries, baggage tags and other information given to tour participants.

tour escort - Person designed as the leader of the group usually for the entire travel experience, although he or she may be assisted by local guides.

tour leader - See tour escort.

tour manager - See tour escort.

tour operator - A company that contracts with hotels, transportation companies, and other suppliers to offer a tour package. Also known as a tour wholesaler.

tour organizer - Person who locates and creates groups for travel arrangements, such as outside sales agents for travel agencies.

tour wholesaler - See tour operator.

tour-basing fare - See inclusive tour (IT) fare.

touring car - An open automobile with a folding top.

tourism - The concept of all the features used for traveling for whatever reasons and the travel industry components as a whole.

tourist - Usually defined as someone who has traveled at least 100 miles from home, or a temporary visitor (staying at least 24-hours at a destination away from home).

tourist card - A document allowing a person to enter a country for a certain period of time. Like a visa, but not as requiring, since a tourist card can often be issued with just proof of citizenship.

tourist class - Accommodations that are below first class, can also be called economy or coach class.

tourist trap - Derogatory term for an area or attraction that has been overrun with tourists and is commercialized to the extent of being unappealing.

tournament - A contest of skill.

tourney - See tournament.

township - A region or district.

TPI - Travel Price Index.

tpl - see triple.

TPM - Ticketed point mileage. The actual mileage between two cities.

TQM - See Total Quality Management.

trade mission - A tour usually planned for business or government representatives to visit a country (or countries) in order to secure new business in foreign markets for their product, destination, or services.

trade name - The name by which an article is known; the name under which a firm does business.

trade route - A way traveled by merchants.

trade show - An exhibit or presentation of products and services, usually in conjunction with an industry's conference, and generally not open to the public. It may also be called a vendor show.

tradewinds - The winds prevailing over the oceans from about 30` north latitude to about 30` south latitude. They blow from the northeast to the southwest in the northern hemisphere and from the southeast to the northwest in the southern hemisphere.

Traffic Conference Areas 1, 2, 3 (TC1, TC2, TC3) - Areas of the world as divided for fare construction purposes: TC1 includes North and South America and Greenland, TC2 includes Europe, Middle East and Africa, TC3 includes Asia and the South Pacific.

trail - A path or route created for use. It may relate to walking, sightseeing, snowmobiling, biking, motorcycling, etc.

training fare - Fare extended to employees for trips that involve training.

traipse - To walk about as without a purpose.

tram car - See streetcar.

tramontane - Beyond the mountains; foreign.

tramway - A railroad in a mine; a streetcar line.

trans-canal - Usually referring to traveling through the Panama Canal.

transaction - Record of business.

transatlantic - Across the Atlantic Ocean.

transcon - Abbreviation for transcontinental.

transcontinental - Across a continent.

Transderm Scop - A band aid type patch placed behind the ear to prevent motion sickness discomfort.

transfers - The services of transportation from an airport, railway station or other terminal to the hotel of the clients.

transient - A traveler passing through a place (for a short stay).

transit point - A passing over point, where a passenger changes only to continue the journey.

transit visa - A visa for entering a country just to travel through it.

transitory - Temporary.

translator - Multi-lingual person who provides the communication between persons who do not speak the same language. It can also be a machine.

transparency - A thin piece of clear acetate used on an overhead projector.

trapshooting - See skeetshooting.

trattoria - An Italian eating house; a restaurant.

travel - To go from one place to another.

travel advisory - A warning or word of caution regarding travel to an area, destination or country.

travel agency - An establishment that has normally met standards for accreditation (in the U.S.-ARC appointment) for the sale of airline tickets and other travel services. It can also be called a travel bureau.

travel agent - Person qualified to sell travel and transportation services and products to the public. Also called a travel consultant, although the latter term usually defines a professional who is secured by travel industry people for specific contract arrangements.

travel bureau - See travel agency.

travel consultant - May also be called a travel agent, but usually means a professional who is hired by travel industry people for specific contract arrangements.

travel counselor - See travel agent.

Travelhost - A company that specializes in publishing magazines for cities/destinations that are usually distributed locally.

travelogue or travelog - A lecture describing travel, usually with slides or movies.

Travelsavers - A consortium, see consortium.

traverse - To cross.

trawler - A fishing vessel which uses a trawl net.

trekking - Making a journey, usually by hiking.

trestle - A supporting framework.

tribune - See dais.

tributary - A stream or river flowing into a larger stream or river.

trip - Generally defined to be travel to a place 100 miles or more away from home and return.

triple - A room for three people.

troglodyte - A cave dweller; a hermit; a brutish or primitive person.

troika - A team of three horses abreast; the vehicle drawn by them (Russian).

trolley - See streetcar.

tropical storm - A storm that has winds under 75 miles per hour.

tropics - Area between the two lines of latitude situated at 23°27' north and south of the Equator: Tropic of Cancer (north) and Tropic of Capricorn (south).

troposphere - The layer of the atmosphere nearest the earth, varying from seven to twelve miles above the surface.

troupe - A traveling company.

TRPB - Triple with bath (see triple).

TRPN - Triple room without bath/shower.

TRPS - Triple room with shower.

trundle bed - A low bed, usually on casters, which can be pushed under a high bed when not in use.

trunk carrier - A major carrier or airline having an extensive route system.

trust territory - A territory that is not self-governing and is administered by a member of the United Nations Trusteeship Council.

truth-in-advertising - Requiring a business to give accurate information on what is being sold.

TSS - Turbine Steam Ship.

TST - Transitional Stored Ticket Record.

tsunami - See tidal wave.

TTGAC - Travel and Tourism Government Affairs Council.

TTL - Total.

TTRA - Travel and Tourism Research Association.

tube - See subway.

tug - A vessel equipped with heavy-duty engines, used for towing.

tuk-tuk - A three-wheeled vehicle used for transportation in Thailand.

tundra - Plains area having the ground frozen beneath the surface even in summer.

turbulence - An irregular condition of the atmosphere characterized by drafts and gusts.

tureen - A large bowl used for serving soup or other foods.

turista - Term used for intestinal problems such as diarrhea and vomiting, also called Montezuma's revenge (Spanish).

turnaround time - Time required to clean, disassemble, and/or remove from a room equipment from one function/guest and reset it for another function/guest. Also used for plane/ship refueling and reprovisioning.

turndown service - Service at deluxe hotels consisting of the bedspread being flipped down in preparation for sleeping, and usually a mint or candy placed on the pillow.

turnover - The replacement rate of employees in a firm or the scope of an operation as measured by the replaced customers being serviced.

turnpike - A road designed for high-speed travel usually requiring a toll to be paid. See also tollway.

turnstile - A device which revolves, usually used at transportation areas to control the entrances and exits of the passengers.

turret - A small tower.

TW - Travel Weekly (magazine).

TWB or TWNB - Twin with bath (see twin).

twin - A room for two people who want separate beds.

twin-screw - Having two screw propellers on either side of the keel, which usually revolve in opposite directions.

twister - One who or that which twists; a whirlwind or tornado.

TWNB - Twin room with bath.

TWNN - Twin room without bath/shower.

TWNS - Twin room with shower.

TWOV - Transit without visa.

TWR - Tower.

tycoon - An exceptionally wealthy businessman.

typhoon - A hurricane occurring in the Pacific, usually during the summer and fall.

tyranny - Government by an absolute ruler.

U   U

U

U-boat - A German submarine.

U-drive - See self-drive.

U-shape setup - Tables set up in the shape of a square-cornered U, with the chairs set all around.

U. K. - See United Kingdom.

U. N. - See United Nations.

U. S. or USA - United States or United States of America. Also called America.

UATP - Universal Air Travel Plan, now called the Air Travel Card. An airline sponsored credit card plan used for airline ticket purchases and accepted by many of the airlines.

Ubangi - A woman of the Central African Republic characterized by pierced lips which are distended by inserting wooden disks.

UBOA - United Bus Owners of America. Now known as UMA - United Motorcoach Association.

UC - Unable to accept request, have not waitlisted.

UCCCF - Universal Credit Card Charge Form.

UFO - Unidentified Flying Object.

UFTAA - Universal Federation of Travel Agents' Associations.

UM - Unaccompanied minor.

UMA - United Motorcoach Association.

umiak - An open, flat-bottomed Eskimo boat.

UMNN - Unaccompanied minor (NN = age).

UMNR - Unaccompanied minor.

UN or UNA - Unable.

unbiased - Free from prejudice.

unchecked baggage - Baggage retained and controlled by the passenger.

undercarriage - The supporting framework beneath an automobile, aircraft or other vehicle.

undercurrent - See undertow.

underdeveloped - Insufficiently or not completely developed.

underground railroad - See subway.

undertow - The current beneath the surface of the water that flows away from the beach.

UNESCO - United Nations Educational, Scientific, and Cultural Organization.

uninterrupted international air transportation - Transportation which does not include a scheduled stopover at any U.S. city of more than 12 hours.

Union Jack - The national flag of Great Britain.

United Kingdom - The geographical and political entity of England, Scotland, Wales, and Northern Ireland (plus some island groups).

United Nations - The international organization of nations established to promote and maintain international peace and security.

universalism - The belief that man should work for the good of all people.

UNK - Unknown.

unlimited mileage - Provision that a rented car can be driven an unlimited number of miles without additional charges.

unrestricted fare - Fare that does not require advance purchase and other requirements.

unscheduled - Not arranged or scheduled in advance.

unspoiled - Uncommercialized, not overdeveloped so as to be frequented by many tourists.

untouchable - Inaccessible; a member of the lowest caste in India that was not to be touched.

untraveled - Not having traveled; unsophisticated.

UPC - Universal Product Code. A bar code of information (price, classification, etc.) that can be read electronically.

upgrade - To change to a better class of service.

uphill - A rising incline.

upkeep - Maintaining the condition; the cost of maintenance.

uproot - To tear away as from a homeland or tradition.

upper and lower beds - Bunk beds.

upscale - That which caters to a more sophisticated or wealthier market group.

upwind - Toward or against the wind.

urban - Characteristic of cities.

urbanite - A resident of a city.

Urdu - An official language of Pakistan.

URL - Universal Resource Locator. A document's address on the world wide web.

US - Unable to accept request, have waitlisted. Also USA Rent-a-Car.

USANTO - United States of America National Tourist Office.

Usenet - A forum which uses the Internet to share information in a text format (like a bulletin board).

user friendly - Referring to computer systems that prompt the user to answer questions rather than relying on formats the user would have to enter.

USS - United States Ship.

USTAR - U.S. Travel Agents Registry. A registered operating name for the group that is working on the Genesis project (See Genesis).

USTDC - United States Travel Data Center.

USTOA - United States Tour Operators Association.

usurp - To seize and hold possession of.

usury - An excessive amount of interest charged for lending money.

UTC - Universal (or Uniform) Time Coordinated. This code may eventually replace GMT. Also stands for Unable To Contact.

UTDN - Unattended Ticket Delivery Network.

utilitarianism - The view that right conduct is determined by the good or usefulness it produces.

utilization rate - Percentage of a car rental company's or individual location's vehicles in use during a specified period.

utopia - An ideally perfect situation or place.

UTR - Unable to Reach.

UTV - Mastercard Universal Travel Voucher. An electronic funds transfer system that allows travel agents/wholesalers to confirm reservations and serves as payment.

UU - Unable.

V-Day - A day on which final victory is achieved.

V-shape setup - See Chevron setup.

V. P. - Vice President.

V.V. - Vice versa, in either direction.

vacancy - Available space.

vacation - A holiday; to take a vacation.

vaccination - Also called an inoculation, usually a medical shot to prevent illness or disease (but can be in tablet or liquid form).

vagabond - One who wanders; a tramp or vagrant; wandering from place to place.

vale - A valley.

valet - One employed for various personal services.

validation - The imprinting of a document.

validator - Machine used to imprint tickets or forms.

validity dates - Dates for which a fare or tour is effective.

valise - A suitcase.

valley - A long and sometimes narrow depression of land, usually between two mountain ranges or ridges.

Value Added Tax (VAT) - Government imposed tax on goods and services.

value season - When rates are lower; the opposite of peak season.

van - A large covered vehicle.

vandalism - Willful destruction of property.

vantage - An advantage; a position affording superiority.

vara - A measurement of anywhere from 32 inches to 43 inches.

variable costs - Costs that change with the number of transactions or in the volume of business.

variety store - A retail store carrying a wide variety of inexpensive goods.

VAT - See Value Added Tax.

vault - To leap; an arched structure; an underground chamber.

VDT - Video Display Terminal. A computer screen terminal, see also CRT.

vector - An entity which indicates direction and magnitude; a line segment that represents an entity; the direction of an object from one point to another.

veer - To change direction.

veld or veldt - The open country.

velocity - Speed.

velodrome - Stadium used for cycle racing.

vender - See vendor.

vending machine - A coin-operated machine which sells gum, candy, or other small items.

vendor - The supplier, seller.

venture capital - Money invested in speculative businesses.

veranda or verandah - A porch or patio usually having a roof.

verbatim - Word for word; the same words.

verboten - Forbidden; prohibited by law (German).

verdant - Green with plants; naive or inexperienced.

verification - Process to substantiate the correctness of what has been presented.

vernacular - The native speech or language of a place; the common name.

vertical drop - Difference in height between the top and the base of the mountain.

vertical file - A group of clippings, pamphlets or other materials kept in an upright position for easy access, as in a library.

vertigo - Dizziness.

vessel - A boat, ship or container to hold things.

vestibule - A hall or antechamber; an enclosed passage between railroad cars.

vet - Abbreviation for veterinarian or veteran. See veteran.

veteran - One who has become thoroughly experienced in a profession; one who has served in the armed forces, especially during a war.

VFR - Visiting Friends and Relatives.

VGML - Vegetable Meal.

via - By way of.

viaduct - A long bridge over a valley or other roads.

viator - One who travels, a wanderer.

VICE - Instead of.

vice versa - In either direction.

vicinity - The nearby area.

Victorian - Pertaining to the time of Queen Victoria of Great Britain (1837-1901); prudish; ornate.

video - The visual communications medium.

videoconference - Meeting in which participants are able to see each other through video links.

vignette - A photograph, a sketch, or a description.

VIL - See villa.

villa - A country house; a mansion; a luxurious home.

vintage - A season of wine-making; a period of time; an age.

VIP - Very Important Passenger/Person.

virus - Any of numerous kinds of organisms that cause disease. In computers a destructive program.

vis-a-vis - Compared to; face to face with.

visa - A stamp or endorsement usually placed in a passport by a consulate allowing a person to enter a country for a certain period of time.

visitor visa - Visa that allows a tourist to enter a country for the purpose of travel.

vista - View of scenery.

vistadome - Special train in Mexico's Copper Canyon area facilitated for viewing the scenery.

VLA - Villa.

volcanism - The phenomena connected with volcanoes and volcanic activity.

volplane - To glide downward in an aircraft; any such gliding plane.

volume incentive - Extra commission or bonuses paid for a certain amount of sales.

voodoo - A religion of African origin characterized by mysterious rites, superstitions, sorcery, commonly practiced in Haiti and other West Indies islands.

vortex - A whirling mass of water or air.

voucher - Document to be exchanged for goods or services, substantiating that payment has already been made. Also called an exchange order.

VSTOL - Vertical/Short Take-Off and Landing.

W W

w/c - Will call.

w/fac - With facilities.

w/o fac - Without facilities.

wadi or wady - The channel of a waterway that is dry except during the rainy season; any oasis.

Wagons-lits - Sleeping cars on the European trains that consist of a private bedroom with accommodations for one, two, or more passengers.

wahines - Hawaiian word for women.

waif - A neglected, homeless person; a wanderer.

waitlist - List established when there are no more ready available spaces; names waiting for cancellations.

waiver - An intentional dismissal of a requirement or right; an express or written statement of the relinquishment.

wake - The waves or smooth water caused by the motion of a ship through water.

walk-in - A guest who did not make previous reservations.

walk-up - Traveler who purchases tickets just prior to departure.

walkabout - Australian word for taking a walk or trip with no specific destination intended.

walked - Term used when a traveler arrives at a hotel with a reservation but no rooms are available; so the hotel pays for the traveler's accommodations at another hotel.

walkie-talkie - A mobile or portable two-way radio/telephone system.

walkout - A worker's strike.

wander - To stroll; to go indirectly or casually.

wanderlust - Desire to wander; a longing to visit faraway places.

wasteland - An area of uncultivated or devastated land.

wat - A Buddhist temple or monastery.

WATA - World Association of Travel Agents.

water closet - Toilet.

water table - The level below which the ground is saturated with water.

waterfront - Section of land adjoining the water.

waterline - Lines on the hull of a ship showing the depth it sinks to when loaded with cargo.

waterman - A boatman.

watershed - An area drained by a stream, system or body of water.

WATS - Wide Area Telephone Service.

way station - A station situated between principal stations.

wayfarer - A traveler.

wayside - The edge of a road or highway.

wayworn - Worn or wearied by travel.

WB - Westbound.

WC - Water or wash closet, term used for a restroom.

WCHC - Wheelchair - passenger completely immobile.

WCHR - Wheelchair.

WCHS - Wheelchair - cannot ascend/descend stairs.

web - Term for the world wide web.

web browser - A software program used to access information on the world wide web.

web site - A specific address on the world wide web for finding information.

weekend rate - Special prices often used to attract leisure travelers to business hotels.

weigh - To hoist or raise a ship's anchor.

well-to-do - Wealthy.

West Indies - A collective name for the group of islands between North and South America located in the Caribbean Sea.

westerlies - Winds that tend to blow from west to east (generally in the temperate zone).

Western hemisphere - See Traffic Conference Area 1.

wet bar - A small drink preparation area in a hotel room.

wet lease - Rental of a vehicle with a crew and all other necessities.

wetback - A Mexican citizen who illegally enters the U. S. often by swimming the Rio Grande River. Often a derogatory term.

wharf - A structure projecting out into a waterway so that vessels may be positioned alongside. See dock.

whistle stop - A town too small to have scheduled stops.

white cap - A wave with a foamy crest.

white-knuckle flyer - Expression for a person who is afraid of flying, such that they grip tightly the arm rests of the seat.

WHO - World Health Organization.

wholesaler - A merchant middleman who sells chiefly to retailers. Also called a jobber.

wide-body - Aircraft that carry a large number of passengers such as 747s, AB3s, and L10s.

widow's walk - A railed observation platform built on the roof of a house. Also called a captain's walk.

wigwam - See tepee.

wilderness - A wild region.

wildlife - Animals or plants that exist in a wild, undomesticated state.

wind shear - Sudden downward draft of air (which has been identified as the cause of some airline accidents).

windchill - The effects of wind speed on a given temperature, expressed as a still-air temperature.

windjammer - A sailing ship or one of its crew.

window - On a computer it is an area of a screen that displays information. Some computer programs provide several windows that can be displayed simultaneously or sequentially.

windward - The direction towards the wind.

Windward Islands - The islands in the Caribbean which include Dominica, Grenada, St. Lucia and St. Vincent.

wing-ding - A social gathering or celebration.

wiretap - A monitor; the device to monitor.

WK - Was confirmed.

WL - See waitlist.

WOAG - Worldwide Official Airline Guide.

workshop - A seminar of training that requires the participants to work on problems or in other ways engage in work details to gain knowledge and/or skills.

Worldspan - Computerized reservation system owned by Delta, Northwest, TWA, and Abacus.

world wide web - Graphical display of information using pictures, text, and sometimes sound - available through the Internet.

write-off - An expense which is tax deductible.

WTCIB - Women's Travellers Center and Information Bank.

WTO - World Tourism Organization.

WTRVW - Water view.

WTTC - World Travel and Tourism Council.

wurst - Sausage-like meat.

www - See world wide web.

X - Connection.

XBAG - Excess baggage.

xenophobia - Fear, distrust, or hatred of foreigners.

XF - Cancelled phone.

XL - Cancel, also cancel waitlist.

XLD - Cancelled.

XN - Cancelled name.

XO - Exchange order. See also voucher.

XR - Cancellation Recommended.

XS - Cancelled segment.

XSEC - See extra section.

XTN - Extension.

XX - Cancelled.

 # Y

Y. M. C. A. - Young Men's Christian Association.

Y. W. C. A. - Young Women's Christian Association.

yacht - A sail, steam, or motorized vessel.

yaw - To deviate from course.

yeoman - A petty officer in the navy.

yeshiva or yeshivah - A Jewish educational institution for studying the Talmud.

yield - The return on an investment; to produce as a result; to give up or give way.

yield management - Pricing according to the return or expected revenue on a seat or other accommodation.

yogwan - A traditional Korean inn.

yokel - A rustic person; a country bumpkin.

youth fare - Fare for persons aged 12-22 or 25 years old.

youth hostel - A student residence or dormitory, see also hostel.

Yucatan - The peninsula of eastern Mexico.

Yule - Christmas.

Yuletide - The time or season of Christmas.

yuppies - Expression for young urban professionals, a market group.

yurt - A domed, portable, cylinder-shaped tent constructed from skins or felt stretched onto a framework of branches, used by various nomadic people in Asia.

Z   Z

Z-time - Zulu time. The same as Greenwich Mean Time (GMT).

zareba or zareeba - An enclosure of thorn bushes or the like, built around a camp or village for protection against enemies or wild animals.

ZD - Budget (car rental company).

ZE - Hertz (car rental company).

Zeitgeist - The spirit of the time.

zenana - In India, the part of the house in which the women and girls of a family are secluded.

zenith - The highest point; the vertical point above one's head.

zephyr - Any soft, mild breeze; a light, fine fabric or yarn.

zeppelin - A rigid dirigible with internal gas cells supporting the long, cylindrical body.

zero-zero - Characterized by weather conditions in which the ceiling and visibility are zero.

ZI - Avis (car rental company).

Zionism - A movement to colonize Hebrews in Palestine; a movement to create a national homeland for Jews in Palestine.

ZIP code - Zone Improvement Plan. The system to improve mail delivery because of an identification number.

ZL - National (car rental company).

ZN - General (car rental company).

zocalo - City square (in Spanish).

zodiac - An imaginary belt encircling the heavens containing twelve constellations and their twelve astrological signs.

zone - A continuous tract or area.

zoning laws - Ordinances which restrict or limit the uses of land areas.

zoo - Zoological garden. A park or area to display animals.

zoology - Study of animals.

zoom lens - See telephoto.

zoomorphic - Representing or using animal forms.

zorbing - A sport that involves rolling down slopes in an inflated ball.

ZR - Dollar (car rental company).

ZT - Thrifty (car rental company).

zwieback - A kind of toasted bread or biscuit.

NOTES

NOTES

TRAVEL INDUSTRY REFERENCES

SOLITAIRE PUBLISHING DISTRIBUTES OVER 45 REFERENCES. CALL (800) 226-0286 (U.S.)/(813) 876-0286 (phone & fax). E-MAIL: PSolitaire@aol.com

AAA Tour Books and Maps - AAA, 1000 AAA Dr., Heathrow, FL 32746-5063. (407) 444-7000. Fax (407) 444-7380. Note: Tour books and maps are free to AAA members.

ABC World Airways Guide, Hotel and Travel Index (Int'l), ABC Rail Guide, ABC Air Cargo Guide, ABC Guide to Int'l Travel, Star Service, - ABC International/Reed Travel Group, Church St., Dunstable, Bedfordshire LU5 4HB, United Kingdom. Call Dunstable (0582) 600111. Fax (0582) 695348.

The Air Charter Guide - 104 Mt. Auburn St., Cambridge, MA 02138. (617) 497-7104. Fax (617) 868-5335. http://www.guides.com/acg

Air Courier Bargains by Kelly Monaghan, available through Solitaire Publishing.

Airline Tariff and Ticketing (Domestic/Int'l versions) - CITC, 55 Eglington Ave. E., Ste. 209, Toronto, Ont., M4P 1G8, Canada. (416) 484-4450. Fax (416) 484-4140. http://www.citcontario.com

ARC Industry Agents Handbook - Airlines Reporting Corp., 1530 Wilson Blvd., #800, Arlington, VA 22209-2448. (703) 816-8000. Fax (703) 816-8104.

American Sightseeing International World Tariff - 490 Post St. #1701, San Francisco, CA 94102. (415) 986-2082. Fax (415) 986-2703. http:// www.sightseeing.com

Amtrak Procedure Manual - National Railroad Passenger Corp., call (202) 484-7540 for offices.

ATPCO Passenger Tariff - Airline Tariff Publishing Co., Dulles International Airport, Box 17415, Washington, DC 20041-0415. (703) 471-7510. Fax (703) 471-1497. http://www.atpco.net

Bed & Breakfasts, Inns & Guesthouses - Ten Speed Press, P.O. Box 7123, Berkeley, CA 94707. (800) 841-2665. Fax (510) 524-4588.

Berlitz Guides - Berlitz Publishing, POB 305, Riverside, NJ 08075. (800) 526-8047. (609) 461-2014. Fax (609) 461-2443.

Birnbaum Travel Guides, Harper Collins Publishers, 10 E. 53rd St., New York, NY 10022-5299. (212) 207-7000. Fax (800) 822-4090. Call (800) 242-7737 to subscribe.

Building Profits With Group Travel - Dendrobium Publishing, available from Solitaire Publishing.

Caribbean Travel Directory Gold Book, Gold Book Publishing, 2655 LeJeune Rd. Ste. 910, Coral Gables, FL 33134. (305) 443-5900. Fax (305) 569-0431. http://www.caribbeantravel.com

Choosing the Right Cruise for You - Distinctive Publishing, POB 17868, Plantation, FL 33318.

CLIA Travel Agent's Manual - Cruise Lines International Assoc., 500 5th Ave., #1407, New York, NY 10010. (212) 921-0066. Fax (212) 921-0549.

Coach Full of Fun, contact Solitaire Publishing.

Complete Book of International Meeting Planning, contact Solitaire Publishing.

Complete Guide for the Meeting Planner - Southwestern Publishing, call (800) 543-0487.

Complete Guide to Incentive Travel, contact Solitaire Publishing.

Condominium Connection Directory - 100 Rancho Rd., #22, Thousand Oaks, CA 91362. (800) 423-2976. (805) 446-2020. Fax (805) 446-2000.

Conducting Tours A Practical Guide - ITP/ Southwestern Publishing, call (800) 543-0487.

Coopetition, contact Solitaire Publishing.

Cruise Hosting - by Brooke Shannon-Bravos - available through Solitaire Publishing.

Culturgrams - Brigham Young Univ., Kennedy Ctr. Publications, 280 HRCB, Provo, UT 84602. (800) 528-6279. (801) 378-6528. Fax (801) 378-5882. http://www.byu.edu/culturgrams

Directory of Int'l Publications for Meeting Planners and the Tourism Industry, contact Solitaire Publishing.

The Disabled Traveler - CITC, 55 Eglington Ave. E., Ste. 209, Toronto, Ont., M4P 1G8, Canada. (416) 484-4450. Fax (416) 484-4140. http://www.citcontario.com

Fearless Flyer - Eighth Mountain Press, 624 SE 29 Ave., Portland, OR 97214. (503) 233-3936. Fax (503) 233-0774.

Fielding's Guides - Fielding Worldwide, 308 S. Catalina Ave., Redondo Beach, CA 90277. (310) 372-4474. Fax (310) 376-8064. http://www.fieldingstravel.com

Fodor's guides - Random House Publishers, 400 Hahn Rd., Westminster, MD 21157. (800) 733-3000. (410) 848-1900.

Forsyth Travel Library has maps, rail passes, and travel guides, 226 Westchester Ave., White Plains, NY 10604. (800) FORSYTH. (914) 681-7250. Fax (914) 681-7251.

Frequent Flyer Guidebook - Air Press, 4715-C Town Center Dr., Colorado Springs, CO 80916. (800) 487-8893. (719) 597-8893. Fax (719) 597-6855.

Frommer's guides - MacMillan Travel, 15 Columbus Circle, New York, NY 10023.

Golf Resort Directory, Travel Publishing, available through Solitaire Publishing.

Gray Line Worldwide Services Directory - 2460 W. 26th Ave., Bldg 1, #300, Denver, CO 80211. (303) 433-9800. Fax (303) 433-4742. http://www.grayline.com

Home Based Travel Agent by Kelly Monaghan, available through Solitaire Publishing.

Hospitality and Travel Automation Directory and Buyers Guide - Garrett Communications Inc., 210 N. Adams St., #1000, Rockville, MD 20850. (888) 427-7388. (301) 738-7927. Fax (301) 738-7896. http://www.garrett-comm.com

Hotel and Travel Index - Reed Travel Group, 500 Plaza Dr., Secaucus, NJ 07096. (800) 360-0015. (201) 902-1600.

How to Get a Job with a Cruise Line - Mary Miller, available through Solitaire Publishing.

How to Open Your Own Travel Agency - Dendrobium Publishing, available from Solitaire Publishing.

Hunter Publishing has maps, videos, dictionaries and guides, 300 Raritan Center Pkwy., Edison, NJ 08818. (732) 225-1900. Fax (732) 417-0482.

Independent Agent Opportunities, contact Solitaire Publishing.

Index to Air Travel Consolidators, contact Solitaire Publishing.

Inn & Travel - Guide to B&Bs and Inns in North America - book and CD-rom versions available through Solitaire Publishing.

Insight guides - American Map Corp., 46-35 54th Rd., Maspeth, NY 11378. (800) 432-6277. (718) 784-0055. Fax (718) 784-1216.

ISMP Start Up Guide to Meeting Planning - contact Solitaire Publishing.

Journal of Travel and Tourism Marketing - International Business Press, an imprint of Haworth Press, 10 Alice St., Binghamton, NY 13904-1580. (800) 342-9678. (607) 722-5857. Fax (800) 895-0582 or (607) 722-6362.

Knopf Guides, 201 E. 50th St., New York, NY 10022. (212) 751-2600. Fax (212) 572-2593.

Let's Go guides - St. Martin's Press, 175 5th Ave., New York, NY 10010. (800) 221-7945. (212) 674-5151. Fax (212) 995-2584.

Lonely Planet guides - Lonely Planet Publications, 155 Filbert St., Ste. 251, Oakland, CA 94607-2538. (800) 275-8555. Fax (510) 893-8563. http://www.lonelyplanet.com

Managing Group Tours - available from Solitaire Publishing.

Michelin Travel Publications - POB 19008, Green-ville, SC 29602-9008. (800) 223-0987. (864) 458-5261. Fax (864) 458-5665.

National Motorcoach Directory - Nat'l Motorcoach Network, Patriot Square, 10527C Braddock Rd., Fairfax, VA 22032. (800) 822-6602. (703) 250-7897. Fax (703) 250-1477.

Nationwide Network - a subscription service for airline and airport briefings and travel alerts, 2060 North Center, Box 3272, Saginaw, MI 48603. (800) 333-4130. (517) 739-9111. http://www.nationwidenetwork.com

Networld (World Manual for Group and Incentive Travel) - 300 Lanidex Plaza., Parsippany, NJ 07054. (800) 992-3411. (973) 884-7474. Fax (973) 884-1711. http://www.networldinc.com

OAG (Official Airline Guides) (publications include Desktop Flight Guides, Travel Planners, OAG - Electronic Edition, and more), 2000 Clear-water Dr., Oak Brook, IL 60521. (800) 942-1888 (IL only), (800) 323-3537, (312) 574-6000.

OCG (Official Cruise Guide) - Reed Travel Group, 500 Plaza Dr., Secaucus, NJ 07096. (800) 360-0015. (201) 902-1800. Fax (201) 319-1947.

Official Steamship Guide International - 9111 Cross Park Dr., #D247, Knoxville, TN 37923. (800) 783-4903. (615) 531-0392. Fax (615) 694-0848.

OHG (Official Hotel Guide) - Reed Travel Group, 500 Plaza Dr., Secaucus, NJ 07096. (800) 360-0015. (201) 902-2000.

Official Tour Directory - Thomas Publishing, 5 Penn Plaza, New York, NY 10001. (212) 290-7355. Fax (212) 290-7288. http://www.vacationpackager.com

The Packing Book - Ten Speed Press, Box 7123, Berkeley, CA 94707. (800) 841-2665. (510) 559-1600. Fax (510) 559-1629. http://www.tenspeed.com

Pelican Publishing Co. has travel and other guides, 1101 Monroe St., Box 3110, Gretna, LA 70054. (800) 843-1724. (504) 368-1175. Fax (504) 368-1195.

Personnel and Operations Manual for Travel
Agencies - Dendrobium Publishing, contact
Solitaire Publishing.

Personnel Guide to Canada's Travel Industry
- Baxter Publishing, 310 Dupont St., Toronto,
Ont., Canada M5R 1V9. (416) 968-7252. Fax
(416) 968-2377. http://www.baxter.net

Prentice Hall offers Hotel Management and
Travel/Tourism books. Call (800) 223-1360.

Professional Travel Counselling - CITC, 55
Eglington Ave. E., Ste. 209, Toronto, Ont.,
M4P 1G8, Canada. (416) 484-4450. Fax (416)
484-4140. http://www.citcontario.com

Profitable Direct Mail for Travel Agents -
available through Solitaire Publishing.

SEA Lead Report - Tour Operators Directory -
SEA Tourism/Travel Research, 3 S. 6th St.,
New Bedford, MA 02740. (800) 445-5046.
(508) 999-3134. Fax (508) 997-6203.

Ski Resort Directory, Travel Publishing,
available through Solitaire Publishing.

Spa Finder - 91 5th Ave., 3rd Floor, New York,
NY 10003. (800) 255-7727. (212) 924-6800. Fax
(212) 924-7240.

Star Service - Reed Travel Group, 500 Plaza
Dr., Secaucus, NJ 07096. (800) 360-0015.
(201) 902-2000. Fax (201) 902-7989.

Stern's Guide to the Cruise Vacation - Pelican
Publishing, 1101 Monroe St., Gretna, LA 70053.
(800) 843-1724. (504) 368-1175. Fax (504)
368-1195.

The Official Outside Sales Travel Agent Manual -
Gary Fee and Alexander Anolik - Solitaire Publishing.

The Tourism Industry: An International Analysis,
CAB International, 198 Madison Ave., 10th Fl., New
York, NY 10016. (800) 528-4841. (212) 726-6490.
Fax (212) 686-7993.

The Travel Consultant's On-Site Inspection Journal,
contact Solitaire Publishing.

Thomas Cook European Timetable, Overseas Timetable, Guide to Airports - Thomas Cook Publications, Box 227, Peterborough, U.K. PE3 6SB. Call
Forsyth Travel Library in the U.S.

Travel Around the World - Weissman Travel Reports,
P.O. Box 49279, Austin, TX 78765. (800) 776-0720.
(512) 320-8700. Fax (512) 320-0016.

Travel Industry Personnel Directory - Chain Store
Guides, available through Solitaire Publishing.

Travel Training Series - Solitaire Publishing,
Box 14508, Tampa, FL 33690. (800) 226-0286.
(813) 876-0286. E-mail: PSolitaire@aol.com

WATA Master Key - WATA (World Assoc. of Travel
Agencies), 14 rue Ferrier CH-102, Geneva,
Switzerland. 731-47-60. Fax 732-81-61.

Weissman Profiles and Reports - Box 49279, Austin,
TX 78765. (800) 776-0720. (512) 320-8700. Fax
(512) 320-0016. E-mail: kgillespie@oag.com

Whitewater Rafting in North America - Globe
Pequot Press, 6 Business Park Rd., Box 833,
Old Saybrook, CT 06475. (800) 243-0495. (806)
395-0440. Fax (800) 820-2329.

World Aviation Directory - McGraw Hill Aviation
Week Group, #900, 1200 G St. NW, Washington, DC
20005. (202) 383-2423. Fax (202) 383-2440.
http://www.wadaviation.com

World Travel and Tourism Review, North American
Office of CAB Int'l, 198 Madison Ave., 10th Fl.,
New York, NY 10016. (800) 528-4841. (212) 726-
6490. Fax (212) 686-7993.

World Travel Guide - SF Communications, 3959
Electric Rd., #155, Roanoke, VA 24018. (800)
322-3834. (540) 772-4500. Fax (540) 772-4505.

Worldwide Brochures Directory (DISKETTE) - 1227
Kenneth St., Detroit Lakes, MN 56501. (800)
852-6752. (218) 847-1694. Fax (218) 847-7090.
http://www.wwb.com

Worldwide Ferry Services - POB 40819, Providence, RI 02940. (508) 252-9896.

INTERNATIONAL VIDEO NETWORK
2246 Camino Ramon
San Ramon, CA 94583
(800) 669-4486
(510) 866-8492

VACATIONS ON VIDEO
7642 E. Gray Rd.
Scottsdale, AZ 85260
(602) 483-1551
Fax (602) 483-0785

AAA VIDEO SERVICES
695 S. Colorado Blvd.
Ste. 270
Denver, CO 80222
(800) 875-5000
(303) 777-1127
Fax (303) 777-3661

QUESTAR, INC.
680 N. Lakeshore, Ste. 900
Chicago, IL 60611
(800) 633-5633
(312) 266-9400
http://www.questar1.com
E-mail: questarchi@aol.com

FORSYTH TRAVEL LIBRARY
226 Westchester Ave.
White Plains, NY 10604
(800) FORSYTH
(914) 681-7250
Fax (914) 681-7251

MENTOR PRODUCTIONS
POB 1148
San Clemente, CA 92674
(800) 521-5104
(714) 498-3954 (phone & fax)

TRAVELVIEW INTERNATIONAL
10370 Richmond Ave., #550
Houston, TX 77042
(800) 862-1305
(713) 975-7077
Fax (713) 975-0331
http://www.travelvideo.com

DESTINATIONS ON TAPE
Publisher's Video Group
112 Main St.
Gilford, CT 06851
(800) 822-4604
(203) 453-8340

COLLETTE TOURS
162 Middle St.
Pawtucket, RI 02860
(401) 728-3805
Fax (401) 728-1380
http://www.
    collettetours.com
E-mail: info@
    collettetours.com

GLOBAL VISIONS TRAVEL
    VIDEOS
Madacy Entertainment
    Group
31312 Via Colinas,
    Ste. 102
Westlake Village, CA
    91362
(818) 991-3600
Fax (818) 991-3408
http://www.
    mandacyvideo.com

LONELY PLANET VIDEOS
155 Filbert St., #251
Oakland, CA 94607
(800) 275-8555
Fax (510) 893-8563

NOTE: Tour companies,
cruise lines, tourist
information offices
and video rental and
sales stores are other
sources.

This list is not all-inclusive. It is not an endorsement of the publications. Changes may occur after printing.

Adventure Travel Business, POB 3210, Incline Village, NV 89450/924 Incline Way, Ste. N, Incline Village, NV 89451. (702) 832-3700. Fax (702) 832-3775. E-mail: rickd@adv-media.com

Air Transport World, Penton Publishing, 1100 Superior Ave., Cleveland, OH 44114-2543. (216) 696-7000. Fax (216) 696-8765. To subscribe call (216) 931-9164.

ASTA Agency Management, Miller Freeman, 1 Penn Plaza, NY, NY 10119. (800) 950-1314, (212) 714-1300, Fax (212) 714-1313. http://www.mfi.com/

Better Business Traveling, 25115 W. Ave. Stanford, #130, Valencia, CA 91355. (805) 295-1250. Fax (805) 295-0787.

Business Travel News, Miller Freeman, One Penn Plaza, New York, NY 10119. (800) 447-0138, (847) 588-0337, Fax (847) 647-5972.

Business Traveler International, 51 E. 42nd St., #1806, New York, NY 10017. (212) 697-1700. Fax (212) 697-1005. http://www.btonline.com

Canadian Travel Press Weekly, Baxter Publishing, 310 Dupont St., Toronto, Ont., Canada. M5R 1V9. (416) 968-7252. Fax (416) 968-2377.

Caribbean Travel and Life, World Publications, 330 W. Canton Ave., Box 2456, Winter Park, FL 32790-3150. (407) 628-4802. Fax (407) 628-7061.

Conde Nast Traveler, 360 Madison Ave., 5th Fl., New York, NY 10017. (212) 880-8800. For subscriptions: (800) 777-0700 or write Box 57018, Boulder, CO 80322.

Consumer Reports Travel Letter, 101 Truman Ave., Yonkers, NY 10703. (914) 378-2770. Fax (914) 378-2000. For subscriptions call (800) 999-7959 or write Box 53629, Boulder, CO 80322.

Cruise Travel, Century World Publishing, P.O. Box 342, Mt. Morris, IL 61054. (800) 877-5893.

Cruise and Vacation Views, Orban Communications, Inc., 25 Washington St., 4th floor, Morristown, NJ 07960. (973) 605-2442. Fax (973) 605-2722. E-mail: cvvoffice@aol.com

Cruising World, #5 John Clarke Rd., Middletown, RI 02842. (401) 847-1588. http://www.cruisingworld.com

Educated Traveler, POB 220822, Chantilly, VA 20153. (703) 471-1063. Fax (703) 471-4807. http://www. educated-traveler.com E-mail: edtrav@aol.com

Endless Vacations, Resort Condominiums International, Box 80229, Indianapolis, IN 46280-0229. (800) 338-7777.

Group Tour Magazine, 2465 112th Ave., Holland, MI 49424. (800) 767-3489. (616) 393-2077 http://www. grouptour.com

Hideaway Report, Harper Associates, Box 50, Sun Valley, ID 83353-0050. (208) 622-3183. http://www. harperassociates.com

Hideaways Guide/Newsletter, Hideaways International, 767 Islington St., Portsmouth, NH 03801. (603) 430-4433. Fax (603) 430-4444. http://www. hideaways.com

International Travel News, 2120 28th St., Sacramento, CA 95818. (916) 457-3643. (800) ITN-4YOU.

Islands, Island Publishing Co., 3886 State St., Santa Barbara, CA 93105. (805) 682-7177. Fax (805) 569-0349. (800) 477-3575. E-mail: islands@ islandsmag.com

Jax Fax Travel Marketing Magazine, Executive Offices, 397 Post Rd., Ste. 102, Darien, CT 06820-1413. (203) 655-8746. Fax (203) 655-6257. http://www.jaxfax.com

Mature Traveler, GEM Publishing Group, POB 50400, Reno, NV 89513-0400. (702) 786-7419.

Meetings & Convention, Reed Travel Group, 500 Plaza Dr., Secaucus, NJ 07096. (201) 902-1700. Fax (201) 902-7900. (800) 446-6551.

Meeting News, Miller Freeman, One Penn Plaza, New York, NY 10119. (800) 447-0138.

Millergram, Bill Miller Cruises Everywhere, POB 1463, Secaucus, NJ 07096. (201) 348-9390 (phone and fax).

National Geographic Traveler, POB 2895, Washington, DC 20077-9960. (202) 857-7000.

Outside, Outside Plaza, 400 Market St., Santa Fe, NM 87501. (800) 678-1131.

Passport, Remy Publishing Co., 401 N. Franklin St., 3rd Floor, Chicago, IL 60610-4400. (312) 464-0300. Fax (312) 464-0166.

Personal Travel Report, Nationwide Intelligence, 2060 North Center, POB 3272, Saginaw, MI 48603. (800) 333-4130. (517) 793-9111. http://www. nationwidenetwork.com

Planet Talk, Lonely Planet Publications, 155 Filbert St., Ste. 251, Oakland, CA 94607. (800) 275-8555. (510) 893-8555. Fax (510) 893-8563.

Porthole, Panoff Publishing, 7100 W. Commercial Blvd., Ste. 106, Ft. Lauderdale, FL 33319. (954) 746-5554. Fax (954) 746-5244. http://www. porthole.com

Recommend, Worth International Communications Corp., 5979 NW 151st St., Ste. 120, Miami Lakes, FL 33014. (800) 447-0123. Fax (305) 826-6950. http://www.gotravel.com

Southern Living Travel Guide, POB 523, Birmingham, AL 35201. (205) 877-6000. Fax (205) 877-6700.

Specialty Travel Index, 305 San Anselmo Ave., #313, San Anselmo, CA 94960. (415) 459-4900. Fax (415) 459-4974. http://www.specialtytravel.com

Tour and Travel News, Miller Freeman, One Penn Plaza, New York, NY 10119. (212) 615-2744. Fax (212) 279-3951. (800) 447-0138.

Tours and Resorts, Century World Publishing, POB 342, Mt. Morris, IL 61054. (800) 877-5893.

Transitions Abroad, 18 Hulst Rd., Amherst, MA 01002. (800) 293-0373. (413) 256-3414. Fax (413) 256-0373. http://www.transabroad.com E-mail trabroad@aol.com

Travel Age, Reed Travel Group, 500 Plaza Dr., Secaucus, NJ 07096. (800) 446-6551. (201) 902-2000.

Travel Agent, 801 Second Ave., 12th Fl., New York, NY 10017. (212) 370-5050. Fax (212) 370-4491.

Travel and Leisure, 1120 6th Ave., 10th Fl., New York, NY 10036. (212) 382-5600. Fax (212) 382-5878.

Travel Books Worldwide, Travel Keys, Box 162266, Sacramento, CA 95816-2266. (916) 452-5200.

Travel Companion Exchange, POB 833, Amityville, NY 11701. (516) 454-0880. Fax (516) 454-0170.

Travel Counselor, Miller Freeman, One Penn Plaza, New York, NY. Editor: (415) 905-4923. Fax (415) 905-2235.

Travel Courier, Baxter Publishing, 310 Dupont St., Toronto, Ont., Canada. M5R 1V9. (416) 968-7252. Fax (416) 968-2377.

Travel Expense Management Newsletter, American Business Pub., 1913 Atlantic Ave., Manasquan, NJ 08736. (732) 292-1100. Fax (732) 292-1111. http://www.themcic.com

Travel Holiday, 1633 Broadway, 43rd Fl., New York, NY 10019. (212) 767-5106. Fax (212) 767-5111.

Travel Smart, 40 Beechdale Rd., Dobbs Ferry, NY 10522. (914) 693-8300.

Travl Tips, P.O. Box 580188, Flushing, NY 11358. (718) 939-2400. Fax (718) 939-2047.

Travel Trade, 15 W. 44th St., New York, NY 10036. (212) 730-6600. Fax (212) 730-7020.

Travel Weekly, 500 Plaza Dr., Secaucus, NJ 07096. (201) 902-1500. Fax (201) 319-1947. http://www.traveler.net/two

Travel World News, 50 Washington St., S. Norwalk, CT 06854-2710. (203) 853-4955. Fax (203) 866-1153. E-mail: pgatt@travelworldnews.com

Traveling Times, 25115 W. Ave. Stanford, #130, Valencia, CA 91355-1290. (805) 295-0175. Fax (805) 295-0787.

Trips, 8 Bernice St. #207, San Francisco, CA 94103. (415) 431-5133. Fax (415) 431-9074. E-mail: office@tripsmag.com

Vacations, Vacations Publications, Inc., 1502 Augusta Dr., Ste. 415, Houston, TX 77057. (713) 974-6903. Fax (713) 974-0445.

COMMUNICATION CODE

Civil aviation throughout the world uses an official phonetic alphabet code for air-to-ground and air-to-air communications. You should use this code to help communicate spellings. For example, spelling the last name "Dabner" would be: "D, as in delta, a-alfa, b-bravo, n-november, e-echo, r-romeo."

A - ALPHA	K - KILO	U- UNIFORM
B - BRAVO	L - LIMA	V - VICTOR
C - CHARLIE	M - MIKE	W - WHISKEY
D - DELTA	N - NOVEMBER	X - X-RAY
E - ECHO	O - OSCAR	Y - YANKEE
F - FOXTROT	P - PAPA	Z - ZULU
G - GOLF	Q - QUEBEC	
H - HOTEL	R - ROMEO	
I - INDIA	S - SIERRA	
J - JULIET	T - TANGO	

TWENTY-FOUR HOUR CLOCK

Most of the world uses the 24-hour clock for scheduling so that AM or PM does not have to be specified. Since it's so universal, it is important to be able to convert AM or PM times into the 24-hour clock and vice versa.

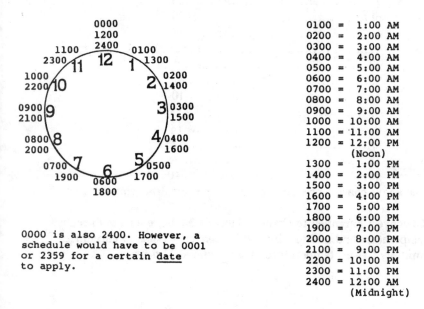

0000 is also 2400. However, a schedule would have to be 0001 or 2359 for a certain <u>date</u> to apply.

0100	=	1:00	AM
0200	=	2:00	AM
0300	=	3:00	AM
0400	=	4:00	AM
0500	=	5:00	AM
0600	=	6:00	AM
0700	=	7:00	AM
0800	=	8:00	AM
0900	=	9:00	AM
1000	=	10:00	AM
1100	=	11:00	AM
1200	=	12:00	PM
		(Noon)	
1300	=	1:00	PM
1400	=	2:00	PM
1500	=	3:00	PM
1600	=	4:00	PM
1700	=	5:00	PM
1800	=	6:00	PM
1900	=	7:00	PM
2000	=	8:00	PM
2100	=	9:00	PM
2200	=	10:00	PM
2300	=	11:00	PM
2400	=	12:00	AM
		(Midnight)	

METRIC CONVERSION TABLES

LINEAR

1 centimeter = .3937 inch	1 inch = 2.54 centimeters
1 decimeter = .328 foot	1 foot = 3.048 decimeters
1 meter = 39.37 inches/1.0936 yards	1 yard = .9144 meters
1 kilometer = .62137 miles	1 mile = 1.6093 kilometers

Hints: A meter is a little over a yard. A kilometer is almost 2/3 of a mile.

WEIGHTS

1 gram = .03527 ounces	1 ounce = 28.35 grams
1 kilogram = 2.2046 pounds	1 pound = .4536 kilograms
1 metric ton = 2,204 pounds	1 ton (2,000 pounds) = .90718 metric tons

VOLUME

1 liter = .8888 quarts liquid (Imperial)	1 quart liquid (Imp.) = 1.136 liters
1 liter = 1.056 quarts liquid (U.S.)	1 quart liquid (U.S.) = .946 liters
1 liter = .220 gallon (Imperial)	1 gallon (Imp.) = 4.543 liters
1 liter = .264 gallon (U.S.)	1 gallon (U.S.) = 3.785 liters

FARENHEIT DEGREES	CELSIUS DEGREES
104	40
98.6	37
95	35
86	30
77	25
68	20
50	10
41	5
32	0
23	-5
14	-10
5	-15
0	-18
-9	-23
-18	-28
-40	-40

The above chart represents approximate equivalent temperatures.

To convert Farenheit to Celsius: Subtract 32 degrees from Farenheit temperature and multiply by 5/9. To convert Celsius to Farenheit: Multiply Celsius temperature by 9/5 and add 32 degrees.

COMPARATIVE CLOTHING AND SHOE SIZES

Shoes - Men's

UK	6	7	8	9	10	11	12
USA	7	8	9	10	11	12	13
Europe	39½	41	42	43	44½	46	47

Shoes - Women's

UK	4	4½	5	5½	6	6½	7
USA	5½	6	6½	7	7½	8	8½
Europe	36½	37	37½	38	38½	39	39½

Shirts - Men's

UK	14½	15	15½	16	16½	17	17½
USA	14½	15	15½	16	16½	17	17½
Europe	37	38	39	41	42	43	44

Blouses - Women's

UK	32	34	36	38	40	42
USA	8	10	12	14	16	18
Europe	38	40	42	44	46	48

Suits - Men's

UK	36	37	38	39	40	41	42
USA	36	37	38	39	40	41	42
Europe	48	49	51	52	54	55	57

Dresses - Women's

UK	10	12	14	16	18	20
USA	8	10	12	14	16	18
Europe*	38	40	42	44	46	48

NOTE: This is the "high" end of comparative sizes. Depending on the country, sizes may be up to 4 less than the number shown (10=8=34 to 38). Since clothing and shoe styles vary, this can only be used to approximate size comparisons.

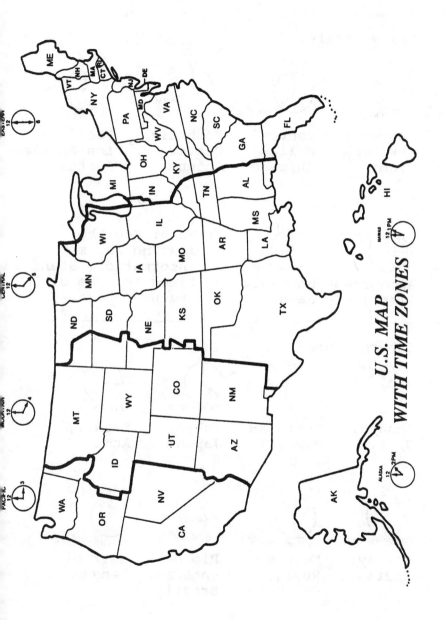

U.S. MAP
WITH TIME ZONES

TIMES AROUND THE WORLD AT A GLANCE

United States

Eastern: **Central:**   **Mountain:**   **Pacific:**
New York   Dallas   Denver   Los Angeles
Miami   Chicago   Phoenix   Seattle

Anchorage   **Honolulu**
Alaska   Hawaii

Note: See the listing for more information. Standard times for the U. S. are used here.

International

London,   **Paris,FR**   **Tokyo,**   **Sydney,**
U. K.   Rome,IT   Japan   Aust.

Bombay,   **Moscow,**   **Rio de**   **Nairobi,**
India   Russia   Janeiro,   Kenya
                            Brazil

TIME ZONES OF THE WORLD

TO USE THE LIST OF TIME ZONES:
1. Find out your country/area's time zone. Check if standard/daylight savings time.
2. Look up the time zone of the destination. Check if standard/daylight saving time.
3. Add the hours difference if the destination is in a later time zone. Subtract the difference if it is in an earlier time zone.

FOR EXAMPLE: It's 1:00 pm in New York City and you want to know what time it is in Zurich, Switzerland. New York City is in EASTERN time zone of U.S., -5 during standard time. Switzerland is +1 during standard time. The difference is 6 hours later (+1 is later than -5), so it is 7:00 pm in Switzerland.

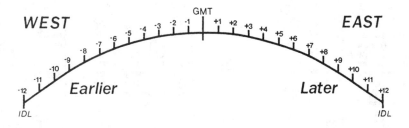

	Standard time	Daylight savings	effective period for daylight savings time*
Afghanistan	+4 1/2		
Albania	+1	+2	Mar. (last) - Oct. (last)
Algeria	+1		
American Samoa	-11		
Andorra	+1	+2	Mar. (last) - Oct. (last)
Angola	+1		
Anguilla	-4		
Antigua(see Leeward Is.)			
Argentina	-3		
Armenia	+3	+4	Mar. (last) - Oct. (last)
Aruba	-4		
Australia-			
Lord Howe Is.	+10 1/2	+11	Oct. (last) - Mar. (last)
New South Wales	+10	+11	Oct. (last) - Mar. (last)
Northern Terr.	+9 1/2		
Queensland	+10		
South Australia	+9 1/2	+10 1/2	Oct. (last) - Mar. (last)
Tasmania	+10	+11	Oct. (last) - Mar. (last)
W. Australia	+8		
Victoria, Cap.Territory	+10	+11	Oct. (last) - Mar. (last)
Austria	+1	+2	Mar. (last) - Oct. (last)
Azerbaijan	+4		
Bahamas	-5	-4	Apr. (first) - Oct. (last)
Bahrain	+3		
Bangladesh	+6		
Barbados	-4		
Belarus	+2	+3	Mar. (last) - Oct. (last)
Belgium	+1	+2	Mar. (last) - Oct. (last)
Belize	-6		
Benin	+1		
Bermuda	-4	-3	Apr. (first) - Oct. (last)
Bhutan	+6		
Bolivia	-4		
Bosnia Herzegovina	+1	+2	Mar. (last) - Oct. (last)
Botswana	+2		

*Parentheses indicate the week in which change normally occurs.

	Standard time	Daylight savings	effective period for daylight savings time*
Brazil-East#	-3	-2	Oct. (second) - Feb. (second)
West	-4	-3	Oct. (second) - Feb. (second)
Territory-Acre	-5		
Fernando De Noronha	-2		

NOTE: Certain states of Brazil remain on standard time.

	Standard time	Daylight savings	effective period for daylight savings time*
Br. Virgin Is.	-4		
Brunei	+8		
Bulgaria	+2	+3	Mar. (last) - Oct. (last)
Burkina Faso	GMT(0)		
Burma(see Myanmar)			
Burundi	+2		
Cambodia	+7		
Cameroon	+1		
Canada -			
Newfoundland	-3 1/2	-2 1/2	Apr. (first) - Oct. (last)
Atlantic area	-4	-3	Apr. (first) - Oct. (last)
Eastern area	-5	-4	Apr. (first) - Oct. (last)
Central area	-6	-5	Apr. (first) - Oct. (last)
Mountain area	-7	-6	Apr. (first) - Oct. (last)
Pacific area	-8	-7	Apr. (first) - Oct. (last)
Yukon terr.	-8	-7	Apr. (first) - Oct. (last)

NOTE: Saskatchewan and certain cities remain on standard time.

	Standard time	Daylight savings	effective period for daylight savings time*
Cape Verde Is.	-1		
Cayman Is.	-5		
Cntrl.African Rep.	+1		
Chad	+1		
Chile(continental)	-4	-3	Oct. (second) - Mar. (second)
Easter Is.	-6	-5	Oct. (second) - Mar. (second)
China	+8		
C.I.S. (Commonwealth of Independent States) -			

see individual states, such as Russia, Azerbaijan, Armenia, Belarus, Georgia, Kazakstan, Turkmenistan, Ukraine, etc.

	Standard time	Daylight savings	effective period for daylight savings time*
Cocos Is.	+6 1/2		
Colombia	-5		
Comoros (see Mayotte)			
Congo	+1		
Congo (Dem. Rep. of)			
Kinshasa	+1		
Kasai, Karu	+2		
Cook Is.	-10		
Costa Rica	-6		
Cote d'Ivoire	GMT(0)		
Croatia	+1	+2	Mar. (last) - Oct. (last)
Cuba	-5	-4	Apr. (first) - Oct. (first)
Cyprus	+2	+3	Mar. (last) - Oct. (last)
Czech Republic	+1	+2	Mar. (last) - Oct. (last)
Denmark	+1	+2	Mar. (last) - Oct. (last)
Djibouti	+3		
Dom. Republic	-4		
Ecuador(continen.)	-5		
Galapagos Is.	-6		
Egypt	+2	+3	Apr. (last) - Sep. (last)
El Salvador	-6		
Eq. Guinea	+1		
Eritrea	+3		
Estonia	+2	+3	Mar. (last) - Oct. (last)
Ethiopia	+3		
Falkland Is.	-4	-3	Sep. (second) - Apr. (third)
Faroe Is.	GMT(0)	+1	Mar. (last) - Oct. (last)
Fiji	+12		
Finland	+2	+3	Mar. (last) - Oct. (last)
France	+1	+2	Mar. (last) - Oct. (last)
French Guiana	-3		

*Parentheses indicate the week in which change normally occurs.

	Standard time	Daylight savings	effective period for daylight savings time*
French Polynesia			
Gambier Is.	-9		
Marquesas Is.	-9 1/2		
Society Is.,			
Tahiti,			
Tuamotu Is.	-10		
Gabon	+1		
Gambia	GMT(0)		
Georgia	+5		
Germany	+1	+2	Mar. (last) - Oct. (last)
Ghana	GMT(0)		
Gibraltar	+1	+2	Mar. (last) - Oct. (last)
Greece	+2	+3	Mar. (last) - Oct. (last)
Greenland			
except Scoresbysund			
and Thule	-3	-2	Mar. (last) - Oct. (last)
Scoresbysund	-1	GMT(0)	Mar. (last) - Oct. (last)
Thule	-4	-3	Apr. (first) - Oct. (last)
Grenada, St. Lucia	-4		
Guadeloupe	-4		
Guam	+10		
Guatemala	-6		
Guinea	GMT(0)		
Guinea-Bissau	GMT(0)		
Guyana	-4		
Haiti	-5	-4	Apr. (first) - Oct. (last)
Honduras	-6		
Hong Kong	+8		
Hungary	+1	+2	Mar. (last) - Oct. (last)
Iceland	GMT(0)		
India	+5 1/2		
Indonesia			
Central	+8		
East	+9		
West(Jakarta)	+7		
Iran	+3 1/2	+4 1/2	Mar. (third) - Sep. (third)
Iraq	+3	+4	Apr. (first) - Sep. (last)
Ireland, Rep. of	GMT(0)	+1	Mar. (last) - Oct. (last)
Israel	+2	+3	Mar. (last) - Sep. (first)
Italy	+1	+2	Mar. (last) - Oct. (last)
Jamaica	-5		
Japan	+9		
Johnston Is.	-10		
Jordan	+2	+3	Apr. (first) - Sep. (third)
Kazakstan			
West	+4	+5	Mar. (last) - Oct. (last)
Central	+5	+6	Mar. (last) - Oct. (last)
East	+6	+7	Mar. (last) - Oct. (last)
Kenya	+3		
Kiribati, Rep. of	+12		
Canton,Enderbury	+13		
Christmas Is.	+14		
Korea, Dem. Rep.	+9		
Korea, Rep. of	+9		
Kuwait	+3		
Kyrgyzstan	+5	+6	Apr. (second) - Sep. (last)
Laos	+7		
Latvia	+2	+3	Mar. (last) - Oct. (last)
Lebanon	+2	+3	Mar. (last) - Sep. (last)
Leeward Is.			
(Antigua, Dominica			
Montserrat, Nevis, St.			
Kitts, Anguilla)	-4		

*Parentheses indicate the week in which change normally occurs.

	Standard time	Daylight savings	effective period for daylight savings time*
Lesotho	+2		
Liberia	GMT(0)		
Libya	+1	+2	Mar. (last) - Sep. (last)
Liechtenstein	+1	+2	Mar. (last) - Oct. (last)
Lithuania	+2	+3	Mar. (last) - Oct. (last)
Luxembourg	+1	+2	Mar. (last) - Oct. (last)
Macedonia	+1	+2	Mar. (last) - Oct. (last)
Madagascar	+3		
Malawi	+2		
Malaysia	+8		
Maldives	+5		
Mali	GMT(0)		
Malta	+1	+2	Mar. (last) - Oct. (last)
Martinique	-4		
Mauritania	GMT(0)		
Mauritius	+4		
Mayotte	+3		
Mexico			
Southern Baja & N. Pacific coast	-7	-6	Apr. (first) - Oct. (last)
Northern Baja (above the 28th parallel)	-8	-7	Apr. (first) - Oct. (last)
General Mexico	-6	-5	Apr. (first) - Oct. (last)
Quintana Roo	-5	-4	Apr. (first) - Oct. (last)
Midway Is.	-11		
Moldova	+2	+3	Mar. (last) - Oct. (last)
Monaco	+1	+2	Mar. (last) - Oct. (last)
Mongolia	+8	+9	Mar. (last) - Oct. (last)
Morocco	GMT(0)		
Mozambique	+2		
Myanmar	+6 1/2		
Namibia	+1	+2	Sep. (first) - Apr. (first)
Nauru, Rep. of	+12		
Nepal	+5 3/4		
Netherlands	+1	+2	Mar. (last) - Oct. (last)
Neth. Antilles	-4		
New Caledonia	+11		
New Zealand (except Chatham Is.)	+12	+13	Oct. (first) - Mar. (sec.)
Chatham Is.	+12 3/4	+13 3/4	Oct. (first) - Mar. (sec.)
Nicaragua	-6		
Niger	+1		
Nigeria	+1		
Niue Is.	-11		
Norfolk Is.	+11 1/2		
Norway	+1	+2	Mar. (last) - Oct. (last)
Oman	+4		
Pacific Trust Territory -			
Caroline Is.	+11		
Marshall Is.	+12		
Kwajalein	-12		
Mariana Is.	+10		
Belau Is.	+9		
Ponape(Pohnpei)	+11		
Pakistan	+5		
Panama	-5		
Papua New Guinea	+10		
Paraguay	-4	-3	Oct. (first) - Feb. (last)
Peru	-5		
Philippines	+8		
Poland	+1	+2	Mar. (last) - Oct. (last)
Portugal -			
Azores	-1	GMT(0)	Mar. (last) - Oct. (last)
Madeira Is.	GMT(0)	+1	Mar. (last) - Oct. (last)
the mainland	+1	+2	Mar. (last) - Oct. (last)

*Parentheses indicate the week in which change normally occurs.

	Standard time	Daylight savings	effective period for daylight savings time*
Puerto Rico	-4		
Qatar	+3		
Reunion	+4		
Romania	+2	+3	Mar. (last) - Oct. (last)
Russia (major cities)			
Moscow,St. Petersburg, Murmarsk	+3	+4	Mar. (last) - Oct. (last)
Samara,Izhevsk	+4	+5	Mar. (last) - Oct. (last)
Chelyabinsk,Perm, Nizhnevartovsk	+5	+6	Mar. (last) - Oct. (last)
Omsk	+6	+7	Mar. (last) - Oct. (last)
Novosibirsk,Krasnojarsk, Norilsk	+7	+8	Mar. (last) - Oct. (last)
Irkutsk,Ulan-ude, Bratsk	+8	+9	Mar. (last) - Oct. (last)
Chita,Yakatsk	+9	+10	Mar. (last) - Oct. (last)
Khabarovsk	+10	+11	Mar. (last) - Oct. (last)
Magadan	+11	+12	Mar. (last) - Oct. (last)
Petropavlovsk	+12	+13	Mar. (last) - Oct. (last)
Rwanda	+2		
St. Pierre & Miquelon	-3	-2	Apr. (first) - Oct. (last)
St. Vincent & the Grenadines	-4		
Samoa(western)	-11		
San Marino	+1	+2	Mar. (last) - Oct. (last)
Sao Tome & Principe Is.	GMT(0)		
Saudi Arabia	+3		
Senegal	GMT(0)		
Seychelles	+4		
Sierre Leone	GMT(0)		
Singapore	+8		
Slovak Rep.	+1	+2	Mar. (last) - Oct.(last)
Slovenia	+1	+2	Mar. (last) - Oct.(last)
Solomon Is.	+11		
Somalia	+3		
South Africa	+2		
Spain - Canary Is.	GMT(0)	+1	Mar. (last) - Oct. (last)
Continental, Balearic Is. and Melilla	+1	+2	Mar. (last) - Oct. (last)
Sri Lanka	+6		
St. Helena	GMT(0)		
Sudan	+2		
Suriname	-3		
Swaziland	+2		
Sweden	+1	+2	Mar. (last) - Oct. (last)
Switzerland	+1	+2	Mar. (last) - Oct. (last)
Syria	+2	+3	Apr. (first) - Sep. (last)
Taiwan	+8		
Tajikistan	+5		
Tanzania	+3		
Thailand	+7		
Togo	GMT(0)		
Tonga	+13		
Trinidad & Tobago	-4		
Tunisia	+1		
Turkey	+2	+3	Mar. (last) - Oct. (last)
Turkmenistan	+5		
Turks & Caicos Is.	-5	-4	Apr. (first) - Oct. (last)
Tuvalu	+12		
Uganda	+3		
Ukraine	+2	+3	Mar. (last) - Oct. (last)

*Parentheses indicate the week in which change normally occurs.

	Standard time	Daylight savings	effective period for daylight savings time*
United Arab Emirates	+4		
United Kingdom	GMT(0)	+1	Mar. (last) - Oct. (last)
U.S.A. -			
Eastern#	-5	-4	Apr. (first) - Oct. (last)
Central	-6	-5	Apr. (first) - Oct. (last)
Mountain#	-7	-6	Apr. (first) - Oct. (last)
Pacific	-8	-7	Apr. (first) - Oct. (last)
#Arizona and parts of Indiana don't observe Daylight Savings Time			
Alaska	-9	-8	Apr. (first) - Oct. (last)
Aleutian Is.	-10	-9	Apr. (first) - Oct. (last)
Hawaii	-10		
U.S. Virgin Is.	-4		
Uruguay	-3		
Uzbekistan	+5		
Vanuatu	+11		
Venezuela	-4		
Vietnam	+7		
Wake Is.	+12		
Wallis and Futuna	+12		
Yemen	+3		
Yugoslavia	+1	+2	Mar. (last) - Oct. (last)
Zaire (see Congo - Dem. Rep. of)			
Zambia	+2		
Zimbabwe	+2		

*Parentheses indicate the week in which change normally occurs.

HINTS ON TIME ZONES AND TRAVELING

FROM THE U.S. TO EUROPE - a majority of flights depart in the afternoon and arrive the next morning.

FROM EUROPE TO THE U.S. - flights normally depart in the morning and arrive in the evening (or night, depending on the destination) on the same day.

FROM U.S. TO AUSTRALIA/NEW ZEALAND/ORIENT - passengers arrive 1 or 2 days later with an actual flying time of about 24 hours.

FROM AUSTRALIA/NEW ZEALAND/ORIENT TO U.S. - passengers arrive the same day or 1 day later.

Crossing the IDL (International Date Line) will take you into the next day or back one day. There will be 24 hours difference (+ or - one hour), depending on the direction of travel.

COUNTRIES, CURRENCIES, AND CURRENCY CODES

Note: Some codes were not available.
*International Standards Organization

COUNTRY CODE-NAME	CURRENCY NAME	ISO* CODE
Abu Dhabi (see United Arab Emirates)		
AF-Afghanistan	Afghani	AFA
AL-Albania	Lek	ALL
DZ-Algeria	Algerian Dinar	DZD
AD-Andorra	Andorra Pesetas	ADP
AO-Angola	Kwanza Reajustado	AOR
AI-Anguilla	East. Carib.Dollar	XCD
AQ-Antarctica	-	
AG-Antigua	East. Carib.Dollar	XCD
AR-Argentina	Peso	ARS
AM-Armenia	Luma	AML
AW-Aruba	Aruban Guilder	AWG
AU-Australia	Australian Dollar	AUD
AT-Austria	Austrian Schilling	ATS
AZ-Azerbaijan	Manat	AZM
BS-Bahamas	Bahamian Dollar	BSD
BH-Bahrain	Bahraini Dinar	BHD
BD-Bangladesh	Taka	BDT
BB-Barbados	Barbados Dollar	BBD
BY-Belarus	Belarussian Rouble	BYB
BE-Belgium	Belgian Franc	BEF
BZ-Belize	Belize Dollar	BZD
BJ-Benin	CFA Franc	XOF
BM-Bermuda	Bermudian Dollar	BMD
BT-Bhutan	Ngultrum	BTN
BO-Bolivia	Bolivanio	BOB
BA-Bosnia Hercegovina	Dinar	BAD
BW-Botswana	Pula	BWP
BR-Brazil	Real	BRL
BN-Brunei	Brunei Dollar	BND
BG-Bulgaria	Lev	BGL
BF-Burkina Faso	CFA Franc	XOF
BU-Burma (see Myanmar)		
BI-Burundi	Burundi Franc	BIF
KH-Cambodia Dem.	Riel	KHR
CM-Cameroon	CFA Franc	XAF
CA-Canada	Canadian Dollar	CAD
CV-Cape Verde	Cape Verde Escudo	CVE
KY-Cayman Is.	Cayman Is. Dollar	KYD
CF-Central African Republic	CFA Franc	XAF
TD-Chad	CFA Franc	XAF
CL-Chile	Chilean Peso	CLP
CN-China	Yuan Renminbi	CNY
CX-Christmas Is.	Australian Dollar	AUD
CC-Cocos Is.	Australian Dollar	AUD
CO-Colombia	Colombian Peso	COP
KM-Comoros	Comoros Franc	KMF
CG-Congo	CFA Franc	XAF
ZR-Congo(Dem.Rep.of)	New Zaire	ZRN
CK-Cook Is.	New Zealand Dollar	NZD

COUNTRY CODE-NAME	CURRENCY NAME	ISO* CODE
CR-Costa Rica	Costa Rican Colon	CRC
CI-Cote D'Ivoire	CFA Franc	XOF
HR-Croatia	Kuna	HRK
CU-Cuba	Cuban Peso	CUP
CY-Cyprus	Cyprus Pound	CYP

Note: The area controlled by the Turkish Cypriot Community uses the Turkish Lira.

CS-Czech Republic	Koruna	CZK
DK-Denmark	Danish Krone	DKK
DJ-Djibouti	Djibouti Franc	DJF
DM-Dominica	East. Carib.Dollar	XCD
DO-Dominican Rep.	Dominican Peso	DOP
Dubai (see United Arab Emirates)		
East. Caribbean	E.Carib.Dollar	XCD
TP-East Timor	Escudo	TPE
EC-Ecuador	Sucre	ECS
EG-Egypt	Egyptian Pound	EGP
SV-El Salvador	El Salvador Colon	SVC
GQ-Equatorial Guinea	CFA Franc	XAF
ER-Eritrea	Ethiopian Birr	ETB
EE-Estonia	Kroon	EEK
ET-Ethiopia	Ethiopian Birr	ETB
European Monetary Cooperation Fund	European Currency Unit	XEU
FK-Falkland Is.	U.K. Pound	FKP
FO-Faroe Is.	Danish Krone	DKK
FJ-Fiji	Fiji Dollar	FJD
FI-Finland	Markka	FIM
FR-France	French Franc	FRF
GF-French Guiana	French Franc	FRF
PF-French Polynesia	CFP Franc	XPF
TF-French Southern Territories	French Franc	FRF
French W.Indies	French Franc	
GA-Gabon	CFA Franc	XAF
GM-Gambia	Dalasi	GMD
GE-Georgia	Lari	GEL
DE-Germany	Deutsche Mark	DEM
GH-Ghana	Cedi	GHC
GI-Gibraltar	Gibraltar Pound	GIP
GR-Greece	Drachma	GRD
GL-Greenland	Danish Krone	DKK
GD-Grenada	East. Carib.Dollar	XCD
GP-Guadeloupe, including St. Barthelemy, French St.Martin	French Franc	FRF
GU-Guam	U.S. Dollar	USD
GT-Guatemala	Quetzal	GTQ
GN-Guinea	Guinea Franc	GNF
GW-Guinea-Bissau	Guinea-Bissau Peso	GWP
GY-Guyana	Guyana Dollar	GYD
HT-Haiti	Gourde	HTG
HM-Heard and McDonald Islands	Australian Dollar	AUD
HN-Honduras	Lempira	HNL

COUNTRY CODE-NAME	CURRENCY NAME	ISO* CODE
HK-Hong Kong	Hong Kong Dollar	HKD
HU-Hungary	Forint	HUF
IS-Iceland	Iceland Krona	ISK
IN-India	Indian Rupee	INR
ID-Indonesia	Rupiah	IDR
IR-Iran	Iranian Rial	IRR
IQ-Iraq	Iraqi Dinar	IQD
IE-Ireland	Irish Pound(Punt)	IEP
IL-Israel	New Shekel	ILS
IT-Italy	Italian Lira	ITL
JM-Jamaica	Jamaican Dollar	JMD
JP-Japan	Yen	JPY
JO-Jordan	Jordanian Dinar	JOD
KZ-Kazakhstan	Tenge	KZT
KE-Kenya	Kenyan Shilling	KES
KI-Kiribati	Australian Dollar	AUD
KP-Korea, Dem. People's Rep.	N. Korean Won	KPW
KR-Korea, Rep. of	Won	KRW
KG-Kyrgystan	Som	KGS
KW-Kuwait	Kuwaiti Dinar	KWD
LA-Laos People's Dem. Rep.	Kip	LAK
LV-Latvia	Lat	LVL
LB-Lebanon	Lebanese Pound	LBP
LS-Lesotho	Maloti	LSL
LR-Liberia	Liberian Dollar	LRD
LY-Libyan Arab Jamahiriya	Libyan Dinar	LYD
LI-Liechtenstein	Swiss Franc	CHF
LT-Lithuania	Litas	LTL
LU-Luxembourg	Luxembourg Franc	LUF
MO-Macau	Macau Pataca	MOP
MK-Macedonia	Macedonia Denar	MKD
MG-Madagascar	Malagasy Franc	MGF
MW-Malawi	Kwacha	MWK
MY-Malaysia	Malaysian Ringgit	MYR
MV-Maldives	Maldivian Rufiyaa	MVR
ML-Mali	CFA Franc	XOF
MT-Malta	Maltese Lira	MTL
MH-Marshall Is.	U.S. Dollar	USD
MQ-Martinique	French Franc	FRF
MR-Mauritania	Ouguiya	MRO
MU-Mauritius	Mauritius Rupee	MUR
XM-Mayotte	French Franc	FRF
MX-Mexico	New Peso	MXN
FM-Micronesia, including Caroline Is., Ponape & Kosrae	U.S. Dollar	USD
MD-Moldova	Leu (plural Lay)	MDL
MC-Monaco	French Franc	FRF
MN-Mongolia	Tugrik	MNT
MS-Montserrat (see Eastern Caribbean)		
MA-Morocco	Moroccan Dirham	MAD
MZ-Mozambique	Metical	MZM
MM-Myanmar	Kyat	MMK

COUNTRY CODE-NAME	CURRENCY NAME	ISO* CODE
NA-Namibia	Namibian Dollar	NAD
NR-Nauru	Australian Dollar	AUD
NP-Nepal	Nepalese Rupee	NPR
NL-Netherlands	Neth. Guilder	NLG
AN-Neth. Antilles	Neth. Ant. Guilder	ANG
Nevis (see Eastern Caribbean)		
NC-New Caledonia	CFP Franc	XPF
NZ-New Zealand	New Zealand Dollar	NZD
NI-Nicaragua	Cordoba Oro	NIO
NE-Niger	CFA Franc	XOF
NG-Nigeria	Naira	NGN
NU-Niue	New Zealand Dollar	NZD
NF-Norfolk Is.	Australian Dollar	AUD
MP-Northern Mariana Is., incl. Mariana Is.,		
except Guam	U.S. Dollar	USD
NO-Norway	Norwegian Krone	NOK
OM-Oman	Rial Omani	OMR
PK-Pakistan	Pakistan Rupee	PKR
PW-Palau	U.S. Dollar	USD
PA-Panama	Balboa	PAB
PG-Papua New Guinea	Kina	PGK
PY-Paraguay	Guarani	PYG
PE-Peru	Nuevo Sol	PES
PH-Philippines	Philippine Peso	PHP
PL-Poland	Zloty	PLZ
PT-Portugal	Portuguese Escudo	PTE
PR-Puerto Rico	U.S. Dollar	USD
QA-Qatar	Qatari Riyal	QAR
RE-Reunion	French Franc	FRF
RO-Romania	Leu	ROL
RU-Russia	Rouble	RUR
RW-Rwanda	Rwanda Franc	RWF
SH-St. Helena	Pound	SHP
KN-St. Kitts & Nevis (see Eastern Caribbean)		
LC-St. Lucia (see Eastern Caribbean)		
PM-St. Pierre & Miquelon		FRF
VC-St. Vincent & Grenadines (see E. Caribbean)		
AS-Samoa(American)	U.S. Dollar	USD
WS-Samoa(Western)	Tala	WST
SM-San Marino	Italian Lira	ITL
ST-Sao Tome & Principe	Dobra	STD
SA-Saudi Arabia	Saudi Riyal	SAR
SN-Senegal	CFA Franc	XOF
SC-Seychelles	Seychelles Rupee	SCR
Sharjah (see United Arab Emirates)		
SL-Sierra Leone	Leone	SLL
SG-Singapore	Singapore Dollar	SGD
SK-Slovakia	Koruna	SKK
SI-Slovenia	Tolar	SIT
SB-Solomon Is.	Solomon Is. Dollar	SBD
SO-Somalia	Somali Shilling	SOS
ZA-South Africa	Rand	ZAR
ES-Spain	Spanish Peseta	ESP
LK-Sri Lanka	Sri Lanka Rupee	LKR

COUNTRY CODE-NAME	CURRENCY NAME	ISO* CODE
SD-Sudan	Dinar	SDD
SR-Suriname	Suriname Guilder	SRG
SZ-Swaziland	Lilangeni	SZL
SE-Sweden	Swedish Krona	SEK
CH-Switzerland	Swiss Franc	CHF
SY-Syrian Arab Rep.	Syrian Pound	SYP
TW-Taiwan	New Taiwan Dollar	TWD
TJ-Tajikistan	Rouble	RUR
TZ-Tanzania	Tanzanian Shilling	TZS
TH-Thailand	Baht	THB
TG-Togo	CFA Franc	XOF
TK-Tokelau	New Zealand Dollar	NZD
TO-Tonga	Pa'anga	TOP
TT-Trinidad & Tobago	Trinidad & Tobago Dollar	TTD
TN-Tunisia	Tunisian Dinar	TND
TR-Turkey	Turkish Lira	TRL
TM-Turkmenistan	Manat	TMM
TC-Turks & Caicos	U.S. Dollar	USD
TV-Tuvalu	Australian Dollar	AUD
UG-Uganda	Uganda Shilling	UGX
UA-Ukraine	Hryvnia	UAH
AE-United Arab Emirates (comprised of Abu Dhabi, Ajman, Dubai, Fujairah, Ras-al-Khaymah, Sharjah, Umm Al Qaiwain	UAE Dirham	AED
GB-United Kingdom	Pound Sterling	GBP
US-United States, incl. Midway Is., Johnson Atoll, Wake Is.	U.S. Dollar	USD
UY-Uruguay	Peso Uruguayo	UYU
UZ-Uzbekistan	Sum	UZS
VU-Vanuatu	Vatu	VUV
VA-Vatican City	Italian Lira	ITL
VE-Venezuela	Bolivar	VEB
VN-Vietnam	Dong	VND
VG-Virgin Is.(Br.)	U.S. Dollar	USD
VI-Virgin Is.(U.S.)	U.S. Dollar	USD
WF-Wallis & Futuna	CFP Franc	XPF
YE-Yemen	Rial	YER
YU-Yugoslavia	New Dinar	YUG
ZM-Zambia	Kwacha	ZMK
ZW-Zimbabwe	Zimbabwe Dollar	ZWD

U.S. STATES AND CAPITALS

THE CAPITAL OF THE U.S. IS WASHINGTON, DC

Alabama - Montgomery
Alaska - Juneau
Arizona - Phoenix
Arkansas - Little Rock
California - Sacramento
Colorado - Denver
Connecticut - Hartford
Delaware - Dover
Florida- Tallahassee
Georgia - Atlanta
Hawaii - Honolulu
Idaho - Boise
Illinois - Springfield
Indiana - Indianapolis
Iowa - Des Moines
Kansas - Topeka
Kentucky - Frankfort
Louisiana - Baton Rouge
Maine - Augusta
Maryland - Annapolis
Massachusetts - Boston
Michigan - Lansing
Minnesota - St. Paul
Mississippi - Jackson
Missouri - Jefferson City

Montana - Helena
Nebraska - Lincoln
Nevada - Carson City
New Hampshire - Concord
New Jersey - Trenton
New Mexico - Santa Fe
New York - Albany
North Carolina - Raleigh
North Dakota - Bismark
Ohio - Columbus
Oklahoma - Oklahoma City
Oregon - Salem
Pennsylvania - Harrisburg
Rhode Island - Providence
South Carolina - Columbia
South Dakota - Pierre
Tennessee - Nashville
Texas - Austin
Utah - Salt Lake City
Vermont - Montpelier
Virginia - Richmond
Washington - Olympia
West Virginia - Charleston
Wisconsin - Madison
Wyoming - Cheyenne

CANADA'S PROVINCES/TERRITORIES AND CAPITALS

THE CAPITAL OF CANADA IS OTTAWA in ONTARIO.

Alberta - Edmonton
British Columbia - Victoria
Manitoba - Winnipeg
Newfoundland - St. John's
New Brunswick - Fredericton
Northwest Territories# - Yellowknife
Nova Scotia - Halifax
Ontario - Toronto
Prince Edward Island - Charlottetown
Saskatchewan - Regina
Quebec* - Quebec
Yukon - Whitehorse

#contains Nunavut - a tentative new territory
*current separatist movement

COUNTRIES/INDEPENDENT STATES WITH
THEIR CAPITALS AND POPULATIONS

NOTE: POPULATION IS GIVEN IN 1,000s.

COUNTRY	CAPITAL	POPULATION
Afghanistan	Kabul	17,080
Albania	Tirana	3,363
Algeria	Algiers	26,581
American Samoa	Pago Pago	53
Andorra	Andorra-la-Vella	64
Angola	Luanda	10,609
Anguilla	The Valley	10
Antigua & Barbuda	St. John's	64
Argentina	Buenos Aires	34,108
Armenia	Yerevan	3,754
Aruba	Oranjestad	80
Australia	Canberra	17,657
Austria	Vienna	8,031
Azerbaijan	Baku	7,499
Bahamas	Nassau	269
Bahrain	Manama	568
Bangladesh	Dhaka	117,787
Barbados	Bridgetown	264
Belarus	Minsk	10,297
Belgium	Brussels	10,101
Belize	Belmopan	209
Benin	Porto-Novo	5,215
Bermuda	Hamilton	60
Bhutan	Thimphu	600
Bolivia	La Paz (adminstrative) Sucre (legislative)	7,237
Bonaire	Kralendijk	10
Bosnia Hercegovina	Sarajevo	3,524
Botswana	Gaborone	1,450
Brazil	Brasilia	155,822
British Virgin Islands	Road Town (on Tortola)	19
Brunei	Bandar Seri Begawan	284
Bulgaria	Sofia	8,427
Burkina Faso	Ouagadougou	9,889
Burundi	Bujumbura	6,134
Cambodia	Phnom Penh	9,568
Cameroon	Yaounde	11,540
Canada	Ottawa	29,248
Cape Verde	Praia	341
Cayman Islands	Georgetown (on Grand Cayman)	32
Central African Republic	Bangui	2,463
Chad	Ndjamena	6,214
Chile	Santiago	14,210
China	Beijing	1,198,550
Colombia	Santa Fe de Bogota (formerly Bogota)	34,520
Comoros	Moroni	484
Congo	Brazzaville	1,843
Cook Islands	Avarua	19
Costa Rica	San Jose	3,505

NOTE: POPULATION IS GIVEN IN 1,000s.

COUNTRY	CAPITAL	POPULATION
Cote d'Ivoire	Yamoussoukro (adminis-trative)	13,695
	Abidjan (commercial)	
Croatia	Zagreb	4,779
Cuba	Havana	10,901
Cyprus	Nicosia	730
Czech Republic	Prague	10,333
Dem. Rep. of Congo	Kinshasa	36,672
Denmark	Copenhagen	5,216
Djibouti	Djibouti	520
Dominica	Roseau	71
Dominican Republic	Santo Domingo	7,769
Ecuador	Quito	11,460
Egypt	Cairo	57,851
El Salvador	San Salvador	5,048
England	London	48,780
Equatorial Guinea	Malabo	356
Eritrea	Asmara	3,436
Estonia	Tallinn	1,476
Ethiopia	Addis Ababa	56,677
Falkland Islands	Stanley	2
Fiji	Suva	797
Finland	Helsinki	5,098
France	Paris	57.903
French Guiana	Cayenne	114
French Polynesia	Papeete, Tahiti	212
Gabon	Libreville	1,011
Gambia	Banjul	1,038
Georgia	Tbilisi	5,471
Germany	Berlin	
	Bonn (administrative)	

Note: By 2002, Berlin will also be an administrative capital.

		81,338
Ghana	Accra	17,000
Gibraltar	Gibraltar	28
Greece	Athens	10,368
Greenland	Nuuk	55
Grenada	St. George's	95
Guadeloupe	Basse-Terre (admin-istrative)	387
	Pointe-a-Pitre (commercial)	
Guam	Agana	146
Guatemala	Guatemala City	10,322
Guernsey	St. Peter Port	59
Guinea	Conakry	5,600
Guinea-Bissau	Bissau	1,050
Guyana	Georgetown	738
Haiti	Port-au-Prince	7,041
Honduras	Tegucigalpa	5,770
Hong Kong (now part of China)		6,189
Hungary	Budapest	10,277
Iceland	Reykjavik	268
India	New Delhi	920,000

NOTE: POPULATION IS GIVEN IN 1,000s.

COUNTRY	CAPITAL	POPULATION
Indonesia	Jakarta	194,440
Iran	Tehran	59,778
Iraq	Baghdad	17,903
Ireland	Dublin	3,582
Israel	Jerusalem	5,462
Italy	Rome	57,269
Ivory Coast (see Cote d'Ivoire)		
Jamaica	Kingston	2,374
Japan	Tokyo	125,200
Jersey	St. Helier	86
Jordan	Amman	5,198
Kazakhstan	Almaty	16.763
Kenya	Nairobi	29,292
Kiribati	Bairiki	78
Korea (Dem. Rep.)	Pyongyang	23,483
Korea (Rep.)	Seoul	44,850
Kuwait	Kuwait City	1,576
Kyrgyzstan	Bishkek	4,476
Laos	Vientiane	4,581
Latvia	Riga	2,530
Lebanon	Beirut	2,745
Lesotho	Maseru	1,700
Liberia	Monrovia	2,700
Libya	Tripoli	4,899
Liechtenstein	Vaduz	31
Lithuania	Vilnius	3,717
Luxembourg	Luxembourg-Ville	407
Macau	Macau	400
Macedonia	Skopje	1.937
Madagascar	Antananarivo	12,092
Malawi	Lilongwe	10,033
Malaysia	Kuala Lumpur	20,103
Maldives	Male	245
Mali	Bamako	8,156
Malta	Valletta	369
Marshall Is.	Majuro	52
Martinique	Fort-de-France	371
Mauritania	Nouakchott	2,211
Mauritius	Port Louis	1,113
Mayotte	Dzaoudzi	94
Mexico	Mexico City	93,008
Micronesia	Pohnpei	105
Moldova	Chisinau	4,350
Monaco	Monaco-Ville	30
Mongolia	Ulan Bator	2,317
Montserrat	Plymouth	11
Morocco	Rabat	26,024
Mozambique	Maputo	17,423
Myanmar	Yangon	41,550
Namibia	Windhoek	1,500
Nauru	Yaren District	10
Nepal	Kathmandu	19,280
Netherlands	Amsterdam	15,385

NOTE: POPULATION IS GIVEN IN 1,000s.

COUNTRY	CAPITAL	POPULATION
Netherlands Antilles	Willemstad	172
New Caledonia	Noumea	183
New Zealand	Wellington	3,592
Nicaragua	Managua	4,500
Niger	Niamey	8,361
Nigeria	Abuja	88,515
Niue	Alofi	2
N. Mariana Is.	Saipan	53
Northern Ireland	Belfast	1,661
Norway	Oslo	4,348
Oman	Muscat	2,096
Pakistan	Islamabad	126,610
Palau	Koror	17
Panama	Panama City	2,631
Papua New Guinea	Port Moresby	3,997
Paraguay	Asuncion	4,642
Peru	Lima	23,088
Philippines	Manila	67,038
Poland	Warsaw	38,609
Portugal	Lisbon	9,902
Puerto Rico	San Juan	3,702
Qatar	Doha	593
Reunion	Saint-Denis	642
Romania	Bucharest	22,731
Russia	Moscow	148,100
Rwanda	Kigali	7,165
Saba	The Bottom	1
St. Eustatius	Oranjestad	2
St. Kitts & Nevis	Basseterre	44
St. Lucia	Castries	140
St. Vincent & the Grenadines	Kingstown	112
San Marino	San Marino	25
Sao Tome & Principe	Sao Tome	125
Saudi Arabia	Riyadh	16,929
Scotland	Edinburgh	5,164
Senegal	Dakar	8,152
Seychelles	Victoria	74
Sierra Leone	Freetown	4,509
Singapore	Singapore	2,986
Slovak Republic	Bratislava	5,368
Slovenia	Ljubljana	1,989
Solomon Islands	Honiara	366
Somalia	Mogadishu	7,114
South Africa	Cape Town (legislative) Pretoria (administrative) Bloemfontein (judicial)	41,245
Spain	Madrid	39,188
Sri Lanka	Colombo	18,00
Sudan	Khartoum	24,940
Suriname	Paramaribo	418
Swaziland	Mbabane	879

NOTE: POPULATION IS GIVEN IN 1,000s.

COUNTRY	CAPITAL	POPULATION
Sweden	Stockholm	8,839
Switzerland	Bern	7,019
Syria	Damascus	15,000
Taiwan	Taipei	21,126
Tajikistan	Dushanbe	5,751
Tanzania	Dodoma (administrative) Dar es Salaam (commercial)	30,340
Thailand	Bangkok	60,000
Togo	Lome	3,928
Tonga	Nuku'alofa	98
Trinidad & Tobago	Port of Spain	1,250
Tunisia	Tunis	8,947
Turkey	Ankara	61,644
Turkmenistan	Ashgabat	4,483
Turks & Caicos Islands	Cockburn Town, Gran Turk	14
Tuvalu	Funafuti	9
Uganda	Kampala	16,671
Ukraine	Kyiv (spelling change from Kiev)	51,728
United Arab Emirates	Abu Dhabi	2,378
United Kingdom	London	58,395
U.S.A.	Washington, DC	264,649
U.S. Virgin Islands	Charlotte Amalie, St. Thomas	102
Uruguay	Montevideo	3,167
Uzbekistan	Tashkent	22,098
Vanuatu	Port Vila	165
Venezuela	Caracas	21,377
Vietnam	Hanoi	70,983
Wales	Cardiff	2,916
Western Samoa	Apia	164
Yemen	Sana'a	14,561
Yugoslavia	Belgrade	10,482
Zambia	Lusaka	8,210
Zimbabwe	Harare	11,215

NOTES

COMPUTERIZATION CODES

As computer/reservation systems vary, these are for example.

AIRLINE ACTION STATUS CODES

DL	DEFERRED FROM WAITLLIST
DS	DESIRES SEGMENT
FS	FREE SALE
HK	HOLD CONFIRMED
HL	HOLDS LIST
HN	HOLDS NEED
HQ	SPACE ALREADY REQUESTED - DUPLICATION
HS	HAVE SOLD
HX	HAVE CANCELLED
IN	IF NOT HOLDING, NEED
IS	IF NOT HOLDING, SELL
IX	IF HOLDING, CANCEL
KK	CONFIRMED
KL	CONFIRMED WAITLIST
LL	ADD PASSENGER TO WAITLIST
NA	NEED ALTERNATE
NN	NEED
NO	NO ACTION TAKEN ON SPECIFIED SEGMENT
OX	CANCEL ONLY IF REQUESTED SEGMENT IS AVAILABLE
RR	PASSENGER HAS RECONFIRMED
SQ	SPACE REQUESTED
SS	SOLD
UN	UNABLE, FLIGHT DOES NOT OPERATE
US	UNABLE TO ACCEPT SALE, FLIGHT CLOSED, WAITLISTED
UU	UNABLE
XL	CANCEL WAITLIST
XX	CANCEL

SPECIAL MEAL REQUEST CODES

BBML	INFANT MEAL	KSML	KOSHER MEAL
BLML	BLAND MEAL	LFML	LOW CHOLESTEROL MEAL
CSML	CHILD MEAL	NLML	NON-LACTOSE MEAL
DBML	DIABETIC MEAL	NSML	NO SALT MEAL
FRML	FRUIT MEAL	SFML	SEAFOOD MEAL
GFML	GLUTEN-FREE MEAL	SPML	SPECIAL MEAL
HFML	HIGH FIBER MEAL	VGML	VEGETARIAN MEAL

COMPUTERIZATION CODES

As computer/reservation systems vary, these are for example.

AIRIMP	ARC/IATA(N) RESERVATIONS INTERLINE MESSAGE PROCEDURES-PASSENGER
ACK	ACKNOWLEDGE
ADB	ADVISE IF DUPLICATE BOOKING
ADNO	ADVISE IF NOT OKAY
ADTK	ADVISE IF TICKETED
ADVN	ADVISE NAMES
ADVR	ADVISE RATE
ADOA	ADVISE ON ARRIVAL
ADV	ADVISE
ARR	ARRIVE,ARRIVED,ARRIVING,ARRIVAL
ASAP	AS SOON AS POSSIBLE
ASC	ADVISING SCHEDULE CHANGE
AVIH	ANIMAL IN HOLD- CHECK AS CARGO
AVS	AVAILABILITY STATUS MESSAGES
BIKE	BICYCLE
BLND	BLIND PASSENGER
BPR	PRERESERVED SEAT/BOARDING PASS (BILATERAL AGREEMENT REQUIRED)
BSCT	BASSINET
CAKE	SPECIAL CAKE/CHAMPAGNE
CBBG	CABIN BAGGAGE
CFY	CLARIFY
CHD	CHILD
CHNT	CHANGE NAME TO
CHTR	CHARTER
COMM	COMMISSION
COND	CONDITIONAL
CTCA	CONTACT ADDRESS
CTCB	CONTACT BUSINESS PHONE
CTCH	CONTACT HOME PHONE
CTCT	CONTACT TRAVEL AGENT PHONE
DAPO	DO ALL POSSIBLE
DCSN	DECISION
DEAF	DEAF PASSENGER

COMPUTERIZATION CODES

DEP	DEPARTS, DEPARTED, DEPARTURE
DEPO	DEPORTEE
DMO	DISTRICT MARKETING OFFICE
DO	DROP OFF
DPST	DEPOSIT
DSM	DISTRICT SALES MANAGER
DSO	DISTRICT SALES OFFICE
EMER	EMERGENCY TRAVEL
EQUIV	EQUIVALENT AMOUNT
ERQ	ENDORSEMENT REQUEST
EXST	EXTRA SEAT
FHTL	FIRST CLASS HOTEL
FLT	FLIGHT
FQTV	FREQUENT TRAVELER
FRAG	FRAGILE BAGGAGE
FRAV	FIRST AVAILABLE
FRST	FIRST RIDER
GPST	GROUP SEAT REQUEST
GRPS	GROUPS
HTL	HOTEL
ID	IDENTIFICATION
IFUN	IF UNABLE
INAD	INADMISSABLE PASSENGER/
INF	INFANT
IRC	INTERNATIONAL ROUTE CHARGE
KP	COMMISSION PERCENTAGE
LHTL	LUXURY CLASS HOTEL
MAAS	MEET AND ASSIST
MSCN	MISCONNECTION
NAC	NO ACTION TAKEN ON COMMUNICATION
NAR	NEW ARRIVAL INFORMATION
NBR	NUMBER
NOCN	NO CONNECTION
NOSH	NO SHOW
NOTR	NO TRAFFIC RIGHTS
NRC	NO RECORD
NRCF	NOT RECONFIRMED
NSST	NON-SMOKING SEAT

COMPUTERIZATION CODES

NTBA	NAME TO BE ADVISED
OPNS	OPERATIONS
ORIG	ORIGIN, ORIGINATED, ORIGINATING
OTHS	OTHER SERVICES - SPECIFY IN FREE FORM AREA
OUT	CHECK OUT DATE
PDM	POSSIBLE DUPLICATE MESSAGE
PETC	PET IN CABIN
PRF	PARTIAL REFUND MESSAGE
PROT	PROTECTED RESERVATION
PUP	PICKUP
PWCT	PASSENGER WILL CONTACT
RDB	REPLY TO DUPLICATE BOOKING INQUIRY
REML/F	REFERENCE MY LETTER/FAX
REQ	REQUEST
REYL/F	REFERENCE YOUR LETTER/FAX
RFD	FULL REFUND MESSAGE
RFI	REQUEST FOR FURTHER INFORMATION
RHYA	RELEASE FOR HANDLING BY YOUR AGENCY
RLNG	RELEASING
RLSE	RELEASE
RQID	REQUEST IF DESIRED
RQR	REQUEST FOR REPLY
RQST	REQUEST SEAT
RR	RECONFIRMED
RS	RESERVED SEAT
SEDM	SCHEDULE EXCHANGE DATA MESSAGE
SHTL	SECOND CLASS HOTEL
SI	SERVICE INFORMATION
SIPP	STANDARD INTERLINE PASSENGER PROCEDURES
SKD	SCHEDULE/SCHEDULE CHANGE
SKED	SCHEDULE
SLPR	SLEEPER BERTH
SMST	SMOKING SEAT
SRVS	SERVICING
SSM	SEGMENT STATUS MESSAGES/SCHEDULE EXCHANGE DATA MESSAGE ID

COMPUTERIZATION CODES

STCR	STRETCHER PASSENGER
STVR	STOPOVER
SUR	SURFACE
TFC	TRAFFIC
THRU	THROUGH
THTL	TOURIST HOTEL
TKNO	TICKET NUMBER
TKTL	TICKET TIME LIMIT
TOTL	TOTAL
TWOV	TRANSIT WITHOUT VISA
UMNN	UNACCOMPANIED MINOR (NN=AGE)
UMNR	UNACCOMPANIED MINOR
UNK	UNKNOWN
VICE	INSTEAD OF
VIP	VERY IMPORTANT PASSENGER
WCHC	WHEELCHAIR-PASSENGER COMPLETELY IMMOBILE
WCHR	WHEELCHAIR-CAN ASCEND/DESCEND STAIRS
WCHS	WHEELCHAIR-CANNOT ASCEND/DESCEND STAIRS
XBAG	EXCESS BAGGAGE
XR	CANCELLATION RECOMMENDED
XTN	EXTENSION

CAR RENTAL COMPANY CODES

DECODING

AD	ADVANTAGE	KG	KEMWEL
AF	AMERICAR	KN	KENNING
AL	ALAMO	LV	ALLSTATE
AN	ANSA	MW	MIDWAY
BL	RED AND BLUE	RR	RENT RITE
CC	TOWN AND COUNTRY	SL	ITS
DS	DISCOUNT RENTALS	TR	TRIANGLE
EC	EUROPEAN	TS	TILDEN
ED	EURODOLLAR	XR	EXCHANGE
EP	EUROPCAR	ZA	PAYLESS
ET	ENTERPRISE	ZD	BUDGET
EX	USA RENT A CAR	ZE	HERTZ
FA	ACE	ZI	AVIS
GO	VALUE	ZL	NATIONAL
HA	HOLIDAY AUTOS	ZN	GENERAL
HO	HOLIDAY RENT	ZR	DOLLAR
IA	INTERAMERICAN	ZT	THRIFTY
IC	INTERCONTINENTAL	ZU	AUTO EUROPE

ENCODING

ACE	FA	HOLIDAY AUTOS	HA
ADVANTAGE	AD	HOLIDAY RENT	HO
ALAMO	AL	INTERAMERICAN	IA
ITS	SL	INTERCONTINENTAL	IC
ALLSTATE	LV	ITS	SL
AMERICAR	AF	KEMWEL	KG
ANSA	AN	KENNING	KN
AUTO EUROPE	ZU	MIDWAY	MW
AVIS	ZI	NATIONAL	ZL
BUDGET	ZD	PAYLESS	ZA
DISCOUNT RENTALS	DS	RED AND BLUE	BL
DOLLAR	ZR	RENT RITE	RR
ENTERPRISE	ED	THRIFTY	ZT
EURODOLLAR	ED	TILDEN	TS
EUROPCAR	EP	TOWN & COUNTRY	CC
EUROPEAN	EC	TRIANGLE	TR
GENERAL	ZN	VALUE	GO
HERTZ	ZE	USA RENT A CAR	EX

CAR RENTAL INFORMATION CODES

CLASS OF CAR
M*	MINI (certain companies)
M*	MIDSIZE/INTERMEDIATE
C	COMPACT
E	ECONOMY
I	INTERMEDIATE/MIDSIZE
S	STANDARD
F	FULL SIZE
P	PREMIUM
L	LUXURY
S	SPECIAL

*as the same code is used, always clarify the situation with the vendor

TYPE OF CAR
C	CAR
B	TWO-DOOR CAR
D	FOUR-DOOR CAR
W	WAGON
V	VAN
L	LIMO
S	SPORTS CAR
T	CONVERTIBLE
R	RECREATIONAL
F	FOUR-WHEEL DRIVE
X	SPECIAL
P	PICKUP
J	ALL TERRAIN
K	TRUCK

TRANSMISSION TYPES
A	AUTOMATIC
S	STANDARD

AIR CONDITIONED
R	AIR CONDITIONED
N	NO AIR CONDITION

SAMPLE VEHICLE TYPE CODES
CCAR	Compact car, automatic transmission, air conditioned
ECAR	Economy car, " " , " "
FCAR	Full size car, " " , " "
ICAR	Intermediate car, " " , " "
LCAR	Luxury car, " " , " "
SCAR	Standard car, " " ,
SFMR	Standard, Four-wheel drive, manual transmission, air conditioned
SPCL	Special car
SSAR	Standard sports car, automatic transmission, air conditioned
STAR	Standard convertible, " " , " "
SVAR	Standard van, automatic transmission, air conditioned
PCAR	Premium car, automatic transmission, air conditioned

HOTEL COMPANY CODES

DECODING

AJ	AMERISUITES	FH	FIESTA AMERICANA
AM	ADAMS MARK HOTELS	FN	FAIRFIELD INN
AN	ANA HOTELS INT'L	FS	FOUR SEASONS
AS	ALL SUITES	FZ	FRIENDSHIP INNS
BB	BARTELL HOTELS	GA	GUESTHOUSE INT'L
BC	COPTHORNE HOTELS	GR	GLOBAL RESERVATION
BD	BED & BREAKFAST DIRECT	GT	GOLDEN TULIP
BH	HAWTHORNE SUITES	HE	HELMSLEY HARLEY
BM	BILTMORE HOTELS	HG	HOMEWOOD SUITES
BP	SHILOH INNS	HH	HILTON HOTELS
BR	RENAISSANCE HOTELS	HI	HOLIDAY INN
BT	BTH HOTELS	HJ	HOWARD JOHNSON
BW	BEST WESTERN INT'L	HL	HILTON INT'L
CC	CLARION COLLECTION	HP	HAWAIIAN PAC. RESOR
CD	CONCORDE HOTELS	HR	HARRAHS HOTELS
CE	SUSSE CHALET	HV	HARVEY HOTELS
CH	CARLYLE HOTEL	HX	HAMPTON INNS
CI	COMFORT INNS	HY	HYATT HOTELS
CN	CONSORT HOTELS	IC	INTERCONTINENTAL
CP	CANADIAN PACIFIC	IG	INSIGNIA RESORTS
CQ	CRESCENT HOTELS	JA	JARVINEN WORLDWIDE
CS	COLONY RESORTS	JH	JOLLY HOTELS
CY	COURTYARD	JV	JACK TAR VILLAGES
CZ	CORPORATE RESORTS	KI	KEMPINSKI HOTELS
DA	DORAL HOTELS	LH	LRI
DE	DELTA HOTELS	LQ	LA QUINTA
DI	DAYS INN	LW	LEADING HOTELS
DO	DORINT HOTELS	LZ	LOEWS HOTELS
DS	DESIGN HOTELS	MC	MARRIOTT
DT	DOUBLETREE HOTELS	MG	MGM GRAND
DW	WALT DISNEY HOTELS	MK	MOVENPICK HOTELS
ED	DISNEYLAND PARIS HOTELS	MN	MONTE CARLO RESORT
EJ	EL SAN JUAN HOTELS	MO	MANDARIN ORIENTAL
EO	ECONO LODGE	NH	NTA HOTEL RYOKAN
ER	ERS	NK	NIKKO HOTELS
ES	EMBASSY SUITES	NO	NEW OTANI
FA	FAIRMONT HOTELS	NR	RAMADA HOTELS
FE	FORTE HOTELS	OB	OBEROI HOTELS

HOTEL COMPANY CODES

OM	OMNI	SJ	SIGNATURE INNS
OO	CROWN STERLING	SK	STAKIS HOTEL GROUP
OR	OUTRIGGER	SL	SWISSOTEL
PA	PARK INN	SO	SONESTA HOTELS
PH	PREFERRED	SQ	SELECT MKTG. HOTELS
PI	PRINCESS HOTELS	SR	SRS HOTELS
PK	PARK PLAZA HOTELS	SS	SUMMERFIELD SUITES
PL	PARK LANE HOTELS	SZ	SLEEP INNS
PO	POINTE RESORTS	TH	COUNTRY COMFORT
PW	PRIMA HOTELS	TI	THISTLE HOTELS
QI	QUALITY INNS	TL	TRAVELODGE
QR	QUALITY HOTEL RES.	TR	TRUST INT'L
RA	RAMADA INNS	UI	UTELL INT'L
RD	RADISSION HOTELS	UK	SWALLOW HOTELS
RE	REGENT INT'L	UR	ULTIMATE RESORTS
RH	REGISTRY HOTELS	VA	VAGABOND INNS
RI	RODEWAY INNS	VB	VACATION BREAK
RL	RED LION HOTELS	VI	VENTURE INNS
RM	ROMANTIK HOTELS	VR	VILLAGE RESORTS
RN	EXPOTEL ROOM CENTER	WC	WORLD CLASS HOTELS
RQ	REGAL HOTELS INT'L	WG	WINGATE INNS
RV	RED ROOF INNS	WI	WESTIN HOTELS
RW	ROBERT F. WARNER	WK	WARWICK HOTELS
RY	ROYCE HOTELS	WL	WELLESLEY INNS
RZ	RITZ-CARLTON HOTELS	WY	WYNDAM HOTELS
SG	SHANGRI-LA HOTELS	XC	HOTELS CAMINO REAL
SI	SHERATON HOTELS	XS	COURTYARD INNS

NOTE: SOME REFERENCES USE THREE-LETTER ABBREVIATIONS
FOR HOTELS. NOT ALL HOTELS ARE LISTED HERE.

HOTEL COMPANY CODES

ENCODING

ADAMS MARK HOTELS	AM	FORTE HOTELS	FE
ALL SUITES	AS	FOUR SEASONS HOTELS	FS
AMERISUITES	AJ	FRIENDSHIP INNS	FZ
ANA HOTELS INT'L	AN	GLOBAL RESERVATIONS	GR
BARTELL HOTELS	BB	GOLDEN TULIP HOTELS	GT
BED & BREAKFAST DIRECT	BD	GUESTHOUSE INT'L	GA
BEST WESTERN INT'L	BW	HAMPTON INNS	HX
BILTMORE HOTELS	BM	HARRAHS HOTELS	HR
BTH HOTELS	BT	HARVEY HOTELS	HV
CANADIAN PACIFIC HOTELS	CP	HAWAIIAN PACIFIC RESORTS	HP
CARLYLE HOTEL	CH	HAWTHORNE SUITES	BH
CLARION COLLECTION	CC	HELMSLEY HARLEY HOTELS	HE
COLONY RESORTS	CS	HILTON HOTELS	HH
COMFORT INNS	CI	HILTON INT'L	HL
CONCORDE HOTELS	CD	HOLIDAY INN	HI
CONSORT HOTELS	CN	HOMEWOOD SUITES	HG
COPTHORNE HOTELS	BC	HOTELS CAMINO REAL	XC
CORPORATE RESORTS	CZ	HOWARD JOHNSON	HJ
COUNTRY COMFORT	TH	HYATT HOTELS	HY
COURTYARD	CY	INSIGNIA RESORTS	IG
COURTYARD INNS CANADA	XS	INTERCONTINENTAL	IC
CRESCENT HOTELS	CQ	JACK TAR VILLAGES	JV
CROWN STERLING	OO	JARVINEN WORLDWIDE	JA
DAYS INN	DI	JOLLY HOTELS	JH
DELTA HOTELS	DE	KEMPINSKI HOTELS	KI
DESIGN HOTELS	DS	LA QUINTA	LQ
DISNEYLAND PARIS HOTELS	ED	LEADING HOTELS	LW
DORAL HOTELS	DA	LOEWS HOTELS	LZ
DORINT HOTELS	DO	LRI	LH
DOUBLETREE HOTELS	DT	MANDARIN ORIENTAL	MO
ECONOLODGE	EO	MARRIOTT	MC
EL SAN JUAN HOTELS	EJ	MGM GRAND HOTEL	MG
EMBASSY SUITES	ES	MONTE CARLO RESORTS	MN
ERS	ER	MOVENPICK HOTELS	MK
EXPOTEL ROOM CENTER	RN	NEW OTANI	NO
FAIRFIELD INN	FN	NIKKO HOTELS	NK
FAIRMONT HOTELS	FA	NTA HOTEL RYOKAN	NH
FIESTA AMERICANA	FH	OBEROI HOTELS	OB

HOTEL COMPANY CODES

OMNI HOTELS	OM	SHERATON HOTELS	SI
OUTRIGGER HOTELS	OR	SHILOH INNS	BP
PARK INN	PA	SIGNATURE INNS	SJ
PARK LANE HOTELS	PL	SLEEP INNS	SZ
PARK PLAZA HOTELS	PK	SONESTA HOTELS	SO
POINTE RESORTS	PO	SRS	SR
PREFERRED HOTELS	PH	STAKIS HOTEL GROUP	SK
PRIMA HOTELS	PW	SUMMERFIELD SUITES	SS
PRINCESS HOTELS	PI	SUSSE CHALET	CE
QUALITY HOTEL RES.	QR	SWALLOW HOTELS	UK
QUALITY INNS	QI	SWISSOTEL	SL
RADISSON HOTELS	RD	THISTLE HOTELS	TI
RAMADA HOTELS	NR	TRAVELODGE	TL
RAMADA INNS	RA	TRUST INT'L	TR
RED LION HOTELS	RL	ULTIMATE RESORTS	UR
RED ROOF INNS	RV	UTELL INT'L	UI
REGAL HOTELS INT'L	RQ	VACATION BREAK	VB
REGENT INT'L HOTELS	RE	VAGABOND INNS	VA
REGISTRY HOTELS	RH	VENTURE INNS	VI
RENAISSANCE HOTELS	BR	VILLAGE RESORTS	VR
RITZ-CARLTON HOTELS	RZ	WALT DISNEY HOTELS	DW
ROBERT F. WARNER	RW	WARWICK	WK
RODEWAY INNS	RI	WELLESLEY INNS	WL
ROMANTIK HOTELS	RM	WESTIN HOTELS	WI
ROYCE HOTELS	RY	WINGATE INNS	WG
SELECT MARKETING HTLS	SQ	WORLD CLASS HOTELS	WC
SHANGRI-LA HOTELS	SG	WYNDAM HOTELS	WY

**NOTE: SOME REFERENCES USE THREE-LETTER ABBREVIATIONS
FOR HOTELS. NOT ALL HOTELS ARE LISTED HERE.**

HOTEL INFORMATION CODES

HOTEL QUALIFIER - LOCATIONS
A	AIRPORT
R	RESORT
M	MALL
C	CITY CENTER
S	SUBURB

MEAL PLANS
A	AMERICAN PLAN
B	BREAKFAST PLAN
C	CONTINENTAL
E	EUROPEAN
M	MODIFIED AMERICAN

ROOM CODES - LOCATION
OF	OCEANFRONT	PS	POOLSIDE
SV	SEA VIEW	BF	BEACHFRONT
MV	MOUNTAIN VIEW	BV	BAY VIEW
GV	GULF VIEW		

TYPE OF ROOM
A	DELUXE
B	SUPERIOR
C	STANDARD
D	MINIMUM

TYPE OF BEDS
2T	2 TWIN BEDS
2D	2 DOUBLES
1Q	1 QUEEN
1K	1 KING

CODES
DBLB	DOUBLE ROOM WITH BATH
DBLN	DOUBLE ROOM WITHOUT BATH/SHOWER
DBLS	DOUBLE ROOM WITH SHOWER
QADB	QUAD ROOM WITH BATH
QADN	QUAD ROOM WITHOUT BATH/SHOWER
QADS	QUAD ROOM WITH SHOWER
QUINB	QUIN ROOM WITH BATH
QUINN	QUIN ROOM WITHOUT BATH/SHOWER
QUINS	QUIN ROOM WITH SHOWER
SGLB	SINGLE ROOM WITH BATH
SGLN	SINGLE ROOM WITHOUT BATH/SHOWER
SGLS	SINGLE ROOM WITH SHOWER
TPLB	TRIPLE ROOM WITH BATH
TPLN	TRIPLE ROOM WITHOUT BATH/SHOWER
TPLS	TRIPLE ROOM WITH SHOWER
TWNB	TWIN ROOM WITH BATH
TWNN	TWIN ROOM WITHOUT BATH/SHOWER
TWNS	TWIN ROOM WITH SHOWER

HOTEL INFORMATION CODES *(continued)*

RATE TYPE CODES

C	CORPORATE
F	FAMILY PLAN
G	GOVERNMENT
P	PROMOTIONAL
T	TOUR
W	WEEKEND
V	CONVENTION
R	RACK
S	SENIOR

RATE ABBREVIATIONS

DLXR	DELUXE
LUXR	LUXURY
MAXR	MAXIMUM
MINR	MINIMUM
ROHR	RUN OF THE HOUSE
STDR	STANDARD
SUPR	SUPERIOR

ROOM LOCATIONS/SPECIFICS

BCH/BCHFT	BEACH/BEACHFRONT	OCNFT	OCEANFRONT
BLCY	BALCONY	OCNVW	OCEAN VIEW
GDN	GARDEN	PLVW	POOL VIEW
GDNVW	GARDEN VIEW	SPC	SPECIAL
HLSDE	HILLSIDE	SVW	SEA VIEW
ISLVW	ISLAND VIEW	TWR	TOWER
LNI	LANAI	WTRVW	WATER VIEW

CREDIT CARD CODES

AC/ACC	ACCESS	DC	DINERS CLUB
AX/AE	AMERICAN EXPRESS	DI/DIS	DISCOVER
BC	BARCLAYS	EC	EUROCARD
CB	CARTE BLANCHE	MC	MASTER CARD
		VI	VISA

OTHER ABBREVIATIONS/CODES

B	BEDS	ON	ON SEASON
COM/COMM	COMMISSION	PH	PENTHOUSE
DLY	DAILY	STE	SUITE
MTH	MONTHLY	TD	TRADE DISCOUNT
OF	OFF SEASON	U	UNITS
		X	EXTRA PERSON

FARE INDICATORS/CODES

Domestic and international airline fares contain codes which in some cases describe the type of fare/its restrictions. The letters and numbers of the fares can be "decoded" to better understand the restrictions. You always have to check the rule for clarification, but a knowledge of fare indicators/codes can expedite fare research. The letters mean different things, depending on their position in the fare code/basis: primary means it's the first letter(s), secondary means it's not the first letter. Example: BLXAP60 is decoded as: coach discount, low season, midweek, advance purchase (and the 60 can mean 60 days advance purchase).

PRIMARY CODES/ INDICATORS

R	SUPERSONIC
P	FIRST CLASS PREMIUM
F	FIRST CLASS
A	FIRST CLASS DISCOUNT
J	BUSINESS CLASS PREMIUM
C	BUSINESS CLASS
D	BUSINESS CLASS DISCOUNT
S	STANDARD CLASS
W	COACH PREMIUM
FN	FIRST CLASS NIGHT
Y	COACH CLASS
CN	BUSINESS CLASS NIGHT
YN	COACH CLASS NIGHT
B	COACH CLASS DISCOUNT
H	COACH CLASS DISCOUNT
Q	COACH CLASS DISCOUNT
M	COACH CLASS DISCOUNT
V	COACH CLASS DISCOUNT
K	COACH CLASS DISCOUNT
L	COACH CLASS DISCOUNT
E	SHUTTLE SERVICE (NO RESERVATIONS)

SECONDARY CODES/ QUALIFIERS

H	HIGH SEASON
K/O	SECOND LEVEL
J	THIRD LEVEL
F/Z	FOURTH LEVEL
T	FIFTH LEVEL
Q	SIXTH LEVEL
L	LOW SEASON
AB	ADVANCE BUY
AP	ADVANCE PURCHASE
G	GROUP
GA	GROUP AFFINITY
GC	GROUP INCENTIVE
GV	GROUP INCLUSIVE TOUR
NR	NON-REFUNDABLE
X	MIDWEEK/EXCEPT
W	WEEKEND
Z	STUDENT/ONLY
U	STANDBY
E	EXCURSION
P	PENALTY
M	MILITARY
CL	CLERGY
IT	INCLUSIVE TOUR
VUSA	VISIT THE USA

WEB SITES

NOTE: http:// has been omitted from these lists to save space. These are just a few of the many sites available. Sites are added constantly, and addresses may change. Create your own list of favorite web sites.

WEB SITES WITH MANY LINKS: http://www.travigator.com
http://www.daemen.edu/pages/dflammger/linkdir.html

AIRLINES

SEARCHES CAN BE MADE BY USING THE WEB SITES:
www.itn.net/airlines
www.yahoo.com/business/corporations/travel/airlines

AEROLINEAS ARGENTINAS	www.pinos.com/Aero/aero.html
AEROMEXICO	www.wotw.com/aeromexico/
AIR ARUBA	www.interknowledge.com/air-aruba/
AIR CANADA	www.aircanada.ca/
AIR FRANCE	www.airfrance.fr/
AIR NEW ZEALAND	www.airnz.com/
ALASKA AIRLINES	www.alaska-air.com/
ALITALIA	www.alitalia.it/
ALM ANTILLEAN AIRLINES	www.empg.com/alm/
ALOHA AIRLINES	www.alohair.com/aloha-air/
AMERICA WEST	www.americawest.com/
AMERICAN AIRLINES	www.americanair.com
ANSETT AIRLINES	www.ansett.com.au/
AUSTRIAN AIRLINES	www.aua.co.at/aua/
AVIANCA	www.avianca.com
AVIATECA	www.flylatinamerica.com/acc_aviateca. html
BRITISH AIRWAYS	www.british-airways.com
BRITISH MIDLAND	www.iflybritishmidland.com
BWIA	www.bwiacaribbean.com
CANADIAN AIRLINES INTL	www.CdnAir.CA/
CARNIVAL AIRLINES	www.carnivalair.com
CATHAY PACIFIC	www.cathay-usa.com
CAYMAN AIRWAYS	www.caymanairways.com
CHINA AIRLINES	www.china-airlines.com/
CONTINENTAL AIRLINES	www.fly-continental.com
DELTA AIRLINES	www.delta-air.com

AIRLINES (continued)

FINNAIR	www.finnair.fi/
GARUDA INDONESIAN	www.indonesianet.com/garudausa/
HAWAIIAN AIRLINES	www.hawaiianair.com
IBERIA AIRLINES	www.iberiausa.com
ICELANDAIR	www.centrum.is/icelandair/
JAPAN AIRLINES	www.jal.co.jp/
KLM ROYAL DUTCH	www. klm.nl/
KOREAN AIR LINES	www.koreanair.com/
LADECO	www.ladeco.com/
LAN CHILE	www.lanchile.com/
LOT POLISH	www.lot.com/
LTU	www.iquest.net/ltu/
MALAYSIAN	www.malaysiaairlines.com.my
MEXICANA	www.mexicana.com
NORTHWEST	www.nwa.com
QANTAS	www.qantas.com.au/
SABENA	www.sabena-usa.com/
SAS	www.sas.se/
SINGAPORE	www.singaporeair.com
SOUTH AFRICAN AIRWAYS	www.saa.co.za/saa/notnet2.htm
SOUTHWEST	www.iflyswa.com
SWISSAIR	www.swissair.com
TAP	www.tap-airportugal.pt
TWA	www.twa.com
UNITED	www.ual.com
US AIRWAYS	www.usair.com
VARIG	www.varig.com.br/
VIRGIN ATLANTIC	www.fly.virgin.com/atlantic/
WESTERN PACIFIC	www.westpac.com

CRUISE LINES

AMERICAN CANADIAN	www.accl-smallships.com
AMERICAN HAWAII	www.cruisehawaii.com
CARNIVAL	www.carnival.com
CELEBRITY	www.celebritycruises.com
CLIPPER	www.clippercruise.com
CLUB MED	www.clubmed.com
COSTA	www.costacruises.com
CUNARD	www.cunardline.com

CRUISE LINES (continued)

DELTA QUEEN STEAMBOAT	www.asource.com/deltaqueen/index.htm
DISCOVERY	www.introweb.com/discovery/
EPIROTIKI	www.epirotiki.com
HOLLAND AMERICA	www.hollandamerica.com
NORWEGIAN CRUISE LINE	www.ncl.com/ncl
PREMIER CRUISE LINE	www.inx.net/bigred
RADISSION SEVEN SEAS	www.asource.com/radisson/
RENAISSANCE	www.rencruises.com/
ROYAL CARIBBEAN INTL	www.royalcaribbean.com
SILVERSEA	www.asource.com/silversea/
STAR CLIPPERS	www.globalint.com/mart/star.html
TALL SHIP ADVENTURES	www.the-wire.com/torbrig/
WINDJAMMER BAREFOOT	www.windjammer.com
WINDSTAR	www.windstarcruises.com
WORLD EXPLORER	www.wecruise.com

TOUR OPERATORS

SEARCHES CAN BE MADE USING THESE WEB SITES:

www.ntaonline	**www.sitravel.com**
www.ustoa.com	**www.vacationpackager.com**
ABERCROMBIE AND KENT	www.abercrombiekent.com
BRENNAN TOURS	www.brennantours.com
CERTIFIED VACATIONS	www.leisureweb.com
CHANGES IN LATTITUDES	www.changes.com/
COLLETE TOURS	www.collettetours.com
CONTIKI	www.contiki.com
DELTA DREAM VACATIONS	www.leisureweb.com/DELTA/
FREEGATE TOURISM	www.freegatetours.com
FRIENDLY HOLIDAYS	www.ten-io.com/friendly/
FUNJET VACATIONS	www.funjet.com
GRAYLINE WORLDWIDE	www.grayline.com
HADDON HOLIDAYS	www.haddon.com
JAPAN AND ORIENT	www.jot.com
JET VACATIONS	www.jetvacations.com
MOUNT COOK LINE	www.mtcook.co.nz/
PACIFIC HOLIDAYS	www.travelfile.com/get/pacifhol
PERILLO TOURS	www.perillotours.com
SUNNY LAND TOURS	www.sunny-land-tours.com
THOMAS COOK VACATIONS	www.tch.thomascook.com/

TOUR OPERATORS (continued)

TOURCRAFTERS	www.tourcrafters.com
TOURLITE INT'L	www.tourlite.com
TRANS GLOBAL VACATIONS	www.tgvacations.com/
VALUE HOLIDAYS	www.valhol.com
ZEUS TOURS	www.zeustours.com

HOTELS

SEARCHES CAN BE MADE USING THESE WEB SITES:
www.all-hotels.com   www.traveler.net/htio/   www.hotelguide.ch/

ADAMS MARK	www.travelx.com/adamsmark.html
ANA HOTELS	www.ananet.or.jp/anahotels/e/
BARCLAY INT'L	www.barclayweb.com
BEST WESTERN INT'L	www.travelweb.com/bw.html
BUDGETEL	www.budgetel.com
CHOICE HOTELS	www.hotelchoice.com
COLONY RESORTS	www.colony-resorts.com
COURTYARD	www.marriott.com/courtyard/
CROWN PLAZA	www.crowneplaza.com/
DAYS INNS	www.daysinn.com
DOUBLETREE	www.doubletreehotels.com
EMBASSY SUITES	www.embassy-suites.com
FAIRFIELD INN	www.marriott.com/fairfieldinn/
FORTE HOTELS	www.forte-hotels.com
FOUR SEASONS	www.fshr.com/
HAMPTON INNS	www.hampton-inn.com
HILTON	www.hilton.com
HOLIDAY INN	www.holiday-inn.com
HOMEWOOD SUITES	www.homewood-suites.com
HOWARD JOHNSON	www.hojo.com
HYATT	www.hyatt.com
INTERCONTINENTAL	www.interconti.com
LOEWS	www.loewshotels.com/
MARRIOTT	www.marriott.com
OMNI	www.omnihotels.com
OUTRIGGER	www.outrigger.com
PARK PLAZA	www.parkhtls.com
PRINCESS	www.princess.com.tr
RADISSON	www.radisson.com
RAMADA	ramada.com

HOTELS (continued)

RED LION	www.TravelWeb.com/rl/common/redlion.html
RENAISSANCE HOTELS	www.renaissance-asia.com
RESIDENCE INN	www.marriott.com/residenceinn/
SANDALS RESORTS	www.sandals.com
SHANGRI-LA HOTELS	www.shangrila.com
SHERATON	www.sheraton.com
SHONEY'S INNS	www.shoneysinn.com/
SONESTA HOTELS	www.sonesta.com
STAKIS HOTEL GROUP	www.co.uk/stakis/hotels.html
SUPER 8 MOTELS	www.super8motels.com/
SUSSE CHALET	www.sussechalet.com
TRAVELODGE	www.travelodge.com
UTELL	www.hotelbook.com
WESTIN	www.westin.com
WESTMARK	www.westmarkhotels.com
WYNDHAM	www.wyndham-recruiting.com/Hotel.htm

CAR RENTAL COMPANIES

ABC RENT A CAR	www.rentabc.com/
ADVANTAGE	www.arac.com
ALAMO	www.goalamo.com
AUTO EUROPE	www.auto-europe.com
AVIS	www.avis.com
BUDGET	www.budget.com
DOLLAR	www.dollarcar.com
EURODOLLAR	www.eurodollar.co.uk/
HERTZ	www.hertz.com
KEMWEL	www.kemwel.com
NATIONAL	www.nationalcar.com
PAYLESS	www.paylesscar.com
RENT A WRECK	rent-a-wreck.com/
THRIFTY	www.thrifty.com
VALUE	www.go-value.com

MISCELLANEOUS WEB SITES OF INTEREST

Microsoft Expedia	www.expedia.com
Travelocity	www.travelocity.com
Air Fares for Less	www.air4less.com
Travel Information System	www.tiss.com/
Consular Information Sheets	travel.state.gov/travel_warnings.html
Federal Aviation Administration	www.faa.gov
Passport Services	travel.state.gov/passport_services.html
U.S. Customs	www.customs.ustreas.gov/
Great Outdoors Recreation	www.gorp.com
Mapquest	www.mapquest.com
Weather Channel	www.weather.com
World Information	www.geopedia.com
City Net Travel Guide	www.city.net:80/
Cybertour of the U.S.	www.std.com/NE/usatour.html
Travel Channel	www.travelchannel.com
Ski Information	www.iski.com
Information on diseases in foreign countries	www.intmed.mcw.edu/travel.html

THERE ARE ALSO HUNDREDS OF WEB SITES FOR DESTINATIONS. CONTACT TOURIST OFFICES FOR ADDRESSES OR USE THE VARIOUS SEARCH ENGINES/ MAIN SITES AVAILABLE.

WORLD FACTS AND TRIVIA

WORLD AREAS AND POPULATIONS

	AREA sq.mi.	sq.km.	POPULATION (in millions)
World Total (land)	57,970,0000	150,142,300	5,384
Asia	17,128,500	44,362,815	3,155
Africa	11,647,720	30,167,594	677
North America	9,363,000	24,250,170	390
South America	6,839,890	17,715,315	302
Antarctica	5,500,000	14,245,000	no indigenous population
Europe	4,057,000	10,507,630	676
Australia	2,967,900	7,686,861	18
Central America	197,480	511,475	32

CONTINENTS, HIGHEST POINTS AND LOWEST POINTS

CONTINENT	POINT	HEIGHT ABOVE SEA LEVEL feet	meters	POINT	BELOW SEA LEVEL feet	meters
Asia	Mt.Everest	29,029	8,848	Dead Sea	1,312	400
South America	Mt.Aconcagua	22,834	6,960	Valdes Pen.	131	40
North America	Mt.McKinley*	20,320	6,194	Death Valley	282	86
Africa	Mt.Kilimanjaro	19,340	5,895	Lake Assal	512	156
Europe	Mt.Elbrus	18,510	5,642	Caspian Sea	92	28
Antarctica	Vinson Massif	16,864	5,140	---	----	
Australia	Mt.Kosciusko	7,310	2,228	Lake Eyre	52	16

*also called Mt. Denali

LARGEST ISLANDS

	AREA sq.mi.	sq.km.
Greenland	840,000	2,175,600
New Guinea	306,000	792,540
Borneo	280,100	725,459
Madagascar	226,658	587,044
Baffin	195,928	507,454
Sumatra	165,000	427,350
Honshu	87,805	227,415
Great Britain	84,200	218,078
Victoria	83,896	217,291
Ellesmere	75,767	196,237
Celebes	69,000	178,710
South Is. (NZ)	58,305	151,010
Java	48,900	126,651
Cuba	44,218	114,525
North Is. (NZ)	44,035	114,051
Newfoundland	42,030	108,858

OCEANS

The largest ocean by surface area is the Pacific Ocean.
It has a maximum depth of 36,200 feet. Next largest
is the Atlantic, with a maximum depth of 30,246 feet.
The Indian Ocean has a maximum depth of 24,442 feet.

SOME MAJOR NATURAL LAKES OF THE WORLD

LAKE	SURFACE AREA sq.mi.	sq.km.	MAXIMUM DEPTH feet	meters
Caspian Sea*	143,240	370,992	3,363	1,025
Superior	31,700	82,103	1,333	406
Victoria	26,820	69,464	279	85
Aral Sea*	24,904	64,501	220	67
Huron	23,000	59,570	750	229
Michigan	22,300	57,757	923	281
Tanganyika	12,350	31,987	4,800	1,463
Baikal	12,160	31,494	5,315	1,620
Great Bear	12,028	31,153	1,356	413
Nyasa	11,150	28,879	2,280	695
Great Slave	11,030	28,568	2,015	614
Erie	9,910	25,667	210	64
Winnipeg	9,417	24,390	92	28
Ontario	7,540	19,529	802	244
Balkhash*	7,115	18,428	87	27
Ladoga	6,835	17,703	755	230
Chad	6,300	16,317	36	11

*salt water

MAJOR RIVERS OF THE WORLD – BY LENGTH

RIVER	LENGTH mi.	km.	OUTFLOW
Nile	4,145	6,673	Mediterranean Sea
Amazon	3,912	6,296	Atlantic Ocean
Mississippi-Missouri	3,740	6,021	Gulf of Mexico
Changjiang (Yangtze)	3,720	5,989	China Sea
Yenisei-Angara	3,650	5,877	Kara Sea (Arctic)
Amur-Argun	3,590	5,780	Sea of Japan
Ob-Irtysh	3,360	5,410	Gulf of Ob (Arctic)
Plata-Parana	3,030	4,878	Atlantic Ocean
Huang He (Yellow)	2,903	4,674	Yellow Sea
Congo (Dem.Rep.of Congo)	2,900	4,669	Atlantic Ocean
Lena	2,730	4,395	Laptev Sea (Arctic)
MacKenzie	2,635	4,242	Beaufort Sea (Arctic)
Mekong	2,600	4,186	South China Sea
Niger	2,600	4,186	Atlantic Ocean
Missouri	2,533	4,078	Mississippi River
Mississippi	2,348	3,780	Gulf of Mexico
Murray-Darling	2,330	3,751	Indian Ocean
Volga	2,290	3,687	Caspian Sea
Madeira	2,013	3,241	Amazon River
San Francisco	1,988	3,201	Atlantic Ocean
Yukon	1,979	3,186	Bering Sea
Rio Grande	1,885	3,035	Gulf of Mexico

10 HIGHEST WATERFALLS OF THE WORLD

WATERFALL	LOCATION	HEIGHT feet	meters
Angel	Venezuela	3,281	1,000
Tugela	Natal, S.Africa	3,000	914
Cuquenan	Venezuela	2,000	610
Sutnerland	South Is., New Zealand	1,904	580
Takkakaw	British Columbia	1,650	503
Ribbon (Yosemite)	California	1,612	491
Upper (Yosemite)	California	1,430	436
Gavarnie	Southwest France	1,384	422
Vettisfoss	Norway	1,200	366
Widow's Tears (Yosemite)	California	1,170	357

OTHER NOTABLE WATERFALLS

WATERFALL	LOCATION	HEIGHT feet	meters
Kaieteur	Guyana	822	251
Bridal Veil (Yosemite)	California	620	189
Victoria	Zimbabwe-Zambia border	355	108

Notes: Iguassu Falls on the border of Brazil, Paraguay, and Argentina features 275 falls that drop from 120 to 240 feet. Niagara Falls on the New York-Ontario border has tremendous volume but only drops a height of between 158 and 167 feet.

MAJOR SHIP CANALS

	LENGTH miles	kilometers
Volga-Baltic	225	362
Baltic-White	140	225
Suez, Egypt	100.7	162
Albert, Belgium	80	129
Moscow-Volga	80	129
Volga-Don	62	100
Gota, Sweden	54	87
Kiel (Nord-Ostsee), Germany	53	86
Panama Canal, Panama	50.7	82
Houston Ship, U.S.	50	81

DESERTS OF THE WORLD

The largest desert is the Sahara, with an area greater than the contiguous United States. The driest place on earth is in the Atacama Desert of Chile - no rainfall was recorded between 1570 and 1971. The highest temperature ever recorded was 136 degrees Farenheit (58 degress Centigrade) - in the Libyan Desert at Al-Aziziya.

U.S. STATES - NICKNAMES

Alabama - Yellowhammer State
Alaska - The Great Land, Last Frontier
Arizona - Grand Canyon State
Arkansas - Land of Opportunity
California - Golden State
Colorado - Centennial State
Connecticut - Constitution State, Nutmeg State
Delaware - Blue Hen State, Diamond State, First State
Florida - Sunshine State
Georgia - Peach State, Empire State of the South
Hawaii - Aloha State
Idaho - Gem State
Illinois - Prairie State, Land of Lincoln
Indiana - Hoosier State
Iowa - Hawkeye State
Kansas - Sunflower State
Kentucky - Bluegrass State
Louisiana - Pelican State
Maine - Pine Tree State
Maryland - Old Line State, Free State
Massachusetts - Bay State, Old Colony
Michigan - Wolverine State
Minnesota - North Star State, Gopher State
Mississippi - Magnolia State
Missouri - Show Me State
Montana - Treasure State, Big Sky Country
Nebraska - Cornhusker State
Nevada - Silver State, Sagebrush State
New Hampshire - Granite State
New Jersey - Garden State
New Mexico - Land of Enchantment
New York - Empire State
North Carolina - Tar Heel State
North Dakota - Flickertail State, Peace Garden State,
        Sioux State
Ohio - Buckeye State
Oklahoma - Sooner State
Oregon - Beaver State
Pennsylvania - Keystone State
Rhode Island - Little Rhody, Ocean State
South Carolina - Palmetto State
South Dakota - Coyote State, Mt. Rushmore State
Tennessee - Volunteer State
Texas - Lone Star State
Utah - Beehive State
Vermont - Green Mountain State
Virginia - Old Dominion State
Washington - Evergreen State
West Virginia - Mountain State
Wisconsin - Badger State, The Dairy State
Wyoming - Equality State

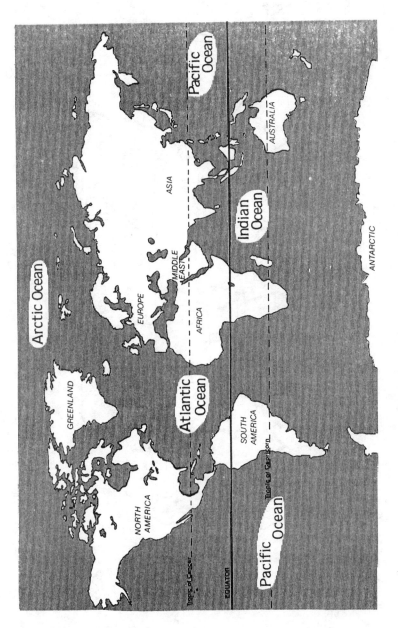

OUTLINE MAP OF THE WORLD

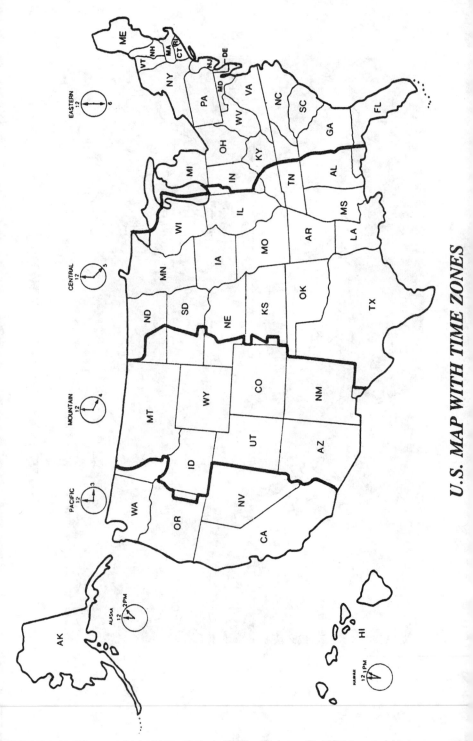

U.S. MAP WITH TIME ZONES

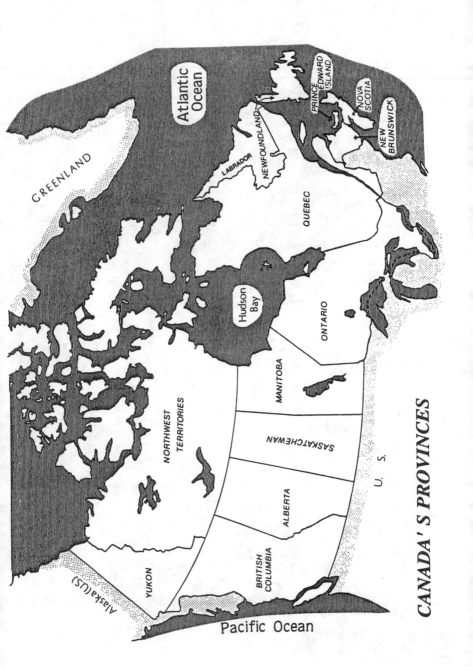

CANADA'S PROVINCES

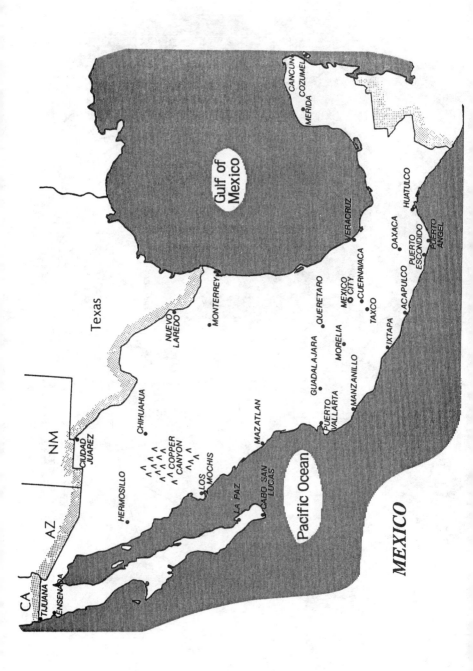

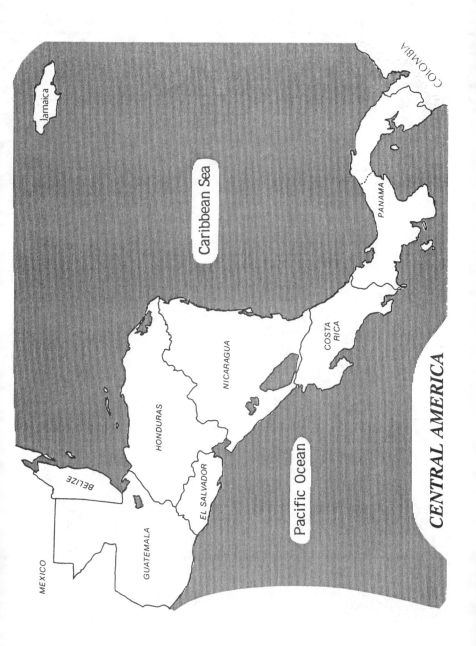

CENTRAL AMERICA

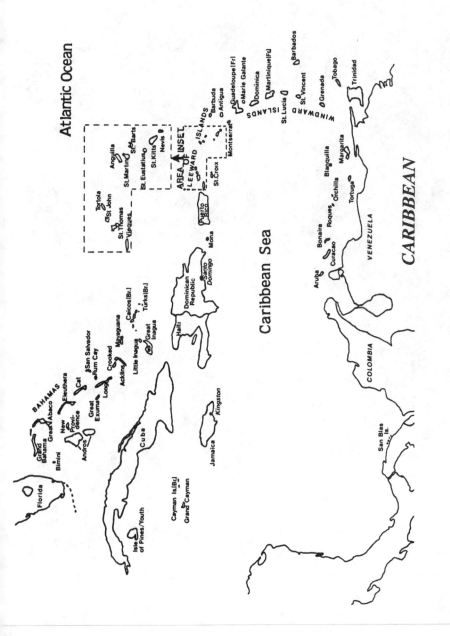

Atlantic Ocean

Florida

Grand Bahama
Bimini
BAHAMAS
New Providence
Andros
Great Abaco
Eleuthera
Cat
San Salvador
Rum Cay
Great Exuma
Long
Crooked
Acklins
Mayaguana
Little Inagua
Caicos (Br.)
Turks (Br.)
Great Inagua

Isle of Pines/Youth
Cuba

Cayman Is.(Br.)
Grand Cayman

Jamaica
Kingston

Haiti
Dominican Republic
Santo Domingo

Mona
Mona

Puerto Rico

Vieques
St. Thomas
St. John
Tortola
Anguilla
St. Martin
St. Barts
St. Kitts
St. Eustatius
Nevis
St. Croix
Montserrat

AREA INSET
LEEWARD ISLANDS

Barbuda
Antigua
Guadeloupe (Fr.)
Marie Galante
Dominica
Martinique (Fr.)
St. Lucia
St. Vincent
Barbados
Grenada
Tobago
Trinidad

WINDWARD ISLANDS

Caribbean Sea

Aruba
Bonaire
Curaçao
Roques
Orchilla
Blaquilla
Margarita
Tortuga

VENEZUELA

San Blas Is.

COLOMBIA

CARIBBEAN

360

COUNTRIES OF SOUTH AMERICA

EUROPE

Atlantic
Ocean

ICELAND

SWEDEN

FINLAND

NORWAY

ESTONIA

N. Ireland
SCOTLAND
NORTH SEA
DENMARK
BALTIC SEA
LATVIA
LITHUANIA

IRELAND
WALES
ENGLAND
Netherlands
•C.I.S.

BELGIUM
GERMANY
POLAND

Luxembourg
CZECH REPUBLIC
UKRAINE

FRANCE
Liechtenstein
SLOVAKIA

Switzerland
AUSTRIA
HUNGARY
Moldova

Slovenia
ROMANIA

Monaco
Croatia
Bosnia & Hercegovina
Yugoslavia

Andorra
San Marino
ITALY
BULGARIA

PORTUGAL
SPAIN
Corsica
ADRIATIC SEA
ALBANIA
Macedonia

Balearic Is.
Sardinia
GREECE
TURKEY

MEDITERRANEAN SEA

Sicily

Malta
Rhodes
Crete

COUNTRIES OF AFRICA

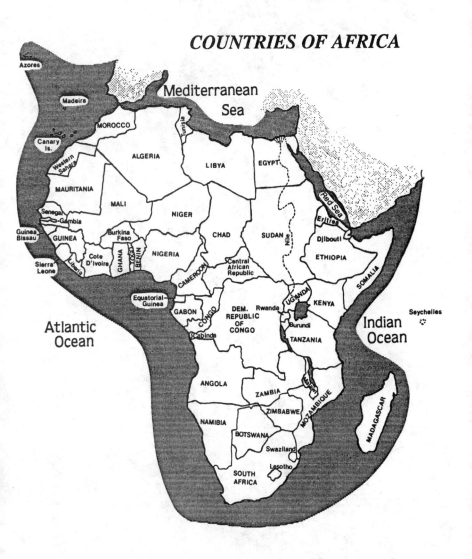

MIDDLE EAST AND ASIA – COUNTRIES

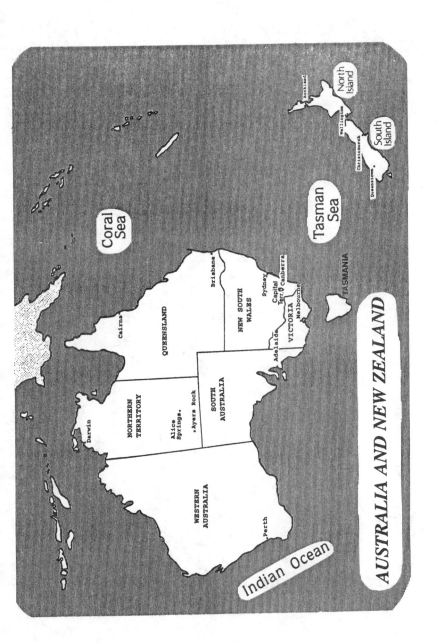

AUSTRALIA AND NEW ZEALAND

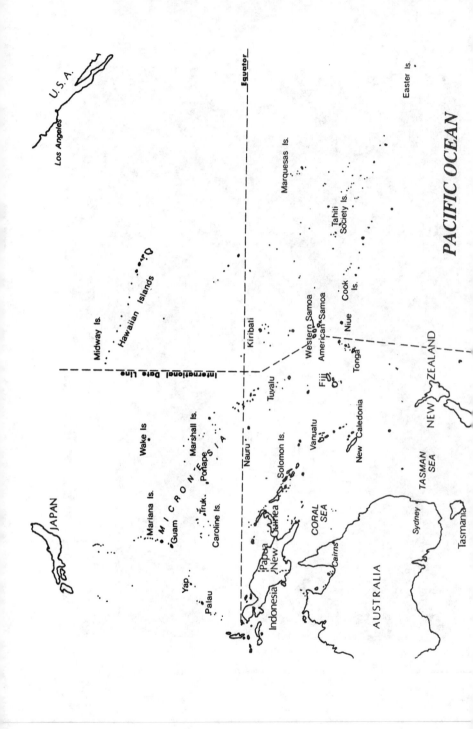

INTERNATIONAL GEOGRAPHICAL TERMS

Terms are followed by the language origin.

Aas	Hills (Danish, Norwegian)
Abajo	Lower (Spanish)
Ada, Adasi	Island (Turkish)
Altipiano	Plateau (Italian)
Altiplano	Plateau (Spanish)
Alv,Alf,Elf	River (Swedish)
Arrecife	Reef (Spanish)
Asa	Hill (Norwegian, Swedish)
Asaga	Lower (Turkish)
Austral	Southern (Spanish)
Baai	Bay (Dutch)
Bab	Gate/Strait (Arabic)
Bahia	Bay (Spanish)
Bahr	Marsh/Lake/Sea/River (Arabic)
Baia	Bay (Portuguese)
Baie	Bay/Gulf (French)
Baizo	Low (Portuguese)
Bakke	Hill (Danish)
Bana	Cape (Japanese)
Banados	Marshes (Spanish)
Bandao	Peninsula (Chinese)
Barra	Reef (Spanish)
Bel	Pass (Turkish)
Belt	Strait (German)
Ben	Mountain (Gaelic)
Bera	Mountain (Dutch)
Berg	Mountain (German)
Bir	Well (Arabic)
Boca	Gulf/Inlet (Spanish)
Boghaz	Strait (Turkish)
Bolshoi/Bolshaya	Big (Russian)
Bong	Mountain (Korean)
Boreal	Northern (Spanish)
Breen	Glacier (Norwegian)
Bro	Bridge (Danish, Nor., Swe.)
Bucht	Bay (German)
Bugt	Bay (Danish)
Bukhta	Bay (Russian)
Bukit	Hill/Mountain (Malaysian)
Bukt	Bay, Gulf (Norwegian, Swe.)
Burnu/Burun	Cape/Point (Turkish)
By	Town (Danish, Nor., Swe.)
Cabo	Cape (Spanish, Portuguese)
Campos	Plains (Portuguese)
Canal	Channel (Spanish, Portuguese)
Cap/Capo	Cape (French, Italian)
Cataratas	Falls (Spanish)
Catena	Mountain Range (Italian)
Catingas	Open Woodlands (Portuguese)
Cayos	Islands (Spanish)
Cerrito/Cerro	Hill (Spanish)
Chai	River (Turkish)
Chott	Salt Lake (Arabic)
Cienaga	Swamp (Spanish)

Ciudad	City (Spanish)
Col	Pass (French)
Cordillera	Mountain Range (Spanish)
Cote	Coast (French)
Cuchilla	Mountain Range (Spanish)
Curiche	Swamp (Spanish)
Dag	Mountain/Peak (Turkish)
Daglari	Mountain Range (Turkish)
Dal	Valley (Norwegian, Swe.)
Dar	Land (Arabic)
Dar'ya	River (Russian)
Dasht	Desert/Plain (Persian)
Deniz/Denizi	Sea/Lake (Turkish)
Desierto	Desert (Spanish)
Detroit	Strait (French)
Djeziret	Island (Turkish, Arabic)
Do	Island (Korean)
Doi	Mountain (Thai)
Eiland	Island (Dutch)
Elv	River (Norwegian, Danish)
Embalse	Reservoir (Spanish)
Emi	Mountain (Berber)
Erg	Dune/Desert (Arabic)
Eski	Old (Turkish)
Est/Este	East (French, Spanish, Port.)
Estero	Estuary/Creek (Spanish)
Estrecho/Estreito	Strait (Spanish, Portuguese)
Etang	Pond/Lagoon (French)
Feng	Mountain (Chinese)
Fiume	River (Italian)
Fjall	Mountain (Swedish)
Fjeld/Fjell	Hills/Mountain (Norwegian)
Fleuve	River (French)
Fljot	Stream (Icelandic)
Fluss	River (German)
Fors	Waterfall (Swedish)
Fos/Foss	Waterfall (Danish, Norwegian)
Gamla,Gamle	Old (Norwegian, Danish)
Gata	Lake (Japanese)
Gawa	River (Japanese)
Gebel	Mountain (Arabic)
Gebergte	Mountain Range (Dutch)
Gebirge	Mountain Range (German)
Gobi	Desert (Mongol)
Goe	Pass (Japanese)
Gol	Lake/Stream (Mongol, Turkish)
Golf	Gulf (German, Dutch)
Golfe	Gulf (French)
Golfo	Gulf (Spanish, Italian, Port.)
Gora	Mountain (Russian)
Groot	Big (Dutch)
Gross	Big (German)
Grosso	Big (Italian, Portuguese)
Guba	Bay/Gulf (Russian)
Gunto	Archipelago (Japanese)
Gunung	Mountain (Malay)
Hai	Sea (Chinese)
Haixia	Strait (Chinese)
Halbinsel	Peninsula (German)

Hamada	Rocky Plateau (Arabic)
Hamn	Harbor (Swedish)
Hamun	Marsh (Persian)
Hanto	Peninsula (Japanese)
Has/Hassi	Well (Arabic)
Hav	Sea/Ocean (Danish, Nor., Swe.)
Havet	Bay (Norwegian)
Havn	Harbor (Danish, Norwegian)
Havre	Harbor (French)
He	River/Stream (Chinese)
Higashi/Higasi	East (Japanese)
Hochebene	Plateau (German)
Hoek	Cape (Dutch)
Hoku	North (Japanese)
Holm	Island (Danish, Norwegian, Swe.)
Hory	Mountains (Czechoslovakian)
Hoved	Cape/Promontory (Danish, Nor.)
Hu	Lake (Chinese)
Huk	Point (Danish, Nor., Swe.)
Hus/Huus	House (Danish, Nor., Swe.)
Idehan	Desert (Arabic)
Ile	Island (French)
Ilet/Ilot	Islet (French)
Indre	Inner (Danish, Norwegian)
Insel	Island (German)
Irmak	River (Turkish)
Isla	Island (Spanish)
Isola	Island (Italian)
Jabal/Jebel	Mountains (Arabic)
Jarvi	Lake (Finnish)
Jaure	Lake (Swedish)
Jiang	River/Stream (Chinese)
Jima	Island (Japanese)
Joki	River (Finnish)
Kaap	Cape (Dutch)
Kai	Sea (Japanese)
Kaikyo	Strait (Japanese)
Kami	Upper (Turkish)
Kanaal	Canal (Dutch)
Kanal	Canal/Channel (Russian, Ger.)
Kao	Mountain (Thai)
Kap/Kapp	Cape (Nor., Swe., Icelandic)
Kaupunki	Town (Finnish)
Kawa	River (Japanese)
Khao	Mountain (Thai)
Khrebet	Mountain Range (Russian)
Kita	North (Japanese)
Klein	Small (Dutch, German)
Ko	Lake (Japanese)
Ko	Island (Thai)
Koh	Island (Cambodian)
Kop	Peak/Head (Dutch)
Korfez/Korfezi	Gulf (Turkish)
Kosui	Lake (Japanese)
Kuh/Kuhha	Mountain Range (Persian)
Kum	Desert (Turkish)
Laag	Low (Dutch)
Lac	Lake (French)
Lago	Lake (Port., Spanish, It.)

Lagoa	Lagoon (Portuguese)
Laguna	Lagoon (Spanish)
Liedao	Islands/Archipelago (Chinese)
Lilla/Lille	Small (Swedish, Danish, Nor.)
Ling	Mountain (Chinese)
Llanos	Plains (Spanish)
Mae Nam	River (Thai)
Man	Bay (Korean)
Mar	Sea (Spanish, Portuguese)
Mare	Sea (Italian)
Meer	Lake (Dutch)
Meer	Sea (German)
Meseta	Plateau (Spanish)
Mis/Mys	Cape (Russian)
Misaki	Cape (Japanese)
Mont/Montagne	Mountain (French)
Montana	Mountains (Spanish)
More	Sea (Russian)
Morue	Hill (French)
Nada	Sea (Japanese)
Nam	River (Burmese, Lao)
Nes	Cape (Norwegian)
Nieder	Lower (German)
Nishi/Nisi	West (Japanese)
Nong	Lake (Thai)
Noord	North (Dutch)
Nord	North (French, German)
Norte	North (Spanish, It., Port.)
Nos	Cape (Russian)
Nur/Nuur	Lake (Chinese, Mongol)
Nuruu	Mountains (Mongol)
Nusa	Island (Malay)
Ober	Upper (German)
Oeste	West (Portuguese)
Ooster	Eastern (Dutch)
Ost	East (German)
Ostrov	Island (Russian)
Ouest	West (French)
Ozero	Lake (Russian)
Pampa	Plain (Spanish)
Pas	Channel/Strait (French)
Paso	Pass (Spanish)
Passo	Pass (Italian, Portuguese)
Pena	Rock/Mountain (Spanish)
Pendi	Basin (Chinese)
Pereval	Pass (Russian)
Peski	Desert (Russian)
Phu	Mountain (Lao)
Pic	Mountain (French)
Pico	Mountain (Port., Spanish)
Pik	Mountain/Peak (Russian)
Piton	Mountain/Peak (French)
Planalto	Plateau (Portuguese)
Plato	Plateau (Russian)
Presa	Reservoir (Spanish)
Presqu'ile	Peninsula (French)
Proliv	Strait (Russian)
Pulou/Pulo	Island (Malay)
Punt	Point (Dutch)

Punta	Point (Spanish, It., Port.)
Qiryat	City/Settlement (Hebrew)
Qum	Desert (Turkish)
Qundao	Islands (Chinese)
Rada	Inlet (Spanish)
Rade	Bay/Inlet (French)
Ras	Cape (Arabic)
Reka	River (Russian)
Retto	Archipelago (Japanese)
Ria	Estuary (Spanish)
Rio	River (Spanish)
Rud	River (Persian)
Sai	West (Japanese)
Saki	Cape (Japanese)
Salto	Falls (Spanish, Portuguese)
San	Hill (Japanese, Korean)
Sanmaek	Mountain Range (Korean)
Schiereiland	Peninsula (Dutch)
Se	River (Cambodian)
See	Sea/Lake (German)
Selvas	Woods/Forest (Spanish, Port.)
Seno	Bay/Gulf (Spanish)
Serra	Mountains (Portuguese)
Serrania	Mountains (Spanish)
Seto	Strait (Japanese)
Shamo	Desert (Chinese)
Shan	Hill/Mtns. (Chinese, Japanese)
Shankou	Pass (Chinese)
Shatt	River (Arabic)
Shima	Island (Japanese)
Shin	Land (Japanese)
Shoto	Islands (Japanese)
Sierra	Mountain Range/Mts. (Spanish)
Sopka	Volcano (Russian)
Spitze	Mountain Peak (German)
Stad	City (Danish, Nor., Swe.)
Straat	Strait (Dutch)
Strasse	Strait (German)
Stretto	Strait (Italian)
Stung	River (Cambodian)
Su	River (Turkish)
Sud	South (Spanish, French, Ger.)
Sul	South (Portuguese)
Sungei	River (Malay)
Sur	South (Spanish)
Suyu	River (Turkish)
Tafelland	Plateau (Dutch)
Tagh	Mountain Range (Turkish)
Take	Peak/Ridge (Japanese)
Tal	Valley (German)
Tell	Hill (Arabic)
Thale	Sea/Lake (Thai)
Tind	Peak (Norwegian)
Toge	Pass (Japanese)
Trask	Lake (Finnish)
Umi	Bay (Japanese)
Vatn	Lake (Norwegian)
Veld	Plain/Field (Dutch)
Vesi	Lake (Finnish)

Vik	Bay (Norwegian, Swedish)
Wadi	Dry River (Arabic)
Wald	Forest (German)
Wan	Bay (Japanese)
Wuste	Desert (German)
Yama	Mountain (Japanese)
Zaki	Cape (Japanese)
Zaliv	Bay/Gulf (Russian)
Zee	Sea (Dutch)
Zuid	South (Dutch)

FOUND AN ERROR?

We've done everything possible to ensure that the information in this book is totally correct, but sometimes errors do occur. If you find that any of the information contained is incorrect or out of date, please let us know so that we can correct our records and ensure the next edition is more accurate. Please fill out the information below and return it to us.

NAME_____

ADDRESS_____

CITY/STATE/ZIP_____

PHONE_____FAX_____

COMMENTS/CHANGES_____

_____

_____

_____

_____

_____

_____

_____

Please mail to: SOLITAIRE PUBLISHING
                POB 14508
                TAMPA, FL 33690 or fax to (813) 876-0286

THANK YOU!

Thank you for having purchased Solitaire Publishing materials. If you would like to receive other items, use the form below or contact us for a current catalog.

SOLITAIRE PUBLISHING   (800) 226-0286 (U.S.)/(813) 876-0286
POB 14508   E-mail: PSolitaire@aol.com
TAMPA, FL 33690-4508

I would like to receive
   The Travel Training Series

Travel Geography	$24.95	_____
Domestic Travel and Ticketing	$29.95	_____
Selling Tours and Independent Travel	$18.95	_____
International Travel and Ticketing	$24.95	_____
Selling Cruises	$15.95	_____
Sales and Marketing	$24.95	_____
The Travel Dictionary	$19.95	_____
COMPLETE SET W/ATLAS & TOTE BAG	$129.95	_____

OTHER ITEMS AVAILABLE:

Building Profits with Group Travel	$29.95	_____
The Complete Guide to Incentive Travel	$45.00	_____
Home-Based Travel Agent	$24.95	_____
A Coach Full of Fun	$19.95	_____
How to get a Job with a Cruise Line	$14.95	_____
Travel Agency Bookkeeping Made Simple	$45.00	_____
Travel Industry Personnel Directory	$31.00	_____
International Golf Resort Directory	$39.50	_____
International Ski Resort Directory	$39.50	_____
World Travel Guide	$159.00	_____
Hammond Explorer Atlas	$10.95	_____
Video on CAREERS IN TRAVEL	$29.95	_____
Video on TOUR LEADERSHIP	$29.95	_____
Video on TOUR WELCOME	$29.95	_____

Shipping: Orders to $60.00 (contiguous U.S.) - add 10% (minimum $4.00), over $60.00 - add 8%. For AK, HI, and Int'l - add $5.00 per item ordered. FL residents add 6.75% tax.

TOTAL = _____

NAME_____
ADDRESS_____
CITY/STATE/ZIP_____
PHONE_____FAX_____